Northern Crossings

Cosmopolitan–Vernacular Dynamics in World Literatures

The four books in this limited series are an outcome of a major Swedish research project called 'Cosmopolitan–Vernacular Dynamics in World Literatures', the aim of which has been to intervene – not least methodologically – in the current disciplinary development of world literature studies. The series is united by a common introductory chapter and approaches the vernacular in world literature across a range of fields, such as comparative literature, postcolonial literature and literary anthropology.

More information on the research project can be found at Worldlit.se.

The books in this series are available as open access through the Bloomsbury Open Access programme and are available at www.bloomsburycollections.com. They are funded by the Riksbankens Jubileumsfond.

Series Editor
Stefan Helgesson

Volumes in the Series

Claiming Space: Locations and Orientations in World Literatures
Edited by Bo G. Ekelund, Adnan Mahmutović and Helena Wulff

Literature and the Making of the World: Cosmopolitan Texts, Vernacular Practices
Edited by Stefan Helgesson, Helena Bodin and Annika Mörte Alling

Northern Crossings: Translation, Circulation and the Literary Semi-periphery
By Chatarina Edfeldt, Erik Falk, Andreas Hedberg, Yvonne Lindqvist, Cecilia Schwartz and Paul Tenngart

Vernaculars in an Age of World Literatures
Edited by Christina Kullberg and David Watson

Northern Crossings

Translation, Circulation and the Literary Semi-periphery

By
Chatarina Edfeldt, Erik Falk, Andreas Hedberg,
Yvonne Lindqvist, Cecilia Schwartz and Paul Tenngart

BLOOMSBURY ACADEMIC
Bloomsbury Publishing Inc
1385 Broadway, New York, NY 10018, USA
50 Bedford Square, London, WC1B 3DP, UK
29 Earlsfort Terrace, Dublin 2, Ireland

BLOOMSBURY, BLOOMSBURY ACADEMIC and the Diana logo are
trademarks of Bloomsbury Publishing Plc

First published in the United States of America 2022
This paperback edition published 2023

Copyright © Chatarina Edfeldt, Erik Falk, Andreas Hedberg, Yvonne Lindqvist,
Cecilia Schwartz and Paul Tenngart, 2022, 2023

For legal purposes the Acknowledgements on p. vii constitute an
extension of this copyright page.

Cover design by Namkwan Cho
Cover image © Shutterstock.com

This work is published open access subject to a Creative Commons
Attribution-NonCommercial-NoDerivatives 3.0 licence (CC BY-NC-ND 3.0,
https://creativecommons.org/licenses/by-nc-nd/3.0/). You may re-use, distribute,
and reproduce this work in any medium for non-commercial purposes, provided
you give attribution to the copyright holder and the publisher and provide a
link to the Creative Commons licence.

Bloomsbury Publishing Inc does not have any control over, or responsibility for, any
third-party websites referred to or in this book. All internet addresses given in this
book were correct at the time of going to press. The author and publisher regret
any inconvenience caused if addresses have changed or sites have ceased
to exist, but can accept no responsibility for any such changes.

Library of Congress Cataloging-in-Publication Data
Names: Edfeldt, Chatarina, author.
Title: Northern crossings : translation, circulation and the literary
semi-periphery / by Chatarina Edfeldt, [et al.].
Description: New York : Bloomsbury Academic, 2022. | Series: Cosmopolitan-vernacular
dynamics in world literatures ; 4 | Includes bibliographical references and index.
Identifiers: LCCN 2021040186 (print) | LCCN 2021040187 (ebook) |
ISBN 9781501374241 (hardback) | ISBN 9781501374289 (paperback) | ISBN
9781501374258 (epub) | ISBN 9781501374265 (pdf) | ISBN 9781501374272 (ebook)
Subjects: LCSH: Swedish literature–Translations–History and criticism. |
Swedish literature–Publishing. | Literature publishing–Sweden. | Translating and
interpreting–Sweden. | Translations–Publishing. | Literature, Modern–20th century–
History and criticism. | Literature, Modern–21st century–History and criticism
Classification: LCC PT9289 .E34 2022 (print) | LCC PT9289
(ebook) | DDC 839.709–dc23/eng/20211027
LC record available at https://lccn.loc.gov/2021040186
LC ebook record available at https://lccn.loc.gov/2021040187

ISBN:	HB:	978-1-5013-7424-1
	PB:	978-1-5013-7428-9
	ePDF:	978-1-5013-7426-5
	eBook:	978-1-5013-7425-8

Series: Cosmopolitan–Vernacular Dynamics in World Literatures

Typeset by Integra Software Services Pvt. Ltd.

To find out more about our authors and books visit www.bloomsbury.com
and sign up for our newsletters.

Contents

Acknowledgements   vii
Series introduction – The cosmopolitan–vernacular dynamic: Conjunctions of world literature *Stefan Helgesson, Christina Kullberg, Paul Tenngart and Helena Wulff*   viii

1   Introduction: The cosmopolitan, the vernacular and the semi-periphery   1
    The state-of-the-art   3
    Sweden, a particular case of the possible   6
    An approach to world systems theory   12
    A collaborative method   18
    Outline of the volume   19

2   Infrastructure of the semi-peripheral exchange   21
    The cosmopolitan infrastructure: Intermediaries institutions, reception   21
    Methodological framework   22
    Publishers of Swedish literature in the UK and the USA   26
    Publishers of Swedish literature in France   33
    Publishers of Italian literature in Sweden   41
    Publishers of Anglophone African literature in Sweden   50
    Publishers of Lusophone literature in Sweden   59
    Publishers of Hispanic Caribbean literature in Sweden   69
    Concluding remarks   77

3   Translators of Nobel Prize literature   81
    Swedish Nobel literature in English: The case of Tomas Tranströmer   83
    Swedish Nobel literature in French: The case of Harry Martinson   88
    Italian Nobel literature in Swedish: The case of Eugenio Montale   93
    Anglophone African Nobel literature in Swedish: The case of Wole Soyinka   99

	Portuguese Nobel literature in Swedish: The case of José Saramago	106
	Maryse Condé: Consecration translators and the prize of the New Academy	113
	Concluding remarks	119
4	Translation strategies to and from the literary semi-periphery: Reduction retention, replacement	123
	Three kinds of translational transformation	124
	Proletarian realism and crime fiction from Swedish to English	127
	Two contemporary Swedish novels in French	139
	Three Italian novels in Swedish	146
	Two Anglophone African novels in Swedish	156
	Two Lusophone novels in Swedish	167
	Three Caribbean novels in Swedish	174
	Concluding remarks	186
5	Positioning the Swedish literary semi-periphery	193
	Three significant features of the Swedish semi-periphery	194
	Swedish literature in English translation 1980–2018	203
	Swedish literature in French translation 1980–2018	209
	Italian literature in Swedish translation 1980–2018	212
	Anglophone African literature in Swedish translation 1980–2018	219
	Lusophone literature in Swedish translation 1980–2018	225
	Francophone and Hispanic Caribbean bibliomigration to Sweden 1980–2018	234
	Concluding remarks	243
6	General conclusion	249

References	253
Index	266

Acknowledgements

This book is available as open access through the Bloomsbury Open Access programme and is available at www.bloomsburycollections.com. The open-access edition of this text was made possible by the Riksbankens Jubileumsfond.

Series introduction
The cosmopolitan–vernacular dynamic: Conjunctions of world literature

Stefan Helgesson, Christina Kullberg, Paul Tenngart and Helena Wulff

'World literature is not an object, it's a *problem*.' This was Franco Moretti (2000: 55), famously, in 2000. But what is the problem of world literature today, two decades later? In broad strokes, the disciplinary challenge would seem to be the same: to devise methods and reading practices that offer alternatives to entrenched national and civilizational frameworks. Scholarship within world literature shares a fundamentally *comparative* urge, whereby different instantiations of literature are considered in conjunction. But 'conjunction' is in fact the nub of the problem, as this is supposedly not just an older version of comparative literature under a new name. Instead, conjunction can be conceptualized through a wide number of temporalities, scales, geographies, generic constellations, languages and ideological perspectives – all of them susceptible to historical change.

Moretti proposed a world-systemic model, inspired by Immanuel Wallerstein, which has since developed into a strong but by no means exclusive or uncontested methodological premise of world literature. Deep-time approaches focusing on imperial formations, translation-based approaches, Alexander Beecroft's (2015) ecologies of literature – all offer distinct ways of investigating conjunction and connection. What they do not always offer is mutual compatibility. Instead, the most productive way to delineate world literature today might be to consider it as a set of procedures and methods rather than a coherent body of theory. As a scholarly field, it provides in the first instance a space of conversation and intellectual exchange *across* specializations that may also enable reconfigured empirical and critical investigations within those specializations.

This give-and-take among different disciplinary locations has shaped the work leading up to the four volumes presented here. Emerging from a long-running project based in Sweden, and involving researchers from comparative literature, anthropology, intellectual history and a range of language departments, the basic methodological wager of our work differs from much else that has been published in the field of world literature. Avoiding hard-wired systemic, deterministic or 'global' claims, what we call the *cosmopolitan–vernacular dynamic* (which can also be read as *vernacular–cosmopolitan*) offers itself not as a distinct theory, but as a methodological starting point – akin to an *Ansatzpunkt* in Erich Auerbach's (1952) sense – from which to explore the resonances and connections between widely diverse literary texts and cultures.

To explain the motivations behind such a methodology, we need to make a detour into the current state of world literature studies. Undergirding this sprawling field is the political and ethical intuition that literary knowledge in our crisis-ridden, globalized and racialized world – even in its (anticipated) post-Covid-19 shape – requires new modes of scholarly attention. To speak from our own contemporary vantage point in Scandinavia, it is clear that the joint impact of the cultural Anglosphere, migration from Europe, the Middle East, Africa and Asia, the cultural policies of the EU and the ubiquitous presence of digital media not only weaken the explanatory value of the nation state and the national language as the privileged loci of the production and reading of literature in Sweden today, but also invite reconsiderations of an earlier literary history in the region. Similar shifts in the production of literature and in the literary imagination can be registered elsewhere across the world, shifts that prompt us to rethink how we read and contextualize literature. The road to such a revised conception of literary studies leads, however, to a garden of forking paths. This is one important lesson to be learned from the twenty-odd years since Moretti's lively provocation in the year 2000.

Common to the turn-of-the-millennium interventions by Moretti and David Damrosch (2003) (less so Pascale Casanova, whose concern was consecration) was an emphasis on circulation – quite literally on how texts move and are received in diverse contexts. This deceptively simple perspective counters what Jerome McGann (1991: 7) once called 'textual idealism', which treats texts as if they were just magically 'there'. Instead, the circulational perspective allows us to engage the material, spatial and historical unconscious of literature as texts in movement. This approach has been developed by Beecroft (2015), Venkat Mani (2017), Sandra Richter (2017) and Yvonne Leffler (2020), among others. Increasingly, as in contributions to Stefan Helgesson and Pieter Vermeulen's (2016) *Institutions of World Literature* or in Ignacio Sánchez Prado's (2018) study of Mexican literature, this tends towards studies of market dynamics and, not least, the sociology of translation (Heilbron 1999, 2020, de Swaan 2001, Sapiro 2008, Buzelin and Baraldi 2016). However, the most rigorous large-scale studies of circulation are to be found within computational literary studies (CLS) which involves an even more fundamental shift towards quantitative methods than the sociology of translation. Not surprisingly, given his coinage of 'distant reading', CLS has become Moretti's (2000: 56–8) main field of activity at the Stanford Literary Lab. Even as the merits and drawbacks of CLS are being debated (Da 2019), the achievements in all these interlinked areas of investigation attest firmly to the *complexity* of studying world-literary circulation. This knowledge is not just readily available, nor does it amount merely to an external study of literature, but it is rather of crucial relevance both to the empirical and theoretical understanding of how literary cultures evolve.

Having said that, a striking alternative development over the last ten years has been the proliferation of interpretive, qualitative methods in world literature studies. Often on the basis of strong theorizations of the world-concept, and sometimes pitched polemically against the circulation approach, researchers have attempted to read 'the world' through specific literary works, rather than through Morettian 'distant reading' (which is ideally suited for digital methods). The epistemic assumption in these interpretive models follows the synechdochal logic of *pars pro toto*, or the part standing in for the whole. Eric Hayot (2012) was early to embark on this path in *On Literary Worlds*, an ambitious but all-too-brief attempt to bring world literature studies – understood as a global extension of literary studies – to bear on, in principle, *any* given work of literature, regardless of origin or period. Emily Apter's (2013) much publicized *Against World Literature* instead championed linguistic specificity – coded as the 'Untranslatable' – as the normative locus of a worldly reading. A related tendency has been the regionally or linguistically restricted conception of literature X *as* world literature, with the Francophone *littérature-monde* as a high-profile example, but also evident in many (not all) titles in Bloomsbury's 'Literatures as World Literature' series. Building on Moretti's world-systemic inclination, the Warwick Research Collective (WReC) has elaborated a significantly different conception of world-literature (with a hyphen) as the aesthetic registration of combined and uneven development in the capitalist world-system – but this, too, has issued in a mode of close interpretive attention to literary texts, rather than distant reading. Other, more or less distinct examples of this interpretive turn in world literature studies can be cited, such as Francesca Orsini's (2015) concept of the multilingual local, pitched in opposition to systemic approaches, Debjani Ganguly's (2016) work on the global novel, Ottmar Ette's (2016) 'transarea' approach (2016), Pheng Cheah's (2016, 2017) phenomenology of 'worlding literature' and Birgit Neumann and Gabriele Rippl's (2017) notes on world-making. A point of relevance to our work is that while the most rigorous systemic approaches, represented here by WReC, speak of world-literature in the singular, the implication of, for example, Hayot's, Apter's or Orsini's perspectives is to consider *literatures* as an inevitably plural phenomenon – even in contexts of exchange and translation. At stake here, ultimately, is the relative theoretical weighting of determinacy and contingency in interpretive practices. Our work does not collectively pursue one or the other of these angles, but most contributions tend to side with contingency and hence the plural conception of literature.

Having said so, it must be stressed that each volume in this series has a distinct methodological profile of its own. As its title indicates, *Northern Crossings* deals with aspects of circulation to and from Sweden – understood in structural terms as a semi-periphery rather than a reified national space. It is in that sense the most systemically oriented volume in this series. *Claiming Space*, by contrast, approaches the narrative inscription of places around the world mainly through interpretive methods. *Literature and the Making of the World* configures its object of inquiry as 'literary practice' (both intra- and extratextual) and combines for that reason text-focused readings with book-historical and anthropological methods of inquiry. *Vernaculars in an Age of World Literatures*, finally, with its focus on the concept of the vernacular, combines interpretive readings with large-scale historical analyses.

As mentioned, it is the working hypothesis of the cosmopolitan–vernacular dynamic that brings these studies together. In the simplest and most general terms, this assumes that literature in different times is shaped through a combination of cosmopolitan and vernacular orientations. Indeed, the cosmopolitan–vernacular dynamic, we claim, *is precisely what is at stake in the world literature field*: not just the outward success or failure of certain texts, genres or literary languages, nor just the 'refraction' of *national* literatures (Damrosch 2003: 281), but rather the always situated negotiation of cosmopolitan and vernacular orientations in the temporal unfolding of literary practice. The further implication – which extends beyond our contributions – is that such a methodology might allow for the articulation of 'universality' after the collapse of 'universalism' (Messling 2019).

Just as importantly, however, the cosmopolitan–vernacular dynamic should be understood as a falsifiable postulation: in the hypothetical case of Beecroft's (2015: 33) 'epichoric', or strictly local, literary ecology it would hardly be meaningful to talk of a cosmopolitan orientation. The opposite point, that there might be texts, genres and modes of writing without any vernacular connection at all, is harder to make – but it is the case, for example, that standard Arabic or *fusha* can function as a cosmopolitan written standard that runs parallel to local (spoken) Arabic dialects (Tageldin 2018). We are not claiming, in other words, that the cosmopolitan–vernacular dynamic *must* apply in all literary contexts. Even more importantly, it does not operate in just one mode, nor is it necessarily always successful. To speak of the cosmopolitan–vernacular dynamic is an open proposition, in the sense that it does not prescribe in advance any particular weighting of cosmopolitan or vernacular tendencies. Although the cosmopolitan–vernacular dynamic is fundamentally a question of how literary values are shaped, just *how* these values should be understood and assessed can only be discovered by examining the particular case.

In adopting the cosmopolitan–vernacular perspective, we acknowledge our debt to Sheldon Pollock (2006), whose magisterial macro-historical analysis of pre-modern literary cultures in South Asia and Europe in *The Language of the Gods in the World of Men* offered a path-breaking comparison not just of the cosmopolitan literatures of Sanskrit and Latin, but more importantly of the historical constructedness of vernacular literatures. *Contra* the Romanticist assumption of vernacular authenticity and immediacy, Pollock (and Beecroft after him) argued that a historical approach to vernacular literatures will show how they tend to be elite projects shaped in reaction against a dominant cosmopolitan Other (such as the literate cultures of Latin and Sanskrit). To *literize* (standardize through writing) and *literarize* languages coded as vernaculars are to be understood as deliberate, politically motivated actions (Pollock 2006: 4–5).

Illuminating though such an explanatory model is, it should not be taken at face value as a transhistorical constant, nor need it be restricted to macro-historical analyses, but can be applied equally to closer textual study. Contrary to Pollock's pre-modern focus, our four volumes engage with literature from the last 200 years (about half of the primary sources are contemporary), an epoch which marks a radical new departure in literary history. This is when *Weltliteratur* was conceptualized in the wake of the accelerating commodification of print literature, the emergence of comparative philology and the entrenchment of (and resistance to) European nationalism and imperialism. It is, hence, an era when cosmopolitan and vernacular orientations in literature have been reconfigured drastically in relation not least, if not only, to the cultural authority of 'the West'. An important aspect of this process has been the accelerating *vernacularization* of languages and literatures in all parts of the world. This needs to be understood in two ways. First, vernacularization entails the positioning of named languages, registers of language or local knowledges as inferior in the field of power, as for instance Aamir Mufti (2016) discusses in the context of India and Pakistan. But, secondly, vernacularization also involves the deliberate elevation of vernaculars, including what we more broadly call the 'domain of vernacularity', as a resource for the construction of national or socially distinct literatures. Given the constitutively relational nature of vernacularization, this process needs to be thought of as unstable: it can change over time (an obvious example being how European vernaculars such as English and French became cosmopolitan, imperial languages), as well as shift momentarily across space (Spanish being transformed into an immigrant vernacular in the United States). Or, as has often been the case in Africa, a *literary* vernacularity has had to be crafted through adopted, formerly imperial languages.

With its connections to comparative philology and the German romantic aesthetics of Herder, Goethe, Schlegel and Schleiermacher, among others (for more on this see Noyes 2015, Bhattacharya 2016, Mufti 2016, Ahmed 2018), post-eighteenth-century vernacularization is a deeply ambivalent affair: its value-coding can be programmatically positive yet grounded in untenable essentializations of race and ethnicity. A particularly effective challenge to this legacy has been the interrogation of language boundaries and 'artefactualized' languages (Blommaert 2010: 4), along with the critique of the 'monolingual paradigm' (Yildiz 2012; see also Bauman and Briggs 2003, Heller-Roazen 2005, Sakai 2009, Minaard and Dembeck 2014, Stockhammer 2015, Gramling 2016, Tidigs and Huss 2017, Helgesson and Kullberg 2018). These debates are relevant to our work, not least since discourses of the vernacular have often been a tool for establishing a monolingual paradigm that effaces translingual conceptions of language (Adejunmobi 2004). Our heuristic employment of the term allows, however, for an alternative take on mono- and multilingualism. If the vernacular indicates a *relation*, it may entail a heteroglossic or translingual register 'within' a named language (vernacular varieties of English, say), as much as an identity as a separate language vis-à-vis a dominant other (which, for example, was the position of Wolof in relation to imperial French). The social dimension of the vernacular also draws our attention to the relativity of communities of comprehension – the intimacy of a vernacular to one group will be perceived as opacity by others. Such fluidity in the definition and nature of the vernacular chimes well with the critique of linguistic 'bordering' (Sakai 2009), but – and this is important – it also factors the wholly contextual dimension of social hierarchies into the analysis. This has two consequences. One is that it acknowledges the de facto importance of artefactualized language, particularly within literature, despite its *theoretical* untenability. In the world of publishing, the authority of standard varieties of English, French or Arabic – including their publishing infrastructures – cannot be wished away. Hence, when terms such as 'centre' and 'periphery' are used in *Northern Crossings* in the context of translational exchanges, this is not a normative judgement, but rather an attempt at descriptively conceptualizing a given state of affairs.

The other consequence is that a social conception of language opens up towards a wider frame of analysis. As argued in *Vernaculars in an Age of World Literatures* and elsewhere in our volumes, the vernacular is not 'just' a linguistic matter, but implies rather an entire domain of vernacularity. This can be understood in metonymic terms as that which relates to proximate, intimate, domestic or local experiences and sensibilities, particularly in their linguistic registration. It has tremendous aesthetic as well as persuasive potential, but is also ideologically ambiguous. As Moradewun Adejunmobi's important work on West Africa shows, it is naïve to assume that promotions of the vernacular are always 'intrinsic and unproblematic exemplars of minority politics' (2005: 179). On the contrary, what she calls 'discourses of the vernacular' have, intermittently, justified asymmetries of power under colonialism, as well as supported the political aspirations of subordinated groups, notably by those 'at the forefront of interaction with the dominant foreign culture' (191). The dynamics of the vernacular will, in brief, always be strictly context-sensitive. From this it follows that an assessment of its political tenor can only be issued *a posteriori*.

If, when we embarked on this project, we found that the vernacular was an ignored or undertheorized term in world literature studies, this has changed to some extent in recent years. An important line of questioning in this regard concerns the extent to which the very term 'vernacular' is possible to use outside of its particular European-latinate genealogy. Tageldin (2018: 115), for one, has observantly noted the instability of the term's field of reference – it is 'terminological quicksand' – but her account of Arabic supports rather than refutes the heuristic value of using the term 'vernacular' comparatively: it is often the case, we find, that when the vernacular transforms into a deliberate literary project, 'middle registers' of writing which fixate the flux of spoken language abound. In literary practice, that is to say, the vernacular oscillates between being a medium and being a citation within the medium. Interestingly, this need not work very differently in oral or performative modes of verbal art, which also exhibit the qualities of craftedness and quotability (see Barber 2007).

Against this backdrop, the value of a 'comparativist assessment of vernacular styles and political practices across the globe', as Sieglinde Lemke (2009: 9) puts it, should be evident.

We should note here that much of the critique *against* world literature as a field of study has argued that the vernacular is what world literature leaves behind. If the basic motivation for world literature as a disciplinary commitment could be described in terms of a cosmopolitan ethics, this has, in turn, often been accused of being an elitist, Eurocentric or politically aloof concern. There is by now an entire subfield of debates in this vein whose most common articulation has been that of postcolonialism 'versus' world literature (Rosendahl Thomsen 2008, Hitchcock 2010, Huggan 2011, Young 2011, Shankar 2012, Spivak 2012, Boehmer 2014, Helgesson 2014, Slaughter 2014, Mufti 2016, Tiwari and Damrosch 2019, 2020, Sturm-Trigonakis 2020). The more recent contributions to this discussion tend, however, also to identify points of convergence between these positions. Our take on this is that if postcolonialism is ideologically primed to speak on behalf of the vernacular (whose proximity to concepts such as the subaltern or indigeneity should not pass unnoticed), an actual attention to vernacular orientations also shows their relevance far beyond strictly postcolonial concerns. We are, in other words, claiming that the cosmopolitan–vernacular optic engages the postcolonial perspective, without effacing or supplanting it.

At this point, however, it is of some urgency also to address the cosmopolitan dimension of our methodology. As mentioned, world literature and cosmopolitanism were revived as concerns in academia more or less in tandem in the post-1989 phase: if world literature is underwritten by a fundamentally cosmopolitan ethos of openness towards the other, it also offers the more philosophical concerns of cosmopolitanism an empirical field of study. Even more importantly, the gradual turn from such philosophically normative approaches to a descriptive conception of cosmopolitanism as 'a characteristic and possession of substantial social collectivities, often nonelite collectivities that had cosmopolitanism thrust upon them' (Robbins and Horta 2017: 3) offers yet further scope for its coupling with world literature. Not unlike Pollock (2000: 593), who considers cosmopolitanism as something people 'do rather than something they declare, as practice rather than proposition', our own work in these volumes is informed not by any *a priori* definition of what a cosmopolitan space or stance is, but, again, by a relational premise: terms such as 'cosmopolitan', 'cosmopolitanism' and 'cosmopolitanization' have meaning only insofar as they set themselves off against other modes of belonging, or, better, other orientations. But to complicate things further, cosmopolitan orientations, insofar as they are verbalized, must have a *specific* linguistic signature; this signature, in turn, might more often than not be positioned as vernacular. Conversely, vernacular orientations may, under the right conditions (such as an attachment to a global language) have a cosmopolitan appeal. An example of the latter could be the Antillean French of Patrick Chamoiseau's Goncourt-winning novel *Texaco* (1992). An example of the former is Rabindranath Tagore's ([1907] 2015) famous lecture in 1907 on world literature, held in the late colonial period when Tagore's Bengali – a formidable language of literature and erudition – was still regarded by the British as a vernacular. It is, in other words, crucial to think of the cosmopolitan and the vernacular orientations as *different* but not as mutually exclusive *opposites*, in a schematic sense. Homi Bhabha (1996), not least, has inspired such a view by speaking of vernacular cosmopolitanism (Werbner 2006). To grasp how these orientations might interact, it is therefore imperative to emphasize that the cosmopolitan–vernacular dynamic is also, and fundamentally, a matter of translation – which could be illustrated by how Tagore's lecture is only accessible to us who are writing this introduction in its English version. As with the vernacular, however, the cosmopolitan tendencies are also ambiguous when translation enters the picture. If cosmopolitan orientations are at work whenever transnational structures or agents – be it anglophone, French, Chinese or any other cross-cultural exportation of literature – exercise their power over less well-endowed literary spaces, it may equally be the case that the cosmopolitan orientation of translational practice creates intercultural channels and mindsets that challenge isolationist tendencies. As Robbins and Horta (2017) explain, cosmopolitanism has always both a positive and a negative definition. In positive terms, it embraces a wider humanity; in negative terms, it fosters detachment. This duality also applies to literary modes of cosmopolitanism, which indicates how *location* must always be factored into the cosmopolitan–vernacular analysis, even if it is a negatively conceived locality (as a consequence of detachment). There is, strictly speaking, no 'world space', no vaguely conceived orbit 'out there' where world literature exists in its separate realm. Instead, any postulation or imaginary of a wider world necessarily implies a particular 'here'. This premise is made explicit in *Claiming Space*, whose readings are organized by way of the two terms 'location' and 'orientation', and in *Literature and the Making of the World*, where the focus on literary practice links the textual and fictive aspects of literature to the emplaced and linguistically inflected work of writers, editors or, in one case, a maker of scrapbooks. The word 'world' emerges here as double-coded, as both the life-world once theorized by Hannah Arendt ([1958] 1998) and others, and as an imagined world with a wider scope – and this imagined world, it turns out, is typically nurtured by modes of writing, much as Don Quixote once mistook his romances for the world.

The world, then, can be made and sustained through literary practice, a perspective which also offers a particularly strong motivation for our incorporation of anthropological approaches to literature in our volumes. Not only is the immediate relevance of anthropology evident when engaging terms such as 'vernacular', 'cosmopolitan' and 'world', but we also claim that the defamiliarizing gaze of anthropology on the literary domain helps literary scholarship to move beyond excessive textualism. The work of Karin Barber (2007) serves as a rich source of inspiration, but there is also a long-running debate on the relation of literature to ethnography (Coundouriotis 1999, Desai 2001, Debaene 2010, Kullberg 2013, Izzo 2019) as well as a subfield of literary anthropology which has grown rapidly in recent years (Rapport 1994, Cohen 2013, Wulff 2017, Hemer 2020, Uimonen 2020). In the latter instance in particular, there has been a consistent development of methods for cultural, temporal and biographical contextualization of literary texts relating to vernacular–cosmopolitan dynamics. A central idea here is that the anthropologist and the author are fellow intellectuals and thus the author's commentary is key to understanding issues such as choice of topic, the writing process, the literary career, the publishing industry and the literary market, as well as the circulation of books. This, juxtaposed with the anthropologist's ethnographic observations, can reveal analytical aspects of world literature that are not obvious from the texts alone. It is for this reason that our volumes integrate contributions that build on anthropological methods, such as ethnographic observations during literary festivals, readings and book launches, combined with extensive in-depth interviews of authors.

Our four volumes will appear in staggered fashion in 2021 and 2022, so depending on when exactly you as reader are encountering this general introduction, not all of them may yet be available. Regardless, we will end by briefly describing their profiles.

As already indicated, *Claiming Space*'s contribution to our larger project is its specification of the cosmopolitan and vernacular vectors in terms of 'location' and 'orientation'. This enables a refined analysis of spatial imaginaries in literature. This volume pays attention to language, forms of aesthetic worlding and processes of translation and distribution, while its edge is turned towards the spatial and territorial politics involved in literary practices and works in the late twentieth and early twenty-first centuries. Locations, we argue, are inhabited or claimed by means of vernacular or cosmopolitan strategies, choices that are also visible in the orientations bound up with these sites. In dialogue with the critical geopolitics of culture, with sociology and anthropology, our attention to literary locations and orientations brings spatial particularity into the reckoning of vernacular and cosmopolitan relationality. Explicitly expressed or implied, manifesting itself sometimes as *dis*location and *dis*orientation, the claiming of space by any symbolic means necessarily is revealed as a constant effect of literary practice.

Vernaculars in an Age of World Literatures attempts to theorize the vernacular. As indicated in the discussion above, our point of departure is that the vernacular is always plural: not limited to language alone but comprising various types of expressions, material objects, people and environments. Moreover, its significance and value change with time and context. From a European point of view, it has been identified with the consolidation of national literatures, but in other contexts it has been associated with diaspora and movements of the marginalized or else, like in early-twentieth-century China, it needs to be adapted to a specific literary and linguistic tradition to be useful as a concept. Sometimes, but not always, it works as an expression of resistance to the hegemony of cultural centres. Yet this seemingly inherent heterogeneity and variability is precisely what makes the vernacular a productive concept for rethinking world literature today. In nine case studies approaching a select number of narratives from the long twentieth century, from more or less marginal contexts, the volume explores how the concept may be put into practice and demonstrates how vernaculars operate within different literary, critical, cultural and political circumstances.

In the collectively authored *Northern Crossings* we analyse cosmopolitanizing and vernacularizing translational processes from the point of view of the literary semi-periphery. Literary traffic to and from Swedish displays a nuanced palette of diverse intercultural relations. The world literary system has hitherto been predominantly described from a binary centre–periphery perspective. A focus on the semi-periphery makes visible other important phenomena in the formation of interlingual literary flows. Our studies show that the logic of integration into new literary cultures does not follow one set of principles or a single pattern. The strategies employed by publishers, translators and other intermediaries in adapting the foreign text to a new literary culture always put the cosmopolitan–vernacular dynamic into play, but exactly what processes are implemented depends on a wide range of variables, such as genre, narrative technique, literary style, textual and authorial position in source and target cultures, publishing agendas, translator profiles and overall relations between specific literary cultures.

Literature and the Making of the World, finally, engages the cosmopolitan-vernacular dynamic by focusing on a range of literary practices and materialities. In its first section, 'Worlds in texts', the world-making potential of place, genre and language is explored in readings of, among other things, French nineteenth-century novels, Lu Xun's 'A Madman's Diary' and Siberian exile writing. The second section, 'Texts in worlds', looks at literary journals, the profession of travel writers, the social world of a scrapbook keeper in Harlem and the trajectory of a contemporary novel in the Indian language Kannada with a view to fleshing out, in an anthropological spirit, the 'world' of world literature as an experiential and embodied category. In contrast to macro-scale varieties of world literature studies, the empirically fine-grained contributions to this volume bring close reading, book history, ethnography and historical contextualization to bear on its selected instances of literary practice.

References

Adejunmobi, M. (2004), *Vernacular Palaver: Imaginations of the Local and Non-native Languages in West Africa*, Clevedon: Multilingual Matters.

Adejunmobi, M. (2005), 'Major and Minor Discourses of the Vernacular: Discrepant African Histories', in F. Lionnet and S. Shih (eds), *Minor Transnationalism*, 179–97, Durham, NC: Duke University Press.

Ahmed, S. (2018), *Archaeology of Babel: The Colonial Foundation of the Humanities*, Stanford, CA: Stanford University Press.

Apter, E. (2013), *Against World Literature: On the Politics of Untranslatability*, London: Verso.

Arendt, H. ([1958] 1998), *The Human Condition*, Chicago, IL: Chicago University Press.

Auerbach, E. (1952), 'Philologie der Weltliteratur', in W. Henschen, W. Muschg and E. Staiger (eds), *Weltliteratur: Festgabe für Fritz Strich zum 70. Geburtstag*, 39–50, Bern: Francke.

Barber, K. (2007), *The Anthropology of Texts, Persons and Publics*, Cambridge: Cambridge University Press.

Bauman, R. and C. Briggs (2003), *Voices of Modernity: Language Ideologies and the Politics of Inequality*, Cambridge: Cambridge University Press.

Beecroft, A. (2015), *An Ecology of World Literature*, London: Verso.

Bhabha, H. (1996), 'Unsatisfied: Notes on Vernacular Cosmopolitanism', in L. Garcia-Morena and P. Pfeifer (eds), *Text and Nation*, 191–207, London: Camden House.

Bhattacharya, B. (2016), 'On Comparatism in the Colony: Archives, Methods, and the Project of *Weltliteratur*', *Critical Inquiry* 42: 677–711.

Blommaert, J. (2010), *The Sociolinguistics of Globalization*, Cambridge: Cambridge University Press.

Boehmer, E. (2014), 'The World and the Postcolonial', *European Review* 22 (2): 299–308.

Boehmer, E. (2018), *Postcolonial Poetics*, Cham: Palgrave Macmillan.

Buzelin, H. and C. Baraldi (2016), 'Sociology and Translation Studies: Two Disciplines Meeting', in Y. Gambier and L. Van Doorslaer (eds), *Border Crossings: Translation Studies and Other Disciplines*, 117–39, Amsterdam: John Benjamins.

Casanova, P. (1999), *La république mondiale des lettres*, Paris: Seuil.

Cheah, P. (2008), 'What Is a World? On World Literature as World-Making Activity', *Daedalus* 13: 26–38.

Cheah, P. (2016), *What Is a World? On Postcolonial Literature as World Literature*, Durham, NC: Duke University Press.

Cheah, P. (2017), 'Worlding Literature: Living with Tiger Spirits', *Diacritics* 45 (2): 86–114.

Cohen, M., ed. (2013), *Novel Approaches to Anthropology: Contributions to Literary Anthropology*, New York: Lexington Books.

Coundouriotis, E. (1999), *Claiming History: Colonialism, Ethnography, and the Novel*, New York: Columbia University Press.

Da, N. (2019), 'The Computational Case against Computational Literary Studies', *Critical Inquiry* 45: 601–39.

Damrosch, D. (2003), *What Is World Literature?*, Princeton, NJ: Princeton University Press.

Debaene, V. (2010), *L'Adieu au voyage. L'ethnologie française entre science et littérature*, Paris: Gallimard.

Desai, G. (2001), *Subject to Colonialism: African Self-Fashioning and the Colonial Library*, Durham, NC: Duke University Press.

De Swaan, A. (2001), *Words of the World: The Global Language System*, Cambridge: Polity Press.

Ette, O. (2016), *TransArea: A Literary History of Globalization*, trans. Mark W. Person, Berlin: De Gruyter.

Ganguly, D. (2016), *This Thing Called the World: The Contemporary Novel as Global Form*, Durham, NC: Duke University Press.

Gramling, D. (2016), *The Invention of Monolingualism*, New York: Bloomsbury.

Hayot, E. (2012), *On Literary Worlds*, Oxford: Oxford University Press.

Heilbron, J. (1999), 'Book Translation as a Cultural World-System', *European Journal of Social Theory* 2 (4): 429–44.

Heilbron, J. (2020), 'Obtaining World Fame from the Periphery', *Dutch Crossing: Journal of Low Countries Studies* 44 (2): 136–44.

Helgesson, S. (2014), 'Postcolonialism and World Literature: Rethinking the Boundaries', *Interventions* 16 (4): 483–500.

Helgesson, S. and C. Kullberg (2018), 'Translingual Events: World Literature and the Making of Language', *Journal of World Literature* 3 (2): 136–52.

Helgesson, S. and P. Vermeulen, eds (2016), *Institutions of World Literature: Writing, Translation, Markets*, New York: Routledge.

Heller-Roazen, D. (2005), *Echolalias: On the Forgetting of Language*, New York: Zone Books.

Hemer, O. (2020), *Contaminations and Ethnographic Fictions: Southern Crossings*, Cham: Palgrave.

Hitchcock, P. (2010), *The Long Space: Transnationalism and Postcolonial Form*, Stanford, CA: Stanford University Press.

Huggan, G. (2011), 'The Trouble with World Literature', in A. Behdad and D. Thomas (eds), *A Companion to Comparative Literature*, 490–506, Oxford: Blackwell.

Izzo, J. (2019), *Experiments with Empire: Anthropology and Fiction in the French Atlantic*, Durham, NC: Duke University Press.

Kullberg, C. (2013), *Poetics of Ethnography in Martinican Narratives: Exploring the Self and the Environment*, Charlottesville, VA: University of Virginia Press.

Laachir, K., S. Marzagora and F. Orsini (2018), 'Significant Geographies: In Lieu of World Literature', *Journal of World Literature* 3 (3): 290–310.

Leffler, Y. (2020), *Swedish Nineteenth-Century Literature and World Literature: Transnational Success and Literary History*, Gothenburg: Göteborg University.

Lemke, S. (2009), *The Vernacular Matters of American Literature*, Basingstoke: Palgrave Macmillan.

Mani, B. V. (2017), *Recoding World Literature: Libraries, Print Culture, and Germany's Pact with Books*, New York: Fordham University Press.

McGann, J. (1991), *The Textual Condition*, Princeton, NJ: Princeton University Press.

Messling, M. (2019), *Universalität nach dem Universalismus: über frankophonen Literaturen der Gegenwart*, Berlin: Matthes & Seitz.

Minaard, L. and T. Dembeck (2014), 'Introduction: How to Challenge the Myth of Monolingualism?', *Thamyris/Intersecting* 28: 9–14.

Moretti, F. (2000), 'Conjectures on World Literature', *New Left Review* 1: 54–68.

Mufti, A. (2016), *Forget English! Orientalisms and World Literatures*, Cambridge, MA: Harvard University Press.

Neumann, B. and G. Rippl (2017), 'Anglophone World Literatures: Introduction', *Anglia* 135 (1): 1–20.

Noyes, J. (2015), *Herder: Aesthetics against Imperialism*, Toronto: University of Toronto Press.

Orsini, F. (2004), 'India in the Mirror of World Fiction', in C. Prendergast (ed.), *Debating World Literature*, 319–33, London: Verso.

Orsini, F. (2015), 'The Multilingual Local in World Literature', *Comparative Literature* 67 (4): 345–74.

Pollock, S. (2000), 'Cosmopolitan and Vernacular in History', *Public Culture* 12 (3): 591–625.
Pollock, S. (2006), *The Language of the Gods in the World of Men*, Berkeley, CA: University of California Press.
Rapport, N. (1994), *The Prose and the Passion: Anthropology, Literature and the Writing of E.M. Forster*, Manchester: Manchester University Press.
Richter, S. (2017), *Eine Weltgeschichte der deutschsprachigen Literatur*, Munich: Bertelsmann.
Robbins, B. and P. Horta (2017), *Cosmopolitanisms*, New York: New York University Press.
Rosendahl Thomsen, M. (2008), *Mapping World Literature: International Canonization and Translational Literatures*, London: Continuum.
Sakai, N. (2009), 'How Do We Count a Language? Translation and Discontinuity', *Translation Studies* 2 (1): 71–88.
Sánchez Prado, I. (2018) *Strategic Occidentalism: On Mexican Fiction, the Neoliberal Book Market, and the Question of World Literature*, Evanston, IL: Northwestern University Press.
Sapiro, G., ed. (2008), *Translatio: le marché de traduction en France à l'heure de la mondialisation*, Paris: CNRS éditions.
Shankar, S. (2012), *Flesh and Fish Blood: Postcolonialism, Translation, and the Vernacular*, Berkeley, CA: University of California Press.
Slaughter, J. (2014), 'World Literature as Property', *Alif* 34: 39–73.
Spivak, G. (2012), 'The Stakes of a World Literature', in G. Spivak, *An Aesthetic Education in the Era of Globalization*, 455–66, Cambridge, MA: Harvard University Press.
Stockhammer, R. (2015), 'Wie deutsch ist es? Glottamimetische, -diegetische, -pithanone, und -aporetische Verfahren in der Literatur', *Arcadia* 50: 146–72.
Sturm-Trigonakis, E., ed. (2020), *World Literature and the Postcolonial*, Berlin: Springer.
Tageldin, S. M. (2018), 'Beyond Latinity, Can the Vernacular Speak?', *Comparative Literature* 70 (2): 114–31.
Tagore, R. ([1907] 2015), 'Vishva Sahitya', trans. R. Das and M. R. Paranjape, in D. Benerjii (ed.), *Rabindranath Tagore in the 21st Century*, 277–88, New Delhi: Springer.
Tidigs, J. and M. Huss (2017), 'The Noise of Multilingualism: Reader Diversity, Linguistic Borders and Literary Multimodality', *Critical Multilingualism Studies* 5 (1): 208–35.
Tiwari, B. and D. Damrosch, eds (2019 and 2020), Special issues on world literature and postcolonial studies, *Journal of World Literature* 4 (3) and 5 (3).
Uimonen, P. (2020), *Invoking Flora Nwapa: Nigerian Women Writers, Femininity and Spirituality in World Literature*, Stockholm: Stockholm University Press.
Warner, M. (2002), 'Publics and Counterpublics', *Public Culture* 14 (1): 49–90.

Warwick Research Collective (WReC) (2015), *Combined and Uneven Development: Towards a New Theory of World-Literature*, Liverpool: Liverpool University Press.

Werbner, P. (2006), 'Vernacular Cosmopolitanism', *Theory, Culture & Society* 23 (2–3): 496–8.

Wulff, H. (2017), *Rhythms of Writing: An Anthropology of Irish Literature*, London: Bloomsbury.

Yildiz, Y. (2012), *Beyond the Mother Tongue: The Postmonolingual Condition*, New York: Fordham University Press.

Young, R. J. C. (2011), 'World Literature and Postcolonialism', in T. D'haen, D. Damrosch and D. Kadir (eds), *The Routledge Companion to World Literature*, 213–22. Abingdon: Routledge.

1

Introduction: The cosmopolitan, the vernacular and the semi-periphery

How do literary texts circulate between languages and literary cultures? Well, it depends. The conditions for adapting stories, plays and poems to new audiences show great variety. This is not only due to different relations between languages, cultures and markets, but also to generic differences and particular shifts in status, values and associations involved in the translational process. In this book, we are looking at a specific kind of translational situation: the literary traffic to and from Swedish.

The Swedish literary market is certainly not a central space in the world literary system, but neither is it a distinctly peripheral one. Alongside a few other literary languages – among them Spanish, Italian, Danish and Polish – Swedish can be placed in the so-called literary semi-periphery, a middle position between the very significant and dominant central languages on the one hand and the dominated peripheral languages on the other (Casanova 2004).

Our collective studies show that one effect of this un-dominant and un-dominated position of literary Swedish – as a source language as well as a target language – is a very nuanced and multifaceted relation to the cosmopolitan and the vernacular. Seen as two ends of a dynamic spectrum between, on the one hand, transnational and ostensibly universal tendencies, and on the other hand, firm anchorage in a particular and limited cultural space, the cosmopolitan and the vernacular have proven productive concepts in understanding the semi-peripheral translational position of literary Swedish. Sometimes, literary translations to and from Swedish have cosmopolitanizing effects, but just as often they tend to vernacularize texts, œuvres and cultural phenomena.

The two fundamental concepts of our exploration are not to be understood as absolutes. Rather than seeking definitions of what the cosmopolitan and the vernacular entail, we want to identify and study the processes and strategies of cosmopolitanizing and vernacularizing. Consequently, we would like to distance ourselves from every use of the vernacular as synonymous with a particular political or cultural entity, such as a region or a nation. Instead, we would like to re-interpret them as terms describing processes in the circulation of literature. Cosmopolitanizing and vernacularizing are movements in two different directions on a scale from the most limited circulation of cultural goods to the largest possible one. Crucially, cosmopolitanization and vernacularization can exist alongside one another (e.g. in a text) and can be differently configured on different levels.

Cosmopolitanizing, when it comes to the circulation of literature, means, as we understand it, adapting a text in a generalist way, playing down its source culture particularities. Vernacularizing, on the other hand, means highlighting these very particularities. These processes do not occur only in translation and translation practices, but also in publishing, framing and marketing of translated literature. Consequently, not only translators but also intermediaries of many different types are involved in the shaping of these processes.

Equally important is that we do not intend to identify or analyse the cultural identities of literatures and authors. Of course, every author is rooted in a specific cultural, political and social environment – or, in the case of migrant or exiled authors, several such environments – but these kinds of environment are not the focus of our study. We are not so much concerned with the authors themselves, but rather with the way that authors and works are handled, presented and processed in the practice of cultural transfer.

We have chosen the semi-periphery as our main focus in this volume. While central and peripheral literary spaces have been defined and, at least to some extent, studied, the semi-periphery has not been taken into due consideration by scholars of world literature. We suggest that the semi-periphery is an ideal point of departure to further the understanding of world literature, because this is a place where the cosmopolitan and the vernacular interact in ways that have not yet been thoroughly explored. As a consequence of this continuing negotiation between the cosmopolitan and the vernacular, the semi-periphery is an area of transition in which the concepts of 'centre' and 'periphery' are questioned. This means that our investigation will also offer a discussion of the centre-periphery model as such.

The state-of-the-art

Although this volume has been conceived and written with an ambition to broaden the research perspectives on world literature, there are a number of similar works that together have paved the way for our contribution. We would like to especially mention the following.

In some ways analogous with our volume, the anthology *How Peripheral is the Periphery? Translating Portugal Back and Forth* (2015) provides an examination of translation flows in and out of the Portuguese cultural system. The discussion's rationale draws from the assumption that Portugal's cultural system should be regarded as semi-peripheral for its intermediary position of cultural and literary transfer. This position derives, in turn, from the historical (as a colonial power) and sociocultural perspectives in which Portugal has, simultaneously, inhabited a central position within the Portuguese-speaking world and a peripheral position within the European context (Maia et al. 2015: xix). The volume has a twofold aim, as it sets out to reflect upon Portugal's position as a place of translation (of import and export) and to critically and theoretically explore the position of the (semi-)periphery, as posed in the title. The case studies cover a rich variety of literary genres and provide an analysis of, e.g., what is translated in and out of Portugal in different historical periods, as well as illustrative examples of imported translations filling a void in the national production. The analytical approach, in some parts, coincides with ours, although the present volume covers more translation flows, while also placing an emphasis on intermediary agents.

The volume *Doing Double Dutch* (2017) presents a substantial study of the circulation of Dutch literature abroad, with a focus on cultural mediators and reception. The theoretical and methodological framework is largely inspired by theories on cultural transfer and the sociology of translation. Drawing on this common ground, the twelve case studies explore a variety of themes with regard to Dutch literature. The analyses are often intertwined with notions and ideas deriving from the fields of reception studies, intermedial studies, adaptation studies, cultural memory studies, etc. The focus of *Doing Double Dutch* differs, however, from the studies included in the present volume, as we take into consideration translation flows both into and out of Sweden. We also address translation to a greater extent, exploring translation strategies in the actual texts, as we recognize the importance of addressing translation not only as a means of circulation but also as a literary strategy.

The same can be said about an older study with a similar scope, the 2008 *Translatio: Le marché de la traduction en France à l'heure de la mondialisation*. This volume, edited by literary sociologist Gisèle Sapiro, presents results from a collective study of the French publishing landscape, but also sheds light on translations from French. The focus of the different contributions is largely the same as in the present volume, including an analysis of the agents of cultural transfer (publishers, translators, institutions, etc.). In the introduction, Sapiro expresses an ambition similar to ours: to use the sociological study of agents as a way to escape from binary oppositions and to arrive at a more nuanced understanding of cultural transfer. Much like *Doing Double Dutch* though, the authors of *Translatio* largely omit the study of translation strategies. Also, while there are a few passages discussing French as a source language for literary translation, the bulk of the volume specifically deals with the French publishing landscape.

In the introduction to *Translation and World Literature* (2019), Susan Bassnett highlights 'the rocky relationship between translation studies and world literature' and the 'lack of communication' between the two disciplines (2019: 1). By underlining the importance of language skills in the field of translation studies and its links to comparative literature, Bassnett outlines how these studies differ from the scholarly background of world literature studies. The essays included in the book put emphasis on translation, including both close and distant reading. For instance, by focusing on the transnational circulation *and* translation strategies in conventional and popular literature, Martín Gaspar's study criticizes the tendency in both fields to concentrate on either innovative and subversive literature or on consecrated 'masterpieces' and other 'world literature-worthy' literature (2019: 107).

The recent volume *Translating the Literatures of Small European Nations* (2020) takes into account several issues that are relevant for the present study. As the title indicates, the studies included in the book explore how so-called 'small-nation' European literatures (i.e. Catalan, Czech, Dutch, Greek, Maltese, Polish, Portuguese, Slovene, etc.) circulate transnationally and how these literatures 'negotiate and seek to overcome the inequality born of these mutual "provincialisms", as expressed in theory, reception and industry practice' (Chitnis and Stougaard-Nielsen 2020: 1). The introduction to the volume reflects on the risk of overestimating the importance of the dominant centre-periphery model but also the opposite risk of underestimating power relations and 'peripheral desires for the centre' (2020: 4). The case studies offer many valuable contributions to the field of circulation studies and to the present volume, for instance Gunilla Hermansson's and Yvonne Leffler's essay on the transnational circulation of nineteenth-century Swedish women writers, and Ondřej Vimr's study on supply-driven translation which addresses the importance of state support for interperipheral circulation. As in the cases of *Translatio* and *Doing Double Dutch*, the volume avoids taking into consideration the textual dimension of translation as well as the notion of the semi-periphery.

Another recent publication, *Scandinavia through Sunglasses: Spaces of Cultural Exchange between Southern/Southeastern Europe and Nordic Countries* (2019), is an outcome of the research group 'Found in translation: Southern Europe/Norden', based at Oslo University. The volume is divided into three sections, of which the first and most substantial one concerns literature. The seven essays included in the section deal with a variety of issues related to representations of the North and South in authorships, literary texts and translations. However, only three of the essays address similar issues as the ones we explore in the present volume: Ingela Johansson's and Marianna Smaragdi's investigation of Swedish literature in Greece and Spain, Hanne Jansen's study of the selection strategies of contemporary Italian literature translated into Danish and Giorgia D'Aprile Østvær's analysis of how culture-specific items in a Swedish novel are translated into Norwegian, English, Italian and Spanish.

Afropolitan Literature as World Literature (2020), the most recent instalment in Bloomsbury's 'Literatures as World Literature' series, takes as its topic the type of cosmopolitan novel that has been published to international best-selling effect in recent decades. Written by authors such as Chimamanda Ngozi Adichie, Teju Cole, Tayie Selasi, Yaa Ghasi and others, the Afropolitan novel, and the ideas associated with it, has been simultaneously acclaimed for presenting alternatives to Afro-pessimism and criticized for its elitism and blindness to African social realities. In his introduction, the editor James Hodapp sets out the terms of the debate and contextualizes the emergence of the genre. Importantly for our purposes in this study, Hodapp suggests that its international success presents 'unique challenges to World Literature systems' (2020: 6). What Hodapp means is that, in what he calls Damrosch's 'model' of world literature (which is Hodapp's point of reference), literary works achieve international recognition *after* national fame. Damrosch's 'world literature', according to this view, is a canon of translated works made up of the best works from various national cultures. As Hodapp rightly points out – and in doing so, reiterates a point made by Graham Huggan, Eileen Julien and others in recent decades – for almost all works that count as African in transnational literary space, the opposite trajectory is the case. Afropolitan works are 'born global', Hodapp writes in a phrase that echoes Rebecca Walkowitz' 'born-translated', and gain traction 'as literature *of* the continent by achieving *outside* the continent' (2020: 6).

Another conceptually important work for our research is one of the latest volumes in the book series 'Literature and Contemporary Thought', *Literature and the World* (2020) by Stefan Helgesson and Mads Rosendahl Thomsen. The volume consists of seven chapters guided by the ambition to critically present some of the main tendencies in world literature studies today and to identify blind spots and problems in its current phase of development. The seven chapters discuss four approaches in relation to world literature: the seasoned national and comparative schools as well as perspectives from postcolonial and translation studies, the scales of the ecologies of literature (Beecroft 2015) and the concept of significant geographies (Laachir et al. 2018). Furthermore, the impact of the methodology of digitization in the humanities and its significance for world literature are emphasized in the chapter 'Media and Method: The Digitized Babel'. Particularly the chapters 'Geographies: Reading the Oceans' – in the way that it clearly shows how the routes of literature cross with the patterns laid out by historical power relations – and 'Translation: Duration and Cosmopolitan Reading' – in its way of elucidating how the complexity of language and the choices of the translator are central issues for world literature studies – have been crucial for our endeavour.

Together, these works show the potential inherent in our perspective on world literature. In the following section, we will further elaborate on the background and object of the present study.

Sweden, a particular case of the possible

In order to analyse the role that translation plays in the semi-periphery and to describe the conditions under which literature travels to and from that position (as well as studying the cosmopolitanizing and vernacularizing processes included in that transition), we have chosen to work with what in Bourdieusian terms might be called a particular case of the possible. The purpose of this volume, then, is to describe and analyse the role of the *Swedish* semi-peripheral position in world literature from different perspectives and on different levels, using both quantitative and qualitative methods, and with an emphasis on the period 1980–2018. Our aim is twofold: to analyse the role that translation plays in the semi-periphery and to describe the conditions under which literature travels to and from that position.

The existing studies of semi-peripheral literary spaces, some of which have been mentioned above, tend to focus on one language or one nation. The scope of the present volume is wider. Sweden, Swedish literature and the Swedish publishing field are used as recurring examples, even though the focus is not on Sweden as such, but rather on the semi-peripheral transitional space as exemplified by the Swedish case. In order to describe the dynamics of this semi-peripheral space, we study literature moving both in and out of Sweden.

In other words, our analysis of a particular case does not mean that we give up the ambition to make generalizable propositions. Rather the opposite, since the comparative method, which treats its object as 'a particular case of the possible', prevents us from unjustifiably universalizing the conclusions. Furthermore, Sweden presents an especially productive case, since its status as a semi-peripheral literary sphere has proven to be remarkably consistent, compared to other languages that have been moving in and out of the semi-peripheral position, e.g. Russian, Japanese, Danish, Polish and Czech.

This understanding of the semi-periphery gives our volume a broad perspective as it involves very different literatures that share a similar position in the literary field and/or interact in different ways with literatures in that same position. The literatures studied are, on the one hand, Swedish literature translated into English and French and, on the other, Caribbean (in Spanish, French and English), Lusophone, Italian and Anglophone African literature translated into Swedish. In the following paragraphs, we will give an introductory overview of these translation flows.

Translations from Swedish to English have lived through some distinct changes since the 1970s. Early in this period, classics and children's literature were dominant categories. Whereas children's literature has kept its central position until today, the extent to which Swedish classics have been translated has fallen significantly compared to other kinds of literature. In the 1980s and the 1990s, there was an increase of contemporary, high prestige Swedish fiction in English, but around the turn of the millennium this genre was overshadowed by suspense fiction. Since 2000, crime novels have been central in the presence of Swedish literature on Anglophone markets. Some of the best-known authors and titles have, of course, been published by big and powerful American and British publishers, but English translations of Swedish literature have predominantly been published by a wide range of small agents, not only based in many different parts of the USA and the UK, but also in India, Australia, New Zealand and Ireland. In recent years, there has also been a distinct increase of English translations published by small Swedish publishers.

Swedish literature translated and published in France is characterized by a large proportion of high prestige literature, by both older canonized authors and contemporary consecrated ones. This can be partly explained by the French literary field occupying such a central position in the world literary space, urging Swedish authors and publishers to put in extra work in order to accomplish translations of high prestige literature. French publishers were also quick to catch on during the boom-like success of Scandinavian crime fiction in the first decade of the twenty-first century. Swedish children's books, on the other hand, saw a somewhat later breakthrough on the French book market than on other comparable markets. Translations play an important role in France, where prestigious publishers market their translations in special series, such as Gallimard's Du monde entier and Le Seuil's Cadre vert. Especially since the 1980s, translations – both from and to French – have enjoyed state support in what has been described as a conscious counter-strategy, in the face of a rising anglo-globalization.

Italian is a rather small language in comparison to other Romance languages such as Spanish and Portuguese, and yet its literature enjoys a prominent position internationally, including in Sweden. To a large extent, Italian literature translated into Swedish consists of older classical works from the Middle Ages and the Renaissance, modern classics from the twentieth century and contemporary literature which has been consecrated by national institutions. Even though literature with a high commercial potential is less represented, translations originating from the Italian language area are available in almost every literary and non-literary genre. The Swedish import from Italian includes mainly novels but also poetry, theatre, graphic novels and children's literature as well as a considerable proportion of non-fiction, such as reportage, religious literature, philosophy, cookbooks and gardening books. Postcolonial writing, which emerged in Italy in the 1990s, has to date left very few traces on the Swedish book market.

Anglophone African literature exemplifies a literary culture that is at once smaller than a language and larger – indeed, much larger – than a nation. Within the segmented thinking common in the publishing world, 'African' – in whatever language – constitutes a significant category for the selection and the marketing of books (Thompson; Huggan). 'African literature' is a niche for publishers, comparable to other niches, and the existence of literary festivals, literary prizes, specialized publishers and book series devoted to this literature are examples of its existence (e.g. Ducourneau). This is the case even when the category is sometimes part of broader labels such as 'postcolonial literature' or 'world literature' (Brouillette; Huggan).

Historically, the discourse of 'African' literature is in significant ways an effect of colonial print culture. From the establishment of the first missionary presses to more developed cultural fields – literary production in what at the time were colonies was imperially structured. One of the lasting effects of this colonial history is that, with the exception of countries such as South Africa and Nigeria, which have large culture sectors, literary fields, at least when it comes to printed matter, are in many places highly transnational – or, as other critics have labelled it: extroverted (Julien 2006; see also Suhr-Sytsma 2018). Two effects of this characteristic relevant for the present study may be noted. First, international writing careers do not develop, as in the case of some of the other literatures investigated here, through national recognition *first* and translation and/or foreign publication *second*. In practical terms, with one single exception – the author Elieshi Lema from Tanzania – all the works included in the material studied here were published first in the UK or the USA. Second (though a related point), in what appears almost an inversion of European authors reaching international fame, acknowledgement in African markets *follows* international fame (Hodapp).

The category 'Anglophone African' as used in this study is, then, intended to combine two ambitions, one analytical and one discursive: on the one hand to capture the number and the rate of Anglophone writers from the African continent who are published in Sweden, and on the other, to discuss the extent to which books by African authors are published and marketed *as* 'African' – that is, whether they are cosmopolitanized or vernacularized.

Like Wendy Griswold in her study of the 'Nigerian literary complex' (2000), we use birth or a prolonged stay in an African country (or the colonies that preceded the independent country) as the selective criteria. This means that Doris Lessing and Alexander McCall Smith, both of whom were born in what was Southern Rhodesia and later became Zimbabwe, and lived longer periods outside the African continent, are defined as 'African' authors – and as a consequence novels by Lessing with no African content or theme are included in the category. For most of the authors, it remains the case that they live in places such as the USA or UK (or like Nuruddin Farah in South Africa or J. M. Coetzee in Australia) or live between continents.

Translated literatures from Portuguese into Swedish, referred to in the present volume as Lusophone literatures, originate from a variety of geographical locations: Angola, Brazil, Cape Verde, East Timor, Mozambique and Portugal. Consequently, this literature also constitutes a non-national literary flow and a culture much larger and more diversified than a single nation. The notion of 'Lusophone' will be used in this volume, strictly as an adjective, when referring to all these literatures written in the Portuguese language (for practical reasons such as not having to constantly list the source cultures). Yet it should be stated that the use of the term here by no means suggests a notion of homogeneity for these diverse cultural expressions, blind to the internal cultural power structures and uneven circulation conditions that clearly exist between these different literary flows in a global perspective. On the contrary, as many researchers have rightly pointed out, an unpolitical and unified cultural conception of 'lusophony' as representing a larger cultural Portuguese-speaking community still needs to be questioned and decolonized (see Almeida 2004, Martins 2012).

For the translations into Swedish, the common denominator of the Portuguese language functions as a predominant organizing factor for how these literatures come to be translated and published. However, a single focus on language cannot present the whole picture of the migration paths of these translations. On the one hand, an approach to the Lusophone literature as an entity is justified because these literatures, to a high degree, share the same limited pole of translators and small-scale niche publishers, as well as enthusiastic cultural mediators promoting its dissemination. On the other hand, African, Brazilian and Portuguese literatures all contain specific interrelations of cultural exchange and historical connections with the Swedish cultural environment, which influence and guide their translational pathways.

With historical roots in colonialism, the Portuguese language is today one of the most spoken and geographically widespread languages worldwide. Nevertheless, when it comes to the Swedish literary market, there is still a modest translation flow. During the period 1980–2018, most of the Lusophone translated authors are men (79 per cent) and belong to the category of contemporary award-winning and highly consecrated authors in their source cultures, as well as in the inner Lusophone market. The novel is by far the most translated genre, although some poetry and children's literature are also published. There is a predominance of translations from Brazilian authors (58 per cent), over Portuguese authors

(28 per cent) and African authors (13 per cent). A tendency that has increased constantly and which has allowed literature from Brazil to be more diversified, in terms of published popular authors, women writers and biographies.

Much as in the preceding sections considering Anglophone African and Lusophone literature, what is considered Caribbean literature written in French, Spanish and English is on the one hand determined geographically by the use of the adjective 'Caribbean', and on the other by the way that the authors are presented to the Swedish readers – as Caribbean authors, which is an important marketing and framing strategy shown to appeal to northern minds. The literatures stemming from this part of the world are homogeneous neither when it comes to languages, genres and literary themes nor when it comes to patterns in bibliomigration (Mani 2014, 2017) to peripheral or semi-peripheral positions in the global translation field. What they have in common is their colonial history of oppression, the use of the colonial languages (sometimes mixed with local varieties as in the case of Maryse Condé, Edwidge Danticat and Junot Díaz) and the fact that the overwhelming majority of the works translated into Swedish are contemporary novels, written by notable writers and translated by highly consecrated translators, whether American or Swedish. Another common feature of Caribbean literatures is that they do not constitute an important literary flow to Sweden in numbers during the examined time span. The importance of French and Spanish as source languages in translation into Swedish has decreased constantly during the last decades, presently not even reaching 3 per cent of the published translations, and Caribbean Spanish and French literature represent a tiny fraction of that percentage. English as a source language for translations into Swedish, on the contrary, covers more than 70 per cent of all translated fiction today and has constantly – compared to French and Spanish – increased during the same time.

However, Caribbean literature in the three different languages represents in fact three different literary consecration cultures, where the French language Caribbean literature can be described as mono-centric, the English language as duo-centric and the Spanish language Caribbean literature as pluri-centric, which means that vernacularizing translation processes differ substantially from one language group to the other (Lindqvist 2019). French and Spanish novels often need to be consecrated within the Anglo-American literary culture before being considered for translation into Swedish. These bibliomigration patterns are formed by double consecration processes, firstly within the centre(s) of the former colonial power (Paris, Madrid, Barcelona) and secondly within the centres of the

Anglo-American literary culture (New York, London). Few Swedish publishers will undertake the costly enterprise of publishing a Caribbean author who has not previously been consecrated by international literary prizes or awards.

An approach to world systems theory

World literature is a system of interconnected literatures; that is the basic realization governing this study. Unlike scholars who have seen 'world literature' as a global canon or mode of reading (Damrosch), or a particular type of literature (Walkowitz, Parks), our approach fits well in a tradition of scholars from the American sociologist and economic historian Immanuel Wallerstein and the Dutch sociologist Abram de Swaan, the Italian-American literary scholar Franco Moretti and the French literary sociologists Pascale Casanova and Gisèle Sapiro (the latter two heavily inspired by Pierre Bourdieu). Wallerstein's 'world systems theory' (1974), a macro-scale approach to world history and social change designed to analyse the division of labour between core, semi-peripheral and peripheral countries, was further developed by de Swaan (2001) into a theory of a global language system, consisting of a hierarchy of languages on four different levels: peripheral, central, super-central and hyper-central. Marxist dialectics is a key ingredient in both Wallerstein's and de Swaan's system: social relations and/or language positions are dependent on economic and political structures.

The thought of a 'world system' was of great importance for the revitalization of the study of world literature, which occurred around the turn of the millennium. In a move that both extended and critiqued postcolonial and comparative literary studies as they had previously been practised, Moretti claimed that world literature should not be regarded as a set of works or a canon; according to him, world literature is not even 'an object, it's a problem, and a problem that asks for a new critical method'. Like world capitalism, Moretti claimed (echoing Wallerstein's Marxist approach) world literature is 'one, and unequal: with a core, and a periphery (and a semi-periphery) that are bound together in a relationship of growing inequality' (Moretti 2000).

The theory of a 'global literary space' was also at the centre of Pascale Casanova's seminal book *La république mondiale des lettres* (1999; *The World Republic of Letters* 2004). Wallerstein's binary opposition between core and periphery is still present in Casanova's work, where dominating literatures are separated from dominated ones and where the state of literature today is the result of a constant fight for symbolic literary power, acquired with the help of aesthetic originality. On the other hand, in *La république mondiale des lettres* there is a strong emphasis on the independence of the literary world: 'its boundaries, its capitals, its highways and its forms of communication do not completely coincide with those of the political or economic world'. Clinging on to this relative independence of literature, Casanova has been described as too idealistic, and her model conspicuously ignores the popular dimensions of literary production and circulation, which are more firmly tied to economic incentives and logics. Several of her colleagues – among them Sapiro – have tried to integrate her vision of the literary world with the practice of literary sociology, including an analysis of the politics of publishing, marketing and framing. For Casanova, the introduction of a literary work in translation is first and foremost an act of aesthetic warfare; for Sapiro, it is also – and perhaps simply – the result of a marketing strategy. Casanova has introduced the overarching vision of how the global literary space works (dominating and dominated literatures, the struggle to define *the literary now*, etc.); Sapiro points to the empirical methods that may be used to analyse these processes.

However, these thinkers' tendency to construct models in terms of binary oppositions, such as dominant and dominated, or distinct categories such as core and periphery (including, but less clearly, the semi-periphery), prove unsatisfying both in terms of description and explanation, and our focus on the semi-periphery (rather than the much more studied centre and periphery) is a way to question this theorization. How, for instance, is translation into Swedish of an Italian literary work – the transfer between two literary languages which both belong to the semi-periphery – best described in terms of the centre-periphery model? And in Casanova's terms: which language (or literary culture) consecrates which through such an act? Or, to take a different example: is the translation of an Anglophone African author's writing appropriately described as the transfer from a 'hyper-central' into a peripheral or semi-peripheral language? Or, again in Casanovan terms: what literary cultures do Anglophone or Lusophone African writers belong to, or Caribbean authors writing in English, Spanish or French?

As these examples – all drawn from the literary translation flows examined in this book – indicate, our quarrel with world systems theory lies on two points. The first concerns the bounding of literatures involved in cultural exchange, the second concerns the relevant scale of comparison.

In world-scale comparisons of translation flows, such as Johan Heilbron's for instance, language is used as the analytical unit. On this basis, languages are grouped with respect to their centrality and their role in the global exchange of literature. English, as stated, is 'hyper-central' due to the proportion of translations, and central languages function as mediators for translation:

> the communication between peripheral [language] groups often passes via a centre ... the more central a language is in the language system, the more it has the capacity to function as an intermediary of *vehicular language*, that is, as a means of communication between language groups which are themselves peripheral or semi-peripheral.
>
> (Heilbron 2000: 15)

We do not question Heilbron's description of the overall dynamics of global translation flows, but his general postulation ignores, and therefore fails to provide the tools to explain, translations that occur without passing through more central languages. In the Swedish literary semi-periphery, as will become clear in the chapters that follow, such literary exchanges make up a significant part of the total volume of translations. An additional drawback of the model is that it leaves uncommented the fact that languages and literatures do not always overlap, as the cases of Anglophone African, Lusophone Brazilian and African literatures and Caribbean literatures in this study exemplify.

From this perspective, Pascale Casanova's modelling of a world literary space, which combines language and territory, is a more flexible approach. Casanova's examples may appear somewhat ambivalent on the centrality of national space but her use of the term 'linguistico-literary capital' ('capital linguistico-littéraire') – that is, the combination of language and what she calls literary resources – indicates there is in principle nothing national about it (2002: 9). And, as Anna Boschetti has emphasized, the Bourdieusian concept of the 'field' itself is not inherently nationalist, even if Bourdieu's own analyses was centred on nationally circumscribed fields (Boschetti 2012: 19–20).

A further indication that language and literary tradition may exist as a fraught whole is, of course, Casanova's insistence that oppositional tendencies help in constituting and perpetuating literary tradition. 'For a language to acquire a high degree of literariness', Casanova writes, 'it has to have a long tradition, one that in each generation refines, modifies, and enlarges the gamut of formal and aesthetic possibilities of the language, establishing, guaranteeing, and calling attention to the literary character of what is written in it' (2004: 18). This refinement, as she clarifies, also includes literary expressions 'written *against*' established norms, as in the case of Anglophone postcolonial literature, which is her example here. However, Casanova's description of literary struggles occurring *in a language* and enriching that language even as they stretch across colonial or national spaces, is difficult to reconcile with her use – and examples – of the terms 'national' literatures, and 'national' versus 'international' writers, as well as the vagueness on the geographical boundaries of literary cultures. Postcolonial literatures offer test cases in this respect. Two examples may be briefly invoked as illustrations.

In her discussion of 'Colombian' literature, Casanova writes that 'One speaks today ... of Colombian literature and of Colombian writers as if they form a politicoliterary entity that is a recognized reality' (2004: 206). Her argument is that this talk ignores the transnational networks and discourses which enable Colombian literary space to form: the large number of exiled writers, the publishers and literary agents in Barcelona and New York, and the literary debates carried out among writers from various Latin American countries. But it is unclear in Casanova's text whether the 'Colombian novel' and the 'Latin American' novel (terms she uses interchangeably, it appears) are the same thing; and how this type of novel relates to the Spanish language in which it is written, and hence to Spanish literary culture. While her basic observation seems to us correct, it is not easy to infer from her account what literary field or fields these authors themselves are located in, help to shape and compete in.

Casanova's discussion of Trinidadian-British author V. S. Naipaul reveals this conceptual imprecision even more clearly. Quoting at length from Naipaul's lecture 'Our Universal Civilization' in which he points out the literary infrastructure needed to support a career in writing – 'To get your name on the spine of the created physical object, you need a vast apparatus outside yourself. You need publishers, editors, designers, printers, binders, booksellers, critics, newspapers, and magazines ... and, of course, buyers and readers ... This kind of society didn't exist in Trinidad' (204) – she argues that it is precisely from the insight into the social and infrastructural character of a literary space that 'dominated national literatures' can be made part of a model of world literary space. 'By describing the dilemmas, choice, and inventions of writers for outlying spaces as a set of mutually related positions' it becomes possible to 'reintegrate' exiled or migrant writers with the 'native lands' from which they have disappeared (204), she writes. What such reintegration means is, however, far from clear. What literary field, or what literary culture, should Naipaul be considered as originating from, and contributing to?

Arguably, one reason for this weakness in Casanova's analytical model is her avoidance of the empirical aspects of literary exchange. Despite her emphasis on the significance of the 'cultural intermediaries' (which serves as a point of departure in Chapter 2 in this volume), her primary focus throughout *La république mondiale des lettres* is on individual authors and nations or literary cultures – a focus that remains in her last book, on translation, *La langue mondiale*. Postcolonial literary scholarship based in print culture and book history has been better equipped to address various instances of non-alignment of language and national field under different rubrics and with more detail. In his study of the postcolonial literary magazines in Mozambique and South Africa, Stefan Helgesson uses the term 'discourse network' to describe the ways in which language and literary infrastructures make up a landscape through which literary content may travel – the point being that the 'discourse network' is reducible neither to the (newly independent) nations as in a 'national culture', nor to the language (Portuguese, English) used for creative expression, nor to the metropolitan locales which enable the circulation of the texts (2008: 11-12). Caroline Davis' studies of the activity of British publishers' activities in late-colonial and early postcolonial African countries have demonstrated the extent to which literary markets were intertwined. To account for this relation of separation and connection, Davis has adjusted Bourdieu's notion of a divided literary economy to speak of a dual market for literature in which the active publishers were able to accumulate both economic and symbolical capital at once, and through the same books, albeit in different places (2012: 346). Key to the conceptual productivity of studies such as these is their grounding in the concrete circumstances of literary production and circulation. The present volume tries to follow a similar course by staying close to the empirical ground. Rather than 'field', then, we reserve the deliberately vague term 'publishing landscape' for the spaces in which the respective translation flows occur.

The second issue – the first one being about the bounding of literatures involved in cultural exchange – concerns the scale at which literary comparisons are made. On the macro scale, analyses of translation flows typically include all *books* in all *genres*, and do not necessarily offer much to explain the ways in which *literary* works are transferred and exchanged, nor do they enable discussion of the different conditions that apply to, say, poetry, fiction, written plays or children's literature. At this aggregated level, accordingly, explanations for trends are correspondingly broad. One example is the demotion of the Russian language from being a central or semi-central one to a semi-peripheral one, which Heilbron explains as caused by the break-up of the Soviet Union (Heilbron 2000: 15). Structural and statistical bird's-eye views like these have their merits, but they also show how explanation is necessarily tied to analytical scale. What global comparison at this level forecloses are aspects such as the significance of literary genres and the key role played by agents and institutions (Franssen 2015, Meylaerts 2018). For our purposes, even studies with a comparative 'world' perspective require a more fine-grained approach. Sapiro's investigation of the translation of French literature in the United States – distinguishing between types of novels translated and publishers putting them on the literary market – and Verboord, Kuipers and Janssen's analysis of interrelated forms of institutional recognition strike us as exemplary in this regard (Sapiro 2015, Verboord, Kuipers and Janssen 2015).

The methodological choices behind our study result from our approach to world systems theory. Accounting for the interaction of the world's literatures arguably constitutes a 'problem' no less today than in 2000, when Moretti formulated his challenge. Case-based theorizations of world literature, such as Walkowitz' or Tim Parks', in which a particular *kind* of literature – the 'born-translated' novel or the 'global novel' – is taken to be typical of our times – or any time – depend on the exemplary nature of the cases presented. Even such a conceptually solid solid understanding of 'world literature' as the one used by Warwick Research Collective (WReC) – for whom the term designates literature which mediates and registers the modern capitalist world system – arguably relies on the premise that certain literary works are *more expressive than others* of the capitalist world (2015: 9). The dilemma of exemplarity in literary study is, as Moretti has recently stated, a version of the dissected meanings of what constitutes the 'normal': the 'frequent-habitual-average' or the 'ideal-normative' (2020: 129).

Quantitative methods are less vulnerable to the problem of exemplarity. In Katherine Bode's view, they also enable valuable inroads in literary study since they begin from a view of literature as a 'system … rather than a collection of individual texts' and use numbers and statistics as useful ways to investigate how the system works as well as test assumptions presented by more conceptual literary study (Bode 2012: 9, 23–4). Data, and use of a quantitative method, are central to our examination of the Swedish literary semi-periphery. As will become apparent, we use meta-data to count in several ways: the number of translations, the number of editions, the percentages of men and women authors, the years between source text publishing and translation. The statistical measures are simple and use meta-data drawn from existing databases such as

Index Translationum, or raw data provided by the national bibliographies and other authorities. The methodological steps taken are described in more detail in each chapter.

Statistical measures are, however, unable to fully answer all the questions that engage us. The analyses of translational strategies, for instance, are brought out through interpretation rather than measurement, and publishers' marketing and framing of authors – particularly in relation to processes of cosmopolitanization and vernacularization – are best discussed through hermeneutic and semiotic reading of individual book covers, blurbs and presentational material.

The aim of the methodological mix employed in this book is to enable a rich description of the literary semi-periphery and the conditions that underlie its literary traffic. In taking this vaguest and least studied literary world system position as our starting point, we also hope to add to an ongoing critical examination of the world systems model, even as we adhere to it.

A collaborative method

Much like WReC, we believe in the potential of collaborative work for the advancement of world literature study. The conception and writing of this volume would not have been possible without the special interests and research experience of the members of our research group. For a single researcher, it would be difficult to master all translation flows analysed in this volume. This has to do with the massive body of material (databases, publishers, translators, institutions) that has to be taken into consideration, as well as the many languages (English, French, Spanish, Italian, Portuguese and Swedish) in which all this literature is written. In other words, the method of co-writing is very much connected to our insistence on the importance of analysis based on empirical study. Research should start with a meticulous study of the object itself – qualitative, but also quantitative – and the more knowledge we are able to accumulate, the more valid our conclusions will be. A group of researchers is of course better suited for this kind of work than a single researcher.

The empirical groundwork of this study has been carried out by the individual scholars. Paul Tenngart has been responsible for supplying data on the Swedish–English translations, Andreas Hedberg has supplied the Swedish–French data, Cecilia Schwartz has been responsible for the Italian–Swedish flow and Chatarina

Edfeldt has contributed with the Lusophone–Swedish observations. Erik Falk has supplied data on Anglophone African literature in Swedish translation, and Yvonne Lindqvist has been responsible for studying English, French and Spanish Caribbean literature in Swedish. In collecting this data we have all followed the same three-level optics. Translational conditions have been observed on the micro, meso and macro levels – that is, on the level of particular books and texts, on the level of publishers and translators and on the level of literary markets and cultures. This three-level model has then also been operational in our collaborative work of interpreting and comparing the collected data, and in describing the translation patterns they illustrate.

Outline of the volume

Northern Crossings investigates the circulation of literature through the Swedish literary semi-periphery from a number of angles, especially during the period 1980–2018.

Chapter 2, in a reference to Pascale Casanova's idea of 'cosmopolitan intermediaries', investigates what might be called the 'cosmopolitan infrastructure', which enables literary texts to cross borders through translation. Chief among the agents making up this infrastructure are the publishers, which are the focus of the chapter, but references are also made to state policies, since translation support programmes and cultural institutes also impact patterns of literary circulation. Publishers are analysed with respect to how they are placed in their respective literary fields, and how they select and market their authors. We investigate cases of what has been called *horizontal isomorphism* (Franssen and Kuipers 2013: 67–9) in which similarly placed publishers translate and put out each other's works, and discuss instances where publishers occupy widely different positions in their respective fields.

Chapter 3 discusses translators of Nobel laureates. The focus in this section lies not so much on the translations themselves but on who are given the task of translating the authors, and whether translation is primarily a way for a translator to bolster his reputation by taking on a highly renowned author, or whether the author stands to gain by being translated by a prominent translator. The guiding assumption behind this discussion of pairings – that translators can themselves bestow symbolic capital on an author – is that in Sweden translation is an established profession which constitutes its own relatively autonomous field, an idea that is elaborated in Chapter 5. In this section, drawing on discussions of the 'economy of prestige' (English 2005), we also explore the possible existence of a 'Nobel effect' – that is, whether laureates experience a translation boom after their award.

In Chapter 4, we look at the translations themselves and the way the translated texts are packaged and presented in the target culture through 'paratexts' – for instance blurbs and publisher profiles. How do the translated texts relate to concepts such as domestication, foreignization (Venuti 1995) and untranslatability (Apter 2013)? In this chapter, we analyse a selection of novels from each translation flow, with a focus on the treatment of vernacular elements, introducing the categories of reduction, retention and replacement – are the elements of a source text that are clearly rooted in the source culture reduced, retained or replaced by the translator? The employment of the three concepts, we suggest, allows for a more detailed analysis than Lawrence Venuti's much-used domesticating/foreignization pair, especially when it comes to the different ways of handling vernacular elements in the source texts. With our wide range of examples of translations to and from semi-peripheral languages and spaces, we are also able to discuss semi-peripheral translation generally. Is semi-peripheral translation (both to and from a semi-peripheral language) a particular kind of translation?

Chapter 5 charts the broader outlines, the trends and some of the changes that occur in each translation flow over the period. Against a background that uses statistics on translation ratios to describe Sweden's position in the world literary space, we sketch the characteristics of each translation flow over the period studied with respect to the kinds of literature and gender bias. Indicators of the profile are genre, the temporal gap between source language publication and target language publication and the ratio of women authors translated. This way, we aim to provide a changing profile of the literary target culture on the Swedish literary market and in concrete ways present the Swedish position as the sum total of a set of relations with other literary cultures in which each literary exchange is driven by its own particular (if not unique) dynamics.

2

Infrastructure of the semi-peripheral exchange

In this chapter, we will examine the meso level of the transnational literary circulation, with a special focus on the semi-periphery. The overall aim is to investigate how cosmopolitanizing and vernacularizing processes are activated in relation to literature entering and exiting the semi-peripheral literary spheres. Our main hypothesis is that the semi-periphery is an intermediate literary space where the boundaries between the cosmopolitan and the vernacular are blurred and, more importantly, where ideas of the cosmopolitan and the vernacular are negotiated and transformed. In order to approach these complex issues, we will examine how the semi-periphery interacts with other literary fields, how it includes literatures from other areas and, vice versa, how it is included in foreign cultures.

According to Nicky van Es and Johan Heilbron (2015), the meso level concerns 'the predominantly national publishing fields', while actors involved in the selection, translation and framing of particular works are analysed on the micro level (298). In this study, the meso level is conceived of as including *both* these levels, since intermediaries tend to be closely related to a specific national or regional publishing field and are therefore an essential part of the *cosmopolitan infrastructure*. The translated texts will be studied in the chapter on the micro level (Chapter 4), as we want to stress the importance of conducting close readings even in studies concerned with the transnational circulation of literature. Consequently, this chapter will discuss the role of the publishing houses. In the next chapter (Chapter 3), we will move on to the translators, and specifically to a discussion of the translators of works by Nobel prize laureates.

The cosmopolitan infrastructure: Intermediaries institutions, reception

According to Pascale Casanova, a language's literariness (i.e. its power, prestige, linguistic and literary capital) is not measured in terms of the number of writers or readers it has but rather in terms of the number of *cosmopolitan intermediaries*, such as publishers, editors, critics and translators (2004: 21). Drawing on this observation, we argue for an extension of this idea to explore the *cosmopolitan infrastructure* in relation to the semi-periphery. The cosmopolitan infrastructure of a region, nation and/or language area includes the *intermediaries* mentioned by Casanova, as well as the *institutions* which proliferate literature (libraries, culture institutes, academies, universities) – all closely engaged with the *vernacular* in the source culture(s) as well as in the target culture(s). The dynamics among such actors – very much influencing the reception of translated literature – is the key interest of our analysis. In the following, we will outline a method for studying these relationships. The method will also be exemplified in the discussion that follows. In our presentation of the method, the focus will be on the publishers. The aim, however, is to provide a methodology that can be applied to other instances of the cosmopolitan infrastructure as well. Moreover, since translation will be given special attention in other parts of this volume, the following method will chiefly concentrate on *selection* and *framing*.

Sweden will be used as an example of a semi-peripheral literary space. The analysis will include examples of Swedish as a target language, but also as a source language. As a literary market, Sweden is relatively open to translated literature, the latter making up quite a large proportion of the books that are published and sold (24 per cent in 2011) (Lindqvist 2016: 75). As a source language of literary translation, Swedish is remarkably common, it is one of the ten most important globally and – like e.g. Russian and Italian – positioned between the hyper-central English, central French and German and peripheral source languages such as Japanese, Romanian and Arabic (Svedjedal 2012: 36). Taken together, the specifics of the Swedish example, both as a target language and a source language, will make it possible to shed additional light on the logics at work in the world system of literary translation, specifically when it comes to semi-peripheral spaces, but also – from the vantage point of the semi-periphery as a transitional space between extremes – regarding world literature in general.

Methodological framework

In the cosmopolitan infrastructure, publishers are intermediaries. In order to study the modes of inclusion – i.e. the strategies through which literary works are selected and framed as vernacular or cosmopolitan – we will investigate 'the process of inscription', in which publishing houses play a key role. According to Lawrence Venuti, this process is initiated as soon as foreign texts are chosen for translation, since these choices necessarily entail an exclusion of other texts as well as an inevitable domestication of the translated text, marking it with linguistic and cultural values that are understandable and attractive to the new audience (Venuti 1998: 67).

Publishing houses are crucial gatekeepers when literature travels from one culture to another, mainly because their selection and packaging reveal inclusion strategies. For instance, in recent years, three Swedish publishers of Italian literature have chosen to present their selection of authors in very different ways, the first one drawing on universality and tradition (Cartaditalia), the second on moral issues and political engagement (Astor), and the third on emotions and entertaining plots (Contempo) (Schwartz 2017). According to van Es and Heilbron (2015: 302–4), this *framing* of foreign literature involves both the publisher's activity and the media reception. They also claim that the framing strategies implemented in the marketing of peripheral literature within the pole of small-scale production (where, according to Pierre Bourdieu [1993: 74–111; 2008], intellectual or aesthetic criteria prevail rather than the law of the market) tend to highlight either the translated work's *cosmopolitan* or *vernacular qualities*. Publishing also involves consecration, a transfer of symbolic capital from the publisher to the translated work as well as from the translated work to the publisher and its repertoire of authors, who themselves were more or less consecrated beforehand (Bourdieu 2008).

Selection

In the following, we will analyse the criteria that have guided publishers' selection of foreign literary works from peripheral and semi-peripheral languages. According to van Es and Heilbron, literary works in peripheral languages are basically chosen because of their success in the source culture – a success that can be either economic or symbolic. In order to discuss these issues, we will use Bourdieu and Gisèle Sapiro's model of ideal-typic writers: the notables, the aesthetes, the popular and the avant-garde writers.

The **aesthetes** (orthodox-autonomous) are authors holding dominant positions while not adapting to the market. These writers have a strong symbolic capital that depends on neither sales nor temporary consecration, such as literary awards. Their counterparts among the dominant writers consist of the **notables** (orthodox-heteronomous), i.e. authors who have become famous thanks to temporary consecration: through literary prizes, successful sales or time-limited positions in institutions or academies.

At the dominated pole, authors are distinguished as belonging to the vanguard or to the popular. The **popular** (heterodox-heteronomous) is represented by authors who have the lowest symbolic capital in the literary hierarchy because they combine a high degree of market adaptation with a strong focus on content. Here we find writers who often live on their writing, but do not have access to literary prestige: popular writers and journalists who write about current issues as well as producing social satire, pamphlets and studies in order to cause scandal. Their non-existent symbolic capital is often replaced with a high degree of social capital. Finally, we have the **vanguard** (heterodox–autonomous) authors who lack formal power but still claim autonomy. These writers represent a subversive idea of literature, which is mainly expressed by attacking the supposedly good taste acclaimed by those at the orthodox pole. However, their attempts to redefine the prevailing aesthetic norms are also aimed at accumulating symbolic capital for themselves.

Our analysis of the selection of the target language will be guided by the following questions: *Were the selected titles successful in their source language? If so, what kind of success did they have: economic (bestsellers) or symbolic (literary awards, critical recognition)?* A second criterion is related to the fact that peripheral literatures are often translated and published by houses close to the pole of small-scale production, with a predominantly literary orientation, the market of symbolic goods in general and the book market in particular being structured around 'the opposition between small-scale and large-scale production/circulation' (Bourdieu 1993: 74–111). Moreover, the publishers tend to make their selections drawing on the elective affinity with similar publishers from foreign literary fields, i.e. *horizontal isomorphism*. These issues are investigated with the help of additional questions: *Do the publishers belong to the pole of the large-scale production or small-scale production? Are there cases of horizontal isomorphism?*

To these questions we will add the following: *How are ideas concerning the cosmopolitan and/or the vernacular reflected in the profiles and practices of the publishers?* Here, the distinction between niche publishers and generalist publishers becomes crucial. In order to find out more about the publisher's profile, their self-perceived function in the literary field and ideas related to the cosmopolitan and the vernacular, the publishers' epitexts – presentation texts on websites, interviews, articles in the press, etc. – provide useful information, especially when it comes to *niche market publishers*, whose identity is often based on translations from a particular language or geographic area. Issues concerning the publishers' peritexts – covers, prefaces, titles, notes, etc. – are also considered as part of the framing strategies.

Framing

As in the case of selection, framing also influences all the instances of the cosmopolitan infrastructure. Works of literature are framed, but so, for example, are institutions. The primary task of the publisher's peritext is that of conveying the text to readers in the receiving culture (Kovala 1996). Van Es and Heilbron argue that translated works from peripheral languages require specific framing strategies, concerning the large-scale vs. small-scale production as well as the work's cosmopolitan vs. vernacular qualities.

We will therefore ask: *Are the works framed within the large-scale pole or the small-scale pole?* At the large-scale pole the framing strategies are recognized when the publishers: a) refer to economic success, best-selling qualities; b) stress that the work is easily accessible; c) compare the work to a more famous author writing in the same genre. For a work framed within the pole of small-scale production, strategies range from presentations underscoring the aesthetic qualities of the work to comparisons pointing out its place within a very particular literary genre.

The framing of literary qualities of works from peripheral languages basically follows two opposite paths: 1) the works' literary qualities lie in the fact that they are *typically* Swedish/Brazilian/Italian/Nigerian etc. This is what we could call the *vernacular qualities*. The other path is quite the opposite in that it underscores the work's *cosmopolitan qualities*: often described as a distinct European/universal/global style (e.g. metaphysical, philosophical, experimental); themes related to migration and cosmopolitanism; comparison with well-known authors and works in the international literary field; the work is regarded as a 'classic', and it is stressed that it is internationally and critically acclaimed (van Es and Heilbron 2015: 303).

Finally, we will ask: *Are the works framed according to their vernacular or cosmopolitan qualities? If so, what are these qualities?* If the cosmopolitan qualities are likely to be more or less the same, we have to be more creative in singling out the vernacular qualities since they might vary from one language to another. In the case of what was regarded as typically Dutch in English translations of literature from the Netherlands, the following features were highlighted: the literary style (a strong realism), the typical culture embodied in the work (Dutch culture), the particular landscapes and, finally, the stories with a Dutch perspective on historical events (the war, colonization etc.) (cf. van Es and Heilbron 2015: 303).

The results are here presented in a discussion of major and minor publishers operating in the chosen 'translation flows' and of the different logics that can be discerned behind their working with translated literature. The period studied is 1980 to 2018, which includes a number of dramatic shifts for the international book market, including an important period of internationalization, spurred on by literary agents and technical innovation. An overall aim is to describe the publishers' choices (chiefly regarding their selection and presentation of foreign works) in relation to the processes of cosmopolitanization and vernacularization. These choices are of course at least partly the result of the dynamics described by Bourdieu:

> In the global structure of the field and at any given moment, each house occupies a specific position with respect to every other depending on its relative wealth in rare resources (economic, symbolic, technical, etc.) and on the power that it confers upon the field; it is this *position* that orients the specific *position-takings* of decision-makers – their stance regarding the publication of French or foreign literature, for example – because it defines a system of objectives and constraints as well as a margin (often restricted) for confrontation and struggle between the players of the publishing game.
>
> (Bourdieu 2008)

Bourdieu also stresses the mutability of the positions occupied by the publishing houses. He attributes changes in editorial policy to changes in the house's position. Hence, a 'movement towards a dominant position' entails a policy shift towards 'asset management' at the cost of innovation, a move from symbolic capital to commercially viable authors. Our analysis will show, among other things, how the selection and framing of translated literature can be related to the position of the target language publisher.

Publishers of Swedish literature in the UK and the USA

The publishing field is often described as made up of, on the one hand, large houses focusing on bestseller genre fiction and economic capital and, on the other, small houses focusing on highbrow literature and symbolic capital. This dichotomic vision cannot, however, do justice to the literary world in its entirety. Occasionally, new players on the field will try to make a name for themselves with the publishing of successful genre fiction more at home at the pole of large-scale production.

An original crime novel, for example, might present an opportunity for such a newcomer, as was the case with Steven T. Murray's English translation of Stieg Larsson's *The Girl with the Dragon Tattoo* (*Män som hatar kvinnor*), the first instalment of the Swedish author's Millennium trilogy. The novel was published by British MacLehose Press as one of its very first titles, the house having been founded by Christopher MacLehose in 2008 as an imprint of Quercus Publishing, itself founded only four years earlier. From the start and up until October 2019, MacLehose Press published more than 230 titles, of which *circa* thirty books were classified as non-fiction. Over a period of almost twelve years, then, the imprint issued more than two hundred titles of fiction. Judging from MacLehose's website presentation, there is no doubt that *The Girl with the Dragon Tattoo* was a crucial early success for the company, pivotal in making its mark on the UK book market. This is how the publisher's history is presented on its official website:

> The MacLehose Press is an independently minded imprint of Quercus Books, founded by Christopher MacLehose and publishing the very best, often prize-winning, literature from around the world; mainly in translation but with a few outstanding exceptions as English language originals.
>
> We published our first books in January 2008, among them a ground breaking thriller by a little-known Swedish author called Stieg Larsson, and since then our list has grown to include writers from almost every continent and some of the very best translators working today. From writers as yet undiscovered in translation, to prize-winning household names; from dazzling literary creations to spine-tingling noir masterpieces, we endeavour to bring a broad spectrum of the very best of foreign literature to English-reading audiences.
>
> Our mission is to 'Read the World', and we hope you will join us on our adventures.
>
> (MacLehose Press, www.maclehosepress.com)

The presentation is very keen on giving the impression that MacLehose offers high-quality books, published with a cosmopolitan outlook on the world. In the short text, the publishers not only express their ambition to publish prize-winning works but also use the phrase 'the very best' three times. Here, MacLehose Press directly positions itself as dealing with notable authors. The ambition to offer a 'broad spectrum' of books from highbrow 'literary creations' to entertaining 'spine-tingling noir masterpieces' shows an interest in both notable and popular writers, but in calling the selected works of suspense novels 'noir masterpieces', the publishers reveal a strategy to also market popular authors as notables.

Apart from this stress on literary quality, MacLehose's presentation shows a distinct ambition to be a major player in publishing and distributing world literature to British readers. They claim to have a mission: to give voice to 'writers from almost every continent' and to give the domestic audience an opportunity to 'Read the World' (this internationalist rhetoric is strongly reminiscent of that used by other publishers, whose claims to 'understand the world' or to publish 'what the world reads' will be analysed below).

At first glance, this publication strategy might seem like a cosmopolitan ambition, but if we go beyond the publisher's self-presentation and take a look at the source languages represented in their backlist and how they are presented, it becomes evident that MacLehose international perspective also can be regarded as vernacular. Their two hundred titles of fiction include literary works originally written in twenty-one languages, including worldwide languages such as Arabic, Chinese and Spanish as well as smaller ones such as Finnish, Estonian, Welsh and Catalan. The fact that the website presentation stresses the ambition to collaborate with 'some of the very best translators working today', confirms a vernacular ambition: MacLehose is keen to come across as treating the original literary works and their vernacular origins with respect. An effect of this broad interest in twenty-one different literary traditions is that English literature tends to be vernacularized by the publisher. With twenty-nine titles of fiction originally written in English, domestic UK literature is just one of many traditions in this publication context, standing side by side with forty-six French, twenty Italian, eighteen Spanish and eighteen Swedish works of fiction.

In the UK distribution of his Nordic noir novels, Stieg Larsson is treated as both notable and popular. *The Girl with the Dragon Tattoo* is described as a masterpiece, but also as a commercial success that made it possible for MacLehose Press to introduce literature from twenty-one languages and even more literary cultures to British readers. MacLehose's marketing of popular writers as notables, together with their emphasis on vernacularity can be compared to the *commercial vernacularization* found in the paratexts and epitexts of other publishers that will be described below.

In relation to the ambition to treat foreign literary works as particular contributions from vernacular cultures, however, a well-spread anecdote surrounding the English translation of Stieg Larsson's first novel is quite paradoxical. According to *New York Times* journalist Charles McGrath, Steven T. Murray refused to be overtly credited with translating *The Girl with the Dragon Tattoo*, which is why the publisher used the translator pseudonym Reg Keeland instead of Murray's name. McGrath argues that Murray was unhappy with Christopher MacLehose's many adjustments of his translation, interventions that the publisher did in order to present the story as accessible to movie executives, hoping to sell the rights to a screenplay (McGrath 2010). That MacLehose ended up publishing the cleaned-up, streamlined version rather than Murray's original translation seems to go against the publisher's ambition to respect the vernacular backgrounds of particular works.

The same year it was issued in Great Britain, 2008, Larsson's novel was published and distributed in the United States by Alfred A. Knopf. Unlike MacLehose Press, Alfred A. Knopf was by then an old, solidly established and financially strong American publisher. The New York company was founded in 1915 by Alfred A. and Blanche Knopf. In 1960, it was acquired by Random House, which in turn was acquired by Bertelsmann in 1998. Since then, Knopf has been an imprint of Knopf Doubleday. From the start, the publisher specialized in highbrow literature, an image they try to maintain in their website presentation:

> Alfred A. Knopf has long been known as a publisher of distinguished hardcover fiction and non-fiction. Its list of authors includes Toni Morrison, John Updike, Cormac McCarthy, Alice Munro, Anne Rice, Anne Tyler, Jane Smiley, Richard Ford, Julia Child, Peter Carey, Kazuo Ishiguro, and Michael Ondaatje, as well as such classic writers as Thomas Mann, Willa Cather, John Hersey, and John Cheever.
>
> (http://knopfdoubleday.com/imprints/#knopf)

The company's special interest in notable authors is clearly underlined in this list of sixteen authors, which includes four Nobel laureates, eight recipients of the Pulitzer Prize and three winners of the Booker Prize. Since 2000, nine titles published by Knopf have been awarded the Pulitzer Prize, including Cormac McCarthy's *The Road* in 2007 and Jennifer Egan's *A Visit from the Goon Squad* in 2011.

If we take a look at the list of authors fronted under the heading 'Authors' on Knopf's website, this massive image of publishing notables is somewhat nuanced. On the first page of writer portraits, at least five of the twenty-four œuvres must be classified as popular rather than notable. Mixed with the likes of Kazuo Ishiguru, Toni Morrison and James Baldwin we find the names of John Grisham, E. L. James, Dan Brown, Stephen King and Alexander McCall Smith. These twenty-four fronted authors also include quite a few non-fiction writers of high esteem, such as John Carreyrou, Erik Larson and David Grann.

In the publisher's list of historically successful œuvres as well as in the list of most fronted contemporary authors, American authors dominate. Only seven out of the twenty-four most visible writers are foreign, and only one of them, Haruki Murakami, writes in a different language than English. Translated literature, then, is by no means put forward as a Knopf specialty. Rather, the publisher's special focus seems to be American contemporary fiction and journalism, but this focus is not stressed as a profile. American literature, culture and politics are elevated to a universal level. In not stressing any kind of vernacular interest, Knopf's website marketing thereby contributes to the cosmopolitanization of American interests.

As we have seen, the minor publishers can turn to translations for the purpose of accumulating symbolic and economic capital (Bourdieu 2008), with the ultimate goal of securing a stable position in the literary field from which competition with older houses is possible. In some cases, though, publishers are motivated by other concerns. This is true of university presses, for whom economic capital might be of secondary importance. In their case, a translation can be made for solely academic purposes, or as a pioneering attempt to introduce an unknown author. One such university press specializing in literary translation is the University of Nebraska Press, founded in 1941 with an explicit ambition very much in line with American university publishers generally. According to their homepage, they run 'a non-profit scholarly and general interest press' that 'extends the university's mission of teaching, research, and service by promoting, publishing, and disseminating works of intellectual and cultural significance and enduring value' (http://nebraskapress.unl.edu). Although this self-imposed mission sounds like a cosmopolitan one – highlighting universal literary values – in the 1970s and 1980s many of the UNP's publications reflected local and regional interests. Many titles were published that studied and presented cultural phenomena from the western USA, especially its Native American heritage. They also published several books by Willa Cather, who is mostly known for her novels on life on the prairie.

Already in the 1960s, however, one could notice a distinct interest in Scandinavian topics at the University of Nebraska Press. Translations of Icelandic sagas, plays by Danish eighteenth-century dramatist Ludvig Holberg and Swedish twentieth-century Nobel laureate Pär Lagerkvist were published, as well as the memoirs of Finnish diplomat Georg Gripenberg. In the 1970s, several books on Icelandic literature were published, and in 1974 a study on Scandinavian migration to the United States. When a selection of Mary Wollstonecraft's letters was published, the collection consisted solely of her letters from Sweden, Norway and Denmark. In 1986, the University of Nebraska Press also launched the book series Modern Scandinavian Literature in Translation. Within the frame of this series, translations of many modern Scandinavian classics were published throughout the 1980s and the 1990s.

Another kind of publisher connected to a university world is the Feminist Press, a part of the City University of New York. The company is explicitly 'non-profit' and 'tax-exempt', and their publications are partly funded by the New York State Council on the Arts (Moa Martinson 1988: 289). Unlike the University of Nebraska Press, however, the Feminist Press has an explicit ideological agenda and is devoted to distributing knowledge on a very specific topic. Their objective is to 'eliminate sexual stereotypes in books and schools'. To this effect, they have published a long list of 'works by women, feminist biographies of women, and non-sexist children's books' since they started in the 1970s. Many of these books are literary works in translation, including two novels by Swedish modern classic Moa Martinson, published by the Feminist Press in 1985 and 1988.

The American Feminist Press can be compared to a British equivalent not connected to a university: the London-based Women's Press, which published one of the above-mentioned translations of Moa Martinson two years after it was issued in the United States. Lacking the funding and channels of a university, the Women's Press does not share the Feminist Press' academic conditions and interests. Their emancipatory ambition is, however, just as evident. They market themselves as 'dedicated to publishing incisive feminist fiction and non-fiction by outstanding women writers from all around the world'. Just like the Feminist Press, their publication list also has a wide generic range: 'Literary and crime fiction, biography and autobiography, books on psychology, health, race and disability, women's studies and cultural, sexual and political theory all have a place within the inclusive publishing space that is the Women's Press' ('The

Women's Press' 2016). The political frame of these publications is made very visible on their covers, on which the company's logotype is placed in the bottom right corner – a flatiron with the publisher's name written on the potentially fiery surface.

The Women's Press was launched in 1977, and it quickly became the second largest feminist publisher in the UK, after Virago, which was founded in 1972. Their first best-selling title was Alice Walker's Pulitzer Prize-winning *The Color Purple* from 1983, a commercial success that opened up large possibilities. According to Simone Murray, the Women's Press developed a unique profile in the 1980s when they promoted 'writing by women from those minority groups marginalized by early second-wave feminism: black women, women from ethnic minorities, working-class women and lesbians' (1998: 176). To achieve this ambition, translations of Scandinavian women writers play a significant role. Apart from Moa Martinson's *Women and Apple Trees* (*Kvinnor och äppelträd*), the publisher has also issued Danish writer Tove Ditlevsen's *Early Spring* (*Det tidlige forår*) and Norwegian writer Cora Sandel's *Krane's Café* (*Kranes konditori*) and her trilogy *Alberta and Jacob* (*Alberte og Jakob*), *Alberta and Freedom* (*Alberte og friheden*) and *Alberta Alone* (*Bare Alberte*).

The Feminist Press and the Women's Press are both results of the influence of feminist theory and politics on the American and British book markets in the 1970s and the 1980s (Murray 1998: 171–2). Still, the fundamental conditions for these two publishers are different. Whereas the Feminist Press is attached to the City University of New York and receives public financial support, the Women's Press is a part of Palestinian businessman Naim Attallah's media group Namara Group. This ownership structure has other kinds of demands than university ambitions and public interests, and the relationship between Attallah and the editors has sometimes been ridden with conflict. In her article on the company, Simone Murray highlights the Women's Press' problematic position between its ideological ambition and the demands of business. She also discusses the special competition between the company and the leading feminist publisher in the UK, Virago.

When Swedish authors such as Moa Martinson are published by university presses or smaller houses with political or ideological ambitions, they are framed in different ways. Commercial vernacularization is not an issue here. Rather, abstruseness or foreign elements are strategically highlighted in order to achieve educational or ideological goals. The semi-periphery is engaged for these idealistic purposes.

Publishers of Swedish literature in France

When it comes to the publishing of Swedish literature translated into French, the market is divided among a large number of publishers, ranging from the very small to – especially when it comes to children's literature – the most important players in the French publishing field. These publishers are characterized by very different amounts of economic and/or symbolic capital, some of them specializing in bestseller authors, others having a very broad catalogue with both bestsellers and high prestige fiction, while some have opted for a clear niche of authors close to the pole of small-scale production described by Robert Escarpit, Bourdieu and his followers.

Among the ten most common publishers of Swedish fiction in translation to French, Éditions du Seuil is (together with Gallimard) the most prestigious, with a central position in the publishing world of the Parisian 'rive gauche'. Together with the competitors Gallimard and Grasset, Le Seuil has jokingly been referred to as 'Galligrasseuil', an imagined oligopoly claiming a large part of the literary market as well as the lion's share of literary prizes, in particular Le Prix Goncourt. This expression of course says a lot about how these publishers are viewed by the average French reader. According to Bourdieu, Le Seuil is one of seven publishers in 'the leading rank' of the French publishing field, together with Gallimard, Flammarion, Grasset, Minuit, Albin Michel and Laffont. They all stand out in their foundation dates (prior to 1946), the size of their personnel (in most cases more than a hundred salaried employees), the number of translated titles they have and the amount of funding they receive for translations. They all have a high degree of symbolic capital, but also a 'high index of commercial success'. Finally, and equally important, they are all situated in Paris, five of them – as Bourdieu especially notes – in the fifth, sixth or seventh arrondissements of the capital (Bourdieu 2008).

Le Seuil was founded in 1935 with the stated aim of publishing works 'that help us understand our time and to imagine what the world needs to become' ('qui permettent de comprendre notre temps et d'imaginer ce que le monde doit devenir'). This, of course, can be understood as an ambition to cosmopolitanize the literary field, to foreground the international qualities of literature and literary communication (to give readers the opportunity to 'read the world', as claimed by the British publisher MacLehose described above). In practice, Le Seuil has developed into an important generalist publisher, although with a couple of clear niches, perhaps most notably translated fiction (in the prestigious series Cadre vert, comparable to Gallimard's Du monde entier) and social sciences (works by, among others, literary sociologists Pierre Bourdieu and Pascale Casanova).

The translation sociologist Gisèle Sapiro has stressed the fact the Le Seuil very early on chose to publish authors from source languages in which other publishers had not yet shown interest, such as German right after the Second World War and the Eastern European languages spoken in countries east of the iron curtain well before the end of the Cold War. With choices like these, Sapiro claims, Le Seuil's clearly cosmopolitan strategy 'cannot be reduced to economics alone but also arose from cultural and political motives and was partly based on elective affinities with publishers from other countries' (Sapiro 2008: 161). In other words, this focus on translation, with clear niches in the form of otherwise-neglected source languages, can be interpreted as a way to accumulate symbolic capital in order to consolidate one's position in the publishing field, very much like the small and innovative publishers described by Bourdieu who, deprived of capital, are 'condemned to a strict observance of universally proclaimed norms', becoming champions of the ideals of the publishing industry (Bourdieu 2008: 135). Translation, as Casanova puts it, is 'a process of establishing value' (2004: 24).

When it comes to translations from the semi-peripheral Swedish, Le Seuil made a couple of early attempts in the 1970s which can be explained according to the logic described by Bourdieu: a re-edition of the script from Ingmar Bergman's movie *Tystnaden* (*Le Silence*/*The Silence*) and a very ambitious anthology of Swedish poetry, *Anthologie de la poésie suédoise*, prefaced by Jean-Clarence Lambert (1971; re-published by UNESCO in 2000, with the added subtitle 'des stèles runiques à nos jours' [from the runestones til today]). However, these attempts do not seem to have been crowned by success (commercial or symbolic), since Le Seuil waited until 1996 before publishing another Swedish author, this time of a completely different kind: children's book artist Anna Höglund (three books, published in the series Seuil Jeunesse, 1996–2000). In the wake of the international success of Nordic crime fiction, the publisher then picked up the pace, introducing five Swedish authors between 1999 and 2008, followed by another three in the early 2010s. In 2006, Le Seuil also published another book by a Swedish author, Björn Larsson's *Besoin de liberté*, written directly in French. The most striking common denominator of these eight authors (of which one is in fact a pair of authors: Cilla and Rolf Börjlind) is that they are crime fiction bestsellers in their source culture, published by large or medium-sized publishing houses. This, of course, can be interpreted as a result of the logic analysed by van Es and Heilbron, that works from peripheral languages (here: semi-peripheral) are chosen as a result of success in terms of economic *or* symbolic capital (here: chiefly economic). It may also be a sign of the changing position of Le Seuil in the French publishing field, having moved further from a position as a small and innovative house towards a position as a major player, rich in both symbolic and economic capital.

The collaborations with Sweden's most important publishers – such as Bonniers and Norstedts – can be interpreted as cases of elective affinities, or horizontal isomorphisms, on Le Seuil's part. Bonniers, Norstedts and Le Seuil are all important generalist publishers, with catalogues spanning from contemporary poetry (small-scale production) to bestsellers (large-scale production), although Le Seuil, with its prestigious translation series and its catalogue of academic literature, seems the most exclusive of the three. The works chosen by Le Seuil from the catalogues of Bonniers and Norstedts are not the ones commonly associated with these important Swedish publishers. More often than for crime fiction, Bonniers and Norstedts are famous for their publishing of high-end novels and poetry by what Pierre Bourdieu has called the 'aesthete' or 'notable' authors. Interestingly, this goes for Le Seuil as well. It seems, then, that Le Seuil wanted to join the race for successful Nordic crime fiction authors, but in order to do so without risking too much, they turned to prestigious publishers mirroring their own status in the literary field. On the other hand, Le Seuil has so far been very reluctant to publish Swedish authors with an 'aesthete' or 'notable' profile; no Swedish author has been included in the translation series Cadre vert, which is somewhat surprising considering the publisher's 'Germanic' and 'pan-European' profile. (Perhaps, though, there will be a shift in Le Seuil's publishing profile. In 2018, they acquired the translation rights to Swedish author Sami Said's novel *Människan är den vackraste staden* [published by the mid-sized Swedish publisher Natur and Kultur in 2018], nominated for both the Swedish August Prize [comparable to the Man Booker Prize or the Goncourt] and for the literary prize of the Nordic Council. Said's novel was published by Le Seuil in 2020.)

In the publishing politics of Le Seuil, then, Swedish literature is typecast as easily accessed popular fiction. At the same time, however, the crime fiction authors chosen by Le Seuil are loaded with literary capital and recognition, with what Pascale Casanova calls 'litterarité' (literariness), something that they are not used to from their source culture. To be in Le Seuil's catalogue of 'polars' (crime novels and thrillers) means being counted among the elite of the genre.

Perhaps as a result of the change of context, the crime novels published by Le Seuil became more critically acclaimed in their target culture, a change in status that would later reoccur for the work of Swedish crime fiction authors Stieg Larsson and Camilla Läckberg when they were picked up by the smaller publisher Actes sud.

That Le Seuil have been careful not to expose themselves to risk is also evident when looking at how they secured control of their two major Swedish authors, Henning Mankell and Håkan Nesser. These authors were already bestsellers and celebrities in their home culture, not just popular in the sense described by Bourdieu but also, using a descriptive label from the same model, notable due to their strong positions in the public sphere. Furthermore, Le Seuil waited for smaller competitors to try out these authors before daring to publish themselves, Henning Mankell's *Mördare utan ansikte* (*Meurtriers sans visage*/*Faceless Killers*) having been published (unsuccessfully) by Christian Bourgois in 1994 and Håkan Nessers' *Det grovmaskiga nätet* (*Le vingt et unième cas*) by Presses universitaires de Caen in 1997. When Le Seuil *did* dare to publish, however, they were very persistent, especially in selling the brand of Henning Mankell, establishing a long-term collaboration or 'constellation of production' (Håkanson 2012: 55) between the Swedish author and 'his' translator, Anna Gibson. Today, Mankell's novels have been translated into thirty-five languages and he has been awarded several international prizes.

Le Seuil's editions of Swedish crime novels are clearly framed within the pole of large-scale production, the black covers (in several cases with photos that are out of focus or taken against a light source, artistic rather than documentary and with no distinguishable localities) making them part of the 'noir et policier' genre, often with special shelves in the French 'librairies'. Referring these novels to the globally successful crime fiction genre also means framing them according to their cosmopolitan qualities (Hedberg 2017, Nilsson 2017). On the other hand, the back cover presentations, which are mostly focused on the plot, tend to mention Sweden or Swedish nature, for example clearly placing the events of the story 'by the forest in the north of Sweden' ('au coin d'un bois, dans le nord de la Suède'), in 'the small city of Ystad' (dans 'la petite ville d'Ystad'), 'on an island in the Baltic sea' ('sur une île de la Baltique') or 'in a small village in the north of Sweden' ('dans un hameau au nord de la Suède'). In the case of Mankell, over the years the paratextual information on the author became more and more respectful, and more and more detailed concerning his identity as a Swedish writer. The back cover presentation of *Svenska gummistövlar* (*Les bottes suédoises*), published the year after his death, ends with a farewell to the author: 'Henning Mankell passed away in Gothenburg on the 5th of October 2015, aged 67' ('Henning Mankell est mort à Göteborg le 5 octobre 2015 à l'âge de 67 ans'). This shows the scope of Le Seuil's investment in Mankell's writing, but it also illustrates how fame and (commercial) success allows for a vernacular framing. With economic success, then, comes the blurring of the line between cosmopolitan and vernacular typical of the semi-peripheral context.

Translated fiction is often confined to independent presses, not expected to sell as well as original language literature, especially so in central language spheres such as the French or Anglophone world. The more central the language sphere, the smaller the proportion of translated fiction on the literary market. Still, translated fiction may come with a high concentration of literary capital, forming a prestigious part of the small-scale literary production. Also, newcomers and independent presses are often the ones to generate movement in the publishing field, much as translations from minor languages, according to Casanova's model, are able to generate movement in the literary culture of the target language.

An example of a French publisher with a clear translation niche is Éditions Gaïa, founded in Larbey, far away from the powerful Parisian publishing houses, in 1991 by the Danish translator Susanne Juul and her French husband, Bernard Saint-Bonnet. Compared to Le Seuil, discussed above, with more than a hundred employees, Gaïa, with fewer than ten, must be considered a small player in the French literary field (since 2005, Actes sud has been a distributor and majority shareholder of Gaïa). In Bourdieu's discussion of the French publishing field, Gaïa (although not mentioned) fits well into a class of 'small, innovative publishers' who may not have much influence in the field but 'are nonetheless its *raison d'être*' since they 'represent its ideals' (in contrast to the established houses, which have turned their editorial policies towards safe investments). Deprived of resources, the small houses are 'condemned to a strict observance of universally proclaimed norms'. Like Gaïa, these houses are '[m]ostly located in the provinces and run largely by women with extensive knowledge of literature'. They are absent from all aspects of the commercial side of the publishing business, and are not able to compete for literary prizes since they lack the resources and networks. On the other hand, they often 'make use of their talent and pioneer audacity to discover minor authors writing in minor languages' (Bourdieu 2008: 135). Consequently, translations make up a sizeable portion of their catalogues.

In Gaïa's case, Juul and Saint-Bonnet very early on opted for Scandinavian literature, with a pronounced ambition to change the public conception of Scandinavia. 'For far too long', they claimed, 'when one spoke of Scandinavian literature, the images that came to the minds of French readers were of landscapes, certainly magical but harsh and ruthless, whose inhabitants were as dark as the polar night. A depressing literature in short' ('Pendant bien trop longtemps, lorsqu'on évoquait la littérature scandinave, les images qui venaient à l'esprit des lecteurs français évoquaient des paysages certes magiques mais rudes, impitoyables, aux habitants aussi sombres que la nuit polaire. Une littérature déprimante en somme'). In order to fight these 'well-anchored clichés' ('clichés bien ancrés'), Gaïa chose to publish more easily accessible fiction, described by themselves as 'novels that make you travel, in the world as well as in thought, the great stories, about personalities that you want to take the time to get to know, to tame and to follow to the end of their adventures' ('des romans qui font voyager, dans le monde comme dans la tête, de grandes sagas, des personnages que l'on peut prendre le temps de connaître, d'apprivoiser, de suivre tout au long de leurs aventures').

It might be said that Juul and Saint-Bonnet shared this ambition with the most successful of French publishers within the 'Nordic niche', Hubert Nyssen, founder of Actes sud, who in Scandinavian fiction claimed to have found the great stories and the strong feelings expressed through landscapes that he found lacking from French literature, which was hampered, as he saw it, by overt philosophical themes and literary experimentation. One might also speak about a case of horizontal isomorphism when comparing Gaïa with the small Swedish publisher Sekwa, with a pronounced ambition to counter a prejudiced perception of French literature, common among Swedish readers, as 'difficult' and 'philosophical' (Hedberg 2016). Both Juul and Nyssen seem to have cultivated an image of cosmopolitanism. They have both shown, in theory as well as in practice, that French literary culture is in need of well-developed contacts with the rest of the world. On the other hand, however, they have time and again chosen to highlight not cosmopolitan but vernacular traits in the source culture texts, i.e. what is different from the literature of the French target culture. This can be interpreted as a natural consequence of the cosmopolitan openness to the world, but also as *commercial vernacularization*, putting the exotic or particular of the other at work for economic purposes. This, then, is another example of the blurring of the line between cosmopolitan and vernacular in a semi-peripheral context.

When it comes to Swedish literature, Gaïa's catalogue presents a broad selection. This is typical of Éditions Gaïa who, within the confines of a clear niche, very much comes off as a generalist publisher. This generalist profile is rather hard to pin down, seeing as it goes against the norm of small publishers, often described as completely dependent on distinct niche marketing. Several of the Swedish authors chosen by Gaïa are best presented as belonging to the field of mid-scale production, not comparable to the bestsellers or notables (as are Mankell and Nesser, published by Le Seuil), nor to the prestigious aesthetes. Exceptions to this tendency are Jonas Gardell, a best-selling novelist and stand-up comedian in Sweden, and Katarina Mazetti, author of children's books as well as light-weight comic novels for adults, also selling well in Sweden and one of Gaïa's greatest successes to date. Neither Gardell or Mazetti, nor Gaïa's only Swedish crime fiction author Kjell Eriksson, were likely published solely for the literary prestige of fiction in translation. Crudely speaking, their success has guaranteed survival for Gaïa's publishing operations. Successful titles such as these seem to be equally important for smaller publishers elsewhere, for example publishing houses working with French literature in translation to Swedish, such as Sekwa mentioned above (Hedberg 2016). This might also explain Gaïa's later choice of publishing the 'feel-good' novels of Mikael Bergstrand, who at least has the potential of developing into another 'Mazetti success' for the publisher (feelgood novels or 'women's fiction' have been described as important future prospects for Sweden's literary export [Hedberg 2019: 28]). Other choices are harder to explain, for example novels by Maria Ernestam and Anna Karin Palm, who are respected authors of romance and adventure novels, but without any overwhelming success in Sweden.

Besides these contemporary authors, Gaïa have opted for two canonized authors from Sweden, Frans G. Bengtsson and Vilhelm Moberg. These authors might be considered as aesthetes, in the sense that they have been given very strong positions in the literary history of Sweden, but at the same time they have been and still are read among larger audiences. In this sense, they can be described as *popular aesthetes*. There is also an epic quality to their fiction, Bengtsson writing (in two volumes) about Viking explorers and Moberg (in four) about nineteenth-century masses of Swedish emigrants to the United States, themes that can be considered vernacular since they are uniquely Swedish or Scandinavian. Both these authors have been translated by Philippe Bouquet, a long-time translator of Swedish fiction and something of an authority when it comes to the cultural ties between Sweden and France. Bouquet's position might in fact help explain the publisher's choice of publishing older Swedish fiction, establishing the prestigious 'production constellation' of Gaïa/Bouquet. Other noteworthy constellations are Gaïa's long-time cooperations with translators Lena Grumbach (for Katarina Mazetti's novels aimed at adult readers) and Agneta Ségol and Marianne Ségol-Samoy (for children's books by the same author).

Looking at how the Swedish novels in Gaïa's catalogue are framed, they are seldom presented as exotic or praised for their *Swedishness*. More often than not, the themes highlighted in the paratexts are universal, even though the authors are specifically presented as Swedish. Cover images usually lack elements that can be connected to specifically Nordic localities, Anna Karin Palm's novel *Les filles du peintre* (*Målarens döttrar*) having been given a cover image by British artist Thomas Gainsborough, and Maria Ernestam's novels (*Les oreilles de Buster/Busters öron* or *Le pianist blesse/Den sårade pianisten*) having covers with drawings or stock photos relatable everywhere.

Moberg's emigrant novels were first (1999–2000) given cover photos from Jan Troell's 1970s film adaptation, and were later (2013) reprinted (now in two massive volumes instead of originally eight) with nautically themed artistic images (sea gulls, a tall ship). This was the second French translation of 'the emigrant saga', the first one (by Marguerite Diehl) having been published by Robert Laffont (1955–1960). Bouquet's translation was also re-published in paperback by Le livre de poche (in five volumes), marking a somewhat surprising success for this 'national epic of Sweden' among French readers (not to mention the French press, that favourably reviewed Moberg's novels). Gaïa presents the novels as 'a unique testimony of Swedish history and a fabulous human adventure' ('témoignage unique de l'histoire de la Suède et fabuleuse aventure humaine'). Still, the vernacular qualities of the novels are played down rather than highlighted, which might also be said about Frans G. Bengtsson's *Orm le rouge* (*Röde Orm/The Long Ships*) even though Gaïa gave this novel a cover image of a Viking ship and presented it as 'a fabulous Viking picaresque' ('un fabuleux roman picaresque viking'). The paratextual focus is on *the adventure*, not the elements of Nordic vernacular culture.

An exception to this rule is Gaïa's edition of Jonas Gardell's trilogy of novels *N'essuie jamais des larmes sans gants* (*Torka aldrig tårar utan handskar*) about the HIV epidemic in 1980s Stockholm. Gardell's novels were published in a single volume, also including a translation of the Swedish edition afterword, emphasizing the trilogy's social history qualities. The translators – once again,

Lena Grumbach, this time in cooperation with Jean-Baptiste Coursaud – are thoroughly presented, more clearly than usual for Gaïa identifying the book as a translation. The back cover presentation says the background of one of the main characters is in 'deep Sweden' ('la Suéde profonde') and mentions the failure of 'the Swedish model' ('le modèle suédois') when it comes to dealing with the epidemic. The vernacular elements of the novels are thus brought to the fore, a strategy otherwise not often used by Éditions Gaïa.

Publishers of Italian literature in Sweden

Italian fiction translated into Swedish is an example of a mutual semi-peripheral exchange in the sense that both languages involved are positioned between the centre and the periphery of the global translation market. Between the years 1980 and 2018, 788 editions of literary works translated from Italian were published by 159 different publishers. One of the most important of these publishing houses is Forum. Founded in 1943, this publisher started out as an imprint of Sweden's largest publishing house Bonniers. Still today, it is part of what has become a powerful conglomerate of publishing houses, Bonnierförlagen. Nevertheless, Forum is presented as 'the small publisher within the large house' ('det lilla förlaget i det stora huset'). A more accurate description would be that of a middle-size publisher. According to the website, Forum publishes sixty to seventy titles per year and has around fifteen employees. In the beginning, the legendary director Adam Helms had the idea to focus on classics (which explains the choice of name) but soon translated fiction became a more important segment for the house: the first title in this category was Ernest Hemingway's *For Whom the Bell Tolls*, which became a huge success. The focus on classics and translations provided a cosmopolitan profile to the publisher, which was the effect of a constriction rather than an independent choice: Forum was not allowed to compete with the mother house Bonniers by publishing Swedish authors (this 'rule' was respected until the 1980s). The cosmopolitan profile of the house was intact in the 1990s, when the motto of Forum was to publish 'what the world reads' ('vad världen läser') (Pettersson 1994: 21). Initially, the house had the ambition to contribute to adult education (*folkbildning*), but there is no doubt that this democratic aim has gradually developed into a more market-oriented profile. In 1994, the director Bertil Käll proudly characterized Forum as a 'publishing house of entertainment literature' ('underhållningslitterärt förlag') which 'takes entertainment seriously' ('tar underhållning på allvar') (Zorn 1994: 8).

Today, the publisher has moved further towards the commercial pole of large-scale production. The overall character of its catalogue reveals that Forum mainly publishes bestsellers and popular fiction, aiming to publish the books you 'talk about during coffee breaks at work' ('böckerna det snackas om på fikarasten'), and reaching a potential audience among those who 'never open a book' ('aldrig öppnar en bok') (https://www.forum.se/om-forlaget/). Yet the company has continued to publish 'serious literature in translation' ('seriös översättningslitteratur') over the decades, and until recently Forum was the publisher of the Portuguese Nobel prize candidate António Lobo Antunes, and still today they issue the works by Claudio Magris.

Parallel to the development towards the commercial pole, in the 1970s Forum started to concentrate on women writers. This female bias was probably inspired by Adam Helms, who immediately after his retirement started a new firm, Trevi, with his former colleague from Forum, Solveig Nellinge. Trevi focused on female authorships and soon became the most important publisher of women's emancipation literature (Andersson 2013: 11), for instance the Portuguese feminist classic *Novas Cartas Portuguesas* 1972. The strong focus on women writers turned out to be very successful, which might explain why Helms' former publishing house was quick to realize the potential of the same concept. In the 1980s, Forum began to explore the upcoming subgenre of women's romance fiction by publishing writers such as Freda Bright and Rona Jaffe, who turned out to be extremely saleable (Pettersson 1994: 20). The real breakthrough of the subgenre took place in 1984 when Forum translated Jackie Collins' novel *Chances* (the Swedish translation of Shirley Conran's *Lace* having been published by the house AWE/Geber the year before).

Only recently have scholars started to investigate in more depth what publishers have known for decades: that translated women's literature is a profitable segment of the book market. A French publisher quoted by Bourdieu claims that 'women's literature and escapist fiction' translated from English is 'the most profitable foreign literature' (Bourdieu 2008: 148). And that this is not a new phenomenon was demonstrated by the research project 'Swedish Women Writers on Export in the Nineteenth Century' led by Yvonne Leffler at the University of Gothenburg. Today, literary agents repeatedly insist on the attractiveness of 'the female perspective' in the translation market (Hedberg 2019: 28). When it comes to Italian literature, however, male authors predominate. Of all translations from Italian to Swedish in the years 1980–2018, only 29 per cent were authored by women, but in the case of Forum the corresponding percentage was much higher, 45 per cent (ten of twenty-two). As a comparison, we can observe that Bromberg, another publishing house of about the same size and with the same number of Italian authors in their catalogue, published fourteen male authors (82 per cent) and only three female (18 per cent) during the same period. Given these figures, Forum outmatches all the other publishing houses in terms of publication of Italian women writers. However, it is not possible to discern any gender pattern in their publications: if the 1980s had a female predominance, the first half of the 1990s shows a clear male bias, which in turn was succeeded by a new female wave in the second half of the 1990s etc. In the years 2009–2018, Forum published only one title by an Italian woman writer.

Among the titles selected by Forum in the 1980s, there are some Italian women writers who anticipated the Jackie Collins trend by using a formula in which feminism was combined with erotic outspokenness, Barbara Alberti and Lidia Ravera. The latter had become worldwide famous thanks to the novel *Porci con le ali* from 1976 (translated into English with the title *Pigs have Wings*, 1977), co-written with Marco Lombardo Radice, about the extravagant sex life of two teenagers. Interestingly, Ravera's novels were translated into Swedish by Si Felicetti, one of the first members of the legendary feminist group Grupp 8. This seems to have influenced the peritext. The flap text presentation of Lidia Ravera claims that 'she has participated actively in the Italian left wing movement, which was so important for the entire European intellectual left' ('hon har deltagit aktivt i den italienska vänsterrörelsen, som betytt så mycket för hela den europeiska intellektuella vänstern'). A belated sister in this category (though lacking Ravera's outspoken feminism) is Melissa Panarello's scandalous novel *100 colpi di spazzola prima di andare a dormire* about a family girl's advanced sex life, which was published by Forum in 2008. Interestingly, Barbara Alberti, another writer published by Forum and belonging to the same category as Ravera, wrote the screenplay when Panarello's novel was transposed into film.

For a publishing house which commits itself to mass-market literature ('underhållningslitteratur'), Forum's selection of Italian writers is surprisingly concentrated on highbrow writers. They are more or less consecrated mainstream authors, which relegates them to the Bourdieusian categories 'notables' (more consecrated) or 'popular' (less consecrated). At the beginning of the studied period, Forum also published a few Italian classics or 'aesthetes': Marco Polo's *Il Milione* (in a translation from 1917), Giuseppe Tomasi di Lampedusa's

Il gattopardo (*The Leopard*) and a retranslation of Sibilla Aleramo's feminist classic *Una donna* (*A Woman*) from 1906. However, these titles disappeared after 1992 and ever since the house has ceased to publish Italian classics. In the 1990s, the majority of Forum's Italian writers (Magris, Bufalino, Maraini, Barbero, Di Lascia) had been awarded some of Italy's greatest literary prizes, while writers translated in the new millennium mainly belong to the populars (Calvetti, Cappellani, Panarello, Faletti, Piazza) or an intermediate zone of 'popular notables', i.e. notables who are very close to the commercial pole (De Carlo, Giordano). This is in line with the general development of the publisher during the last two decades. The divide between the popular and the notables is actually blurred; a more appropriate categorization for the literature that is translated from Italian would be what Gianluigi Simonetti calls 'nobile intrattenimento' (2018: 227), the noble entertainment.

Even though *horizontal isomorphism* is applied in the case of Forum, as it publishes Italian authors from the largest publishing houses, similar to Forum's mother house Bonnier (Rizzoli, Bompiani, Feltrinelli, Mondadori, etc.), it is clear that of these publishers' wide-ranging catalogues, the house tends to select the more commercial titles. Forum's development might in some regards be compared to the French publisher Le Seuil's (that has been described above); both houses, in the process of accumulating capital, introduced themselves as innovative, while at the same time observing the core values of literature. They both did this by focusing on translation. Over time, however, their selection became more and more confined to literature regarded as commercially viable.

According to van Es and Heilbron (2015), peripheral titles will be framed in order to emphasize either symbolic or economic qualities. Interestingly, Forum's inclination towards the commercial pole is not always reflected in the packaging of the books of Italian provenience. Especially in the 1980s and 1990s, the economic qualities – such as references to sales figures – were not particularly highlighted in the peritext. Only occasionally did the texts on the flaps and back covers refer to a works' best-selling qualities, for instance the number of languages that the title had been translated into previously. Making comparisons with internationally acclaimed authors, which is another way of signalling economic quality, is very uncommon. In the examined volumes there was only one case: Gesualdo Bufalino is described as 'Italy's Graham Greene'. A more usual strategy is to describe writers as part of the Italian literary forefront: 'one of the most important authors in contemporary

Italy', and similar formulaic expressions aiming to cover *both* economic and symbolic qualities are frequently employed, and they are often intertwined as in the case of Francesca Duranti's novel which is described as an 'intellectual entertainment novel' that had been praised by both critics and ordinary readers.

More than the economic qualities, the Italian titles are highlighted for their symbolic qualities and the framing is definitely cosmopolitan. For instance, Italian fiction, especially in the 1980s and 1990s, were given covers with paintings by famous European artists such as René Magritte, Vincent van Gogh and Marc Chagall. Often, the publisher chose the same cover as the original. In recent years, however, a tendency to deviate from the original packaging has emerged, which indicates a greater distance between the source and target culture. In the packaging of the novels published in the new millennium, there are several cases in which the cover has undergone major changes. The Italian edition of Paolo Giordano's novel *La solitudine dei numeri primi* (English translation in 2009, *The Solitude of Prime Numbers*) features a close-up of a brown-eyed girl on the front cover, which was rejected by Forum in favour of two espresso cups seen from above with eyes reflected on the beverage's surface. This choice evidently underlines the source text's Italian origin, which at the beginning of the new millennium was cherished for its coffee culture. According to the dictionary *Svensk ordbok*, the Italian terms *espresso* and *cappuccino* entered Swedish in the 1960s, but the Italian coffee boom took place around the new millennium, when barista training and competitions became popular in Sweden.

Even more striking are the transformations of Gianrico Carofiglio's legal thrillers, which were all soberly packaged in the Italian editions from Sellerio (a publishing house which applies a homogenized packaging of all their publications), while the Swedish editions (notably inspired by the English ones) have photos of lonely women and men in sunglasses. Both transformations signal a greater tendency to promote Italian literature with regard to stereotypes, a *commercial vernacularization*, which has become a more recurrent strategy in Forum's peritexts.

Even though Forum has made use of this commercial vernacularization, the cosmopolitan qualities generally prevail on the flap texts, blurbs and back covers. In many cases, especially in the first two decades, Italy is only mentioned with regard to the author's nationality or the work's economic success, while the descriptions of the content generally do not draw on Italianness. 'Cosmopolitan' traits and issues – such as references to the world, universality, the human existence, classics, intellectuality – are highlighted in formulations such as 'the Western human being of our time' 'vår tids västerländska människa', an 'intellectual adventure' (Duranti), 'a onebook campaign against national chauvinism' (Magris), 'in this old continental culture' (Magris), 'strong inner drama' (Tamaro), 'in the labyrinths of human existence' (Tamaro), 'an unconventional picture of our rather insane world' 'en okonventionell bild av vår tämligen vansinniga värld' and 'a modern classic' (Benni).

Additionally, the portraits of the authors bear signs of a strong cosmopolitan bias in that they are framed within an international setting: Andrea De Carlo 'has travelled and worked in Europe, North America and Australia' 'han har rest och arbetat i Europa, Nordamerika och Australien', Stefano Benni is 'a cult figure even in some places outside his homeland' 'en kultfigur på sina håll också utanför hemlandet', while one of the most recent Italian authors of Forum's catalogue, Emma Piazza, is presented as 'a South European cosmopolitan' 'en sydeuropeisk kosmopolit'. Especially Claudio Magris is depicted as an intellectual, not only in words regarding his erudition and professional titles (professor of German literature, author of works about Habsburg, translator of Kleist and Schnitzler), but also in the way he is literally portrayed: the front cover of his work *Microcosm* features a photo of the author himself sitting in a café with a newspaper on his lap and a contemplative gaze – an image of the European intellectual à la Jean-Paul Sartre. In the paperback edition, this idea was reduced to the image of a cup of espresso and a newspaper. To summarize, Forum, especially in the 1980s and 1990s, chose to frame Italian literature as cosmopolitan, and even though this cosmopolitanization is still practised, the emphasis on the vernacular Italianness is becoming more frequent.

Among the Swedish publishers with a large catalogue of translated Italian fiction, one of the smallest is Contempo, which mainly publishes works that belong to the pole of large-scale production. For this reason, there are no cases of horizontal isomorphism or elective affinity; rather, if we want to stick to the mathematical terminology, it is a case of anti-isomorphism since this small house publishes novels that are edited by Italy's largest houses Feltrinelli, Einaudi, Rizzoli, Mondadori and Bompiani.

Contempo was founded in Stockholm in 2011 (with its first titles released in 2013) by Göran Emitslöf and his daughter Malin Emitslöf. According to Göran Emitslöf, the rise of Contempo was inspired by a meeting with the director of the Italian Cultural Institute in Stockholm, Paolo Grossi, who was also involved in the foundation of at least three other publishing houses with an Italian focus: Laurella & Wallin, Astor and Cartaditalia (cf. Schwartz 2017). As the name Contempo indicates, the house concentrates on contemporary Italian novels, all of which have achieved economic and/or symbolic success in their homeland. Until 2018, Contempo had published fifteen titles by ten authors and among their writers there were names of well-established middlebrow Italian, mainly male, writers such as Sandro Veronesi, Marco Missiroli and Paolo Cognetti. On its website, Contempo is presented as a *connoisseur* of Italian literature as it states that its activity is conducted 'in close contact with the Italian book market' and it is also stressed that the publishing house has 'translated and published several acclaimed Italian literary stars'. The strategy is clearly that of publishing literature which has been successful in the source culture, a strategy that is often described as a way to gain fast recognition outside national borders (Dubini 2009: 5). A similar method was applied by Forum in the 1980s and 1990s, but there might be a commercial reason why it was abandoned. In order to attract a Swedish audience, it is not enough to claim that a writer was successful in his or her source culture, at least this tactic does not seem to work when it comes to Italian literature in Sweden.

In an interview, Göran Emitslöf admits that Contempo is 'struggling to be exposed as a publishing house' and that it is 'extremely hard' to reach out to the Swedish book market. Actually, Contempo's publications have had very little visibility in the Swedish media and book market. Not only do their titles receive hardly any reviews (blogs included), but the firm has also failed to pinpoint Italian writers who really excite Swedish readers, such as Silvia Avallone and Elena Ferrante. In Contempo's latest publication, Paolo Cognetti's *Le otto montagne*, which was awarded the prestigious Premio Strega and became an international bestseller, the peritext draws parallels to Ferrante by highlighting that it is 'a modern Italian masterpiece about the viability of friendship' and the 'encounter between two boys from different backgrounds that will develop and challenge them throughout the whole life'. Several blurbs from international and Italian press follow this description, with one asking: 'Is Cognetti the new Ferrante?'

Focusing on a single language area, the company employs a clear niche strategy, but its ambition to publish *best-selling notables* seems to collate with two different literary systems: the Italian source system in which these authors have a good reputation and a considerable readership, and the Swedish system in which the names are unknown. These authors have to compete with already well-established Anglophone writers, as a critic of Sandro Veronesi's novel *Caos calmo* indicates:

> Fast vi lever ju, för att komma med en originell observation, i en globaliserad värld. Denna italienska bästsäljare, filmatiserad av Nanni Moretti, påminner snarare om en viss sorts engelska förebilder som undantagslöst också blir filmatiserade – Nick Hornbys böcker, till exempel, eller David Nicholls 'En dag'.
>
> (Although, to offer an original observation, we do live in a globalized world. This Italian bestseller, adapted to the movie screen by Nanni Moretti, is rather reminiscent of a certain kind of English work, that also, without exception, are made into movies – Nick Hornby's novel for example, or David Nicholl's *One Day*.)
>
> (*Expressen*, 5 March 2013)

Another peculiarity regarding Contempo is that it not only tries to introduce new names, but the house also 'rescued' some authors who had been published and subsequently dropped by a larger Swedish company (Melania Mazzucco, Niccolò Ammaniti and Margaret Mazzantini). This publishing pattern actually goes against the common notion of small publishing houses as discoverers of unknown but promising authors (Sapiro 2008: 157), who, if they are successful, will be contracted by larger firms.

As in the case of Forum, most Italian writers published by Contempo belong to the category of *best-selling notables*, i.e. commercially successful and award-winning authors with a great deal of focus on plot. The choice of a more or less pronounced *figure idéal-typique* reflects the determination to provide a coherent image of Italian writers. According to Siri Nergaard, a publishing house's decision to concentrate exclusively on a particular geographic region represents 'a strong ideological position' (2013: 193). The object of Nergaard's study is for many reasons an older sibling of Contempo: Iperborea, an Italian publisher focusing on literature from the Nordic countries and applying 'localizing' translation and packaging strategies by 'insisting on geographical, national and cultural origin' (2013: 198). Iperborea itself was inspired by the French publisher Actes sud, using a similar strategy when framing and presenting literary translations, often from the Scandinavian countries (Nergaard 2004). Even in the case of Contempo, the Italian focus gives rise to some clichés about the country in the epitext. For instance, on its website, Contempo puts emphasis on Italy as the homeland of conflicting and strong emotions, which is reflected in the country's literature where everything is 'always portrayed with passion, in love and hate, life and death, pleasure and pain' (https://www.contempo.se/om-forlaget/).

Moreover, publishing houses' emphasis on a particular region or country tends to homogenize the selected titles and reduce the distance between them by creating 'family resemblances' (Nergaard 2013: 192). Similar family resemblances are highlighted in the peritext of Contempo's titles, where a couple of frequently repeated themes interconnect very different stories and writers: life, family bonds, love, sex and passion, i.e. typical ingredients of *Italianness*. 'Life' is often described as something that starts anew after a crisis. The peritexts are pervaded with expressions such as 'to find new lust for life' 'the beginning of a travel towards a new life', 'the dream of a better life'. Similarly, words that denote love, desire, sex and passion can be detected on almost every back cover. Margaret Mazzantini's *Splendore*, for instance, is described as 'a love novel on forbidden love' between two boys 'who develop a loving friendship which during the teenage leads to sexual attraction'. Interestingly, the peritexts refer to love and passion even when these are not very dominant themes in the novels, for instance in the case of Melania Mazzucco's *Vita*, a novel about Italian emigrants in New York at the beginning of the twentieth century.

Even though Contempo does not explicitly highlight the Italian origin of the works and the authors (which would be superfluous since it only publishes Italian novels), the focus on the above-mentioned themes (life, love, family) is used to make the reader associate with the most positive elements of Italianness. The strategy is then to interconnect these 'good' qualities with typical formulations referring to economic qualities, i.e. *commercial vernacularization*. The house actually applies the large-scale publishing house's typical strategies, by insisting on their focus on bestsellers. Under their logotype, a short but very telling text explains that 'Contempo publishes Italian literature in Swedish. The authors represent a selection of contemporary bestsellers in Italy and in many other countries' 'Contempo ger ut italiensk litteratur på svenska. Författarna är ett urvalav samtida storsäljare i Italien och många andra länder'. The peritexts always refer to the successful sales of the title in Italy and/or abroad, the many languages that the titles have been translated into, and other qualities that highlight the book's capacity to reach a broad audience. A synthesis of all these elements is found in the text on the back cover of Margaret Mazzantini's *Splendore*:

Margaret Mazzantini har skrivit sex romaner varav tre är filmatiserade. Alla filmer har maken Sergio Castellito regisserat och i två av dem spelar Penélope Cruz huvudrollen. Mazzantinis stora genombrott kom med romanen *Non ti muovere* (Rör dig inte). Boken är översatt till fler än 30 språk och blev film år 2004. Margaret Mazzantini har belönats med flera prestigefyllda litterära priser.

(Margaret Mazzantini has written six novels of which three have been filmed. All the films have been directed by her husband Sergio Castellito and in two of them Penélope Cruz plays the leading role. Mazzantini's great breakthrough was with the novel *Non ti muovere* (Do not move). The book has been translated into more than 30 languages and became a film in the year 2004. Margaret Mazzantini has been awarded several prestigious literary prizes.)

Moreover, Contempo's covers are colourful and richly illustrated, always in a way that denotes or reproduces an aspect of the content. For example, Mauro Covacich's *A perdifiato*, in which the main character is a Marathoner, has a runner on the cover, while Niccolò Ammaniti's *Io e te*, about a schoolboy who hides in the basement during the winter holidays, features a pair of eyes under a staircase on the front cover. This focus on the plot utterly underscores Contempo's orientation towards the commercial pole. A considerable part of the back cover texts summarizes the plot in the most exciting way possible, often with direct references to entertainment literature, as in the cases of Veronesi's *The Power of the Past*, which is claimed to have 'a thriller's spectacular twists'; Mazzucco's *Sei come sei*, which is described to be 'as exciting and dramatic as an adventure novel'; and Igiaba Scego's postcolonial novel *Adua*, which is defined as 'captivating and intriguing'. By a generous use of affective adjectives, the novels in Contempo's catalogue are described as 'thrilling,' 'moving' and 'heart-stopping'. The peritexts' framing of Italian *notables* as *populars* is a recurring tendency which might be explained by the ongoing popularization of the literary field (Franssen 2015).

Publishers of Anglophone African literature in Sweden

Anglophone African literature is at once a literature written in a hyper-central language, with very few exceptions first published in one of the global literary centres, and, at the same time, an expressive mode at the margin of world literary space. English is for all intents and purposes the necessary condition for this literature's mobility through the world's publishing systems and its visibility to institutions that receive and recognize literature, as is publication by houses in London and New York. Despite recent efforts, such as Nigerian publisher Cassava Republic's decision to establish offices both in Lagos and London to connect book markets, or the earlier establishment of African Books Collective, a distribution network that aims to sell African books on American and other international book markets, African publishing makes up a minimal percentage of the world's total output of books, and local- or national-language books seldom travel beyond national borders (Bgoya and Jay 2013, Bosch Santana 2018, Wallis 2018).

The Swedish case illustrates this situation well. In the period studied here, 430 editions of translated African literature (novels, short story collections, poetry and drama) were published in Sweden. Out of a translation total of a little more than thirty thousand editions, this means African literature accounts for around 1.5 per cent. The pattern fluctuates slightly between years and decades, for instance, the 1990s ended at the slightly lower level of 0.5 per cent, but the proportion of African literature in Swedish publishing remains relatively stable. Virtually all the novels translated were first published by British or American publishers, which confirms the importance of the global centres of publication. One of the very few exceptions to the rule, which may be recounted since it reminds us that books also travel along more individual routes, is Tanzanian author Elieshi Lema's novel *Parched Earth*. First published in 2001 by the publishing house that Lema herself founded in Dar es Salaam, E&D Ltd, it was translated into Swedish and published in 2004. It has not found a British or American publisher but has recently, somewhat unexpectedly, been translated into French, and published by *Présence Africaine* (2016).

Given the small volume of translated Anglophone African literature on the Swedish literary market, it is noteworthy that the total is shared among a relatively large number of publishers, although the number (around forty) seems small in comparison to Italian literature described above. A small niche market, the publishing of Anglophone African literature is not dominated by houses with an 'African' profile; nor is Anglophone African literature primarily presented to the Swedish audience through book series, as is the case, for instance, in France (Ducourneau 2011: 50). The literary output is clearly divided into large-scale/small-scale literature, but several publishers also work across the poles. For instance, Tranan, a small publisher with a marked 'world literature' profile and the ambition to introduce literature from less well-known literary cultures, publishes twenty-one Anglophone African literary works in the period, all of which belong in the category of literary fiction. Bromberg, another small publisher specializing in literary fiction from many parts of the world, in similar fashion concentrates on literature with high symbolic capital but has a much narrower focus: one author, J. M. Coetzee, accounts for twenty-two of their total of twenty-eight published works (the other authors being Athol Fugard and Buchi Emecheta). At the other end of the publishing spectrum, popular publisher Damm's Anglophone African publishing is limited to best-selling Alexander McCall Smith, and B. Wahlström's to Wilbur Smith. Working at both ends of the literary-popular spectrum, Bonniers published a great deal of the Anglophone African literature during the period, and combined highly literary fiction, such as Nadine Gordimer and Nuruddin Farah, with 'mid-brow' authors such as Chimamanda Ngozi Adichie, even making an attempt to break into the popular Anglophone African literary segment through the publication of McCall Smith's *Drömguden* (2007, *Dream Angus*). The crossover pattern can also be observed in the case of significantly smaller publishers such as Weyler, which publishes highly consecrated South African author Marlene van Niekerk, author of *Agaat*, alongside popular crime writer Deon Meyer (both of whom write in Afrikaans but are translated from English). To further illustrate the publishing of African literature in Sweden in the period, it will be useful to compare two publishers at opposite ends of the publishing poles, Bonniers and Modernista.

Bonniers is one of Sweden's oldest publishing houses. Founded from a bookseller business in 1839, it has long been one of the biggest and most important publishers in Sweden. Throughout its history, it has published numerous canonized Swedish authors – in the nineteenth and early twentieth centuries August Strindberg, Ellen Key and Nobel prize laureates Selma Lagerlöf and Pär Lagerkvist, among others. This history has made Bonniers into one of the most prestigious publishers in Sweden. Bonniers also maintains a leading position in translating foreign quality literature into Swedish, for example with the famous Panache publication line, which started in 1946 and which contains many Nobel Prize laureates, the majority of which were published long before the year of the prize (Ruëgg 2020).

Like many international publishing houses, over the last decades Bonniers has gone through changes that have to do with its position and role, as well as its internal organization. Bonniers has, through mergers, acquisitions and restructuring, gone from being a privately owned publishing house to a large corporate media conglomerate. The transformations have not followed a single logic but have shifted from expansion of activities in the 1990s to contraction in the following decade. Parallel to these developments, Bonniers – again like several other European and American houses – has been engaged in vertical integration, i.e. buying and/or controlling distribution and sales of books.

Being one of the major publishing houses in Sweden, Bonniers publishes broadly and in many different genres from poetry to crime fiction. For example, at its small-scale pole it publishes poetry ranging from the highly experimental, and sometimes controversial (vanguard authors such as Johan Jönson), to the established (notables such as Aase Berg and aesthetes such as Witold Gombrowicz); at its popular, large-scale, pole, Bonniers is home to a number of crime writers and authors of romantic prose, such as American bestsellers Dennis Lehane and John Grisham, Swedish (and internationally successful) authors such as Lars Kepler (pseudonym for Alexander Ahndoril and Alexandra Coelho Ahndoril) and American Nora Roberts and British Penny Vicenzi, whose romances have sold millions of copies globally. Between the extremes of the publishing spectrum, Bonniers has a large segment of literary fiction which attracts critical acclaim because of its literary value while at the same time finding success with readers. This category of the novel, among which are found Man Booker Prize laureates, can be exemplified by authors such as Salman Rushdie, Roberto Bolaño and Marlon James internationally, and Jonas Hassen Khemiri, one of the stars of contemporary Swedish literature, nationally.

Bonniers' broad profile makes its Anglophone African publishing pattern interesting. As Sarah Brouillette and various others have noted, postcolonial literature (the umbrella term under which African literature is often included) is internationally very often a niche market, which is indicated by the existence of specialized publishers, imprints or book series devoted to literatures from particular regions (Brouillette 2007: 44–75). When it is not, as is the case with Bonniers, the question arises what authors are published, and how they are marketed. To what degree are these authors presented as belonging to a certain country, region or culture? What does the relation between the vernacular and the cosmopolitan look like in the presentation of these authors?

In the period 1980–2018, Bonniers published eight African authors writing in English: Nadine Gordimer, Damon Galgut, Nuruddin Farah, Ben Okri, Chimamanda Ngozi Adichie, Alexander McCall Smith, Petina Gappah and Dinaw Mengestu. In total, the publishing amounts to twenty-five editions – a little more than 7 per cent of the total publishing output of African authors translated from English. The selection of authors presents no singular focus on the part of the publisher, which includes both notables such as Nadine Gordimer, popular writers such as Alexander McCall Smith and 'mid-brow' writers such as Chimamanda Ngozi Adichie and Petina Gappah.

Being a distinctly cosmopolitan publisher in its selection of authors, it is interesting to examine how Bonniers have portrayed their authors in the epitextual material which surrounds the publishing. The case of Nadine Gordimer offers a good entry point. Gordimer is a long-standing commitment for Bonniers, and she was one of the first African authors to be translated into Swedish. Gordimer's novelistic debut, *Lögnens dagar* (*Lying Days*), was published in 1955, two years after its original publication. After the first translation, Bonniers remained a faithful and rather swift publisher of Gordimer's works, releasing them onto the Swedish market a year or two after their original publishing. *A World of Strangers* (1958) was published as *Främlingars värld* (1959); *Occasion for Loving* (1963) as *Tillfälle att älska* (1965); *The Late Bourgeois World* (1966) as *En bortgången värld* (1967), *The Conservationist* (1974) as *Bevararen* (1975), to give examples from Gordimer's early career. An exception to this pattern was *The Guest of Honour* which was originally published in 1970 and published by Bonniers in 1977.

In their presentation of Gordimer, Bonniers has been careful to describe her authorship in ways that connect locality to universal themes. Thus, for instance, the publisher's web page briefly recounts her life (born in the Transvaal, discontinued studies at the University of the Witwatersrand) and stresses her artistic concern with the local conditions of apartheid, while simultaneously generalizing this thematic as an exploration of the interaction of public and private life (https://www.albertbonniersforlag.se/). The framing of her novels has put equal emphasis on the vernacular and the cosmopolitan qualities of her writing. *Börja leva* (*Get A Life*), for instance, is described as involving a South African ecologist and as thematizing how 'existence is fundamentally transformed' in moments of crisis ('hur tillvaron ohjälpligt förändras när allt ställs på sin spets').

That the transcendence of the local situation is important, and that vernacular attachment may indeed stand in opposition to the general is indicated by the quotation from the British newspaper *The Times* included on the web page to market the novel, which states that Gordimer's 'rootedness in a political time, place and destiny never overshadows her multifaceted talent as a writer' ('starka förankring i en politisk tid, dess och plats och öde har aldrig överskyllt hennes mångfacetterade begåvning som författare'). *The House Gun*, to take another example, is, according to a critic cited on the publisher's website, said to take place in a post-apartheid South Africa where 'years of racial conflict vibrate under the surface' ('år av rasmotsättningar vibrerar under ytan'), and thematizing deeply existential – placeless – conditions ('tillvarons själva grundvillkor, varhelst människorna lever sina liv').

The examples indicate that for Bonniers the particularities of a South African context are not seen as intrinsically good, but have to be communicated in a cosmopolitan literary form in order to reach the target language reader. This cosmopolitanization of Gordimer's work differs from the commercial vernacularization instigated by Le Seuil and Forum described above. Presumably, this has to do with Gordimer's status as a Nobel Prize laureate, dubbing her work as 'pure literature' (and raising it above the work of the authors vernacularized by Le Seuil and Forum). The early introduction of Gordimer to Swedish readers, and the dedication to the translation of works by this highly consecrated author, have generated a great deal of symbolic capital for Bonniers and contributed to its prestige. Gordimer was awarded the Booker Prize (UK, 1974), the Premio Malaparte (Italy, 1985) and the Nelly Sachs Prize (Germany 1986) – before she was awarded the Nobel Prize in 1991 for her 'epic writing' in the service of ('great benefit to') 'humanity'.

In view of the total of Bonniers' Anglophone African publishing, the long-standing commitment to a renowned author appears a singular case, and regardless of what type of writer is involved, the house's publishing strategy seems rather more erratic and discontinuous. The fate of Nuruddin Farah, a writer with a stature comparable to Gordimer's, illustrates this well. Farah, originally from Somalia and for many years a resident of South Africa, had his first novel, *From a Crooked Rib*, published by Heinemann in the African Writers Series 1970. His next novel, *A Naked Needle*, was published in 1976, also by Heinemann, after which followed a series of trilogies – a format which came to be seen as a Farah trademark. 'Variations on the theme of African Dictatorship', which includes *Sweet and Sour Milk* (1979), *Sardines* (1979) and *Close Sesame* (1983), was Farah's first trilogy; the second, 'Blood in the Sun', encompasses *Maps* (1986), *Gifts* (1993) and *Secrets* (1998); the 'Past Imperfect' trilogy, which is his latest, includes *Links* (2003), *Knots* (2007) and *Crossbones* (2011). Farah's most recent novels, *Hiding in Plain Sight* (2014) and *North of Dawn* (2018), are free-standing novels. Farah's productivity is matched by his international literary standing. He has been awarded a number of literary prizes, among them the

Neustadt Prize, and the Tucholsky Prize (awarded by the Swedish section of PEN International) and his name is regularly mentioned in speculation before the Nobel Prize (e.g. Smith in *The New York Times*, 19 May 2004). The website of his present publisher, Penguin Random House, presents him through quotations by author colleagues such as Nadine Gordimer and Salman Rushdie (https://www.penguinrandomhouse.com/authors/241845/nuruddin-farah).

Bonniers published the first Swedish translation of Farah's work *Kartor* (*Maps*) – the first novel in the 'Blood in the Sun' trilogy – in 1987, one year after its original publication. Over the following decade, they published the subsequent instalments in the trilogy: *Gåvor* (*Gifts*) in 1990, and *Hemligheter* (*Secrets*) in 2000. After the completion of the 'Blood in the Sun' trilogy, the publishing of Farah's novels in Swedish became more scattered. Bonniers published *Länkar* (the first of the 'Past Imperfect' Trilogy) in 2006 but did not follow up with the subsequent novels; instead, their next translation was *Adams revben* (*From a Crooked Rib*), released in 2008, after which the publisher seems to have lost interest in Farah. Bonniers' handling seems to be an example of how a major publisher picks up a foreign author for symbolic reasons but then drops the same author for economic reasons. More recently the small publisher Modernista has taken over the publishing of his work, re-issued the 'Blood in the Sun' trilogy and translated his most recent novel *Hiding in Plain Sight* (*Dolda i det fullt synliga*, 2018).

Whatever the explanation for Farah's more recent fate at the hands of Bonniers – be it increasing pressure on books to perform well economically or something else – the release of a highly consecrated writer appears to foreshadow what has later befallen less renowned but acclaimed writers such as Ben Okri, Dinaw Mengestu and Petina Gappah. Okri, a Nigerian author, had his Booker Prize-winning *Den omättliga vägen* (*The Famished Road*, 1992) published in 1993 by Wiken but was later taken up by Bonniers through *Farlig kärlek* (1997; *Dangerous Love*, 1996). The title remains the publisher's only effort with Okri; despite the fact that the author, who has written eight novels to date, has been translated into twenty languages, received several literary awards and is housed by large publishing corporation Penguin, Bonniers has discontinued the publishing of his novels. Mengestu, an Ethiopian/American author with two novels behind him, likewise, has seen Bonniers publish his first novel – *Att tyda luften* (*How to Read the Air*, 2010) – in 2012, but show no interest in his following novel (*All our Names*, 2015). Gappah, whose latest novel, *Out of Darkness, Shining Light*, is her fourth literary work, and who is published by major American publishing house Simon and Schuster, has only had two titles translated into Swedish and published by Bonniers: *Sorgesång för Easterly* (*Elegy for Easterly*, 2009) and *Memorys Bok* (*The Book of Memory*, 2015).

The lack of publishing continuity contrasts with Bonniers' presentation of their Anglophone African authors. All are apparently selected on the basis of literary merit rather than economic success (a number of literary prizes mentioned, even if some of these may also hint at increased sales figures) and are described as significant literary voices which (like Gordimer) combine vernacular and cosmopolitan traits in their writing. Gappah, though, is partly described as a satirist, dealing with particular versions of eternal themes – struggling lives under the Mugabe regime; a setting in a prison's death row in Harare – and as an important author ('stilsäker [...] väsentligt författarskap'), Mengestu as a sensitive author grappling with existential issues from a particular migrant experience ('sensibel skildring av att försöka förstå de skeenden som format en människa').

Bonniers' presentation of Chimamanda Ngozi Adichie crystallizes in more positive ways what may be seen as the publisher's rhetorical split between emphasizing the literary value of an author, but evaluating her with regard to sales. Adichie, whose books have sold millions of copies around the world, is presented on the publisher's web page as primarily a qualitative writer (the Orange Prize, National Book Critics Circle Award, *The New York Times*' Best Books, and the MacArthur Foundation Genius Grant are mentioned, even if the range of translations are also noted), and her novel *Americanah* is compared with Balzac's work in its ability to capture the atmosphere of an era through the literary depiction of a few individuals' lives ('skildra ett helt samhälle och en tidsanda genom några få, utmejslade öden').

Modernista is one of Sweden's smaller publishers, focusing on translations, especially from English. One of the strategies of this publisher has been to re-issue Swedish and international books which are considered classics – and to do this within different genres of literature. Thus Modernista has translated and published Plato's *The Republic* and Nietzsche's *Thus Spake Zarathustra* and *On the Genealogy of Morals*, as well as Scott Fitzgerald's *The Great Gatsby*, Charles Dickens' *Hard Times*, short stories by Katherine Mansfield and Virginia Woolf's *The Waves*. Modernista has also launched re-editions of minor or major classics by Swedish authors, such as Selma Largerlöf, Birgitta Trotzig and Jan Myrdal.

The re-issuing of classic works may be interpreted in different ways. It may be, as Gisèle Sapiro puts it, a way by which literatures are allowed to exist – and perhaps only exist – in terms of 'past symbolic capital' (2015: 321). It may also be a way for a publisher to accumulate its own literary capital with relative speed through the taking over of what were once other publishers' backlists. A publisher's build-up of reputation is a time-consuming and high-risk activity in which the investment in authors gradually yields returns in the form of symbolic capital (e.g. Bourdieu 2008, Thompson 2010: 219–20). Since Modernista, which was founded in 2002, has not yet had the time to accumulate that capital through nurturing their own authors' literary careers, the acquisition of rights to publish Swedish or foreign classics appears, in this context, a process by which the accumulation of literary capital is accelerated. In comparison to Bourdieu's typical case, however, Modernista's position-taking appears somewhat less risky in that the publisher continuously receives support from the state-sponsored Kulturrådet and very often re-publishes older translations.

In the period covered, Modernista published eleven titles by Anglophone African authors, all of them in the last years of the period (2014–2017). Of these, Nuruddin Farah and Ngugi wa Thiong'o represent more than half of the outlet (the other authors being Ben Okri, Amadi Elechi, Ayi Kwei Armah). It may be noted that the publishing is all-male, a profile which is closely connected to – if not explained by – the fact that, except for Ben Okri, the works issued are almost all by authors long hailed as writers of 'classics', most of whose works were originally published in the 1960s and 1970s. Elechi's novels published by Modernista, for instance, were originally published by Heinemann's Educational Publisher in the 'African Writers Series' (*The Concubine*, 1966; *The Great Ponds*, 1970), as were Farah, even if Modernista's selections are later works, originally published by Arcade publishers in the United States (since 2010 part of Skyhorse publishing).

Modernista's selection of Anglophone African 'classics' – or works written by authors also considered to have produced 'classics' – is matched by the publisher's presentation of these authors. Farah is described as 'long seen as one of Africa's most significant writers' ('Sedan länge räknas han till de mest betydande afrikanska författarna') and his Neustadt Prize is mentioned, alongside the explanation that it is one of the world's most prestigious literary prizes ('en av världens mest prestigefyllda priser'). The publisher's presentation of *Secrets* draws attention to the distinctly vernacular – or rather national – qualities of the novel. It is set, the text states, in a society on the brink of civil war where familial bonds have become ideology ('blodsband har blivit ideologi') – all the while excerpts from reviewers and author colleagues demonstrate the literary quality of the writing, and the value of the singular artistic practice of Farah. A quotation from Salman Rushdie labels Farah as one of Africa's best contemporary writers; an excerpt from a review in the *Guardian* states that Farah is one of Africa's great writers and a cosmopolitan voice in English language fiction; and Swedish critic Viola Bao is quoted as saying the value of Farah's art lies in the connection of individual lives and larger political circumstances. Bao's description somewhat echoes the presentation of Gordimer as a vernacular author who speaks to the world.

Modernista's presentation of Ngugi is similar to Farah's and his authorship closely connects regional (African) politics and great art. Ngugi is said to be a great African author, polemicist and satirist, and several of the descriptions of his literary works include references to speculation about Ngugi as a possible Nobel Prize laureate. His *Kråkornas herre* (*Wizard of the Crow*, 2006) is described as a great allegory about the African postcolony ('storslagen allegorisk skildring [...] av en afrikansk nation i efterdyningarna av kolonialismen'), and both *The River Between* and *A Grain of Wheat* are presented as deeply rooted in the Kenyan context ('Två Gikuyu-stammar i Kenya'; 'Kenyas frihetskamp på femtiotalet') while dealing with universal themes like the power of collective stories ('de kollektiva berättelsernas inneboende kraft'), betrayal and love lost. A number of quotations from international and Swedish press accompany the presentation of his novels, many of which reference both the historical background against which Ngugi writes, and his literary craft. A common trait for these Anglophone African writers translated into Swedish, then, is that they are presented as rooted in the vernacular, the foreignized context of the African continent, while still speaking to readers all over the world in a cosmopolitan literary form.

Publishers of Lusophone literature in Sweden

Literatures written in Portuguese – so-called Lusophone literatures – translated into Swedish originate from four different continents: Europe (Portugal), Latin America (Brazil), Asia (East Timor) and Africa (Angola, Cape Verde and Mozambique). Despite its geographical diversity and abundance this literature is, with 317 translated literary works during the period 1980–2018, a peripheral phenomenon in the Swedish book market. When looking at the publishing landscape of translated Lusophone literature, a significant majority of the publishers are thus to be found in the small-scale publishing industry. Out of these, quite a few are 'micro-publishers' with only very few titles per year. 'Micro-publisher' is used in this text as defining a small-scale company with modest annual sales, often operating on a one-person level and with only one (or even fewer) titles published per year. As noted by Ann Steiner, the distinction between a small publisher and a micro-publisher can be difficult to define. One definition presented by Steiner draws upon the publishers' size through measuring their economic turnover, that is, less than ten million Swedish crowns for the 'small publisher' and under one million for the 'micro-publisher' (2019: 131). The predominance of small-scale houses also emerges when looking at the publishing houses responsible for hosting the most titles and authors of Lusophone literature in their backlists. During the period studied here, the niche publisher Tranan ranks first with thirty-two titles (with very few second editions) and seventeen different authors, and a micro-publisher such as Almaviva, with twelve titles and seven authors is also among the most prominent in number of published titles (as will be addressed more thoroughly below).

With a niche profile focusing on translations of 'literature of quality from all over the world' ('översatt kvalitetslitteratur från hela världen' – Tranan's web page https://tranan.nu/om-tranan), the publishing house Tranan hosts several Brazilian authors, e.g. Clarice Lispector, but also the Angolan writers Ondjaki and Pepetela, the Cape Verdean Germano de Almeida, as well as the East Timorese Luís Cardoso. Clarice Lispector holds a predominant position in the Brazilian literary canon, as well as being highly consecrated and translated outside Brazil. With growing international recognition and symbolic capital, Lispector qualifies for the category of *aesthetes* and she has grown to be one of Tranan's most prestigious profile authors, with seven published titles, some with several editions. Furthermore, Tranan has also introduced contemporary Brazilian authors such as Adriana Lisboa and João Paulo Cuenca. These authors are considered to belong to the new generation of writers in Brazil awarded prestigious national literary prizes, for example Prêmio Jabuti. All the Lusophone writers Tranan publishes from Africa and Asia: Ondjaki, Pepetela (Angola), Germano de Almeida (Cape Verde) and Luís Cardoso (East Timor) belong to the *notables*, as the most contemporary consecrated authors of their source cultures and are translated internationally. Likewise, in the inner transcontinental Lusophone book market, these authors have high sales numbers, are awarded prestigious literary prizes and are published by large-scale publishing houses in Portugal and Brazil.

Adding to the picture of Lusophone literature predominantly being hosted by small-scale publishers is the fact that Portuguese and Brazilian classics and their most canonized authors (*aesthetes*), such as Fernando Pessoa, Eça de Queirós and Machado de Assis are published by the small publishing house Pontes. As a consequence of this picture, only a few Lusophone writers or single titles are published by Swedish large-scale or mid-scale publishing houses. It is mainly the two internationally recognized Portuguese authorships, the Nobel Prize laureate of 1998 José Saramago (thirteen translated titles) and the 'considered' Nobel candidate António Lobo Antunes (fourteen translated titles), which are published by Wahlström & Widstrand and Forum, respectively, both parts of the large publishing house Bonniers. Bonniers also published one title each of the Brazilian authors Milton Hatoum in 2010, *Den förtrollade staden* (*Orfãos de Eldorado*), Michel Laub in 2014, *Att falla* (*Diário da Queda*) and Patrícia Melo in 2000, *Lögnens lov* (*Elogio da Mentira*). Also, the large-scale publisher Norstedts has published single titles by Brazilian authors during the period. The publishing of these single titles is possibly an attempt to introduce and launch these globally successful authors into the Swedish market, although none of the titles were followed up with a second translation. In the border zone between middle-size and small-range publishers we find the well-established publishing houses Ordfront and Leopard, which launch approximately thirty titles per year, and have published the internationally recognized Mozambican author Mia Couto. Leopard – which will be further studied below – has also published a recent successful novel by the Angolan writer José Eduardo Agualusa.

To complete this brief overview of the Swedish publishing landscape of Lusophone literature we have to address the case of the Brazilian worldwide best-selling author Paulo Coelho. In terms of number of titles and editions of Brazilian literature translated into Swedish, Coelho dominates completely. In the investigated period (1980–2018), he is the author of 61 (33 per cent) out of a total of 186 editions of Brazilian literature. Coelho is published by the publishing house Bazar, which is closer to the commercial pole of the publishing field. Coelho is then the only author writing in Portuguese who qualifies as a *popular* author in the Swedish market. We will take a closer look at two instructive examples of publishers of Lusophone literature in Sweden, the mid-scale publisher Leopard and the micro-publisher Almaviva.

The publishing house Leopard was founded in 2001 by the Swedish internationally best-selling author Henning Mankell and editor Daniel Israel. They both formerly came from the publishing house Ordfront – with a similar size and profile as Leopard – where Israel held the position of publishing director and Mankell was the signed global best-selling author of Nordic noir novels. Henning Mankell is also known for introducing the world famous Swedish police inspector Kurt Wallander in his novels. In an interview in the Swedish daily *Aftonbladet* that very same year, Mankell explained that their intention with the new publishing house was to launch translations of fiction from Africa and Asia. The name of the label, Leopard, is derived from Mankell's novel *Leopardens öga* (1990) (*The Eye of the Leopard*) and symbolizes the Leopard's ability to survey its surroundings when lying down in a spot where it has a great overview of the terrain (interview with Mankell, *Aftonbladet*, 6 June 2001). During the last two decades, in tune with Mankell's personal political and social commitments, Leopard has developed into a publishing house with a strong community-oriented profile of sociopolitical consciousness, publishing around thirty titles per year.

Since then, Leopard's original scope of literature from Asia and Africa has been broadened with non-fiction genres (e.g. debate, history and popular science), which focus on social equality issues and questions with reference to both Swedish society as well as the larger world. Leopard's current catalogue includes a variety of topics concerning social engagement, for example anti-colonialism, globalization, racism, human rights, feminism and LGBT issues, as well as fiction from Sweden, Africa, Asia, Arabic countries and Latin America. Leopard's publishing list of non-Swedish writers includes Maryse Condé, Assia Djebar, Achmat Dangor, Emmanuel Dongala and Frantz Fanon. Also included in Leopard's catalogue are two prominent African authors writing in Portuguese: José Eduardo Agualusa from Angola and Mia Couto from Mozambique.

The trajectory of Mia Couto's authorship into the Leopard publishing house is an interesting one, simultaneously representing a translational path of an already globally translated and successful writer – translated into more than forty languages – and a personal networking path. Mankell had a long-standing commitment to African independence and development and a lifelong and special personal relationship to Mozambique (cf. Helgesson 2018: 92). For many years, Mankell lived partly in Maputo where he worked as a director of the theatre house Teatro Avenida and where he cultivated a close friendship with Mia Couto. Three of Couto's previous novels were published by Ordfront, before he followed Mankell to his new publishing house.

Leopard's backlist includes two novels by Mia Couto: *Sjöjungfruns andra fot* (*O outro Pé da Sereia*; Caminho 2006), published in 2010, with a reprint and a paperback edition in 2014 and *Jesusalem* (*Jesusalém*; Caminho 2009) published in 2015. By José Eduardo Agualusa, Leopard has also published one title: *En allmän teori om glömska* (*Teoria Geral do Esquecimento*; Quetzal 2012) in 2017. However, it was not Leopard that introduced Agualusa authorship to the Swedish audience. The micro-publisher Almaviva had previously published four titles of his work, which will be addressed below. Leopard's publishing of Agualusa's novel followed upon its international success of being awarded the English PEN Translates award, and the International Dublin Literary Award (former IMPAC Dublin Award), as well as being shortlisted for the 2016 Man Booker International Prize. Likewise, Mia Couto, has been awarded important literary prizes within the Lusophone publishing circuit as well as international ones. Couto received the most prestigious Portuguese literary award, the Camões Prize, the important Neustadt International Prize for literature in 2014 and was a finalist for the Man Booker Prize in 2015. Agualusa and Couto are arguably the two most renowned and successful Lusophone African writers in the current international publishing market, both in number of translations into other languages, as well as in symbolic capital accumulated from critical attention. Furthermore, in their source cultures and in the transcontinental Lusophone publishing circuit they are published by the most prominent and large-scale publishing houses, e.g. in Portugal, by Caminho/Leya (Couto) and Quetzal (Agualusa) and in Brazil, both by Companhia das Letras. When these publishers launch new titles by Couto and Agualusa they are treated as 'big books', meaning that, in anticipation of a big success, they invest in 'a larger print run, more marketing events, and prioritized sale pitch' (Steiner 2018: 121). While the average print run of a new novel by the publisher Caminho/Leya in Portugal is between two to three thousand, the first edition of a new novel by Couto is often printed in thirty thousand copies.

Leopard's web page frames Mia Couto and Agualusa accordingly, on literary merits and quality, as being the foremost representatives of Portuguese-speaking Africa: Mia Couto is considered 'the foremost author of Portuguese-speaking Africa' ('den främsta författaren från det portugisiskspråkiga Afrika') and Agualusa 'one of the foremost literary voices of Angola and the Portuguese-speaking world' ('en av de främsta litterära rösterna från Angola och den portugisiskspråkiga världen') (https://leopardforlag.se/). The claim of being 'the best and foremost' author representing a country or a language area seems to be a common strategy used by a smaller publisher when highlighting the literary quality of an author. The presentations on the website are short and include mentions of literary awards and the positions as finalists for the Man Booker Prize.

Leopard's description of the three novels sums up the vernacular plot, but then stresses the cosmopolitan value and the universal human condition as its subject matter, rather than suggesting a vernacularized exotification of the novel's content. As can be seen in the description of Agualusa's novel: 'The result is a fascinating and playful novel, both comic and tragic, and at the same time a tender depiction of human vulnerability' ('Resultatet är en fascinerande och lekfull roman, både komisk och tragisk och på samma gång en ömsint skildring av människans sårbarhet') (https://leopardforlag.se/). Likewise, in the presentations of Couto's novels the universal human condition is highlighted: 'Sjöjungfruns andra fot [The Mermaid's Second Foot – the novel is not translated into English] is a poetic novel that questions perceptions of identity, race and tradition' ('*Sjöjungfruns andra fot* är en poetisk roman som ifrågasätter uppfattningar om identitet, ras och tradition'). Leopard's presentation of the authorships and novels is thus on par with their expressed niche profile of cosmopolitan concern for social equality issues from a global perspective. Nevertheless, questions must be raised regarding the lack of continuity in publishing the novels of Mia Couto by Leopard, just as in the case with Bonniers' publishing of Nuruddin Farah, described above. Despite additional titles, including a paperback edition of Couto's first novel, Leopard has not published any more of his novels since 2015. Since the year 2015, coinciding with Mankell's death, the publishing house has continued the clear cosmopolitan profile of social engagement in global issues. However, the percentage of socially engaged non-fiction has lately increased substantially in proportion, arguably at the expense of the continuity of publishing African authors such as Mia Couto.

Having accumulated a large amount of symbolic and economic capital in the transcontinental Lusophone literary circuit and symbolic capital internationally, Mia Couto and Agualusa fall into the category of notables. Nevertheless, when migrating into the Swedish book market, through Leopard, this means being published by a medium/small-size niche publisher. This is in line with the overall arrangement of the Swedish publishing of Lusophone literatures, where even culturally consecrated, canonized and best-selling authors are generally published at the small-scale pole of publishing. At the same time, this also follows a recognizable pattern of African literature being published on the international market by a niche publisher of postcolonial African and Asian novels (Brouillette 2007).

Another notable feature of published Lusophone literature on the Swedish market is the relatively large proportion of micro-publishers in the overall small-scale production. Four micro-publishers, Lusima böcker, Panta rei, Diadorim Edition and Almaviva, are responsible for 10 per cent of the published titles and 16 per cent of the introduced authorships during the studied period. These small enterprises are all niched in Lusophone literatures and operated by a single woman who assumes the multiple roles of translator, editor, designer, marketing director and publisher. Lusima böcker ('böcker' meaning books), operated by Inger M. Alves, introduced and published one title each of the notable Portuguese writers Gonçalo M. Tavares (the publishing house Tranan has followed up with two titles) and Alice Vieira. Panta rei, managed by Gunilla Winberg, has published titles by the Angolan writers Pepetela, José Luís Mendonça, Maria Celestina Fernandes and Paula Tavares and the *aesthete* Brazilian writer Jorge Amado. Ulla M. Gabrielsson, the originator of the publishing house Diadorim editions, specializes in poetry and has translated and published the poets Ana Luísa Amaral (Portugal) and several titles by the Brazilians Ferreira Gullar and Gui Mallon. If we also add to this group of four micro-publishers the small-scale publisher Pontes (publisher of Fernando Pessoa and the Lusophone *aesthetes*), which is managed by Margareta Marin, they are responsible for a fairly large proportion of the publications in general and of the translated poetry in particular. In common for these micro-publishers are the structure of a 'one-woman enterprise' assuming all these different roles of cultural mediation through their own personally created networks and attachments: Inger M. Alves worked as an interpreter and lived for many years in Portugal, Gunilla Winberg worked on solidarity and development work for SIDA (The Swedish Governmental Development Agency) in Angola, and the poet and translator Ulla M. Gabrielsson has lived in Brazil. Their cultural mediator profiles could well be described as 'smugglers', defined recently by Roig-Sanz and Meylaerts, as non-profit promoters of cultural exchange and creators of 'their own norms, circuits, channels and forms' (2018: 3) and as 'mediating in channels of exchange in which translated literature has a low economic value but a high symbolic one' (14). The driving force behind these micro-publishers is clearly not commercial or economic; instead, it is a personal engagement with and commitment to the translational dissemination of Portuguese-speaking cultures and literatures. This description is also very true for the micro-publisher with the most Lusophone titles in their backlist, Almaviva.

The publisher Almaviva was founded in 2000 by the award-winning translator and editor Marianne Sandels. With a total of eleven published translations from the Portuguese language, and as the host of seven different authorships, Almaviva is, in spite of its very small-scale production, a major player in terms of the number of Lusophone titles disseminated in Sweden. On Almaviva's web page, Sandels explains the reason for her interest in Lusophone literature as an interest in Portuguese culture as a niche with high-quality literature and an interesting history (seafarers, colonizers and missionaries), which is not sufficiently presented to the Swedish and Nordic audiences. Since the beginning, Almaviva's ambition has broadened this scope to encompass the larger Portuguese-speaking world and its inner cultural, social and historical affinities and interconnectedness (Almavivas' web page, http://www.almavivabok.se/om_almaviva.html).

Marianne Sandels started off as a translator of poetry, and before establishing Almaviva she translated several Portuguese poets published by other houses. Almaviva's backlist includes four books by José Eduardo Agualusa: two collections of chronicles and texts, *Dansa igen: berättelser och krönikor från den portugisisktalande världen* (2002), *Praktisk handledning i konsten att* sväva (2011), and two of his well-known novels, *Kreolska riket* (*Nação criola*) in 2003 and *En främling i Goa* (*Um Estranho em Goa*) in 2006. Regarding Portuguese writers, Almaviva published two titles of prose by the *notable* Almeida Faria and four titles of translated poetry by four contemporary poets: Eugénio de Andrade, Ana Luísa Amaral, Nuno Júdice and Vasco Graça Moura. Furthermore, the backlist includes a collection of poems from the Mozambican poet José Craveirinha. This selection of contemporary authors all belong to the well-known and (symbolic) *notables* authors in their source cultures and in the inner Lusophone circuit. However, it is always difficult to connect the literary production of even successful poets to economic large-scale publishing. These Portuguese poets belong to the notables through critical recognition, rewarded prices and as translated into several languages. Likewise, the poet Craveirinha must be considered as the most consecrated poet in Mozambique, often considered the father of Mozambican poetry and crucial for the development of Mozambican literature, as well as being the receiver of the prestigious Portuguese Camões Prize. (For a discussion on Craveirinha's translational dissemination beyond the Portuguese linguistic circuit, e.g. Sweden, see Helgesson 2018: 85–99.)

In line with fostering a niche profile towards Lusophone culture and literature, all Almaviva's publications include a personal written introduction by Sandels, thorough bio-bibliographical notes on the author, descriptions of the literary text with culturally specific sociopolitical and historical contextualization and accentuates the text's importance in the source cultures. The editions aim to distinguish themselves in the market by exhibiting a stylish overall uniform design in the book covers and extra care in paper quality. John Eyre has designed all the covers in a uniform style and font, with pictures of, e.g. landscapes or paintings covered with a watercolour-like matte surface, creating a sophisticated impression. Two of the covers (Almeida Faria and Agualusa) have reproductions of modernist paintings of the Portuguese Amadeo de Souza-Cardoso, and two (Agualusa and Craveirinha) have African motifs, while others show serene landscapes, connoting an overall prevailing *cosmopolitan* impression with *vernacular* elements. For these qualities Almaviva was rewarded a 'honorable mention for an ambitious series with good quality' ('hedersomnämnande för en ambitiös serie med god kvalitet') by the jury of Svensk Bokkonst in 2001 (http://www.almavivabok.se/). 'Svensk Bokkonst' is a non-profit association that every year gives out rewards to stimulate and inspire the book industry to increase quality in the production of books in Sweden.

Looking at the framing of the publications on the web page, they all, to some extent, emphasize the *vernacular* qualities, as they include and enhance cultural affinities between the author/literary text and major specific historical and political contexts, such as Portuguese colonialism, fascist regime, the Carnation Revolution and African national independence. Moreover, the framing enhances culture-specific concepts such as the well-known melancholic mood of 'saudade' and mythical connections to the sea (seafarer), as expressed in the introduction to the anthology of poems *Vintergatan asfalteras i vitt* (2012) by Amaral, Judice and Moura: 'represents the lyrical tradition of their homeland in a multifaceted way [...] some poems characterized by melancholy and longing, the saudade one meets in fado songs' ('representerar sitt hemlands lyriska tradition på ett mångfacetterat sätt [...] vissa dikter präglade av melankoli och längtan, den *saudade* man möter i fadosånger') (http://www.almavivabok.se/).

Interestingly, Almaviva's descriptions of Agualusa's works and authorship differ in focus and perspective from the framing of the Leopard editions. If Leopard presented him as being one of the foremost African authors writing in Portuguese, with universal qualities, Almaviva portrays him as a voice of – and transnational traveller in – the historical and cultural interconnectedness of the Portuguese-speaking world and cultures. By focusing on how Agualusa lived and studied in Angola, Portugal and Brazil and how his novels and short prose texts take place in various parts of the Portuguese-speaking world (http://www.almavivabok.se/), the peritexts frame Agualusa as a representative of a larger transcontinental Portuguese-speaking community that extends beyond an exclusively vernacular regional image of Angola. In describing the publications, Almaviva combines vernacular qualities with references to the authors' affiliations with cosmopolitan traits, such as highlighting connections with classical mythical motifs and the writing and writers of Western and European cultures. The overall framing, then, of Almaviva's packaging of the books and their descriptions on the web page's peritext contains an entanglement of enhancing vernacular and cosmopolitan qualities in order to simultaneously present a unique and original literature that qualitatively connects to the larger circuit of world literature.

The publishing landscape of translated Lusophone literatures in the Swedish market is mainly populated by male authors (75 per cent) from the categories of notables and aesthetes in their Portuguese-speaking source cultures, and they are almost exclusively published in the small-scale publishing field, in which the niche micro-publishers play a prominent role. Horizontal isomorphism is only to be found in two cases of Portuguese writers, José Saramago and António Lobo Antunes, and in single titles by Brazilian authors, published by the large-scale publishing houses Wahlström & Widstrand, Forum, Bonniers and Norstedts. The micro-publishers' management through a non-commercial personal commitment to disseminating the Portuguese-speaking cultures opens up possibilities to discover authorships through their direct networking activities without this literature being previously translated and circulated in central languages such as English or French. As such, they can play an important role as introducers of authorships that later get picked up by more established publishers, as in the cases (referenced above) of Agualusa (from Almaviva to Leopard) and Gonçalo M. Tavares (from Lusima böcker to Tranan). At the same time, the scarce economic circumstances of these small-scale publishers make them highly dependent on state institutional support of different kinds to cover the costs of their translations and publications. An investigation into the number of Portuguese and Afro-Portuguese literary works translated into Swedish which received publication grants indicates a high degree of dependency on institutional support for these titles. Most of the titles published between 2000 and 2018 received financial support from either the Swedish Arts Council (Kulturrådet) or from Portuguese cultural institutes (see Schwartz and Edfeldt forthcoming). Furthermore, the micro-publishers have limited resources for marketing, and encounter difficulties in attracting media attention and getting their titles reviewed in the major papers. These editorial circumstances point to an overall lack of autonomy in, and an uncertainty about the continuity in publishing of, the translational flow from peripheral literatures to the Swedish market, such as in the case of Lusophone literatures.

Publishers of Hispanic Caribbean literature in Sweden

Hispanic Caribbean literature translated into Swedish is a rather marginal literary phenomenon in terms of the number of translated novels – during the investigated period (1980–2018) less than one novel a year, twenty-eight novels in total. This is probably due to the fact that bibliomigration (cf. Mani 2014) patterns are complex and heterogeneous (Lindqvist 2019), which in turn can be partially explained by the pluri-centrality of the Hispanic language and literary consecration and the fact that many Hispanic authors live in English-speaking parts of the world and also write in English. As discussed in the case of Anglophone African literature, sustainable definitions of Caribbean literature are hard to pin down. The only reasonable way of defining Caribbean literature is that it is presented as such to the Swedish reading public, whether the authors write in Spanish, English or French. This definition goes hand in hand with the development within translation studies to consider translations as facts of the target culture (Toury 1995, 2012), emphasizing the norms and aesthetics of the receiving culture in the bibliomigration process. Having said that, what is nevertheless clear is that the majority of the translated authors are Cuban. The favoured position of Cuban literature in Swedish translation among Hispanic Caribbean literature might partially be explained by the favourable political and cultural relations between the Swedish Social Democratic governments and the Cuban regime during the 1980s and 1990s (Ahlmark 1997: 161). Moreover, a third of the twenty-eight studied novels have English as their source language. It is mostly the Cuban immigrant writers living in the United States or in Europe who write in English, but even so, they are presented to the Swedish readers as Cuban writers. Judging from the sum up of the source languages of the novels in the study it seems as if writing in English is also favoured by the selected translated female authors.

When examining the Swedish publishing field in search of a niched publishing house for Hispanic Caribbean literature, it becomes clear that it simply does not exist. Caribbean literature is not a self-evident category in the publishing field nor in the Swedish National Bibliography. Therefore, the publication data of this study is based on numbers from the database *Världslitteratur.se* (worldliterature.se). The site is part of a project run by the Världsbiblioteket (World Library) in Stockholm. Its aim is to promote world literature – defined as African, Asian and Latin American literature – and to represent the authors and their translated works in print and online. The account which follows is presented in descending order of the numbers of publications by the involved publishing houses. Since the numbers are fairly low, no percentages will be employed in the account.

One of the most important publishers of Spanish Caribbean authors in Swedish translation counting numbers of novels, Bazar, was founded in 2002 as a Nordic publishing house including Norway, Sweden and Finland. In 2003, Denmark was also included. Today, only the Swedish section of the house has survived. The Danish branch was shut down and shortly after the Norwegian branch was purchased by Cappelen Damm publishing house. Since 2019, the remaining Swedish branch has been part of the rapidly growing Strawberry Publishing.

Bazar mainly publishes translated literature and explicitly describes their publishing strategy as promoting the best and most popular foreign literature ('det bästa och mest populära i utländsk skönlitteratur'), i.e. the best-selling foreign literature. Bazar's profile authors are – according to their website – populars such as Paulo Coelho (described as 'our biggest author' ['vår största författare'] and 'one of Bazar's strongest brands' ['Ett av Bazars starkaste varumärken']), Cecilia Samartín and Bernard Cornwell. Together with an ambition to promote the best-selling foreign literature and the earlier sale possibilities in the other Nordic countries, Bazar's publishing strategy forms a good candidate for being qualified as very close to the commercial pole of the publishing field. They work according to a short production cycle with close contact to an already established demand. Bazar is focused on more short-sighted economic capital than long-sighted cultural capital. They do not invest in building literary careers; rather they build on other charismatic consecrators' work. At the same time, however, Bazar's operations seem to be governed by an ambition to internationalize the Scandinavian book market. This is done, however, by describing the authors not as representatives of exotic source cultures, but rather as border-crossers and champions of a cosmopolitan literary art. This is especially clear in the publisher's presentation of Paulo Coelho, whose native country (of Brazil) is not even mentioned – on the other hand, he is described as 'an international bestseller' and as a writer who has 'inspired people all around the world'.

Another publisher of Caribbean fiction in translation to Swedish is Tranan, whose business model differs radically from Bazar's. Tranan focuses primarily on 'literature of quality from the world' ('kvalitetslitteratur från hela världen') (https://tranan.nu/om-tranan/), their selection favouring translated fiction from Africa, Asia and Latin America and other regions less represented within the Swedish literary culture. Tranan is a relatively small publishing house with a production rate of twenty-five titles a year. Their first novel was published in 1992. From the start, Tranan was exclusively aimed at publishing translated Chinese literature (hence the name Tranan, meaning 'the crane'). That market strategy changed over time and today their profile authors are, among others, the Brazilian novelist and short story writer Clarice Lispector, the Chilean novelist Roberto Bolaño and the Chinese novelist and Nobel Prize laureate Mo Yan. The high profiled series of anthologies with short stories Berättarserien (The storytelling series), started in 2004 with the title China Narrates (Kina berättar) and today has a total of twenty-five anthologies with short stories from different languages and cultures. Comparing Tranan publishing house with Bazar, the former constitutes the best candidate for being characterized as the 'discovery type' of publisher in the Bourdieusian sense (1986: 2001), i.e. a house that discovers and introduces quality literature from more peripheral literary cultures from a Swedish perspective. Among Caribbean writers, Tranan has published the Cuban poet and novelist Wendy Guerra's novel *Alla ger sig av* (*Todos se van*) and – through its imprint Trasten, publishing books for children and young adults – her compatriot Teresa Cárdenas' novels *Slaven* (*Perro Viejo*) and *Brev till mamma* (*Cartas a mi mama*). Both can be described as notable according to Bourdieu's model of ideal-type writers. Tranan's take on internationalization is different from Bazar's, very much emphasizing the source culture of its athors (e.g. China Narrates) and proudly stating that they have published more than three hundred books from seventy-five countries, translated from almost forty languages. The same is true for the children's books imprint Trasten, described as 'the publisher who breaks the boundaries to let the world take place in the book shelves of Swedish children'.

The two publishing houses represent what Bourdieu would call two different kinds of symbolic 'bankers' within the Swedish publishing field, offering as security their accumulated symbolic capital (cf. Bourdieu 1993: 77). Classifying the two quantitatively most important publishing houses based on yearly output of titles, yearly revenue and independence and numbers of members of the editorial board (cf. Steiner 2012: 233, Ruëgg 2020: 136), the size and range of the two publishing houses also differ from medium to small. It is important to keep in mind that publishing houses often change ownership relations as well as their profile and publishing lines over time. However, counting the sum of the output of titles published by the thirteen different publishing houses involved in Hispanic Caribbean translations into Swedish the medium range publishers except for Bazar, for instance Leopard and Forum, together dominate the output, often just publishing one translated title by the same author. The large publishing conglomerates Bonniers and Norstedts together published nine out of twenty-eight titles, and small houses produced eight titles. Medium-sized publishing houses thus published the majority of the translated Hispanic Caribbean literature in Sweden, but the differences are not very significant. These numbers confirm the heterogeneous nature of the publishing of this kind of literature.

Moreover, examining the relationship between the publishing houses within the Hispanic, Anglo-American and the Swedish literary spaces, the picture is even more heterogeneous, which makes it virtually impossible to trace cases of horizontal isomorphism, where publishers tend to make their selection drawing on the elective affinity with similar publishers from foreign literary fields. A general purview of the publishing houses in the three concerned literary spaces examined gives no clear picture. It seems that literary consecration by means of prizes and awards is more influential when it comes to Spanish Caribbean literature in Swedish translation.

Within the Hispanic context, rather small publishing houses placed in Havana are represented, for example Édiciones Union, Éditorial Lettras Cubanas and Édición Homenaje del Ministerio de Cultura as well as large Mexican publishing concerns, for instance E.D.I.A.P.S.A. (Edición y Distribución Ibero Americana de Publicaciones. S. A.) and Spanish large and middle-range houses such as Alfaguara, Planeta and Anagrama. Among the American and English language publishing houses we find large conglomerates including Faber & Faber, Penguin and Bloomsbury, as well as the smaller Duke University Press and originally Hispanic niched American publishing houses such as Knopf publishing.

The following will explore the findings of the studied authors by means of the categorization into ideal-type writers, i.e. aesthetes, notables, popular and vanguards, the number of translated novels per author and the source languages of the source texts – three important variables in the study of translation bibliomigrancy. It should also be noted that in the group of a total of twenty-eight translated Hispanic Caribbean novelists in Swedish, the gender distribution is surprisingly balanced: eight female and nine male authors were translated during the research period. According to the distinction of the writers in the four categories it is shown that the notables are the most translated into Swedish. They constitute roughly half of the translated authors during the research time span, for example Teresa Cárdenas, Wendy Guerra, Ana Menédez, Senel Paz, Esmeralda Santiago and Carlos Somoza. However, these characterizations are approximations. Several authors could belong to different categories at different times in their careers. Nevertheless, one of the criteria for being characterized as a notable is that the writer in question has become famous thanks to temporary consecration through literary prizes or successful sales. This selection of authors for translation concurs very well with the general translation policy in the Swedish translation field – in order to be selected for translation you have to be highly consecrated within the source culture or write in English – English being the most translated literary source language. A favourable condition for the Hispanic writers to get translated is to also have been translated into English prior to the Swedish translation, a kind of double consecration (cf. Lindqvist 2019).

A good example of the notable category is Esmeralda Santiago. She was born in Puerto Rico in 1948 but moved to New York as a teenager. She graduated from Harvard in 1974 and currently, with her husband, runs a production company for documentaries and motion pictures named Cantomedia. She also works as a publisher and is very active politically. Santiago has written four novels and one has been translated into Swedish: *El sueño de América* in 1996 (*Américas Dröm*; America's dream), published at Bra böcker 1997 in translation by Maria Ortman – a charismatic translator with a long career in translation spanning more than fifty years.

Thematically the writing of Esmeralda Santiago deals with cosmopolitan issues such as immigration and the vulnerability of women. She writes 'memoirs', a kind of autobiographical fiction. Santiago is considered one of the most important and commercially successful voices within the Nyorican movement – a cultural movement created by poets and writers with Puerto Rican roots in New York during the 1970s. The cover of *Américas dröm* adorned by a close-up photograph of a beautiful dark skinned young woman captured with a blurry lens conveys the thematic exoticism of the novel – a fact underlined by the retention of the Spanish spelling of the protagonist's name on the cover and the presentation of the author on the inside of the dust jacket, which stresses that she is born in Puerto Rico, but which also underlines her double appurtenance in Hispanic and Anglo-American culture in citing her activities as an essayist and journalist in major American newspapers such as *The New York Times* and *The Boston Globe*. Esmeralda Santiago writes her novels in Spanish and then translates them herself into English, thus taking part in two literary markets and consecration cultures. The back cover of the dust jacket is covered by a text excerpt from the novel describing the married lover of the protagonist América as:

> en man som kvinnor älskar att se svettas. Fukten på hans hud framhäver armmusklerna, de kraftfulla låren, den eleganta kurvan mellan baken och övre delen av ryggen ...
> (a man that women love to watch sweating. The moisture on the skin highlights the muscles of his arms, the strong thighs, the elegant curve from his behind up his back ...)

The text ends with a short sentence describing the maltreatment occurring in the relationship: 'Slaget skickar iväg henne så att hon faller raklång på den grusiga vägen' (The blow sends her falling flat on the gravel road). Hence the text on the back of the dust jacket somehow contradicts the exotic romantic blurriness of the front cover and also frames the narrative as an account of vernacular Latino machismo.

Furthermore, the second largest category – the aesthetes – is made up of five authors: Julia Alvarez, Jorge Onelio Cardoso, Heberto Padilla, Junot Díaz and René Vásquez Díaz. They all write in Spanish with the exception of one writer, who writes both in English and Spanish (Junot Díaz). These authors hold dominant positions in the source culture but do not adapt to the market. They are fewer in number in Swedish translation than the notables, probably because they are more esoteric in their consecration. The author chosen here as an example due to his large number of published novels is René Vásquez Díaz (b. 1952), originally from Cuba, but living in Sweden since the 1970s. Vásquez Díaz writes in Spanish and publishes his novels in Spanish in Sweden. They are then translated into Swedish by Elisabeth Helms and published again. Elisabeth Helms is a highly consecrated translator in the Swedish literary translation field who has received several translation prizes, for instance the Elsa Tulin Prize, which is a life achievement prize from the translation union Författarförbundets översättarsektion. Possibly the relation between Vasquez Díaz and Helms can be described as a budding production constellation, i.e. a relation dominating the translation field when it comes to the number of novels published. Vasquez Diaz has published more than ten novels, the latest written in Swedish. He also works in poetry and has written a crime novel, a cookery book and several non-fiction literary studies. His three most well-known novels make up the Cuba Trilogy which consist of the novels *Hägringens tid* (1987, *La era imaginaria*; *The Time of Mirage*), *Kärleksblommans ö*, (1994, *La isla de Cundeamor*; *The Island of the Love Flower*), and *Dårskap och Kärlek* (2003, *El amor que se nos va*; *Foolishness and Love*), all published by Bonniers.

The Vásquez Díaz' consecration in Sweden is subtle, and not as formal as for most of the notables, and consists in his appointment in 2011 to the annual writer's award of the Publishers of the Swedish region Skåne. Vásquez Díaz was a board member of the Swedish Writer's Union during the period 2005–2012. He also works as a translator and has translated several high prestige Swedish authors into Spanish, among others Artur Lundqvist and Birgitta Trotzig. A more elusive form of consecration lay in the selection of Vásquez Díaz twice as host for the very popular radio programme *Sommar* (Summer) in Sweden, most recently in 2006. He has, however, also received awards internationally, for example in France, where he received the Radio France International Juan Rulfo Award in 2007. The Prize is the result of a cooperation between the institutions of the Romance languages in Paris, El Instituto Cervantes and the Spanish version of Le Monde Diplomatique. René Vásquez Díaz' literary authorship deals with both cosmopolitan and vernacular themes, but he is mostly framed as a Cuban immigrant author. Cosmopolitan themes include political opposition, betrayal, migration and love. Vernacular themes are reminiscences from his native Cuba, particularly expressed in his Cuba Trilogy, and contemplations of important Swedish authorships and their qualities.

Two categories remain to comment on: the popular and the vanguard. They both have two representatives each in the group. The popular authors are Cecilia Samartín and Diana Chaviano; the vanguards are Pedro Juan Gutiérrez and Junot Díaz. Popular writers are those within a dominated position who combine a high degree of market adaptation with a strong focus on content. The Hispano-American author Cecilia Samartín – living in the United States but originating from Cuba – is an illustrative example of the popular, ideal type of writer. All her published novels are translated from English, despite the Spanish titles in Sweden, for instance *Señor Peregrino* (2010) translated by Maria Cederroth and Lasse Lindström, which in the source text publication was entitled *Tarnished Beauty* and *Women in White* published in Sweden as *Doña María. Kvinnor i vitt* – a clear exoticizing framing strategy since the words *Señor* and *Doña* are kept in Spanish replaced and added in the Swedish title. The covers in warm yellow colour tones also clearly denote the exotic plot setting. Cecilia Samartín is a worldwide success story. In Norway, she is particularly popular, with more than four hundred thousand copies of her books sold, more than the Swedish crime fiction author Stieg Larsson and Dan Brown. Despite her worldwide success she is – as might be expected according to the hierarchization of literary prestige (Casanova 2004) – far from a critic's favourite. The critic Kerstin Johanson (2011) writes in a review of the novel *Dreamhart* that the novel is shallow and the characterizations '[…] tunnare än röken från en Havannacigarr' (thinner than the smoke from a Havana cigar) (*Helsingborgs dagblad*, 21 March 2011).

An interesting finding among these authors is that the popular writers in the studied group write solely in English, but the vanguards write in both Spanish and English. The vanguards even mix English and Spanish and several varieties of the two. They represent a subversive idea of literature either in defying supposedly good taste or breaking prevailing conceptions of good literary language of the orthodox pole. An example of a vanguard writer defying literary good taste is the Cuban Pedro Juan Gutiérrez (b. 1950), author of the novel *Dirty Havana – the Havana Trilogy*. The novel was published in 2010 in Sweden by Lind & Co publishing house – a general publishing house, which started in 1999 and which today is one of the largest independent publishing houses in Sweden. The novel was translated into Swedish by Peter Landelius. He is a very prolific and extremely well-renowned translator who has translated more than forty novels into Swedish and served as an ambassador in several Latin American countries during the period 1980–2001.

Gutiérrez is a precursor of the literary movement 'Dirty Realism' and is often described as 'the Bukowski of the Caribbean'. He lives in Cuba and has been internationally consecrated on several occasions. He was for instance awarded the Spanish literary prize Alfons Garcia Ramos in 2000 and the Prix des Amériques Insulaires et de la Guyanne in 2008. Gutiérrez has altogether written five novels, fourteen collections of poems and a large number of travelling accounts and other journalistic texts. *The Havana Trilogy* was forbidden in Cuba for a long time, but has been translated into fifteen different languages, among them Swedish and English. An interesting detail showing the impact of Anglo-American culture and literature in Sweden and of the importance of double consecration is that the title of the English translation from 1998 is kept in the Swedish version – *Triologia sucia de la Habana* published by Anagrama in Spain in 1998 became the *Dirty Havana Trilogy* in the English translation at Faber & Faber and *Dirty Havana - Havannatriologin* in the Swedish version kept segments of the American title on the Swedish cover – possibly left over from the double consecration preceding the Swedish translation. Gutiérrez's thematic sphere deals with sex and drugs and sex again. In that sense, the themes are cosmopolitan. However, the novel is framed on the dust jacket as a challenge to the official image of Cuban socialist society – a thrilling mixture of drugs, sex and politics set in Havana – a strongly commercialized vernacularization:

> Dirty Havanna är en vildsint hedonistisk och kompromisslöst frispråkig skälmroman från Kuba. Berättelserna i boken bygger på författarens egna erfarenheter och väjer inte för någonting. Dirty havanna är totalförbjuden på Kuba eftersom den motsäger den officiella bilden av det socialistiska idealsamhället. Här ges röst åt ett folk som i tilltagande yttre förfall med alla medel kämpar för sin överlevnad och tvingas till prostitution och andra former av kriminalitet. Misären är påtaglig, men också uppfinningsrikedomen, livsviljan och kåtheten.
>
> (Dirty Havana is a wild, hedonistic and without compromise outspoken picaresque novel from Cuba. The narratives in the novel are based on the personal experiences of the author and do not avoid anything. Dirty Havana is strictly forbidden in Cuba, since it contradicts the official image of the ideal socialist society. The novel gives voice to people who, facing constantly increasing exterior decay, fight for their survival with every possible means, and are forced into prostitution and other forms of criminality. The misery is palpable as well as the ingenuity, the willpower and the sexual steam.)

In 2019 the *Triologia sucia de la Habana* was published in Cuba for the first time by Ediciones Unión. An observation comparing the two accounted for Cuban trilogies in Swedish translation – the aesthete and the vanguard – is that Swedish readers can take part in both an aesthetic and somehow distant romanticized childhood and adolescent narrative in the first case, and the darker sides of human nature played out in the capital Havana in decay and challenging the official image of the socialist society.

Concluding remarks

Our main hypothesis in this chapter has been that the semi-periphery is an intermediate literary space where boundaries between the cosmopolitan and the vernacular are blurred and, more importantly, where ideas of the cosmopolitan and the vernacular are negotiated and transformed.

In many cases, the analyses of the selection and framing of translated works have confirmed this main hypothesis. For instance, we have seen that a combination of cosmopolitan and vernacular values has been referred to in the launching of Anglophone African writers in Sweden. In the case of Gordimer, the large publisher Bonniers has added a cosmopolitan framework to the vernacular particularities of her novels. When launching three Lusophone novels in Swedish translation, the mid-sized publisher Leopard has chosen epitexts that sum up the plots, focusing on vernacular elements. At the same time, however, they stress that the themes of these stories are cosmopolitan, in the sense that they deal with the human condition. In the case of the small-scale publisher, however, it is not easy to say whether the French publisher Gaïa's framing of Swedish literature in translation should be conceived of as cosmopolitanizing or vernacularizing with commercial purposes; in the cases studied, a consistent strategy has not been identified.

A rhetorical figure that occurs in the self-presentations of several of the publishers studied is the claim that the act of publishing translations is a way to connect the reader to the world. The British publisher MacLehose insists on having a cosmopolitan outlook on the world. In the 1990s, the motto of the Swedish publisher Forum was to translate 'what the world reads'. Similarly, the Swedish children's book publisher Trasten (an imprint of the small house Tranan) claims to aspire to 'break the boundaries' and to 'let the world take place in the book shelves of Swedish children'. This image draws on the conception of literature as a cosmopolitan phenomenon, on literature as 'literary' rather than 'national'. It is also consistent with Casanova's description of the ongoing struggle to de-nationalize literary establishments through the inclusion of authors or literary works that have already escaped the confines of national boundaries. By referring to this kind of struggle, the publishers are trying to present themselves as active subjects in the realization of literature's potential as a border-crossing and liberating phenomenon.

As shown in the examples above, another conclusion is that the blending of the cosmopolitan and the vernacular concerns all kinds of publishers, from large scale to small-scale houses. We have seen many examples of small publishers performing the same kind of actions as were once associated with large publishers with a commercial or generalist profile. For instance, some authors chosen by smaller publishers such as MacLehose, University of Nebraska Press, Bazar, Gaïa and Contempo do not belong to the small-scale pole of production in their source culture. Rather, they are best-selling writers in the mid- or large-scale category. Small publishers have turned out to be of two kinds: those who publish small-scale literature and those who publish mid- or large-scale literature. The best example of this tendency concerns Caribbean literature translated into Swedish by two small publishers: the high-prestige publisher Tranan and the more commercially focused Bazar. Therefore, in these cases, the 'rule' of horizontal isomorphism does not apply. The lack of horizontal isomorphism is especially evident when a very small publisher, even a micro-publisher such as Almaviva in the case of Lusophone literature, can become one of the leading publishers of translations from a whole language area.

Another action often associated with large publishers is the tendency to abandon semi-peripheral or peripheral authors after just one or a few titles (as Bonniers did with Farah and Norstedts with Melania Mazzucco). This strategy was used by some smaller houses in the analysed translation flows, for instance Leopard and Couto. (We have also seen examples of the opposite: Le Seuil remained faithful to Mankell, and Forum to Magris.) The more peripheral the source language, it seems, the harder it is for a translated author to survive in the target culture, and in the catalogue of his or her target language publisher, especially when sales are unsatisfactory.

It has not always been possible to distinguish between economic and symbolic qualities, since they are often combined and intertwined, both in the publishers' selection and in their framing. We have also noted that the borders between the ideal-typical authors which were once outlined by Bourdieu tend to become less visible. In our attempts to categorize the chosen authors and the ways in which they are framed, we have often felt compelled to combine categories, ending up with amalgams such as 'popular aesthetes' (Vilhelm Moberg) and 'popular notables' (De Carlo, Giordano). We have also seen how British publisher MacLehose transforms Swedish noir into notables and vice versa, and how Italian notables are described as typical 'popular' writers by Swedish publishers.

Coming back to the notion of the semi-periphery and its status as a 'transitional space', we have shown that this is true in the case of Sweden and Swedish literature. The semi-peripheral Swedish translation field allows for both domesticating and foreignizing of translation and framing in a way hardly possible in central or hyper-central target cultures, where domestication is a prerequisite (Casanova 2015). Looking at Swedish as a source language for literary translation, we have found a similar tendency for both domesticating and exotification to be possible, although for different reasons. This, presumably, is because the semi-peripheral Swedish culture is sufficiently familiar in the target cultures that have been studied.

3

Translators of Nobel Prize literature

The Nobel Prize in Literature, awarded by the Swedish Academy in Stockholm since 1901, has been described by the French world literature scholar Pascale Casanova as 'a prime, objective indicator of the existence of a world literary space'. There is, she claims, an almost 'unanimous belief' in the universality and autonomy of this prize, which is 'one of the few truly international literary consecrations, a unique laboratory for the designation and definition of what is universal in literature'.

Consequently, authors that have been awarded the Nobel Prize are ideally suited as objects for the study of high prestige literature, regarded as 'literary' by the establishments of what Casanova has called 'the world republic of letters'. This is especially true since there is no other agreed-upon definition of what constitutes 'high prestige literature'. The Nobel Prize, then, may be used as an objective indicator for this kind of literature (Casanova 2014: 195).

The Swedish Academy is one of the Royal Academies of Sweden and one of the most powerful cultural institutions in Sweden today, administering a wide range of cultural and literary events, prizes and scholarships. Among them, the Nobel Prize in Literature is the most famous worldwide, partly due to the large sum of money that the prize consists of and the festivities surrounding the prize ceremony in the City Hall of Stockholm on 10th December each year. For more than a hundred years, Academy members have discussed and decided on what should be considered as high-prestige literature. In recent years, the Academy and the prize have been the subject of considerable debate and turbulence. In 2018, the prize was cancelled, due to a crisis of trust between the Nobel Foundation and the Swedish Academy. In 2019, the Academy decided to grant two literature prizes, honouring the work of Olga Tokarczuk and Peter Handke. The prize attributed to the latter spurred renewed debate (cf. Sapiro 2020: 197–226).

In this segment, we will contribute to describing the specificity of this kind of literature through an analysis of cultural transfer and translation. What are the bibliomigration patterns for high-prestige literature? What kinds of translators and cultural transmitters are attracted to Nobel Prize authors, or to authors of the kind that tend to be awarded the Nobel Prize? What is the motivation behind the translation of such authors?

To further analyse the position of the translators, we will make use of Casanova's model of different mediator types. Because translation is a way of transferring literary capital, Casanova claims, 'the value of translation and its degree of legitimacy will depend on the capital of the translator-consecrator' (Casanova 2002: 17–18). In order to fully understand the role of specific translators, Casanova further claims, they have to be situated 'within a context, a continuum of functions and agents'. Along this continuum, Casanova identifies three types of mediators, the *ordinary*, the *consecrated* and the *institutional* ones. The ordinary mediators (e.g. translators) are 'almost invisible', lacking the power to consecrate literature by themselves. They are specialists who simply provide 'information about literary innovations in the countries they visit or know'. At the other extreme of the continuum are the consecrated or charismatic mediators, whose power to consecrate 'depends on their own consecration' as writers or as other important actors in the literary field. These mediators consecrate on their own behalf, while the institutional mediators ('the third pole') belong to the academic or scholarly establishment, and consecrate mainly as representatives of these establishments. In the cases below, we will chiefly discuss the consecrated (charismatic) and the institutional mediators.

In order to analyse the translators' careers diachronically, we will also apply Yvonne Lindqvist's model of translator consecration, in which the translator goes through several stages: *the investment phase*, with a low degree of consecration, through *the initiation phase*, getting reviews and commissions from well-respected publishing houses, onto *the recognition phase*, receiving grants and prizes, and finally *the confirmation phase*, with honorary appointments and board memberships (Lindqvist 2021a). While high-prestige literature is often described as being consecrated by critics and literary institutions, the opposite is equally true, i.e. the prestige of institutions such as the Swedish Academy is very much dependent on their connection to a certain kind of literature. In the following, we will describe how this kind of literature is handled by the literary establishment, through an analysis of the translation and cultural transfer of works by five Nobel Prize laureates (Tomas Tranströmer, Harry Martinson, Eugenio Montale, Wole Soyinka and José Saramago) and one often recurring candidate often shortlisted for the prize (Maryse Condé). So far, only sixteen women have been awarded the prize, which has limited our possibilities to analyse the work of contemporary female Nobel laureates.

Swedish Nobel literature in English: The case of Tomas Tranströmer

When he received the Nobel Prize in 2011, Swedish poet Tomas Tranströmer (1931–2015) was widely translated and well known in the international community of poets and poetry readers. In an article from 2010, Niklas Schiöler counts sixty languages in which Tranströmer's dense and metaphor-driven poems have been made accessible (Schiöler 2010: 134), and the award has added several new languages to that list. From the point of view of poetry, the Swedish poet has had a large readership throughout the world. From the point of view of literature in general, the number of translators having transformed his lyrical imagery into other languages has been enormous. Poetry translations are often published as short, separate texts in journals and anthologies, a fact that prompts more translators to have a go at a couple of favourite poems.

The significant number of Tranströmer translations also has to do with the fact that he was himself a frequent translator of poetry. His first collection of poems, *17 dikter*, was met with great critical acclaim when it was published in 1954. With this debut, Tranströmer's name was instantaneously established as one of the most important voices in Swedish postwar poetry. Around the same time, he published his first translations – a collection of contemporary Greek poetry, translated in collaboration with Mikael Fioretos. During the following decades, Tranströmer frequently published translations of separate poems, mainly from British, American and Hungarian originals (Schiöler 2010: 134).

English language literary markets are often described as less open for import than markets that are less dominant in the international literary space. When it comes to Tomas Tranströmer this is not the case. His poetry was translated as early into English as into German – in the mid-1960s – and since then publications in the UK and the USA have appeared more or less evenly, with an exceptional peak in 2011 as a result of the Nobel Prize. Until 2019, thirty-eight books of Tranströmer poems had been published in English, starting with the American compilation *Twenty Poems* from 1970. Most of these titles have been published in Great Britain and the United States, but they also include Canadian, Irish, Danish and Swedish books. Apart from the single-authored collections, the

Swedish poet has appeared in seven anthologies. One memoir has also been translated – *Memories Look at Me* (2011), originally published in Swedish in 1993. Not counting single contributions in journals, sixteen different translators have made Tomas Tranströmer's poetry accessible to Anglophone readerships. Some parts of the poet's œuvre have been more acknowledged than others. The original collection *Sanningsbarriären* (originally published in Swedish in 1978), for example, inspired three different English publications between 1980 and 1985: Robert Bly's translation *Truth Barriers*, published in San Francisco in 1980, Robin Fulton's *The Truth Barrier*, published in London in 1984, and John F. Deane's versions in *The Truth Barrier*, published in Ireland in 1985. Similarly, the collection *För levande och döda* from 1989 prompted three publications between 1994 and 1996, all entitled *For the Living and the Dead*, with translations by John F. Deane, Joanna Bankier and Don Coles, respectively.

The first Tranströmer book in English was Robert Bly's translation *Twenty Poems* from 1970. This collection was the result of a special kind of relationship between author and translator which had started six years earlier. Bly was born in Minnesota in 1926 and graduated from Harvard in 1950. A couple of years later he returned to the Midwest and settled on a farm in Minnesota. In 1958, he and a friend, William Duffy, started the literary journal *The Fifties*, a couple of years later renamed *The Sixties* (and later *The Seventies*). Here, the two editors published translations of a whole range of poets who were hardly known in the United States at the time, for example Pablo Neruda, César Vallejo and Georg Trakl. Through the journal, Bly and Duffy also issued books, for example the Tranströmer volume *Twenty Poems*, published by the Seventies Press. In 1962, Bly's first collection of his own poetry was published – *Silence in the Snowy Fields*. It was followed by *The Light Around the Body* (1967), which received the National Book Award for Poetry. Since then, Bly has been quite a productive poet, publishing a couple of original volumes each decade. His latest collection is *Stealing Sugar from the Castle* from 2013, a compilation of older and new poems. The same year, he received the Robert Frost Medal for his lifetime achievement in American poetry. Bly's most widely spread book, however, is the prose work *Iron John: A Book About Men* from 1990, a non-fiction analysis of an old folktale and parable according to the ideas of the 'mythopoetic men's movement', in which Bly was a leading figure in the 1980s and the 1990s.

Bly's and Duffy's journal also included Scandinavian poetry. Being of Norwegian descent, Bly had spent some time in Oslo in the mid-1950s to learn the language of his great grandfather (Schmidt 2001: 8). After this personal achievement, it was a rather small step to developing reading skills in Swedish as well. In the winter of 1964, Bly heard about a new Swedish poet and became curious. He drove into Minneapolis and borrowed Tranströmer's second collection *Den halvfärdiga himlen*, published two years earlier, from the University of Minnesota library. When he came back to his farm, a letter from the Swedish poet was waiting for him in his mailbox. Tranströmer had come across some poems by Jim Wright that he wanted to translate into Swedish, and since he did not know where Wright lived, the Swedish poet tried to reach him through his publisher, the Sixties Press, which was run from Bly's home (Schmidt 2001: 8). When Bly responded to Tranströmer's letter presenting his own ambitions to translate poems from *Den halvfärdiga himlen*, an intense and productive literary collaboration began and a lifelong friendship was born.

From the mid-1960s onwards, Tomas Tranströmer and Robert Bly translated each other. Tranströmer not only published separate translations from Bly in literary magazines. In his own collection *Stigar* from 1973, he included several poems by Bly. In a peritextual comment concluding the book, Tranströmer writes that Bly's poems are so close to him that he feels as if they are his own. 'It doesn't matter', he adds, 'who wrote them originally' (Tranströmer 1973, our translation). The two poets and translators met for the first time in the summer of 1965, and after that they visited each other quite often. First and foremost, however, they communicated via letters. The compilation *Airmail: the Letters of Robert Bly and Tomas Tranströmer*, edited by Thomas R. Smith and published by Greywolf Press in 2013, offers a unique insight into the poet–translator relationship, with plenty of tangible interlingual and intercultural problems concerning vocabulary, metaphors and poetic diction but also more fundamental aspects of translating and being translated by a close friend (Smith 2013).

Bly's first years as a Tranströmer translator were very productive. In the early 1970s, three collections were published: *Twenty Poems*, by Bly's own Seventies Press in 1970; *Night Vision*, by the London Magazine in 1972; and *Elegy: Some October Notes*, by Sceptre Press in 1973. In the anthology *Friends, You Drank Some Darkness* from 1975, presenting the Swedish poets Harry Martinson, Gunnar Ekelöf and Tranströmer for an American audience, Bly's translations represented the latter poet, and in 1980 his version of Tranströmer's *Sanningsbarriären*, *Truth Barriers*, was published by the San Francisco publisher Sierra Club Books. In 1987, a volume of *Selected Poems* was issued by the Ecco Press in New York, and in 2001 Bly's latest Tranströmer collection, *The Half-*

Finished Heaven, was published by the Minnesota-based Graywolf Press. A second edition of the latter title was issued in 2017. This makes Robert Bly the second most frequent Tranströmer translator into English, only surpassed by Robin Fulton, who was responsible for twelve whole editions of Tranströmer collections between 1972 and 2019.

In a comparison of four Tranströmer translators into English – the Americans Robert Bly and Samuel Charters, the Canadian Don Coles and the Scottish Robin Fulton – Niklas Schiöler observes that Bly's versions are the most extensive, using significantly more characters and words than any of the others. In the poem 'Vermeer', for example, Schiöler finds these quantitative differences:

Tranströmer (1986): 1179 characters, 252 words
Fulton (1987): 1222 characters, 266 words
Coles (1996): 1290 characters, 277 words
Charters (1987): 1289 characters, 280 words
Bly (1995): 1433 characters, 305 words

(Schiöler 2010: 167)

A comparison between Tranströmer's, Fulton's and Bly's versions of the poem's first stanza illustrates the latter's stylistic characteristics as a translator. The Swedish original reads:

Ingen skyddad värld ... Strax bakom väggen börjar larmet
börjar värdshuset
med skratt och kvirr, tandrader tårar klockornas dån
och den sinnesrubbade svågern, dödsbringaren som alla måste darra för.

(Tranströmer 1986)

Fulton keeps the impression of brevity and directness:

No protected world ... Just behind the wall the noise begins,
the inn is there
with laughter and bickering, rows of teeth, tears, the din of bells
and the deranged brother-in-law, the death-bringer we all must tremble for

(Fulton 1987)

Bly, on the other hand, changes the tone of the speaker's voice, making the poem more conversational:

It's not a sheltered world. The noise begins over there, on the other side of
the wall
where the alehouse is

with its laughter and quarrels, its rows of teeth, its tears, its chiming of clocks, and the psychotic brother-in-law, the murderer, in whose presence everyone feels fear.

(Bly 1995)

It seems then that Bly's translations are the ones farthest away from the Swedish originals. But that depends on what kind of origin you refer to. In a letter from 1974, Tomas Tranströmer writes that Bly's translations are true to his own creative moments of writing the poems: 'Other translators give a pale reproduction of the finished poem but you bring me back to the original experience' (Smith 2013: 77). This impression is in line with an idea Tranströmer expressed when receiving the Neustadt International Prize for literature in Germany in 1990. Here, the Swedish poet suggests that the original poem and the translation are only two different manifestations of a third, invisible poem:

[T]he poem as it is presented is a manifestation of another, invisible poem, written in a language behind the common languages. Thus, even the original version is a translation. A transfer into English or Malayalam is merely the invisible poem's new attempt to come into being.

(Tranströmer 1990)

The invisible poem is the real original. Tranströmer's and Bly's versions are just two different, but equally valid manifestations of it.

Even apart from his Tranströmer books, Robert Bly is a very productive translator, with more than forty collections of poetry translations between 1961 and 2019. Outside Swedish, he translates from German, Norwegian, Spanish, French and Russian. He has also published several books of English translations – or 'versions' as he sometimes calls them – of classical Latin, Hindi, Urdu, Persian and Japanese poets in collaboration with translators more familiar with the source language. These collections have been published in the USA as well as in the UK, mainly by a wide range of small and specialized publishers. Bly has also translated one title of prose fiction, Norwegian author Knut Hamsun's novel *Sult*. Bly's version *Hunger* was first published by Farrar, Straus and Giroux in New York in 1967, and later re-issued in 2008. This translation was also used by Duckworth and Pan in their distributions of the novel in the UK in 1974 and 1976, respectively.

In adding so much of his own poetic temperament to the Tranströmer poems, Robert Bly makes the Swedish poems less rooted in the source culture vernacular. But that is not to say that he necessarily makes Tranströmer's lyrical texts more cosmopolitan. Rather, Bly's distinct and radical transformations seem to rely on a shared understanding between poet and translator that both the Swedish poem and its English translation are merely different vernacular versions of a common cosmopolitan – or even universal – aesthetic entity that exists beyond every particular manifestation. Tranströmer and Bly seem to agree that poetry translation is a very special kind of interlingual communication that must be separated from other kinds of literary translations.

Swedish Nobel literature in French: The case of Harry Martinson

The fifth Nobel Prize in Literature to be awarded to a Swedish writer, and the third to be awarded to a member of the Swedish Academy itself, was jointly received by the Academy members Eyvind Johnson (1900–1976) and Harry Martinson (1904–1978) in 1974. (Selma Lagerlöf [1858–1940], the first female [and the first Swedish] recipient, was awarded the Prize in 1909 but was not elected into the Swedish Academy until 1914.) They both belonged to a generation of so-called 'proletarian writers', literary autodidacts having risen to fame in the 1930s. Both Johnson and Martinson can also – somewhat surprisingly considering their humble beginnings and their rootedness in a vernacular proletarian context – be described as cosmopolitan writers, having spent most of their youth abroad in order to escape poverty and abuse, Johnson in the literary metropoles of Berlin and Paris, Martinson as a stoker and self-proclaimed 'geosopher' or 'citizen of the world'. These nomadic existences are mirrored in the international transmission of their work, both being translated into world languages – English and French – very early on in their careers, even before Danish, Norwegian and other Nordic languages, thus reversing the traditional bibliomigration patterns of Swedish writers (as well as the international careers of contemporary 'proletarian writers' such as Ivar Lo-Johansson and Vilhelm Moberg), who tend to depend on Danish and German as 'transit languages' on the path towards international fame (Lönnroth 1990: 38).

Before the Nobel Prize, Martinson was the most translated of the two, having been published in fourteen languages (among them Dutch, Czech and Russian) in the period 1934–1974 (Johnson was published in ten languages between 1927 and 1974). Johnson, however, took more immediate advantage of the Prize; translations of his work were published in fifty-six editions in the 1970s, 1980s and 1990s, while translations of Martinson were limited to thirty-eight editions (according to the catalogue of the National Library of Sweden). It may be said, however, that Martinson triumphed in the long run; since the turn of the millennium, he has completely overshadowed Johnson in the international market (twenty-eight editions in the period 2000–2020, compared to twelve for Johnson). Overall, Johnson's work has been published in 106 editions in thirty-one languages, Martinson's in 110 editions in twenty-eight languages. Compared to other Swedish Nobel Prize laureates, this makes them considerably less successful than, e.g. Selma Lagerlöf (awarded the Prize in 1909 and very much dominating the scene with 1,813 editions in fifty-three languages), Pär Lagerkvist (1951: 374, 45) and Tomas Tranströmer (2011: 187, 42).

Martinson was awarded the Nobel Prize 'for writings that catch the dewdrops and reflect the cosmos', a prize motivation mirroring Martinson's work, which spans from meticulously detailed nature poems (as in the collection *Natur* from 1934, not translated into English in its entirety) to progressive travel writings (as in *Kap Farväl* from 1933, published in English as *Cape Farewell* in 1934) and from autobiographic and socially engaged novels (such as *Nässlorna blomma* from 1935, published in English as *Flowering Nettle* in 1936) to the ambitious science fiction space epic *Aniara. En revy om människan i tid och rum* (1956; *Aniara: A Review of Man in Time and Space*, 1963 and 1991). On the French book market, very much operated from the Parisian literary circles where Eyvind Johnson had spent part of his youth, Martinson was introduced in 1938 to Étienne Avenard's translation of the travel book *Resor utan mål* (1932), given the (literally translated) French title *Voyages sans but* 1938. Johnson – who has been described as an important literary innovator, almost postmodern in his interest for metafiction – was given an eleven-year head start, since his novel *Stad i ljus* (1927) had already been published as *Lettre recommandée* (translated by the Swedish expatriate Victor Vinde) in 1927. In the remaining decades of the twentieth century, however, as well as at the beginning of the twenty-first, the two writers would follow similar paths in the French metropolis. They have both been published in thirteen editions, their impact was clearly affected by the Nobel Prize in 1974 (although for Johnson, this effect was somewhat delayed – interestingly, the opposite of the same situation globally, where Johnson was the one whose work was immediately favoured by the Prize), and they have both enjoyed a surprising comeback since the turn of the millennium. In the following paragraphs we will elaborate on these trajectories, while focusing mainly on Martinson's career. However, Johnson's work and impact will be an obvious point of reference.

Starting at the end, the rise of both Martinson and Johnson in the 1990s and 2000s can be explained with reference to the work of Philippe Bouquet (b. 1937), the most diligent and arguably the most important translator of Swedish fiction to French in the last half-century. His personal bibliography comprises 161 book-length translations published between 1980 and 2016 (bibliography supplied by Philippe Bouquet to the authors [2020]). As in the case of many other literary translators, however, translation has not been Bouquet's livelihood. Instead, he has worked as a professor of Scandinavian languages at the University of Caen in Normandy, where he received his doctorate in 1976 after defending a thesis on the Swedish proletarian writers, among them Martinson and Johnson (entitled 'L'individu et la societé dans les œuvres des romanciers prolétariens suédois').

Bouquet was one of several translators with a university background who were engaged by publishing houses in the 1980s, creating a wave of translations of Swedish and Scandinavian fiction on the French book market (Ballu 2016: 912). Judging by Pascale Casanova's model of different mediator types, these translators can be described as 'institutional consecrators', who are able to consecrate in the name of an institution such as a university or an academy with high prestige. In Bouquet's case, however, the institutions were of secondary importance, the University of Caen lacking the prestige of the Sorbonne, and the small or mid-scale publishers with which he collaborated, the likes of Gaïa Éditions and Actes sud, hardly being comparable to the elite houses of the Parisian rive gauche.

In his memoir-like book *Tankar vid en prisutdelning* (Thoughts at an Award Ceremony, 2004; the award mentioned in the title of the book is Ivar Lo Johanssons personliga pris [The personal prize of Ivar Lo-Johansson], in 1995 jointly received by Philippe Bouquet and the Swedish literature scholar Stig-Lennart Godin). Bouquet explains how he came to learn Swedish and become a translator of Swedish literature. Training to become a language teacher, he had to learn a third language, besides English, and chose Swedish because he considered it easier than German. He found himself instantly attracted by this Nordic language, finding it 'simple, beautiful, melodic and expressive'. However, the decision to write a thesis on the Swedish proletarian writers was not his own, but a suggestion from his supervisor. In his memoirs, he nevertheless claims to have found an elective affinity with Martinson, Johnson and their colleagues. This, Bouquet claims, was especially true when it came to their ideas on the purpose of literature and of literary creation. Literature, Bouquet insists, must have a meaning in relation to the outside world. Much like the work of the proletarian writers, literary creation should always include 'an element of protest or concern'. Art is not timeless; to claim this, according to Bouquet, is to negate its connection to humanity and to human experience which is always 'extremely connected to time and place' (2004: 33–4). Exhausted from ten years of work on his dissertation, Bouquet turned to translation as a recreational activity, because he thought 'it might be fun'. It ended up becoming, as he describes it, a lifelong 'vice' or 'disease', taking up his spare time from work as a university teacher (39). This enthusiasm for translation is mirrored in Bouquet's multifaceted bibliography. He started out with well-respected and consecrated authors such as the proletarian writer Ivar Lo-Johansson and the existentialist novelist Stig Dagerman, but did not, a couple of years later, shy away from revising and completing an older translation of the crime fiction novels of Maj Sjöwall and Per Wahlöö or introducing the thriller writer Jan Guillou to the French audience.

Nevertheless, the subject of his doctoral thesis has remained a recurring point of reference, and Bouquet has always come back to the proletarian writers, for instance translating the so-called emigrant saga of Vilhelm Moberg (telling the story of Swedish immigrants to America in the nineteenth century) and the short stories of Lo-Johansson. Therefore, it was hardly surprising when Bouquet took on the 1974 Nobel laureates, starting with Johnson in the 1990s and moving on to Martinson by the turn of the millennium. As shown above, Johnson and Martinson had been translated earlier, but Bouquet is the most prolific translator of both writers. Étienne Avenard, artist, journalist and translator of the travelogue *Resor utan mål* in 1932, never returned to Martinson's work. Neither did the French linguist Pierre Naert, based in Sweden, who (together with his wife Denise) translated the novel *Vägen till Klockrike* (*Le Chemin de Klockrike*) in 1951 or Carl Gustaf Bjurström, Swedish expatriate and influential cultural transmitter, who translated the novel *Nässlorna blomma* (*Les orties fleurissent*) in 1978 (with Jean Quveval).

Bouquet's first choice from Martinson's catalogue was the novel *Vägen ut*, a sequel to the autobiographic *Nässlorna blomma*, published as *Il faut partir* in 2002. He then carried out a complete revision of Naert's translation of the realist novel *Vägen till Klockrike* (re-published as *La societé des vagabonds*, 2004) before moving on to the space epic *Aniara* (*Aniara. Une odyssée de l'espace*, 2004), a complicated 103 canto poetry cycle which he translated with the Swedish scholar and writer Björn Larsson. In 2013, finally, Bouquet published a collection of a hundred Martinson poems, translated with Caroline Chevalier.

In *Tankar vid en prisutdelning*, Bouquet describes Martinson as an 'author of world format', a wise man and a mystic reaching out to readers everywhere, but who, nevertheless, despite the Nobel Prize, has not achieved the global acclaim he rightfully deserves. This last fact, Bouquet explains, can be partly understood as a result of Martinson being 'very hard to translate'. (This clearly separates him from the latest Swedish Nobel Prize laureate, poet Tomas Tranströmer, famous for his 'translatability', whose work had already been published in fifty languages before he received the prize.) Bouquet, however, claims to be attracted by this difficulty. As a translator, he has been drawn to what is foreign and intellectually challenging. And Martinson, who 'speaks to the world', is at the same time a spokesman for a 'uniquely Swedish vision' (Bouquet 2004: 96). (This, according to Bouquet, is not the paradox it seems to be, since all great art is local, and since the specificity of a literary work is exactly what attracts readers everywhere [2004: 33].) To translate from Swedish to French might prove difficult enough – French, as Bouquet explains, being an abstract and analytical language whereas the Scandinavian languages are concrete and synthetic – but Martinson makes it even harder as a result of a number of stylistic traits, such as his fondness for compounds and neologisms. For a speaker of Swedish, the possibility to compound new words is almost unlimited, while in French, this is just not done. Translating Martinson into French, then, often means translating single words into expressions or groups of words, which of course changes the rhythm and overall feeling of a text.

Defending his continuous efforts with 'difficult' and vernacular literature, Bouquet speaks about translation as a calling. The world of translated literature, he claims, should be 'a domain of one hundred flowers'. Not all types of literature can be disseminated with the help of literary agents. While 'the bestsellers always find their way', there is a need for a specific kind of translator, disregarding fame and profit. This, Bouquet claims, echoing Pascale Casanova's words in *La langue mondiale* (2015), is a fight against globalization (2004: 96). While the bestsellers are 'globally attractive' in their universality, the work of Martinson and others, with all their vernacular abstruseness, remains true to what it means to be human (Bouquet 2004: 33).

Being an academic and an intellectual, Bouquet's background is typical for translators of semi-peripheral high-prestige literature, and for what Casanova has called the institutional consecrators. He also has a lot in common with other translators of Martinson's work, for example those translating to English and German. For translations to the latter languages, however, fellow authors seem to have played a more important role for the introduction of Martinson's work (e.g. Edzard Schaper to German, Hugh MacDiarmid to English). This is especially true when it comes to the English language literary field, where Martinson's translators were consecrated by their own literary outcome rather than by belonging to important institutions. Also, there seems to be no one with the same dominant position and the same perseverance as Bouquet. An important common denominator for Martinson's translators is that most of them are not professional translators, in the sense that translation is their livelihood. Rather, they are poets or university teachers. It seems, then, that translation of high-prestige literature is very much dependent on the unpaid work of individuals who consider translation as a calling or, as Bouquet puts it, as an incurable disease.

Italian Nobel literature in Swedish: The case of Eugenio Montale

This section investigates the Swedish translators of Eugenio Montale, one of the foremost Italian twentieth-century poets, who received the Nobel Prize in 1975. Drawing on the positions and literary careers of these mediators, the focus is on their power to consecrate a foreign poet from a semi-peripheral language area and, vice versa, Montale's power to consecrate his translators.

Eugenio Montale (1896–1981) made his debut as a poet in 1925 with the volume *Ossi di seppia* (*Cuttlefish Bones*), which was received with enthusiasm by Italian critics. In the same year he signed the Manifesto of the Antifascist Intellectuals, a courageous position-taking that would cause him severe trouble when Mussolini's grip on Italy became stronger. The manifesto was initiated by the philosopher Benedetto Croce as a response to Giovanni Gentile's proclamation of the Manifesto of Fascist Intellectuals in the same year. Together with poets such as Giuseppe Ungaretti and Salvatore Quasimodo, Montale was regarded as a representative of the Italian modernist current *hermeticism*, a condensed form of symbolism with pre-existentialist elements. It should be mentioned, however, that today hermeticism is thought to be far too limited to describe the complexity and the many oscillations of Montale's poetry.

Shortly after his debut, Montale entered the space of world literature as a result of single poems that had already been published in French and English in 1928, and they were soon followed by translations into several other languages long before he received the Nobel Prize. According to Barile (1977), single poems by Montale were translated into German (1932), Greek and Romanian (1938), Serbo-Croatian (1939), Bulgarian and Hungarian (1941), Spanish (1948), Swedish (1957), Russian (1958), Catalan, Japanese and Danish (1960), Czech (1965) and Portuguese (1970). The first book-length translation appeared in 1948 when Gallimard published *Ossi di seppia* in French translation (*Os de seiche*). Today, volumes dedicated to Montale's poetry are represented in at least twenty-nine languages, with Swedish in shared fifth place; a search on WorldCat.org shows 107 English entries, ninety-eight French, forty-nine German, forty Spanish and seven Romanian and Swedish (the search was limited to 'books' with Montale as the author [20 April 2020]). This reflects the importance of Montale in central and semi-peripheral language areas. It is noteworthy that Montale enjoys a very privileged position in the English language area as he is actually one of the most translated Italian authors of our time. In terms of the number of editions, Montale is only preceded by Luigi Pirandello, Alberto Moravia, Italo Calvino and Dario Fo, as shown by Robin Healey (2019: xiv). The first book-length translation of Montale's work into English occurred in 1959, with a selection by Edwin Morgan published by the University of Reading. This first volume was followed by a very large number of editions: there are sixty editions (including reprints) that are entirely dedicated to poems by Montale. Even though the number of editions reached a peak in the 1970s (sixteen editions), it should be underlined that the Genoese poet's work still attracts readers, publishers and translators: since 1990 no less than twenty-five Montale editions have been published in the English-speaking world. In this sense, Montale could be considered a cosmopolitan writer, but also in the sense that his writing, even in the first Ligurian phase, explores inner landscapes rather than the surrounding nature.

Even though Montale's popularity is indisputable, it can be noticed that initially, in Sweden, he was treated with suspicion and scepticism. Instead, the Swedish literary establishment fully embraced the poetry of Montale's younger adept, Salvatore Quasimodo, a hermetic who had recycled himself into a socially engaged poet after the Second World War. Before he received the Nobel Prize in 1959, Quasimodo was the poet on everybody's lips in Sweden (Westerström 2013: 351), while Montale was first translated into Swedish in 1960, i.e. the year after his Sicilian colleague was awarded the prize. A few attempts to introduce the poet to a Swedish readership were made by the Italianist Gösta Andersson who published one of Montale's poems, 'Riviere', in the daily paper *Svenska*

Dagbladet (14 April 1957), and a month later, the same paper published a longer introduction to his work by the respected Rome correspondent Martha Larsson (Schwartz 2015). The Swedish attention to Montale could therefore be referred to as a 'Nobel effect', meaning that the prestigious prize to Quasimodo had positive consequences even for writers from the same language area (Gunder 2011).

To date, there have been at least seven Swedish translators of Montale, as follows (with the number of translated poems in brackets): Gösta Andersson (16), Sture Axelson (43), Östen Sjöstrand (2), Lars-Håkan Svensson (2), Lasse Söderberg (1), Estrid Tenggren (3) and Anders Österling (17). It is worth noticing that all translators but one are male, which reflects an imbalance that is recurrent among Swedish translators of Italian poetry. In the period 1900–2015, the proportion of female poetry translators was 33 per cent (Schwartz 2019).

In the following, the focus will be on the three most prolific translators: the poet Sture Axelson, the academic Gösta Andersson and the poet, critic and permanent secretary of the Swedish Academy, Anders Österling. It will be argued that even though their translations might have contributed to one of the highest forms of consecration to Montale – the Nobel Prize – it could also be noticed that these translators turned to Montale at a time when their careers were in need of recognition and symbolic capital.

At first glance, it seems that these translators could be easily categorized according to Casanova's model of mediator types. Based on their position in the literary field, translators have more or less power to consecrate foreign authors (2010: 299–302). Following this model, both Österling and Axelson would be categorized as charismatic mediators, while the academic Gösta Andersson would be placed at the institutional pole. But a closer look at their careers reveals a far more complex picture; in the following, each translator is presented according to the chronology of their Montale volumes.

The first Swedish book-length volume with Montale's poetry was published in 1960 by Gösta Andersson (1913–1997), who was born in a small village (Norrby) in the middle of Sweden as the son of a master tailor. After his studies at Uppsala University he gained a position as a lecturer of Swedish language and literature at the University of Rome during the years 1940–1947. During his stay in Italy, Andersson debuted as a translator of the novel *Yu-ri-san, la pittrice di crisantemi* (Yu-ri-san, the chrysanthemum painter, which in Swedish received the title *Av främmande ras*, of foreign race, written by the fascist apologete Mario Appelius). Even though it has not been possible to examine the underlying motives for this translation, the possibility should not be excluded that the novel was suggested to Andersson by a representative of Mussolini's regime, imposing foreigners to spread Italian literature abroad (cf. Rundle 2010). When Andersson returned to Sweden in 1948, he made his living mainly as a school teacher, but he also initiated and held language courses in Italian on Swedish radio. At the same time, Andersson continued his academic career by writing theses on Croce and Pirandello. Having received his PhD in 1966, he taught Italian at Catholic University (Washington DC) and New York State University. On his return to Sweden in 1971 he gave courses in the Department of Romance Languages at Stockholm University. When he passed away in 1977, he had witnessed Montale receiving the Nobel Prize in Literature.

Interestingly, Andersson published his first Montale translations in 1957 and three years later the first volume was issued, i.e. *before* he received his PhD and entered the academic world. This fact suggests that at the time he translated Montale, he was not to be regarded as an institutional mediator but as rather close to the pole of the ordinary mediator. Moreover, the volume was issued by the newly started publishing house Italica, directed by Giacomo Oreglia, who had become a very influential cultural mediator between Italy and Sweden. In order to consecrate the volume, Oreglia chose a charismatic mediator as the writer of the preface, Montale himself, which suggests that it was Montale who consecrated Gösta Andersson and Italica rather than the other way around. A similar pattern is visible in the cases of Sture Axelson and Anders Österling, who both translated Montale when their own literary careers were on the ropes.

In 1967, a second volume entirely dedicated to the work of Montale was translated by the poet Sture Axelson. The volume included a selection of poems from *La bufera e altro* (1956), and it was published by the small but prestigious house FiB:s Lyrikklubb. The translator, Sture Axelson (1913–1976), was born in Linköping, as the only child of a railway man and his wife. After language studies at Uppsala University, he received a PhD in Latin in 1944 and positions as a teacher in classical languages at upper secondary schools. In parallel to teaching, Axelson began a career as a poet. From his debut in 1938 until his fifth collection in 1965, Axelson was published by Sweden's major house, Bonniers. After the fifth volume, though, Bonniers started refusing Axelson's manuscripts. This was probably because the aesthetic ideals that Axelson's own poetry represented – a nostalgic and often idyllic nature poetry far from any experimental tendency – had become desperately outdated (Hertzman 2013). The remaining volumes were issued in cheap editions by the small publisher Zindermans. This suggests that in 1967, when the Montale volume was published, Axelson was in a difficult situation in his literary career, at a 'forced turning point', i.e. a radical change in the career that is not self-initiated but '*forced* on some, by external events and/or the actions of others' (Hodkinson and Sparkes 1997: 39). Moreover, his rheumatism, from which he suffered from a young age, became worse. As Axelson became increasingly disabled, he was forced to retire early in 1968, but that did not prevent him from composing and translating poetry. In two Zinderman editions from 1973 and 1974, that is, the years before Montale received the Nobel Prize, Axelson included no less than twenty-two poems by the author in the volumes. These were very modest publications which were practically ignored by the literary establishment. When Montale received the Nobel Prize in 1975, Axelson, who was the most prolific Swedish translator of the Genoese poet, seemed almost forgotten. He passed away in 1976.

The third Montale collection was translated by Anders Österling and published in 1972 by Oreglia's Italica. The volume was successfully launched at the Italian Cultural Institute in Stockholm, on an evening to which the director Lucia Pallavicini had invited the capital's literary celebrities: members of the Swedish Academy, the president of the Swedish PEN Club, the editors and literary critics of the largest Swedish newspapers, as well as university scholars and students. The event drew some attention to the new Montale volume. In a very positive review in *Svenska Dagbladet*, Åke Janzon described Österling's translations as 'excellent', 'admirable' and 'extraordinary', but his colleague in *Dagens Nyheter*, Ingemar Wizelius, was less dazzled: 'In Österling's version, Montale therefore appears […] with sweeter and more melodious contours than he actually has'. This critique of Österling's style was not unfounded (Smedberg Bondesson 2010), and yet it echoes an opinion of his poetry that was widespread in literary Sweden.

Anders Österling (1884–1981), grew up in a wealthy bourgeois home in Helsingborg. He made his debut as a poet in 1904 and at the age of thirty-five he was elected a member of the Swedish Academy, of which he was the permanent secretary during the years 1941–1964. Österling's capacity for work was immense: alongside the duties in the Swedish Academy, he published poetry and translations and reviewed three or four literary works a week. There is no doubt that Österling had a very large amount of prestige, which gave him a central position in Sweden's literary field (Westerström 2013). However, there was a weak point in Österling's impressive curriculum that concerned his own authorship. After a brilliant debut as a poetic prodigy, he was soon to be associated with an excessively idyllic and idealistic form of expression; his poetry became increasingly perceived as beautifully rhymed verse without much substance. When modernism rolled into Sweden, he had, so to speak, ended up on the wrong train: his beautiful and evocative images of nature were exactly the kind of poetry that had become most heavily criticized by the younger writers (Westerström 2013: 353). This somewhat negative attitude towards Österling's poetry materializes in the short and often disparaging lines with which his work is addressed in Swedish literary manuals, for instance Staffan Bergsten's brief description of Österling in *Den svenska poesins historia* (2007). Conversely, Österling retained his reputation as a translator and introducer of foreign literature (Westerström 2013: 192).

Österling's habitus included a lifelong passion for Italian literature, but he could also express severe judgements about it. For instance, he argued, in 1921, that 'Italy's modern poetry has its greatest weaknesses in the cosmopolitan susceptibility and the temptation to produce viable export literature, which can be read in Paris as well as in Milan' (1921: 140–1, our translation). With this view of Italian literature, it is not surprising that Österling would become an advocate of the Italian realists who debuted in the 1930s and 1940s. As already mentioned, he was sceptical about Montale and *hermeticism*, which he conceived as too pessimistic and introverted, but in 1960 Österling translated a few poems by the author, which must be regarded as a sort of Italian Nobel effect after the award to Salvatore Quasimodo in 1959, and in 1972 he completed the volume for Italica. At the time, Österling was an old man (eighty-eight years), who was no longer the permanent secretary of the Swedish Academy and whose poetry had not been taken into serious consideration for decades. His power to consecrate Montale, who had become a poet recognized worldwide, was limited. It is even questionable whether the Nobel Prize contributed to the consecration of Montale; rather it confirmed his status in world literature. Yet it should not be denied that the (former) centrality of Anders Österling in the literary field, not least as a member of the Swedish Academy, was decisive for the numerous reprints of his versions in newspapers and anthologies, while the translations of the more marginalized Gösta Andersson and Sture Axelson remained less widespread and reviewed.

To conclude, the Swedish Montale volumes did not coincide with the peaks of the translators' careers. Rather, their initiatives to translate an internationally consecrated author such as Montale conferred literary prestige on the translators themselves, as they were undertaken in the 'initiation phase' (cf. Lindqvist 2021a) or at the end of their careers.

From the cosmopolitan-vernacular perspective it is noticeable that one of Montale's translators, Österling, was overtly against the cosmopolitanism of Italian literature as he preferred its more regional and rural expressions. Even though the Ligurian landscape and the sea were at the centre of Montale's debut, the barren nature of the region was rather an exploration of the inner landscape of isolation and despair, far from Österling's idyllic and idealistic world view.

In Sweden, the announcement of the Nobel Prize to Montale was received with little enthusiasm and it certainly did not cause any Nobel effect in terms of new translations. In 1975, Bonniers issued a new edition of Österling's volume that had previously been published by Italica. Thereafter, only three single poems have been translated into Swedish, one in 1976 and two in 2019. This brief analysis suggests that an explanation could be the translators' lack of power to consecrate. In fact, in languages to which Montale was translated by more aesthetically congenial translators, such as Danish and English, his poetry constantly gave rise to new interpretations and translations.

Anglophone African Nobel literature in Swedish: The case of Wole Soyinka

When Wole Soyinka was awarded the Nobel Prize in 1986 as the first African author, it was according to the motivation of the prize committee, for a literary art that 'in a wide cultural perspective and with poetic overtones fashions the drama of existence'. The award confirmed his position as a writer of and for the world; from this moment on, Soyinka was considered a 'universal genius', as Caroline Davis put it, as an 'international writer' in Pascale Casanova's formulation, or, more critically, according to Emily Apter, as one of the internationally recognized authors of 'Global lit' (2012: 34, Apter 2001: 2, Casanova 2004: 110).

However, Soyinka's publishing history and the international reception of his work gives nuance to the narrative that such phrases seem to imply. In the case of Soyinka's introduction to Swedish audiences, which is the focus here, the selection of works for translation, the wordings of the reviews and the different positions of the translators engaged in bringing his writing onto the Swedish literary market demonstrate at once both a rather limited and a varied approach to his literature.

Wole Soyinka's first published works were a few poems printed in the magazine *The Horn*, set up at the English department of University College,

Ibadan (UCI) in 1962. Shortly after, three plays were published by the Ibadan-based and short-lived publisher Mbari Publications, a publishing outfit growing out of the influential literary magazine *Black Orpheus* and the Mbari Artists and Writers' Club which was also located in Ibadan. Catering to a local readership, Mbari's publishing also allowed Soyinka's works to begin enjoying an international readership, since Mbari also reached British and American readers and thereby constituted a 'crucial prelude to being published in London and New York' (Suhr-Sytsma 2013: 44).

Soyinka's more substantially international career began with his affiliation to Oxford University Press (OUP) and the publishing of the plays *The Lion and the Jewel* and *A Dance of the Forests* in 1963 (Davis 2012: 354). Benefiting from an imperial structure with offices in the UK, Nigeria and Kenya, and sales outlets in Uganda and Tanzania, OUP launched Soyinka for several literary markets at once. In the newly independent African countries, the author was published and marketed for an educational market, while in the UK, Soyinka was presented as a highly literary writer. As book historian Caroline Davis has shown, for the publisher this double strategy was not altogether easy to maintain. The reader and editor Rex Collings, for instance, wrote in a letter in support of contracting Soyinka that '[*The Lion and the Jewel*] is not alas an altogether suitable play for schools – but nor is an unexpurgated Macbeth' (Davis 2012: 354). In the end, however, the play was highly successful and OUP managed to make substantial profits out of its school book publishing in Africa, and simultaneously accumulated symbolic capital in the UK by taking on new literary talents.

From 1963 to 1969, OUP published seven of Soyinka's plays but was later replaced as a publisher by Methuen and Collings. Methuen published the poetry collection *Idanre and Other Poems* (1967) and continued to publish works such as *Madmen and Specialists* (1971), *Bacchae* (1973) and *Camwood on Leaves* (1973), whereas Collings published *Poems from Prison* (1969), *The Man Died* (1972) and *Season of Anomy* (1974). The two houses remained Soyinka's most prolific first publishers even if they were complemented by occasional outputs from Deutsch and Hans Zell. Soyinka's novel *The Interpreters* was also published as a reprint in the successful 'African Writers Series' with its recognizable coloured logo, even if, as its long-term editor James Currey has stated, the author resented being included in the 'orange ghetto' as a representative of 'African' literature (Zell 2011: 69).

Soyinka's identity as an African writer has proved to be a matter of recurring debate. At the African Writers Conference organized in Kampala in 1962,

Soyinka rejected the epithet through a quip that has become famous: 'African authors do not have to justify their Africanness just as tigers have no need to profess their "tigritude"'. In the mid-1970s, he was attacked by writers Chinweizu, Jemie and Madubike for his alleged 'Euro-modernism' in an article in the literary magazine *Okike*, which was edited by Chinua Achebe. In the article, which later became part of a book, they made the claim that Soyinka was a 'point man and demolition expert' to a cultural British imperialism set on blocking a nationalist movement (Feuser 1988: 557).

The debate over Soyinka's authenticity as an African writer in Nigeria, Anglophone Africa and beyond provides an ironic backdrop to the Swedish reception and subsequent Nobel award. Where the Swedish Academy in its motivation can rightly be said to emphasize cosmopolitan and human qualities in referencing Soyinka's 'wide cultural perspective' and his thematizing the 'drama of existence', for many other Swedish groups the Nobel Prize was primarily a (long overdue) literary prize to Africa, a sentiment Soyinka, according to Raoul Granqvist, acknowledged through his dedication of the prize to Nelson Mandela (1988: 468).

Soyinka was first introduced to Swedish readers through the anthology *Afrika berättar* (Africa narrates) in 1961. The anthology was edited by Per Wästberg, at the time twenty-seven years old, and published by Cavefors, a newly founded publisher located in the southern university town of Lund and headed by Bo Cavefors, also in his twenties. Wästberg, who would later become one of Sweden's leading intellectuals and a member of the Swedish Academy, was introduced to Soyinka by the Nigerian artist Ben Enwonwu, and formed a close friendship with the author (Wästberg 2007: 239). In Cavefors, Wästberg found a publisher with the courage to take on a new kind of publishing venture. Cavefors, on the other hand, saw in Wästberg an editor with a topic suitable to launch a radical new publishing house (Svensson 2015).

After the early introduction of Soyinka to a Swedish audience through two poems – in fact, the translation of Soyinka's 'Abiku' for Wästberg's anthology is a world first – and with the exception of the play *Swamp Dwellers*, which was translated for a performance on Swedish radio in 1967, more than a decade would pass before the next Swedish translation of Soyinka (Granqvist 1988: 472). But between 1972 and 1977 four of Soyinka's works were translated. One of Sweden's most important houses, Wahlström & Widstrand, published a collection of poetry entitled *Oguns skugga* 1972 (a collection of poems from *Idanre and Other Poems* and *A Shuttle from the Crypt*), and Cavefors the three novels *Röster ur förändringen* in 1975 (*The Interpreters*), *Laglöshetens tid* in 1975 (*Season of Anomy*) and *Mannen dog* in 1977 (*The Man Died. Notes from Prison*). Around ten years after this concerted effort, around the time of his Nobel award, and now in the absence of Cavefors which had foundered, Wahlström & Widstrand published new editions of these works (*Oguns skugga* in 1983, *Mannen dog, Röster ur förändringen* and *Laglöshetens tid,* all 1986). Soyinka's first autobiography, first published in 1981, was published by the same publisher as *Aké: barndomsåren* in 1987, the year after the Prize.

Given Soyinka's literary reputation and his growing body of work, the delay in Swedish translations after the first publications appears somewhat puzzling, especially given the fact that Soyinka had a presence of sorts in Sweden, shown, for instance, by the fact that he participated in the 1967 Scandinavian-African Writers' Conference organized by the Nordic Africa Institute. Even more so is the selection of works, which almost completely bypasses Soyinka's dramatic texts. Apart from *The Swamp Dwellers*, none of the plays published by OUP, for instance, were translated.

However, it seems clear that the omission was not caused by ignorance or lack of appreciation. The Nobel Committee's phrase the 'drama of existence' may be vague as evidence of the Committee's appreciation for the playwright, but reviews of his novels in Swedish newspapers regularly mention his versatility as a writer, his abilities as a dramatist and his success on international stages. One reviewer in 1984, for instance, noted Soyinka's performances in New York, and expressed a wish for Swedish translations of his plays (*Svenska Dagbladet*, 2 February 1984). The absence of Soyinka's drama in the Swedish literary market may in fact be due to concerns that have little to do with aesthetic preference. Estrid Tenggren, one of Soyinka's early translators, has reported that she translated three of Soyinka's plays in the 1970s for Cavefors (*Arbetet*, 18 October 1986). Furthermore, in a small advertisement by Bo Cavefors in *Aftonbladet* towards the end of 1979, the publisher stated his intention to publish some of Soyinka's plays. Two volumes of drama would appear the following year, Cavefors wrote. The volumes never appeared, however, and in 1981, Cavefors ceased to exist.

Whatever the reasons, Swedish publishers' near-exclusive focus on Soyinka's prose contrasts with his position in the Anglophone world. In Nigeria (and other African countries), Soyinka has frequently directed his own plays (and acted in a few of the performances) – a position that has allowed him to adapt his plays to current political situations in order to criticize power – and in Britain, Soyinka's drama and his directing are widely known, a reputation first established, of course, by OUP's marketing of him as a playwright, and further extended by Soyinka's position at the Royal Court Theatre where two of his plays were performed during one of his early stays in the country (Gibbs 1986: 3–17). That James Gibb's 1986 book on Wole Soyinka is published in Macmillan's 'Modern Dramatists' series, which include titles on Arthur Miller and Henrik Ibsen, is a further indication of his place in the British cultural landscape.

Nevertheless, the selective transfer of Soyinka's writing into the Swedish language is in line with how he is received in many other parts of the world. In France, Soyinka was first published as a novelist, with *Les Interprètes* (*The Interpreters*) in 1979, followed by *Aké* in 1984, before *Une Saison d'Anomie* (*Season of Anomy*) and *La Danse de la forêt* (*A Dance of the Forests*), both 1987. An indication that the Nobel Prize may have played a part in the publishing of the latter two is the fact that Soyinka's Nobel lecture was translated in 1987 (as *Que ce passé parle à son present*). The first German edition of Soyinka's work appeared in 1977, through East German publisher Volk and Welt's translation of *Season of Anomy* as *Zeit der Gestzlosigkeit*. This is the only exclusively GDR-published edition. West German editions of Soyinka's work were published from 1979 through *Die Plage der tollwütigen Hunde* (*Season of Anomy*) and *Der Mann is Tot* and *Die Plage* (*Season of Anomy*). Whether a 'Nobel effect' can be detected in the more even-paced trickle of Italian translations is uncertain, but on the Italian literary market, too, Soyinka is primarily a novelist: *Gli interpreti* (*The Interpreters*) appeared in 1979, *Stagione di anomia* (*Season of Anomy*) in 1981 and *Aké* in 1984, *L'uomo è morto* (*The Man Died*) in 1986 and *La morte e il cavaliere del re* (*Death and the King's Horseman*) in 1993.

If the number and the selection of Swedish translations do not do justice to the range and variety of Soyinka's writing, the different positions of translators that engage with his work demonstrate a variety that suggests Soyinka's place in the Swedish literary field spans the highbrow and the popular, the literary and the anthropological. Apart from Wästberg's anthology, the first translations of Soyinka were by Estrid Tenggren who translated *The Interpreters, Season of Anomy* and *The Man Died* with assistance from Eivor Olerup.

Tenggren had a background as a school teacher and began working with a printer in Lund in the late 1940s, the town where Cavefors would later set up business and with which she would become associated. Around this time, she made her first translations, and over her career she would focus on Italian and French poetry and novelists from central Europe. One of her late efforts is the much-reviewed translation of Nabokov's *Invitation to a Beheading* (translated as *Inbjudan till en halshuggning*, 2002) (Schwartz 2018). Although her reception in the early phase of her career is difficult to measure through reviewers' comments since translation work was seldom commented upon at the time – a fact which illustrates what Lawrence Venuti has called the 'invisibility' of the translator – by 1961, Tenggren was recognized enough for an article in one of the major newspapers to refer to her as an established, skilled and sensitive translator of contemporary Italian poetry (*Svenska Dagbladet*, 23 October 1961).

Östen Sjöstrand, who translated and prefaced Soyinka's poetry in the collection *Oguns skugga*, was a very different type of literary mediator. Sjöstrand was a poet himself translated into several languages, and was a respected introducer of French and Italian poetry. He was a frequent traveller to the Mediterranean and well versed in several languages. Coming from a well-situated home with a father in publishing, albeit in the entertainment segment of the field, Sjöstrand began his critical career at the big regional newspaper *Göteborgs-Posten* in 1947, made his debut as a poet two years later and published close to twenty poetry collections with the publisher Bonniers during his career (Schwartz 2018). Sjöstrand became a member of the Swedish Academy in 1975.

In an article in the literary magazine *Artes* in 1983, Sjöstrand presents his view of Soyinka's poetry. Comparing him both to Eliot and René Char, Sjöstrand describes Soyinka as a 'difficult' and 'complex' poet well worth the reading effort, a master of the discipline of form and fundamentally anchored in the Yoruba culture which, he stresses, is not frozen tradition but a living, 'existential reality'. For Sjöstrand, Soyinka is also a writer whose poetry is full of 'direct, not to say muscular, strength'. It is the latter quality in particular that puts him in 'world literature' – a term Sjöstrand does not explain but which seems to imply a canon of the world's great works (Sjöstrand 1983: 64, 66, 67).

Sjöstrand's article, published three years before Soyinka's Nobel Prize, offers a valuable inroad to Soyinka's poetry, but is silent on the labour of translation. Compared to Estrid Tenggren's comments on Soyinka's prose, published in a newspaper interview after the author's award, it well illustrates the translators' different positions in the literary field. In her after-the-fact interview, Tenggren remarks on the difficulty of translating Soyinka and her continuous conversation with him about particular words and phrases. She also speaks of her high regard for his writing and claims that he is 'better than Gordimer and Brink' (*Arbetet*, 18 October 1986). Sjöstrand's translations, Cecilia Schwartz has suggested (2018), probably contributed to Soyinka's award, in which case it is conceivable that his elaboration in *Artes* may have played its part.

If Sjöstrand was instrumental in Soyinka's award, he was almost certainly not alone. Per Wästberg, Sjöstrand's colleague in the Swedish Academy and the first introducer of Soyinka to a Swedish audience, reviewed the new edition of *Oguns skugga* for *Dagens Nyheter*, Sweden's largest newspaper, and referred to the author as 'probably the best' (*främste*) of the contemporary African writers. Artur Lundkvist, also an Academy member, in his 1976 review of *Laglöshetens tid* (*Season of Anomy*) – in a phrase that showed his particular brand of exoticism – had already called Soyinka the 'most powerful and sophisticated author from black Africa' (Lundkvist 1976: 3, Alvstad and Lundahl 2010).

Two later translators of Soyinka may be mentioned briefly since they represent yet again different types of mediators. Björn Ranung, who translated Soyinka's essay *Isara: A Voyage around Essay* in 1990, was a latecomer to Soyinka's work as a translator, but had been familiar with his work and with Nigeria for a long time. Ranung was a multitasker: he became a doctor of anthropology with experience of fieldwork in Nigeria and eventually curator at the Ethnographic Museum of Sweden. A man of many talents, he produced graphic prints and practised calligraphy. He played instruments, notably the harmonica and the Spanish guitar – an instrument that, he has recounted, caused some amusement when he played it in Nigeria during his anthropological work. In later life, Ranung was appointed 'riksspelman' (a badge of honour for folk music musicians) in harmonica. His literary output reflects his wide-ranging interests which include anthropological chapters and prefaces, exhibition catalogues and illustrations (*KulturNav*, 2019).

Lennart Olofsson, who translated Soyinka's memoir *Aké* (1983), is also the translator of Nuruddin Farah's Blood in the Sun trilogy: *Maps* (translated as *Kartor*, 1987), *Gifts* (*Gåvor*, 1990) and *Secrets* (*Hemligheter*, 2000). Apart from this venture into African literary fiction, however, Olofsson's professional translation has been almost purely of crime fiction and thrillers. Olofsson is the translator of Conn Iggulden, Stephen King, John Grisham, Harlan Coben and David Baldacci, among others.

Against the background of Wole Soyinka's early introduction to Swedish audience – made possible by one of Sweden's leading intellectuals and an entrepreneurial publisher – the long delay before further translations followed appears somewhat surprising. It is also noteworthy that, on the Swedish literary market, Soyinka is published primarily as a novelist (and later as an autobiographer), even as critics frequently point to his literary versatility and his recognition as a playwright. This framing is in sharp contrast to the

English-speaking world where Soyinka is known as a dramatist – a reputation that forms from the very first publishing of his works by Oxford University Press. However, it is in line with how he is introduced and published on several other national literary fields. While the selection of titles for Swedish publishing narrows the author's range, the different types of translators who transfer his work into Swedish in a different manner indicate Soyinka's breadth, and his somewhat elusive position on the national field. Tenggren and Olofsson, the first a professional translator with a specialization in poetry and prose from the Mediterranean, the second a translator of popular literature with a long list of crime fiction and thriller authors behind him, belong to Casanova's category of *ordinary* translators, despite their differences, even if Tenggren's recognition would eventually move her closer to a position as a *consecrated* translator. Sjöstrand, poet and member of the Swedish Academy embodied the *consecrated* type of translator, while Ranung, musician and anthropologist, although having an institution behind him, partly defies neat categorization.

Portuguese Nobel literature in Swedish: The case of José Saramago

When the Nobel Prize was awarded to the author José Saramago in 1998, he was the first Portuguese language recipient of the prize. The absence of a literary Nobel Prize laureate from the Portuguese-speaking world was by then something extensively discussed, often with much indignation, especially in the Portuguese and Brazilian public media and literary establishments. Consequently, for the Portuguese literary sphere the award given to Saramago meant an important and eagerly awaited symbolic and cultural recognition. In a special issue of the literary magazine *Colóquio/Letras*, dedicated to Saramago and published in 2000, Maria Alzira Seixo (1999) said: 'The spell of the evil eye was broken, what we for a long time disbelieved had happened at last' ('Quebrou-se o enguiço, aquilo em que já desacreditávamos aconteceu enfim'). However, on the Brazilian literary circuit, critics continue to analyse and discuss the reasons behind not being considered for this recognition. In the aftermath of the scandal and crisis of the Swedish Academy in 2018, which severely damaged its reputation and brought into question the integrity of its members, some critics also started to establish a link between its lack of legitimacy and the failure to reward female and non-European authors (see e.g. Albuquerque 2019 and Almeida 2019).

In this part we will explore the 'Nobel Prize effect' on Saramago's pathway of Swedish and wider international circulation together with his road within the Swedish literary circuit leading up to the Nobel Prize. We will suggest that Saramago's Nobel Prize came about through a combination of favourable circumstances, like the reciprocal consecration pathway of Saramago's novels and the career development of his professional translator Marianne Eyre, together with strong institutional support, such as being published by a renowned large-scale publishing house with a capacity for marketing and attracting media attention. Admittedly, members of the Swedish Academy have stated that a translation into Swedish is not a prerequisite for being eligible for the prize and that in such an eventuality they would arrange for interesting authorships to be translated (Interview with Per Wästberg in the television programme *Malou efter tio*). Nevertheless, it is obviously a great advantage for the candidate if the Academy has access to high-quality translations of a work if they do not possess the competence to read it in its original language. The importance of a skilful translator with accumulated intercultural transfer competence in the process of consecrating José Saramago's authorship in the Swedish landscape cannot be underestimated (cf. Roig-Sanz and Meylaerts 2018: 14). Into this equation for a reciprocal consecration pathway, we also must take into consideration the other widely critically acclaimed Portuguese writer besides Saramago, António Lobo Antunes. In many ways, Antunes' translations into Swedish are just as important for the consecration path of the translator Marianne Eyre as for the accumulated prestige that contemporary Portuguese literature acquired in the 1990s in Sweden. This mutual consecration pathway is the logic behind the inclusion of António Lobo Antunes' translations in the rationale of this text.

At the time of the prize, the editorial circumstances in the Swedish book market for Saramago and Antunes were very similar. While Portuguese-language literature was (and still is) generally published in the small-scale pole of publishing, Saramago and Antunes constituted rare exceptions as both were published by the publishing houses Wahlström & Widstrand and Forum, both belonging to the large-scale Bonnier Group. They both received high media attention, high praise from the literary establishment and were both translated into Swedish by the prominent translator Marianne Eyre.

For several years before Saramago received the prize he and António Lobo Antunes were frequently mentioned as candidates in the Swedish media speculations about the prize. Having two possible and qualified candidates for the prize promoted in the media by influential critics was something that gave extra weight to the request for a Portuguese prize winner. The media often created a rivalry between the two camps where critics and researchers discussed the advantage of one over the other. Obviously, this rivalry situation also stemmed from the implicit consensus that the time had come for Portuguese language literature to finally receive the prize. However, that would probably mean that it would take a long time until another Portuguese author would again be up for consideration. One example of these strong positionings in favour of Antunes and Saramago was expressed by Pascale Casanova in her seminal study *La république mondiale des lettres*. She writes: 'It is to be regretted, however, that in choosing between José Saramago and António Lobo Antunes the Swedish Academy should have privileged the more "national" of the two and the upholder of a conservative aesthetic of the novel. Antunes, an innovator, the creator of new literary forms, is unquestionably the only true Portuguese "classic of the future"' (Casanova 2004: 377). However passionately convincing this statement may seem, when looking at the facts surrounding domestic controversies and the full picture of Saramago's writing, it seems unfair to regard him as 'national' and 'conservative'. On the contrary, Antunes and Saramago have been equally critically acclaimed as innovators of literary form and language, as well as being considered equally politically controversial in their source culture (as will be addressed further below).

Saramago received the Nobel Prize at the age of seventy-six with the motivation: 'Who with parables sustained by imagination, compassion and irony continually enables us once again to apprehend an illusory reality' (https://www.svenskaakademien.se/en). Saramago was an autodidact from a modest background with parents who were illiterate. He began his writing career working for newspapers and translating. In 1975, he had to resign as deputy editor-in-chief of the daily paper *Diário de Notícias* due to his political activities and his membership in the Communist Party. This was just one of several high-profile political controversies in which he would be implicated in his home country. Saramago wrote poetry, drama and essays, and in the early 1980s his novels received national awards and were translated mainly into Western European languages.

Comparing José Saramago's pathway to global circulation in translation before and after the Nobel Prize reveals some interesting results. At the time of the Nobel Prize, Saramago had already written several of his major successes which were translated into many European languages. According to the online 'Translation database' provided by the Portuguese DGLAB (Direcção-Geral do Livro, dos Arquivos e das Bibliotecas), for example: *Memorial do Convento* (1982) was translated into twenty-nine languages, *História do Cerco de Lisboa* (1989) into fifteen languages and *O Evangelho segundo Jesus Cristo* (1991) into fourteen languages. A 'Nobel Prize effect' on the dissemination of Saramago's novels is noticeable in the significant increase in translated publications after 1998: 144 translations in the period 1970–1998 and 342 in the period 1999–2020. However, the 'effect' is primarily manifested in the fact that several of his titles are now available in non-Western languages, such as Hebrew, Bengali, Arabic, Mandarin, Japanese, Hindi, Urdu, Thai and Korean (translational database, DGLAB, https://dglab.gov.pt/ [accessed 14 September 2020]). A complementary search in WorldCat.org reveals even more translations (subsequent to 1998) into languages such as Indonesian, Russian, Persian, Turkish, Vietnamese and Punjabi, among others (accessed 14 September 2020).

In Sweden, four of Saramago's novels were published before, and one in the same year as he was awarded the Nobel Prize. In 1988, his most successful work in sales and translations *Memorial do Convento* (1982) was published with the Swedish title *Baltasar and Blimunda*, followed by *Historien om Lissabons belägring* in 1991 (*História do Cerco de Lisboa*, 1989), *Evangeliet enligt Jesus Kristus* in 1993 (*O evangelho Segundo Jesus Cristo*, 1991) and *Blindheten* in 1997 (*Ensaio sobre a Cegeira*, 1995). Marianne Eyre was the translator of the first two novels, published by the large firm Wahlström & Widstrand and re-published in more editions. In the early 1990s, Portuguese literature received some growing attention in the form of special issues, published in the literary journals *Allt om böcker* (no. 6, 1991) and *Ariel litterär tidskrift* (no. 4–5, 1994). In both these, however, greater focus was placed on António Lobo Antunes' authorship. Antunes' first translation into Swedish was published as early as 1985, and when Saramago received the prize he already had seven titles translated into Swedish by Marianne Eyre. The reason Marianne Eyre interrupted the translation of Saramago's third novel into Swedish, *Evangeliet enligt Jesus Kristus* (*O Evangelho Segundo Jesus Cristo*) was her personal religious concerns over the content. Instead, it was published with a new translator, Henrik Berggren, who would translate the following eleven titles by Saramago, published in Sweden until 2020.

The novel *O Evangelho Segundo Jesus Cristo* caused great controversy and scandal in Portugal and in the Catholic world through containing a critical reconstruction and reimagining of Jesus' relationship to God and canonical events. Following its publication there was a heated debate in the press about Saramago's alleged heresy, and Portugal's Minister of Culture vetoed the nomination of the novel to the newly established European Union Literary Prize. In the aftermath of these controversies, Saramago exiled himself to Lanzarote in Spain. This literary scandal also received attention in Sweden. In the context of commemorating the 5th anniversary of the Fatwah against Salman Rushdie, Saramago was asked to write an exclusive piece on sin for the culture section of a Swedish daily newspaper. The article entitled 'Kätteri – en mänsklig rättighet' (Heresy – a human right) was translated by Marianne Eyre and published in the daily paper *iDag*. In introducing Saramago's text his case was compared to Salman Rushdie's for attracting similar religious criticism, although from a Christian perspective, and states: 'Suddenly, the seventy-year-old Saramago became one of the most controversial writers of the 90s' ('Plötsligt blev den drygt sjuttioårige Saramago en av 90-talets mest kontroversiella författare') (*iDag*, 14 February 1994). Evidently, the political controversy in the demand for creative freedom of literary expression in Saramago's novel was not something held against him in the selection process of the Academy four years later.

The translator Marianne Eyre started her successful career by publishing both her own poetry and translations of poems in the *Amnesty Bulletin*. She was involved in the founding of Swedish Amnesty, and in 1975–1976, she worked at Amnesty's international office in London. Her first book translations included both testimonies of political repression (from South Africa and China), published by the small-scale pole of publishing and novels by Ismail Kadaré and Régine Deforges, published by the renowned large-scale publishing house Bonniers. From early on she thereby established a professional relationship with the large-scale publisher that would later publish both Saramago and Antunes. Through her committed work within Amnesty, she made personal contacts and became close friends with several political prisoners from different parts of the world, including several who were imprisoned in Brazil (Widestam 2001). In the late 1970s, she worked in Brazil, where she encountered and learned the Portuguese language.

In the early 1980s, Eyre translated her first books from Portuguese (e.g. the Portuguese Almeida Faria and Brazilian Clarice Lispector) which would later be her main source language. In 1985, the first translation of António Lobo Antunes' *De förrådda* (*Os Cus de Judas*, 1985) was published by the publisher Forum. This novel would be followed by another thirteen titles. Due to Marianne Eyre's retirement, Antunes' last three translated titles, published between 2008 and 2015, were translated by another established translator of Lusophone literature in the Swedish field, Örjan Sjögren. In the 1980s and 1990s she also translated the novels by Saramago which led up to his Nobel Prize.

Besides the translations of Antunes and Saramago, Marianne Eyre also translated Brazilians such as Augusto Boal, Fernando Morais, António Linto and Clarice Lispector, and three titles of the Mozambican Mia Couto. Through her early establishment with large-scale publishers the majority of these titles have also been published in the large-scale publishers, thus contradicting the usual publishing pattern of Lusophone literature in Sweden. Eyre also collaborated with other productive translators of Lusophone literature, such as Örjan Sjögren and Marianne Sandels in anthologies and literary journals, Eyre is thereby one of the most important contemporary cultural mediators and transmitters of Lusophone literature in Sweden.

In an interview article with Eyre from 1996, two years before Saramago's Nobel Prize, in the daily paper *Dagens Nyheter*, Stefan Helgesson pointed out that she 'belongs to the tens of translators in this country whose work is regularly praised to the heavens' and that he considered her personal international social commitment an important explanation of her skill (*Dagens Nyheter*, 5 June 1996). Consequently, Eyre was often mentioned and praised in book reviews, and in *Handbok för inkvisitorer* (*O Manual dos Inquisidores*), she got her own printed personal dedication from Antunes (Antunes 1996). Quotes of her translation skills from reviews have also made their way onto covers, such as the dust jacket of Saramago: 'In addition, brilliantly translated by Marianne Eyre' ('Därtill briljant översatt av Marianne Eyre') (Saramago 1993).

Accompanying these translations, Eyre started to receive the most prestigious translation awards in the Swedish literary circuit. In 1989, she was awarded the Translations Award of Samfundet de nio (The Nine Society) and in 1992 Albert Bonniers 100-årsminne (award in memory of Albert Bonnier's centenary). This latter prize is awarded to writers and illustrators, and since 1991 also translators. Eyre was the second translator to receive this award. In 1993, she received the prize 'for excellent translations into the Swedish language' by the Swedish Academy. In 1997, Eyre received the Letterstedtska priset för översättningar (Letterstedska Prize for translations), awarded by the Royal Swedish Academy of Letters for the translation of Lobo Antunes' *Tingens naturliga ordning (A ordem natural das coisas)*. In 2001, Eyre received the Elsa Thulins översättarpris (Elsa Thulin's Translator's Award) from the Swedish Writers' Union, for outstanding authorship with the motivation: 'Marianne Eyre – a safe pilot for large ships in difficult-to-understand waters. For a dedicated act of translation during which she with unusual power and passion placed herself at the poets' disposal, from the nameless prisoner of conscience to the prestigious António Lobo Antunes' ('Marianne Eyre – en trygg lots för stora skepp i svåröverskådliga farvatten. För en hängiven översättargärning under vilken hon med ovanlig kraft och lidelse ställt sig till diktarnas förfogande, från den namnlöse samvetsfången till den ryktbare António Lobo Antunes') (https://oversattarsektionen.se/utmarkelser/elsa-thulin-priset/pristagare/marianne-eyre). As we can see in this motivation there is an outspoken connection between Eyre's international solidarity commitment and her translation activity in the recognition she receives from the literary establishment.

In investigating the consecration processes of translators in the Swedish literary translation field, Yvonne Lindqvist has pointed out different steps corresponding to an accumulation of symbolic capital in the form of translation awards, prizes and different possibilities for sustainment and governmental funding, which allowed for being a full-time translator (Lindqvist 2021a). According to these measurements, Eyre has received the highest degree of consecration possible in the Swedish translation field as she was awarded the most prestigious prizes and is one of the very exclusive few granted the Official Artist Salary – guarantee of income (*inkomstgaranti*) – from the Swedish government as a translator. This consecration process of Marianne Eyre in the Swedish translation field then developed reciprocally with the recognition of literary quality in the writings of both the Nobel laureate Saramago and Lobo Antunes, leading up to the Portuguese Nobel Prize in the Swedish literary landscape.

After the Nobel Prize, Saramago's novels were published in Sweden with an increased publishing consistency in new translated titles and of re-editions. Saramago did not suffer from the legendary post-Nobel writer's block as he produced many more literary texts before his death in 2010. The novels he wrote in the 2000s were all translated into Swedish with a minimum time gap: *Grottan* in 2001 (*A Caverna*, 2000), *Dubbelgångaren* in 2003 (*O Homem Duplicado*, 2002), *Klarsynen* in 2006 (*Ensaio Sobre a Lucidez*, 2004), *Dödens nycker* in 2008 (*As Intermitências da Morte*, 2005). In 2010 the memoir *Små minnen* (*As Pequenas Memórias*, 2006) was his last work published by a large-scale publisher. The very last translation to date, *Kain* (*Cain*) was published after Saramago's death in 2013 by the small publisher Tranan. Although Saramago was published with a higher consistency after the prize, this trend seems to have lasted for a decade and applied mainly to his novels written in the 2000s. On the other hand, in regard to the translation consistency of António Lobo Antunes' novels, after the Nobel Prize a slight decrease could be seen as early as the 2000s, and this became even more notable after 2010. In 2014, a new niche publisher Modernista relaunched his authorship and re-published *De förrådda* (*O Cus de Judas*). The title was followed up in 2017 by Modernista, republishing and repackaging three of Antunes novels in 'The Benfica Trilogy', which prompted the critic Claes Wahlin to write a celebratory review in the daily paper *Aftonbladet* with the headline 'Ge honom Nobelpriset!' (Give him the Nobel Prize!) (*Aftonbladet*, 26 June 2017).

Maryse Condé: Consecration translators and the prize of the New Academy

Maryse Condé (b. 1937) is one of the most noteworthy contemporary Caribbean writers today writing in French. Her production comprises twenty novels, three autobiographical works, eight children's books and a large number of essays and short stories. Additionally, she is in fact the most translated Caribbean author into Swedish. One of the most salient themes in the literary production of Maryse Condé is the search for 'the origin', which can be understood as a vernacular experience. In her native Guadeloupe, as in the rest of the Caribbean, black blood symbolizes centuries of oppression and exploitation. Condé's novels narrate tales of the abusive colonial power and strong women. In an interview, Condé underlines that the most important thing when writing a Caribbean novel is to capture the soul and structure of the Caribbean narrative. You have to get hold of the Caribbean way of telling a story (Wolf 1999: 6). That is why her novels mix chapters narrated in the first and third persons and intermingle male and female voices.

Condé is read within many different cultures. She is widely translated into English, German, Dutch, Italian, Spanish, Portuguese, Japanese and Swedish. According to Sapiro and Bustamante (2009), the number of languages that a novel is translated into gives a rough estimation of the consecration of the author within the world literary field. Condé is thus a highly consecrated author. Her most prolific translator into English is her husband Richard Philcox. Into Swedish, Condé's novels have so far been translated by three different translators: Helena

Böhme (b. 1961), Kristina Ekelund (b. 1958) and Svante Hansson (b. 1938). A fourth translator, Gunnel von Friesen (b. 1939), translated the youth novel *À la courbe du Joliba* (*At the Joliba Curve*) at Papamosca publishing house in 2007. According to the model of translator consecration (Lindqvist 2021a), which identifies four phases of accumulated translation capital in the Swedish literary translation field (investment, initiation, recognition and confirmation) and which in ascending prestige distinguishes between acknowledged translators, rewarded translators and (state) subsidized translators, Böhme and Ekelund belong to the recognition phase as acknowledged translators. They have worked for many years in the field and have published several book-length translations. However, neither of them has been awarded translation prizes or awards available in the field, nor received scholarships from the union or subsidies from the state – tokens which distinguish acknowledged translators from rewarded and subsidized ones. They translate authors that can be described as aesthetes or vanguard, according to the Bourdieusian model of ideal-typic writers. From this point of view, Hansson is entering the field as a temporary visitor, more acknowledged for his translations of non-fiction.

Helena Böhme has translated five of Condé's seven novels into Swedish. She has also translated several short stories by Condé published in the literary journal *Karavan*. Condé's second novel in Sweden, *Traversée de la mangrove* (*Färden genom mangroven*; *Crossing the mangrove*), which Böhme translated and was used to introduce Condé at the annual book fair in Gothenburg, was published by Leopard publishing house in 2007. Still, translation is not Böhme's livelihood; she also holds a position at the municipal library of Stockholm. She has a bachelor's degree in French and translation from Stockholm University and attended the master class in literary translation at the University College of Södertörn during the years 2000 to 2002. Böhme also translated novels by the French authors Alice Ferney and Marie Desplechin at the beginning of her translation career. Her translations have been very well received by the Swedish press.

Kristina Ekelund, the second important translator of Condé's work in Sweden, works mainly with French as a source language. She is particularly interested in North African literature written in French and has translated, introduced and promoted Magreb literature in Sweden, for example the Moroccan authors Driss Chraibi and Damia Oumassine but also Belgian and French writers, for instance Sandrine Bessora and Marie Darrieussecq. She holds a bachelor's degree in French and Classic languages and studied at the master class in literary translation at the University College of Södertörn in the period 2000–2002. She has taught translation classes at Uppsala University and participated in round table talks discussing African literature at the Gothenburg Book Fair in 2010. Her production of translations amounts to eleven novels and two non-fiction book publications.

The third translator of Condé's novels into Swedish, Svante Hansson, translated the novel *Ségou: Tome 1. Les Murailles de terre* as early as in 1989 under the title *Segu*. The novel *Ségou* consists of two volumes. The first volume, *Ségou: Les murailles de terre*, was published in France by Éditions Robert Laffont in 1984 and the second volume, *Ségou: La terre en miettes*, in 1985. Only the first tome was translated into Swedish. Hansson's experience as a literary translator was at the time rather restricted. He worked as a teacher in political sciences and translated non-fiction literature from the Scandinavian languages, English and French. His translation of Segu was published by Hammarström & Åkerberg publishing house in 1989 and re-published by Leopard in 2008 under a new exoticizing title: *Segu. En afrikansk släktsaga* (*Segu: An African Family Saga*). The first publication was financed by funds from the Swedish government agency SIDA, Swedish International Development Cooperation Agency. These economic instigations might explain why this novel 'travelled' so quickly to Sweden. In most cases, bibliomigration from this part of the world has been proven to require a much longer time span (cf. Lindqvist 2019).

Common features for the three Condé translators are firstly that none of them work solely with translation: Böhme is a librarian, Ekelund and Hansson are teachers. Secondly, they translate authors that can be described as either aesthetes or vanguard. Thirdly, Ekelund and Böhme have educational backgrounds that are similar in more than one respect. They both studied at Stockholm University and they both attended the master class in literary translation at the University College Södertörn during the same time span (Kleberg 2007). This master class ran during the period 1998–2012 and is today considered as an invaluable plant school for future literary translators, supervised by some of the most prominent Swedish translators of the time, for example Anders Bodegård, Ulrika Wallenström and Jan Stolpe and with close connections to the publishing houses. The master class gave students access to the publishing business, since their supervisors were also important 'node persons' (cf. Svedjedal 2012: 64) for different language spheres within the Swedish literary culture, so-called *charismatic translators* with the power to consecrate newcomers in the field. Each student applied with and worked with a specific translation during the master class, with the explicit aim of getting this translation published. The translation project of Helena Böhme, for example, was *Färden genom mangroven* (*Crossing the Mangrove*) – a very well received work when published by Leopard in 2007.

After the book fair in Gothenburg in 2007 and ever since, Condé has been frequently mentioned in the annual Nobel Prize speculations in the Swedish press (cf. Flakiersk 2007, Jonsson 2007, Erenberg 2011, Strängberg 2012) – speculations that were further strengthened when the literary journal *Karavan* published a special issue dedicated to her work. Condé also had a history of winning prestigious literary prizes, such as the Grand Prix Littéraire de la Femme in 1986, the Prix Alain Boucheron in 1987 and the Prix de l'Académie Française in 1988. The publishing trajectories of her novels are also a testament to her significant reputation. Three years after the first publication of the novel *Traversée de la mangrove*, it appeared in the Gallimard Collection Folio for modern classics. To be included in such a modern classics collection is regarded by many as a sure sign of consecration. In 1993, Condé was the first female ever to be awarded the highly prestigious American Puterbaugh Prize for the total of her literary production, and in 1999, she received the Marguerite Yourcenar Prize for Francophone writers living in the United States. The French state further honoured Condé with the Commandeur de L'Ordre des Arts et de Lettres in 2001 and she was appointed Chevalier de la Légion d'Honneur in 2004. These prizes and honours bear witness to Condé's consecration within both the French and Anglo-American cultures. A paperback edition of the novel *Segou* in the English-speaking world by Penguin appeared in 1996 – another sign of the high prestige of Maryse Condé's authorship within the English language sphere. Since her first appearance at the Book Fair in Gothenburg, Sweden in 2007, Condé has visited Sweden several times, participating in book launches and literary talks, for instance in 2012 at the International Writers' Stage at the Stockholm Culture House – a literary institution that has invited interesting authors from all over the world since 1998. Some Nobel laureates have even appeared on that stage prior to winning their prize, for instance the two recent laureates Olga Tokarczuk and Svetlana Aleksijevitj in 2011. Maryse Condé, on the other hand, was shortlisted for the Man Booker International Prize in 2015 and then, in 2018, she was awarded the New Academy Prize in Literature.

The New Academy was born in response to the cancellation of the Nobel Prize of literature of 2018. It was founded by the journalist and author Alexandra

Pascalidou as a non-profit organization, not affiliated with either the Nobel Foundation or the Swedish Academy. The explicit intention of the New Academy was to emphasize that literature promotes democracy, openness, empathy and respect (Perera 2018) and was – in contrast to the traditional selection process of the Royal Swedish Academy – more democratic, with a three-step voting procedure for the prize, inviting the general reading public to participate instead of just a restricted number of Academy members. As the critic Erika Harlitz-Kern remarked:

> For the Nobel Prize in Literature to regain its international reputation, the ivory tower that the Swedish Academy has become needs to come down. The New Academy is not intended to be the solution to the crisis surrounding the Nobel Prize in Literature. But it can be an important step on the way towards a rejuvenation of the Nobel Prize.
>
> (Harlitz-Kern 2018)

Firstly, librarians from all over Sweden were asked to nominate two authors of their choice. The result of this first step was a list of 155 authors, which was curated to forty-seven authors based on the number of nominations. This long list is in fact a general representation of appreciated authors and literature in the Swedish libraries of today. It contains thirty women and seventeen men. Sweden and the United States had most of the nominations: twelve each. The United Kingdom followed with five nominations. Of the American authors nominated, five were women working within a wide span of literary genres, including names such as Jamaica Kincaid, Patti Smith and Donna Tartt. Traditionally the Nobel Prize in Literature favours male, white and French authors, but in contrast, on this list France was represented solely by one male author, Édouard Louis, and two female writers, Nina Bouraoui of North African descent, and Maryse Condé from Guadeloupe. Some of the Swedish authors nominated were Johannes Anyuru, Jonas Hassen Khemiri and Agneta Pleijel, also defying the Nobel norm. Compared to the typical Nobel Prize laureate, Louis, Anyuru and Khemiri, for example, are very young. While they have been hailed for their stylistically well-crafted and original novels, they are still very much at a formative stage of their writing careers.

Secondly, readers could vote for their favourite author on the website of the New Academy. More than thirty thousand people voted. Thirdly, a panel made up of the editor and independent publisher Ann Pålsson, the literature professor Lisbeth Larsson, the literary critic and translator Peter Stenson and the library director Gunilla Sandin appointed the winner from a shortlist of two female and two male writers. The shortlisted writers were Haruki Murakami, Kim Thúy, Maryse Condé and Neil Gaiman. However, Haruki Murakami declined his nomination, leaving three candidates for the prize. Murakami's reason for this renouncement was that he wanted to concentrate on his writing far away from the spotlight of the media (Wrede 2018) and – one might suspect – with the ambition to be awarded the ordinary Nobel Prize in literature in the future, which probably would not be helped by the prize of the New Academy. A critic in one of the most renowned daily newspapers in Sweden, *Dagens Nyheter*, claimed that Murakami would be 'fried' if he won the prize of the New Academy (Magnusson 2018), a claim that equally concerns the other nominees and most certainly the final recipient of the prize.

The goal of the New Academy was to achieve a prize sum of a million Swedish krona by means of crowdfunding, which would pay for the prize and the festivities surrounding the prize ceremony. The final prize sum eventually amounted to 320,000 Swedish krona (just over 30,000 euros; Wrede 2018), which makes this literary prize one of the better paid ones after the Nobel Prize (800,000 euros) and the Planeta prize (600,000 euros) in Spain. On 9 December 2018 Maryse Condé received the alternative Nobel Prize in Stockholm. In an interview, Condé underlined that for her there is no difference between the Nobel Prize and the alternative Nobel Prize. She considers the prize she received to be a great honour (Wrede 2018). The Prize motivation by the New Academy read:

> Maryse Condé is a grand storyteller. Her authorship belongs to world literature. In her work, she describes the ravages of colonialism and the postcolonial chaos in a language which is both precise and overwhelming. The magic, the dream and the terror is as also love constantly present. Fiction and reality overlap each other and people live as much in an imagined world with long and complicated traditions as the ongoing present. Respectfully and with humour she narrates the postcolonial insanity disruption and abuse but also human solidarity and warmth. The dead live in her stories closely to the living in a multitudinous world where gender, race and class are constantly turned over in new constellations.
> (http://www.mynewsdesk.com/se/pressreleases/maryse-conde-receives-the-new-academy-prize-in-literature-2018-at-berns-stockholm-on-december-9-2810518 [accessed 6 May 2020])

Two days after the prize ceremony the New Academy was dissolved, having served its purpose.

Concluding remarks

Our discussion of Nobel Prize laureates and their translators emphatically shows that high-prestige literature in translation is a field for enthusiasts. Among the translators discussed, only a few are or have been writers and translators exclusively (among them Robert Bly and Anders Österling). Most have translated in their free time away from work as teachers, publishers and librarians. They have been paid for their efforts, but translation alone has not been enough for them to earn a living. It seems, then, that the dichotomy of symbolic and economic capital is confirmed. In most cases, translations of high-prestige literature also seem to exist in a world of its own, a *circuit lettré* independent from the circulation pattern of other types of literature.

There are, of course, exceptions to this rule, some of which have been mentioned in our discussion. For example, Philippe Bouquet, the foremost translator of Swedish literature into French since 1980, has fluctuated between high-prestige literature on the one hand and thrillers and crime fiction on the other. This may have to do with the semi-peripheral position of the Swedish language. On the one hand, Swedish was in the 1980s such a small source language in the French literary market that it was possible for one translator to dominate the scene, and to translate works of several different genres. On the other hand, Swedish literature was sufficiently well known and integrated in the cultural transfer processes of Western Europe for publishers to be willing to try out both popular fiction and high-prestige literature.

We have also discussed the phenomenon of consecration, and its relations to various institutions and to literature itself. It is commonly stated that literature is consecrated by institutions of various kinds; they might be academies or societies but also publishers and individuals such as writers and translators. We have studied these processes with the help of Pascale Casanova's model of different mediator types, 'institutional consecrators', 'ordinary mediators' and the 'consecrated' or 'charismatic consecrators', the latter category having the largest amount of consecrating power. A poignant example was the publishing of Maryse Condé's novel *Traversée de la mangrove*, in Gallimard's prestigious Collection Folio for modern classics. Another one was the fact that Eugenio Montale was translated by Anders Österling, a member of the Swedish Academy and therefore a powerful 'institutional consecrator' (although Montale's breakthrough in Sweden turned out to be rather limited).

Several of our examples illustrate the central role of literary translators in and around the Nobel Prize. Translators give access to literature from elsewhere, and members of the Swedish Academy and its Nobel Prize committee are among the recipients of this access, directly or indirectly. But translators are not only important in the process leading up to the award; they also help creating distributional effects after a prize is given. Without translators, the Nobel Prize would be a far less important event in the continual formation of world literature.

However, it is of equal importance to stress literature's capacity to consecrate those who handle it – publishers, academies, translators, etc. Having worked with translations of Tomas Tranströmer's poetry has very much altered Robert Bly's reputation, at least in Tranströmer's home country of Sweden. Giving the literary prize of the New Academy to Maryse Condé might be seen as an attempt to restore the reputation of Sweden's literary establishment after the crisis in the Swedish Academy, by associating the former with a postcolonial literary perspective. Moreover, the analysis of Montale's three Swedish translators show that they all turned to his poetry when their own careers were in need of symbolic capital. In other words, there exists a dialectic of consecration, where literature is consecrated by different actors in the literary field, while at the same time altering the position of those very actors.

Lawrence Venuti has described translations as either domesticating or foreignizing. Adding to this, there seems to be an overwhelming consensus that central or hyper-central language spheres tend to favour domesticating translations, while there is a higher tolerance for foreignizing ones in peripheral or semi-peripheral literary cultures. This might very well be the case, but our analysis above has shown that translators of high-prestige literature, regardless of the target language, above all seem concerned with preserving the integrity and character of the source culture text. However, this can be done in different ways. Robert Bly's English translations of Tranströmer's poetry, for example, are significantly wordier than the original. Anders Österling's Swedish translations of Eugenio Montale, on the other hand, seem designed to convey the status and value of the original by adapting it to a high-prestige (and somewhat archaic) poetic idiom typical of the target culture. In some cases – e.g. Philippe Bouquet's French translations of Harry Martinson's work – the translator's attempt to remain true and respectful towards the original can be regarded as a kind of foreignizing, in the sense that the translator wants the source text to retain its nature. In other cases – e.g. Österling's translations of Montale – the same ambition can result in a specific kind of domestication.

When it comes to translated high-prestige literature in general, the act of translation is more often than not made explicit. The name of the translator might even be printed on the book cover. Translations are published in prestigious series, such as the French 'Cadre vert' (Le Seuil) and 'Du monde entire' (Gallimard). When translators in this field are interviewed, or otherwise given the opportunity to elaborate on their profession, there is often an expectation that they will provide a kind of meta-language of translation, which they also tend to do. The Swedish Nobel Prize laureate Tomas Tranströmer talks about the 'invisible poem' as a true original, of which the source language text and the target language poem are two different versions. This kind of meta-language or philosophy of translation does not seem to be expected from translators of crime fiction or children's books, even though they too need to reflect upon their work.

Our analysis has shown the specificity of high-prestige literature, as seen from the perspective of the translator. We have given examples of how this kind of literature is handled by the literary establishment, but also how this very establishment is altered by this handling. Our analysis also stresses the fact that literary prestige is *created*, and that the autonomy of high-prestige literature is consequently being emphasized by the literary establishment.

4

Translation strategies to and from the literary semi-periphery: Reduction retention, replacement

The dynamics between the cosmopolitan and the vernacular are manifested in the publications themselves – in the actual literary texts and in the verbal and visual information surrounding them in afterwords, dust jacket presentations and cover images. On this micro level, we find the results of translators' creative decisions in transferring the story, drama or poem into new languages as well as editorial interventions in presenting the literary text to new audiences. Examining these changes between source and target texts involves identifying and analysing strategies of transformation. In the translation process, the source text is transformed in order to function on a new literary market addressing new readers. When literary works are published anew in different cultural environments, Isabel Hofmeyr writes in *The Portable Bunyan: A Transnational History of The Pilgrim's Progress*, they change shape. Exploring African versions of John Bunyan's seventeenth-century Christian tale, Hofmeyr shows how imaginary worlds 'are excised, summarized, abridged, and bowdlerized by the new intellectual formations into which they migrate' (Hofmeyr 2004: 2–3). These changes are not neutral. They reshape the literary works according to certain conceptions of the world. They confirm, create or adjust ideas about the source culture, the target culture and their interrelations.

One crucial condition affecting these transformations is the general relation between source and target languages, cultures and literatures that forms the fundamental conditions for the particular translation. In other words, the source and target languages' respective positions in the world literary system are highly important factors as they shape the way in which literary works are made accessible for new audiences. Whether the translation is made from a dominating or a dominant literary culture strongly affects the micro-level transformations. As David Damrosch observes, 'provincial or subordinate

Western writers are always particularly liable to be assimilated to the immediate interests and agendas of those who edit, translate and interpret them' (Damrosch 2003: 24–5). How this liability impacts on literature as it migrates from the semi-periphery to other parts of the world literary system – other semi-peripheral positions, peripheries and centres – is one of the key questions to be explored in this chapter.

The semi-peripheral position is not, however, the decisive factor when it comes to how the literary works are transformed in the translation process. Our studies show that other factors are more important in prompting transformation strategies: the literary status of the work, the scope of distribution, the level of narrative localization and the level of un-standardized language used in the source text all have very strong impact on translators and editors in making the text accessible for the target audience.

Three kinds of translational transformation

Translational transformations have distinct effects on any literary text's relation to the cosmopolitan and the vernacular. It is the source text's rootedness in its original vernacular context – linguistically, socially, culturally – that needs to be dealt with in order to make it understandable for readers who are not parts of or familiar with that context. By necessity, the translation process thus leads to a new dynamic between cosmopolitan and vernacular tendencies. In our material, this transformation is far from univocal. Some of the texts are made less vernacular and more cosmopolitan; others are, on the contrary, vernacularized. More often than not, though, the translations studied here contain instances of both: while some transformations cosmopolitanize the text, others make it more vernacular.

We have identified three different approaches used by translators to deal with the texts' relations to source culture vernaculars: *reduction, retention* and *replacement*. In reducing the text's vernacular anchorage, translators lift the text's significance from the culturally specific to a more general level. In this way, editors and translators create access for new readers by neutralizing elements that they think readers would find strange or incomprehensible and which thus would obscure their understanding of the work. The source culture vernacular is faded, leaving room for an understanding unlimited by culture-specific knowledge and familiarity. In retaining the source culture vernacular, translators and editors stress the fact that the publication is a result of a translational process. The target text reader is reminded that underneath the text he or she is actually reading there is another text belonging to a different linguistic and cultural context. The foreignness of the work's setting, ideas or narrative techniques is highlighted, and the distance between the reader and the author is pointed out. The literary text becomes a passage into the unfamiliar, or, as Damrosch has phrased it in *What is World Literature?*, a window on the world (2003: 15). In replacing source culture specificities with target culture connections and associations, on the other hand, elements from the target vernacular are implemented in the text or the book, establishing a link between the foreign work of literature and the reader's own experiential sphere. The connections to the source culture vernacular are weakened, and new connections to the target culture vernacular are created.

In introducing the processes of reduction, retention and replacement, we propose another way of analysing translational strategies than the long-lived binary optic derived from Friedrich Schleiermacher's nineteenth-century theory on two available kinds of translations (Snell-Hornby 2006: 8). Rather than working with two reciprocally exclusive alternatives – as in Gideon Toury's *adequacy* and *acceptability* (2012) and Lawrence Venuti's *domestication* and *foreignization* (1995) – we would like to study three different ways of dealing with the source text's anchorage in the source culture vernacular. There are three geocultural positions involved in the translational process – the source culture vernacular, the target culture vernacular and the cosmopolitan – and since translators and editors may choose to reinforce any of these, there is one kind of cosmopolitanization and two different kinds of vernacularization available. Reduction is a cosmopolitanizing strategy in which the target text is made less rooted in any vernacular and thus geoculturally generalized. Retention is a process of vernacularization in which the source culture vernacular is strengthened, whereas replacement performs a very different kind of vernacularization by adding distinct connections to the target culture vernacular.

The three transformational strategies are executed on different levels and in different aspects of the publication and the literary work. The most direct and visible transformation occurs in the peritexts. Distinguished from the epitexts, the peritexts are the kinds of paratext that according to Gérard Genette are parts of the volume as such, such as introductions, afterwords, endnotes, footnotes, covers and dust jacket presentations (1987). The peritexts accompany the literary work, offering the reader a way into the work (in covers, introductions and dust jacket presentations), explanations and digressions along the way (in notes and other kinds of interruptions by editors and translators) and afterthoughts (in afterwords and other information placed at the end of the volume). In these peritexts, editors and translators have a great opportunity to guide the reading of the target text in different directions and thereby shape the reader's notion of the semi-peripheral context in which the literary work was produced. It's on this peritextual level that it becomes most evident that the target text functions differently in the receiving culture than the source text functions in the source culture.

Added peritexts – as well as omitted and replaced peritexts – are also examples of changes in format: the literary work is manifested in a different kind of book than the source text. However, format changes also occur on many other levels and aspects of the book and the work. Sometimes editors decide to make volume changes. A trilogy can be merged into one volume and a long novel can be divided into several books, and a single part of a series of works can be published separately. The number of chapters can also be transformed: long chapters can be divided into several chapters and several short chapters can be merged into longer ones. More often, such alterations take place within chapters when source text divisions into sections and paragraphs are adjusted. A kind of format change that can occur on different levels is abbreviation. Whole chapters, sections and paragraphs as well as single sentences, phrases and words can all be omitted from the target text. A more special kind of format change is the treatment of illustrations, which can be omitted, added or replaced.

On a more fundamental level, the translation process necessarily and evidently entails a change of language. There are no direct equivalences between any distinct languages: whatever word or phrase the translator chooses it will never have the exact same significance as the source language word or phrase, and quite often there is not even a reasonably equivalent counterpart to be used in the target language in order to convey the source text meaning. Untranslatables are found in every language (Apter 2013), but the non-equivalence between languages has more fundamental effects on literary translation than the problem of transferring particularly difficult and specific concepts, words and phrases. Two essential literary devices – style and narrative technique – are intimately connected to the imminent features of each particular language, so that the language shift always also results in stylistic and narrative transformations. The stylistic characteristics of a specific source text will never be exactly the same in the target text. The translator can never be required to find more than an approximation of the style used by the author. The same is true for narrative techniques: some narrative effects are not that difficult to transfer, but others are deeply connected to the source language grammar and its domestic literary tradition.

Peritextual transformations as well as changes in format, language, style and narrative technique may also result in thematic alterations. Since the theme of a literary work is an abstraction produced by the interpretation of the totality of its different parts, and also a result of contextualization, every single change in the immediate context of the work and in the work itself will have a potential impact on what the story, drama or poem is understood to be about. Often, these thematic changes do not consist of drastic shifts from one theme to another, but rather slight modifications of balance and emphasis, but since the theme of a literary work is essential for the reading experience, even small thematic changes may have a fundamental impact on how it is perceived. Many of the above transformations may also have generic implications. Peritextual presentations and volume changes as well as stylistic, narrative and thematic alterations might turn the literary work into another literary genre. Simplification of a complex narrative technique, for example, will make the target text become another kind of novel than the source text, and an introductory comparison of the translated work with a well-known target culture classic can make it represent a very different kind of literature than it normally represents in the source culture literary tradition.

On the following pages we will explore the processes of reduction, retention and replacement in our six different translational flows to and from the semi-peripheral Swedish. Since these micro-level transformations are to be found in the textual details of the translations, we have been forced to drill deep into a few examples rather than offering a generally valid overview. However, our ambition has been to widen the significance of our observations by comparing the existence of reduction, retention and replacement in different kinds of translations within each flow.

Proletarian realism and crime fiction from Swedish to English

The translational flow from the semi-peripheral Swedish to the hyper-central English language will be discussed via two very different examples. A whole category of social realist modern classics – proletarian fiction – will illustrate small-scale distribution of translated Swedish literature in the UK and the USA, whereas a single novel will illustrate the international commercial success of the Nordic noir genre. The first kind of translation is characterized by an extensive use of retention. Initially, we expected that the translation of the international bestseller would show opposite characteristics. Our study shows, however, that this is not the case.

In the history of English translations of Swedish literature between 1980 and 2018, a particular kind of publishing organization not covered by Lawrence Venuti's study of US translations (1995) plays a specific role – university presses. With a continual contribution of approximately two titles per year, this kind of publisher provides the British and North American reading public with Swedish literary classics and aesthetically high-end contemporary titles. Being able to focus on educational and scholarly values rather than commercial outcomes, these non-profit presses can afford to be quite small: as many as twenty-three different publishers are responsible for the seventy-nine translations from Swedish published by US and UK university presses from 1980 to 2018.

A closer look at US translations of Swedish working-class novels from the 1930s illustrates the general translational features of these university press titles. This kind of literature has a central position in Swedish twentieth-century literary history, with a distinct connection to the particularly Swedish version of the welfare state. From 1983 to 1991, six translations of classic Swedish proletarian novels originally published in the 1930s appeared in the United States: Jan Fridegård's *I, Lars Hård* (1983; *Jag Lars Hård*, 1935) and *Jacob's Ladder & Mercy* (1985; *Tack för himlastegen*, 1936, and *Barmhärtighet*, 1936), translated by Robert E. Bjork and published by the University of Nebraska Press; Moa Martinson's *Women and Appletrees* (1985; *Kvinnor och äppelträd*, 1933) and *My Mother Gets Married* (1988; *Mor gifter sig*, 1936), translated by Margaret S. Lacy and published by the Feminist Press, an imprint at the City University of New York, and Ivar Lo-Johansson's *Breaking Free* (1990; *Godnatt, jord*, 1933) and *Only a Mother* (1991; *Bara en mor*, 1939), translated by Rochelle Wright and Robert E. Bjork, respectively, and published by the University of Nebraska Press.

Contrary to Lawrence Venuti's general characterization of American twentieth-century translations, all these translations contain an extensive use of foreignizing effects that strongly retain the particularities of the source culture vernacular. One reason for this is the fact that there is a historical gap between the source and target texts. All the novels are canonized working-class narratives in the history of Swedish literature, and the US translators and editors treat them as foreign classics that require proper and respectful introductions. This explanation is confirmed by a comparison with earlier translations of Swedish working-class novels from the 1930s. In the more contemporaneous translations, the strategy of reducing and replacing the source culture vernacular is distinctly more evident than in the later translations. However, there is a more important reason why the publications from the 1980s and the 1990s include such a high degree of foreignization. Unlike the earlier translations, the later ones are all published by university presses, and all three translators are academics. For Robert E. Bjork, Margaret S. Lacy and Rochelle Wright, literary translation is a parallel pursuit alongside their main occupation as university professors, and their teaching experience and academic knowledge about Sweden make a distinct mark on the American versions of these Swedish classics.

The strategy of retention is most evident on the level of language by the frequent inclusion of Swedish words in the English target texts. Some of the translators keep the Swedish currency and area units throughout the stories, some keep colloquial Swedish words and oral expressions, and many words, especially for Swedish kinds of food and drink, make the texts bilingual. Many of these Swedish words and expressions are kept to insert a foreign flair into the narratives and remind the readers of the novels' settings rather than out of necessity. One example is Margaret S. Lacy's decision to keep the Swedish filler *ja* in *Women and Appletrees*. This little colloquial word, almost void of semantic substance, crops up in italics on each and every page of the translation, constantly destabilizing the English norm and continuously reminding the reader that the novel is set in another culture and was originally written in another language. In her afterword, Lacy explains this strategy with her intention of catching 'the sing-song music' of spoken Swedish (Martinson 1985: 200). The translator wants to keep the oral rhythm of Moa Martinson's prose. Her decision to retain all the jas in Martinson's Swedish novel is thus also a question of style. Domestically, Moa Martinson is well known for her personal prose style, which has been seen as gnarly and ungainly in a way that conveys the tough physical lives of her protagonists. Lacy wants to transfer this style to her translation, but by retaining the filler in italics throughout the novel the translator is reinforcing the idiosyncratic characteristics of Martinson's style, adding a bilingual quality to the prose. This effect is most apparent in the dialogue:

'Have you read all of them?' [...]

'*Ja*, sure, the whole lot. There aren't as many as it looks. Do you like to read?'

'*Ja-a*, stories for sure, but I haven't time.'

'Time, *ja*, well, I probably shouldn't have that either, but one can always find some time.'

(103)

(–Har du läst allt det här? [...]

–Ja visst, alltihop, det är inte så mycket som det ser ut. Tycker du om att läsa?

–Ja-a, berättelser förstås, men jag har inte tid.

–Tid ja, det skulle väl inte jag ha heller, men alltid har man någon stund [...].)

(126)

But the retained Swedish filler is also used by the anonymous narrator:

> She remembered the alley quarrels, where sexual intercourse was openly derided as the most repulsive thing in creation, she remembered, *ja*, she remembered the boy from the painting, but then her thoughts quieted down, and she dreamed vague, unspeakable dreams.
>
> (81)

(Hon minns grändernas trätor, där samlagsakten öppet hånades som det vidrigaste i skapelsen, hon minns, ja, hon minns gossen från tavlan, men då stillnar tankarna och Ellen drömmer vaga, outsägbara drömmar.)

(100)

The target text becomes much more deviant from the stylistic norm of realist novels than the source text, and the retention strategy thus heavily increases the stylistic peculiarities of the narrative.

Lacy's description of spoken Swedish is also an example of a peritextual retention of the source vernacular. Swedish is described as a special kind of foreign language with distinct tonal particularities. All the six translations are accompanied by quite extensive introductions or afterwords, all of which underline the fact that the authors and novels are Swedish. The foreign country comes across as a peculiar place, and when Jan Fridegård's trilogy is described as depicting 'Swedish peasant life' (Fridegård 1983) and Lo-Johansson's *Breaking Free* is said to portray life 'on a large baronial estate in Sweden' (Lo-Johansson 1990) the novels are clearly presented as dealing with conditions somewhere else. This effect is most evident in the foot- and endnotes that annotate all the target texts. *Women and Appletrees, My Mother Gets Married, I, Lars Hård* and *Jacob's Ladder & Mercy* have seven, fifteen, eighteen and thirty-six footnotes, respectively, and *Only a Mother* and *Breaking Free* have thirty-two and fifty-eight endnotes. Many of these notes contain extensive presentations of Swedish phenomena explaining events, behaviour and references in the novels. They strongly reinforce the impression that the narratives belong to quite another cultural context than the one American readers are familiar with.

The inclusion of foot- and endnotes also affects the format of the publications. Apart from added paratexts, the literary texts themselves become interwoven with continual asterisks or numbers that break the fluency of narrative prose. Especially the inflicted numbers add an academic character to the publications. These books not only offer literary stories originally written in another language but also non-fictional, learned information about the source culture. This added academic dimension of the publication also has generic effects, since the notes tend to push the books from the genre of literary fiction towards the genre of ethnography. In the explanatory notes, an ethnographic gaze is frequently used to describe seasonal feasts and traditions, often in relation to food and drink. In a note to Ivar Lo-Johansson's *Only a Mother*, for example, the translator Robert E. Bjork explains:

> Lutfisk: A traditional Swedish Christmas dish made of salted and dried stockfish soaked in a solution of lime, soda, and water for several days. On Christmas Eve, it is boiled and served with a white sauce.
> (Lo-Johansson 1991: 487)

In this very detailed explanation of a quite insignificant reference in the story, the translator adopts the role of a cultural cicerone, guiding the reader through the cultural landscape of the source culture. Rather than offering necessary information to avoid a potential misunderstanding of the novel, Bjork uses Lo-Johansson's story to enlighten the American reader about any Swedish cultural phenomena touched upon in the narrative. He grasps the opportunity to teach.

A couple of these notes are added in order to retain the original theme of the novels. For example, Rochelle Wright's first note in *Breaking Free* is a long and detailed explanation of the uniquely Swedish economic system of rural labour that was kept intact up until the mid-twentieth century. This national system is the most crucial context for the way the source text has been read in Sweden: the novel predominantly thematizes the human effects of these social and economic conditions. But in order to retain this particular theme, Wright is obliged to temporarily turn the novel into a book on the history of Swedish farm labour.

The Swedish vernacular is also retained by peritextual connections to other source culture phenomena. Addressing an American audience in introductions and afterwords, the translators need to contextualize the novels by linking them to Swedish circumstances that might already be known by the readers. This creates a general and prototypical notion of Swedish culture. A recurring vision in Moa Martinson's *Women and Appletrees* is, for example, said to be 'as arresting as Ingmar Bergman's Dance of Death in *The Seventh Seal*' (Martinson 1985: 207). For a Swedish reader, the connection between Martinson and Bergman is surprising. The self-taught writer of realist novels on the everyday struggles of working-class women belongs to a completely different part of Swedish twentieth-century culture than the bourgeois director of aesthetically ambitious films. This kind of cultural comparison can perhaps reveal similarities and patterns unnoticeable within the source culture, but the construction of a slim canon of source culture phenomena leads to a merging of very disparate expressions into a unified and univocal cultural space. In the Martinson–Bergman connection, the central target culture perspective comprises and evens out the source culture periphery in a way that confirms and reinforces the hierarchical cultural relation between the United States and Sweden.

This effect is most evident in the foot- and endnotes, where references, events and behaviour deemed inaccessible for the target reader are explained in an ethnographic way that establishes general ideas of the foreign culture. For example, Lacy explains the expression 'old mother of First Farm' thus: 'Mother is used to designate the wife of a farmer who owns a sizeable farm. She retains this designation after the death of her husband' (Martinson 1985: 92). Notable here is the use of present tense. The note explains what certain Swedes *do* and how the social structure of the Swedish countryside *is* arranged, but Lacy's translation appears fifty-two years after the source text was published in Sweden. Furthermore, the explanatory note refers to an episode in the novel that takes place in the nineteenth century. Describing the rural custom in the present tense a hundred years later gives a strong impression of an unchanged social praxis, untouched by historical development and maintained by a Swedish cultural particularity.

The most annotated translation of all six publications is Rochelle Wright's *Breaking Free*. In this novel by Ivar Lo-Johansson, Wright has included fifty-eight endnotes explaining a wide range of aspects of Swedish culture and society.

Wright's decision to include all these notes strongly emphasizes the notion of cultural difference: the American reader needs this extensive help in order to understand the foreign narrative. But the frequent comments also indicate a possibility to construct a comprehensive overview of a foreign culture. Every single cultural or societal phenomenon hinted at by Lo-Johansson comes forth as explainable and translatable. Sweden can be summarized and understood. These notes thus reinforce the centre's self-imposed mandate to define and control the cultural peripheries. Just like domestication and invisible translators, foreignization and highly visible translators reinforce cultural hierarchies – not by understating the role of the literary interlocutor, but, on the contrary, by emphasizing and confirming his or her power to define the less central cultural space. In other words, the translational strategy of retaining source culture specificity runs the risk of othering and diminishing the semi-periphery.

The target dust jacket covers do not univocally confirm this heavy tendency of retention. Only Nebraska University Press editions of Ivar Lo-Johansson's novels retain their vernacular source culture setting. Whereas the original covers from 1933 and 1939 lift up the proletarian lives to an existential level with the help of graphically striking visual symbols, the US publisher uses Swedish artist Sven Ljungberg's engravings to illustrate how the socioeconomic misery described in the novels is distinctly connected to a particular social and physical milieu.

The University of Nebraska Press' editions of Jan Fridegård's trilogy exemplify, however, the opposite process. In his engravings for the Swedish originals, artist Stig Åsberg connects the protagonist's conflict with society to three distinct physical milieus. On the US covers, on the contrary, Christine Mercer's drawings underline the individually psychological and existential dimensions of Lars Hård's problems. On these dust jackets, then, the vernacular Swedish setting of Jan Fridegård's novels is reduced.

The American and British covers of Moa Martinson's novels deviate more distinctly from the strong retention strategy in the actual texts. Both of them use classic paintings by women artists. With German painter Paula Modersohn-Becker's painting *Mädchenbildnis mit gespreizter Hand vor der Brust* from 1905 the characters of Martinson's *Mor gifter sig* are elevated to a cosmopolitan level of women's hardship, at least for those readers who know that Modersohn-Becker was German and not Swedish. The specific source culture conditions are thus reduced, and the significance of the narrative is generalized. With American artist Mary Cassatt's *Baby Reaching for an Apple* from 1893, the vernacular setting of *Kvinnor och äppelträd* is replaced by a historical frame from the target culture. In one respect, however, these covers do confirm the retention strategy used by the respective translators. All target covers except *Women and Apple Trees* include the name of the translator. Robert E. Bjork, Rochelle Wright and Margaret S. Lacy are not invisible, either in or on the covers of these books.

The small-scale distribution of Swedish proletarian classics has a distinct contrast in Reg Keeland's translation of Stieg Larsson's *Män som hatar kvinnor* (2005), *The Girl with the Dragon Tattoo* from 2008, which was published in the UK by MacLehose Press and in the USA by Alfred A. Knopf. As one of the pivotal titles in the international boom of Nordic noir (crime stories in books, television and films set in Scandinavia), Larsson's thriller represents a totally different kind of literary export from Sweden: mainstream entertainment with a broad audience, not necessarily lowbrow in every cultural context, but definitely wide-brow. In the British and American editions of the thriller, there are no introductions, no afterwords and no footnotes. Another distinct contrast to how Bjork, Lacy and Wright treat the proletarian novels is the fact that Reg Keeland makes himself quite independent and creative in transferring the Swedish story into English.

Keeland's text is a strongly shortened version of Larsson's novel, not on the level of events and characters, but on the detailed level of narration. In the majority of the paragraphs there are significant abbreviations of Larsson's way to narrate the story, for example in the very first paragraph of the prologue:

Stieg Larsson:

Kommissarien, som visste att samtalet skulle komma efter postutdelningen vid elvatiden på morgonen, drack kaffe medan han väntade. Detta år ringde telefonen redan halv elva. Han lyfte luren och sa hej utan att presentera sig.

(Larsson 2005: 5)

Reg Keeland:

The old policeman was sitting with his coffee, waiting, expecting the call.

(Larsson 2008: 1)

Literal translation with omitted information in bold:

The Detective Superintendent, **who knew that the call would come after the post had arrived at 11 am**, had a coffee while he waited. **This year the phone rang at half past ten. He lifted the hook and said hello without presenting himself.**

Usually, these continuous and quite evenly distributed abbreviations of Larsson's prose make the paragraphs shorter and thereby increase the narrative pace of the story. Keeland's version becomes faster, more action-driven and less reflexive than Larsson's. A telling example is found a couple of pages into the novel's first chapter, when the protagonist Mikael Blomkvist is answering questions from the Swedish press after he has been found guilty of libel:

Stieg Larsson:

"Men du glömde bort att man som journalist faktiskt måste kunna belägga sina påståenden", sa Hon från TV4 med en antydan till skärpa i rösten. Påståendet kunde knappast förnekas. De hade varit goda vänner. Hennes ansikte var neutralt men Mikael tyckte sig kunna urskilja en antydan till besviket avståndstagande i hennes ögon.

Mikael Blomkvist stannade kvar och besvarade frågor i ytterligare några plågsamma minuter. Den fråga som låg outtalad i luften men som ingen reporter kom sig för att ställa – kanske därför att det var så generande obegripligt – var hur Mikael hade kunnat skriva en text som så fullständigt saknade substans. Reportrarna på plats, undantaget vikarien på *Dagens Industri*, var alla veteraner med bred yrkesbakgrund. För dem låg svaret på frågan bortom det begripligas gräns.

Reg Keeland:

"But how did you come to forget that journalists actually have to back up their assertions?" *She* from T.V.4. Her expression was neutral, but Blomkvist thought he saw a hint of disappointed repudiation in her eyes.

The reporters on site, apart from the boy from *Dagens Nyheter*, were all veterans in the business. For them the answer to that question was beyond the conceivable.

Literal translation with omitted information in bold:

"But you forgot that as a journalist you have to be able to back up your assertions", said *She* from TV4 **with a hint of sharpness in her voice. Her statement could hardly be denied. They had been good friends.** Her face was neutral but Mikael thought that he could detect a hint of disappointed distancing in her eyes.

Mikael Blomkvist stayed and answered questions for a couple more painful minutes. The question that lay unuttered in the air but that no reporter came around to ask – perhaps because it was so embarrassingly unconceivable – was how Mikael could have written a text that was so completely devoid of substance. The reporters on site, apart from the stand-in from *Dagens Industri*, were all veterans in the business. For them the answer to that question was beyond the conceivable.

Reg Keeland's abbreviations are so extensive and frequent that it is not unfair to call *The Girl with the Dragon Tattoo* an abridged version of Larsson's novel, solely concentrated on transmitting the fundamental story to British and American readers. The story behind the translator's pseudonym Reg Keeland, and the way this anecdote emphasizes the role of the publisher Christopher MacLehose and plays down the responsibility of the real translator, Steven T. Murray (see Chapter 2), gives a plausible explanation of this extensive slimming of the text. Furthermore, Christopher MacLehose has explained that his initial intention when he changed Murray's translation was indeed to attract film producers to Larsson's story (McGrath 2010). Moviemakers are of course less interested in the stylistic qualities of a narrative than in its events and characters.

In omitting the verb 'sa' (said) at the beginning of the quoted dialogue above, Keeland adds a stylistic characteristic to the novel. The short, no-nonsense sentence '*She* from T.V.4.' infers a hardboiled, ballsy dimension into the narration that does not exist in Larsson's Swedish text. Another detail in the above quote that adds to the dominant tendency to simplify the text is Keeland's change of newspapers from Larsson's *Dagens Industri* to *Dagens Nyheter*. Both are names of real Swedish national papers, but *Dagens Nyheter* has already been mentioned in the translation. Keeland probably does not want to burden the English-speaking reader with too many foreign words and cultural references. Therefore, the two daily papers are merged into one. This is therefore a kind of simplifying that does not involve shortening the text.

Most of Keeland's abbreviations make the novel less particular and more generic. This effect is also the consequence of the radical changes in titles and covers from the Swedish originals to the UK and US versions. One of the things Larsson insisted on when he submitted his manuscript to the Swedish publisher Norstedts was that the title of the book was not changed (Cochrane 2011). Larsson died before the book was published, but the publisher did keep his title *Män som hatar kvinnor* (literally 'Men who hate women'), a title that stands out among the vast jungle of best-selling suspense novels in the bookshop. With the English title *The Girl with the Dragon Tattoo*, everything that is special and significant in the Swedish title is not only long gone but also replaced by opposite connotations. Larsson's indirect but distinct contempt of male aggression towards women has been turned into a very conventional objectification of a female body. The differences between Swedish and British front covers have the same effect. The Swedish book shows a female face with eyes forcibly closed with the help of two pieces of coarse, hardwearing tape, while the British cover shows the back and side of a female head with open eyes, and a naked female back, adorned with a discreet tattoo. Whereas the Swedish version shows a human victim of violence, the British cover is a display of a sexualized female body that is possibly also a victim of violence.

The changes of titles and cover images leads to a reduction of the Swedish vernacular. With its title and violent image, the Swedish cover refers to and enhances the role of statistics in the novel. Each of the novel's four parts is introduced with figures on male violence towards women in Sweden: '18% of the women in Sweden have at one time been threatened by a man', '46% of the women in Sweden have been subjected to violence by a man', '13% of the women in Sweden have been subjected to aggravated sexual assault outside of a sexual relationship' and '92% of women in Sweden who have been subjected to sexual assault have not reported the most recent violent incident to the police' (Larsson 2008: 7, 119, 255, 415). The word 'men' in the Swedish title thus particularly refers to men in Sweden, and the abuse executed on the female face on the Swedish book cover refers to the statistics of male aggression in Sweden that run through the book. With the British and American title and covers this focusing upon and visualization of Swedish violence is omitted.

Furthermore, on the Swedish back cover there is an old photograph of a couple of wooden houses on the waterfront of the Stockholm archipelago. For a Swedish audience, this picture shows a prototypically Swedish traditional idyll. This stereotypical notion of unicultural harmony is exactly the national myth that Stieg Larsson explodes with his story on murder, rape, ruthless capitalism and Swedish Nazism. This photograph is not used on the British and the American books. Larsson's novel's intense connections to Swedish history, Swedish historiography and Swedish self-conceptions are thus further reduced. The removal of the name of the daily paper *Dagens Industri* is an example of how Keeland's strategy of simplification affects the vernacular anchorage of Stieg Larsson's novel. The names of two Swedish daily papers are one too many. In omitting one of them the Swedish vernacular space is made smaller, less nuanced and unified.

It is not fair to say, however, that the continuous slimming of Larsson's prose leads to an extensive reduction of vernacular Swedish references. In shortening the text, Keeland seldom takes the opportunity to reduce the many distinct references to specifically Swedish phenomena. Place names such as Fridhemsplan, Bellmansgatan, Gamla Stan, Riddarfjärden, Slussen, Bullandö, Arholma and Ängsö are kept in their original versions and referred to without explanation (Larsson 2008: 13–17, 248). Similarly, names of TV shows and magazines such as *Rapport, Aftonbladet, Ordfront Magazine* and *E.T.C.* are not removed or explained (248), although they are slightly adjusted in the latter two cases, since these magazines are called *Ordfront Magasin* and *ETC* in Swedish. Keeland also keeps *en passant* references to domestic business legends Erik Penser and Peter Wallenberg without enlightening the English-speaking readers in any way about their significance in Swedish financial history (248), and Stieg Larsson's playing around with references to domestically well-known Swedish children's books only needs a very slight clarification:

> Berömmelsens baksida var att den andra kvällstidningen inte kunde avhålla sig från att sätta rubriken *Kalle Blomkvist löste fallet*. Den raljerande texten var skriven av en äldre kvinnlig kolumnist och innehöll ett dussin hänvisningar till Astrid Lindgrens unge detektiv.
>
> (Larsson 2005: 15)

> The down side of his celebrity was that the other evening newspaper could not resist using the headline "*Kalle Blomkvist solves the case*". The tongue-in-cheek story was written by an older female columnist and contained references to the young detective in Astrid Lindgren's books for children.
>
> (Larsson 2008: 11)

Keeland makes sure that the reader is aware that the name is a reference to children's literature, but even though he does not expect his readers to have any knowledge of the Kalle Blomkvist character as such, he does not tune down but rather expands the reference. Neither Steven T. Murray, Reg Keeland nor Christopher MacLehose thus reduce the narrative's rootedness in the Swedish vernacular society, history and culture. Keeland has simplified the prose and the narration, but not the narrative's setting.

Unlike the translations of modern proletarian classics, then, the translation of Stieg Larsson's contemporary Nordic noir thriller does not respect the original Swedish text as such. Keeland has no problem changing, cutting and adjusting the creative work of Larsson. But this lack of reverence towards the author's narrative style does not affect the novel's rootedness in its original vernacular context. Why? Because cultural and geographical exoticism is a central part of the international attraction of Nordic noir fiction. It is exactly the distinct connections between the fictional world of *The Girl with the Dragon Tattoo* and the semi-peripheral cultural context of its Swedish origin that make it an international success. Whereas the retention strategies in Robert E. Bjork's,

Margaret S. Lacy's and Rochelle Wright's translations of Swedish proletarian realism have an educational purpose, the lack of reduction and replacement in Reg Keeland's translation of Stieg Larsson's crime novel has an entertaining and atmospheric function.

Two contemporary Swedish novels in French

To illustrate the Swedish–French translational flow, two novels will be compared: the first one is a popular novel in large-scale circulation, the second is a debut novel aimed at an audience of higher prestige. The French translation of the first includes significant examples of reduction and replacement, whereas the translator of the latter is much more prone to using the strategy of retention.

The early 1980s proved a turning point for the French translation market, not least when it came to translations of Scandinavian and Swedish fiction. Since the Second World War, the publishing of Swedish fiction in France had been mostly limited to the major Parisian publishing houses, who chose to publish a small number of authors, heavily invested in symbolic capital. Success was at best limited, although many ambitious translations were made, including novels by Birgitta Trotzig, a catholic writer and Swedish expatriate living in Paris, and the poetry of Gunnar Ekelöf – both highly consecrated authors in their source culture. In the 1980s, however, the French publishing market was rejuvenated by a number of small, some of them soon to be medium-sized presses, including several who chose to focus on translations. As a result, the number of literary works translated from Swedish rose dramatically, reaching a first peak of sixty editions per year by the middle of the 1980s (to be compared with less than twenty editions per year during the years 1945–1975). With this increase in the number of translations came a wider selection of authorships and genres that distinctly transformed the image of Swedish literature in France.

Swedish author Katarina Mazetti (b. 1944) made her debut in the 1980s as an author of children's books. In the 1990s, she went on to write cross-over fiction and finally achieved great success with the novel *Grabben i graven bredvid* (1998; English translation *Benny & Shrimp*, 2008), a romantic story about the culture clashes between life in the urban middle class and the realities of the countryside, aimed at an adult audience. Almost half a million copies have been sold in Sweden alone, and it has been translated into thirty-three languages. (It was also made into a commercially successful movie in 2002.) The novel's main character is the librarian Desirée who falls in love with a farmer, Benny, an unlikely mate in many ways, since their lives are very different. Mazetti tells the story from two perspectives, letting Desirée speak in one chapter and Benny in the next. They often get to narrate the same events, forming much of the basis of the book's comic effect.

The first of Mazetti's books to be translated into French was the children's book *Köttvars trollformler* (1991; French translation *Trucs et ficelles d'un petit troll*, 2002), published by France's biggest publishing house Hachette. But it was the small publisher Gaïa, specializing in Scandinavian fiction, that managed to secure the rights for *Grabben i graven bredvid*, published (with a literally translated title) as *Le mec de la tombe d'à côté* (which translates as 'The Bloke in the Next Grave', a title chosen because the main characters first meet in a graveyard) in 2006 and translated by Lena Grumbach (translator of a large number of highbrow Swedish novels but also of Stieg Larsson's successful Millennium crime series) and Catherine Marcus. This first French edition went on to sell more than thirty thousand copies and the pocket edition, published in 2009 by Actes sud – another publisher specializing in Scandinavian fiction and also (since 2005) the main shareholder of Gaïa – sold another three hundred thousand. The book was adapted into both a French theatre play and a French TV film screened by TF1, France's most popular domestic network.

When it comes to the French edition of *Grabben i graven bredvid*, one might first consider the novel's changed position and presentation on the literary market compared to the Swedish original. *Grabben i graven bredvid* was published by the mid-sized publisher Alfabeta. The text is printed on 185 pages, Desirée's chapters opening with a few lines of poetry written by the character. On the front cover, there is a somewhat out-of-focus photo of a cow's head, colourized in red, on a monochrome yellow background. On the back cover, the novel is described as '[e]tt tragikomiskt vardagsdrama om kärlekens möjligheter och omöjligheter' (a tragicomic everyday drama about the possibilities and impossibilities of love).

Since Gaïa is a small firm, based in southern France (which is a rare choice, the French book market being very much centralized to Paris), the French translation of Mazetti's novel had a hard start, compared to the original, which could benefit from its publisher's relatively central position in the literary field. Gaïa chose a somewhat different angle for the marketing of Mazetti's novel. The text is printed on 245 pages, which means significantly less text per page compared to the original, and on terracotta coloured or pinkish paper. The paper matches the all-pink back cover and the front cover's drawing of a pink rose losing its petals one by one, placed beside another drawing, this one of a young woman. On the back cover, the novel is described as a '[r]oman d'amour drôle tendre, à l'humour décapant [qui] touche pourtant là où ça fait mail: ce fossé qui sépare les categories sociales. On ne peut plus contemporain ... ' (a funny and tender love story, with disarming humour [...] that nevertheless touches where it hurts: the gap between the social classes. It doesn't get more contemporary ...).

It might be said, then, that the French edition highlights the romantic 'love story traits' of Mazetti's novel, chiefly through the illustrations (the rose and the petals being signs for love and for the hesitation and problems that come with it). This also means, of course, that *Le mec de la tombe d'à côté* is pratextually defined as a book for female readers (a marketing choice not made as clearly by Alfabeta when publishing the original version). The back cover presentation of the French edition does not, on the other hand, differ in any significant way from the source language version. However, the choice of the word 'drôle' (funny) sets a somewhat lighter mood than the Swedish 'komisk' (comic). Other translated editions of Mazetti's novel have been given covers similar to the Swedish original, thus highlighting the elements of satire and culture clash rather than romantic love, for example the Italian version 'O me o muuh' (It's me or mooh), with a front cover photo of a cow sticking out its tongue.

When it comes to the text of the novel, the overall strategy for the translators Grumbach and Marcus when confronted with specificities of the source culture vernacular seems to be a combination of reduction and replacement (the translated text being almost completely devoid of retentions). Often, in the spirit of reduction, names for specifically Swedish phenomena are changed to more general terms: DN (abbreviation for *Dagens Nyheter*), Sweden's biggest morning paper, is reduced to 'journal' (newspaper [interestingly, however, in a later chapter the translators have kept the name *Dagens Nyheter*]), Föreningsbanken (an important Swedish bank) is changed to 'banque' (bank), 'X2000' (the express train operated by Sweden's government owned railway company) is changed to 'train express' (fast train), Bingolotto (a popular Swedish game show involving lotteries) is changed to 'le tirage du Loto' (the lottery draw) and lutfisk (a Swedish Christmas dish made from dried whitefish treated with lye) is changed to the general 'morue' (meaning cod).

Somewhat more complicated, but also a kind of reduction, are mentions of specifically Swedish phenomena and traditions which are explained in the text by the translators. For example, the expression 'det medhavda' (literally 'that which have been brought', which for a Swedish reader cannot mean anything else than the liquor bottle that has been secretly brought to a party) which Grumbach and Marcus explain as 'la bouteille que quelqu'un avait apportée' ('the bottle that someone had brought') or 'Grindslanten' (a painting by the nineteenth-century Swedish artist August Malmström, having been reproduced in very large numbers and, for a Swedish public, being almost synonymous with 'kitsch'), explained as 'ce chromo populaire avec des enfants qui se bagarrent devant une grille à la campagne' (that popular print of children fighting in front of a countryside gate).

In a number of cases, Grumbach and Marcus have opted for a different technique when faced with Swedish phenomena not easily understood by a French audience, that of replacement. For example, 'radhus' (the Swedish kind of terraced house or 'row house', often used as a symbol for a typically Swedish family life) is replaced by pavillon (a word used for a single family detached residence, but which comes with roughly the same associations for the French reader). Similarly, the term 'dansband' (used to signify a specifically Swedish and Scandinavian music genre, often danced to in pairs and with a main audience of middle aged [or older] adults) is replaced with 'les vieux standards de bal musette' (the old standards of the *bal musette*, bal musette signifying an evening of dancing in pairs, often accompanied by accordion music and aimed at approximately the same audience as the Swedish 'dansband' events), 'glögg' (a Swedish Christmas drink made from red wine and spices) is replaced with 'vin chaud' (a similar but not identical French drink) and 'mazarin' (a Swedish pastry filled with almond paste) is replaced with 'gateau étouffe chrétien' (cake *étouffe chretien*, étouffe chrétien being a French expression signifying something dense and filling).

In conclusion, Grumbach and Marcus' translation seems bent on familiarizing Mazetti's novel for larger groups of French readers. Foreign elements are largely played down, and, if it were not for the Swedish proper names and landscapes (and of course for the short back cover presentation of Mazetti as a Swedish journalist and author), one might suspect that *Le mec de la tombe d'à côté* is a French original. Gaïa's edition is also (somewhat in contrast to the Swedish original) clearly defined as a romantic novel for female readers. Judging by the sales numbers (thirty thousand copies of the original edition and three hundred thousand of the pocket book) and the continuing popularity of Mazetti's work in France, this transformation strategy seems to have been a success.

Den drunknade (*The Drowned*, 2011) is Therese Bohman's (b. 1978) debut novel. It was published in 2010 by Norstedts, one of Sweden's most important publishers. Bohman tells the story of Marina, an art student of Stockholm University who travels to the south of Sweden to spend some time with her older sister Stella, who lives in a summer house with the rather famous novelist Gabriel. As the days pass, there are signs that Gabriel might be abusing Stella, but Marina nevertheless becomes more and more enthralled by the unpredictable man. Later that summer, Stella tragically drowns in the nearby lake. Marina suspects that Gabriel has something to do with her sister's death, but nevertheless finds it hard to tear herself away. The novel is written in poetic prose, often centred around images of vegetation, death and decline, and uses the art of the English Pre-Raphaelite painters as an important intertext (the cover illustration is an 1855 painting in a similar style, *La jeune martyre* by the French artist Paul Delaroche).

Bohman's short debut novel, 171 pages in its first edition, somewhat surprisingly (given the rather complicated writing, suspenseful but lacking a traditional intrigue) became an international success story, quickly translated into four important languages, French (2011), English (2011), Dutch (2012) and German (2012). This success can be partly explained by the paratexts of the translated editions. The German version, *Die Ertrunkene*, for instance, has borrowed the style of the book cover design from successful Swedish crime novels by authors such as Henning Mankell and Camilla Läckberg, showing a small red cabin by a lake, dramatically tinted in dark blue. The red cabin can be seen as a reference to the popular German vision of Sweden as a countryside idyll, very much influenced by the children's books of Astrid Lindgren (author of, e.g. the Pippi Longstocking-books). The German reader, then, might suspect that Bohman's novel will show this idyll being threatened by dark forces, expectations which are not easy to conform with the story of *Den drunknade*, which is completely devoid of red cabins and criminals, at least in the crime story sense of the word. The cover of the English translation instead shows a greenhouse seen from the exterior, which fits well with the novel's style and story (which in the back cover text is described as combining 'hothouse sensuality with ice-cold fear on every page'). But in a review (from *The Oprah Magazine*), also quoted on the back cover, Bohman is, very surprisingly for a Swedish reader, compared to 'Nordic noir' phenomenon Stieg Larsson, and *Den drunknade* (*The Drowned*) is compared to Larsson's international bestseller *Män som hatar kvinnor* (*The Girl with the Dragon Tattoo*). If the reader is expecting the same kind of thrill that can be found in the adventures of Mikael Blomkvist and Lisbeth Salander, the main characters in Larsson's novel, she or he will be sorely disappointed.

Symptomatically, Bohman's English translator Marlaine Delargy, is also the translator of crime novels by Anne Holt, Åsa Larsson and Johan Theorin, as well as the successful horror novels of John Ajvide Lindqvist (author of the vampire novel *Låt den rätte komma in* [*Let the Right One In*]). Bohman's French translator, Carine Bruy, has almost exactly the same profile, having translated crime fiction and thrillers, as well as Ajvide Lindqvist's *Låt den rätte komma in* (*Laisse-moi entrer*) and *Hanteringen av odöda* (*Le retour des morts*). In other words, both Delargy and Bruy have managed to secure a position at the very centre of the international 'boom' of Swedish fiction, Bruy having also translated the immensely popular comic writer Jonas Jonasson, author of *Hundraåringen som klev ut genom fönstret och försvann* (*The Hundred-Year-Old Man Who Climbed Out the Window and Disappeared*). More interesting, however, is that Bohman's rather highbrow debut novel has been placed in this context of international bestsellers.

The French edition of *Den drunknade*, *La noyée* (212 pages), was published by the small and prestigious firm Éditions Balland (based, like the majority of French publishers, in Paris Latin Quarter). The cover photo shows the hand of a person trying to climb out of the water onto a wooden jetty. The choice of image echoes the German edition, suggesting that a murder has been committed, a fact not established in the novel. The front cover clearly states (in contrast to Gaïas edition of Mazetti's *Le mec de la tombe d'à côté*) that the book is a translation, naming the translator and the original language ('Traduit du suédois par Carine Bruy' [Translated from Swedish by Carine Bruy]) and also stating that *La noyée* is part of Balland's series of 'littérature étrangère' (foreign literature). This means assigning Bohman's novel a place close to the pole of small-scale production, the French foreign literature series being characterized by linguistic and national diversity but also by the absence of bestsellers. On the other hand, the back cover text describes the novel as a 'bestseller' in Sweden, a claim that might be contested, since the sales figures of *Den drunknade* were very modest compared to the likes of Stieg Larsson and Camilla Läckberg (even though Bohman's novel sold enough copies to be re-published in a pocket book edition). The rest of the back cover text gives a rather precise summary of *Den drunknade*, without the spectacular (and rather stretched) comparisons of the English edition.

When it comes to Bruy's translation and to the transformation strategies of reduction, retention and replacement, it is clear that *Den drunknade* does not present the same difficulties as Mazetti's *Grabben i graven bredvid*. Bohman's writing often lacks distinct elements of the source culture vernacular. However, there are a number of cases where Bruy has chosen to reduce the foreignness of Bohman's text. For example, the term 'torp' (signifying a small cottage in the countryside, a kind of leased farm often paid for with manual work on the owner's [the farmer's] field) is simply replaced by 'ferme' (meaning 'farm', which is something else), 'funkisförortstallar' (literally 'the pine trees of the suburbs built in functionalistic style', a clear reference to the suburbs of Stockholm, built in the 1950s and 1960s, whose bright and functionalistic apartment buildings are often interspersed by sparse pine forests) is replaced by 'arbres typiques des banlieus' (which means 'the trees typical of the suburbs') and 'rötmånad' (literally 'the month of rottenness', a Swedish word for the late summer weeks, mostly in August, when temperatures rise and food easily goes bad) is replaced by 'canicule' (which simply means 'heatwave').

More interesting, however, are the nine footnotes in the French translation. These notes, together with the front cover's clear identification of the novel as a translation, retain the cultural specificities of Bohman's Swedish original and stress the cultural differences between Sweden and France. The inclusion of notes serves to remind the reader that what she or he is reading is a *translation*, that there is an *original* text. One might say that the footnotes indicate that the reader is in fact reading two texts at the same time, the original and the translation (Kullberg 2011: 56). Thus, Bruy has chosen the opposite strategy compared to Mazetti's translators Grumbach and Marcus. *La noyée* is clearly aimed at a different audience than *Le mec de la tombe d'à côté* – not the reader typical of the pole of large-scale production, but rather the 'sophisticated' reader of the series of foreign literature published by highbrow editors such as Gallimard and Seuil, readers who care about the cultural capital inherent in translated fiction.

In several of Bruy's notes, the original text is clearly mentioned. When Bohman quotes a song lyric by the British post-punk band New Order, Bruy adds a note saying 'En anglais dans le texte' (In English in the [original] text) and also includes a French translation (as well as the explanation that all the notes are written by the translator). The same strategy is used when Bohman later quotes the British poet Algernon Charles Swinburne. When a French language book title is mentioned, *Une étude sur la peinture symboliste* (which seems to be a made up title), the footnote explains: 'En français dans le texte' (In French in the [original] text). Other footnotes include explanations of Swedish expressions and phenomena, such as *Dagens Nyheter* (the title of Sweden's largest morning paper) and 'Söder' (explained as 'abréviation de Södermalm, quartier sud de Stockholm', meaning 'abbreviation of Södermalm, the southern part of Stockholm city centre'). Rather than reducing or replacing, then, Bruy has chosen to keep expressions from the original that are highlighted with explanations, thus retaining the vernacular elements of the original text.

In conclusion, Carine Bruy and Éditions Balland have chosen a middle way compared to the German and English editions of *Den drunknade*. Bohman's novel is described as a bestseller, the front cover clearly highlighting the (very sparse) crime fiction elements of the story. At the same time, *La noyée* is paratextually identified as a highbrow translation, which is further emphasized by the translator's footnotes.

Three Italian novels in Swedish

The next translational flow to be studied is one between two semi-peripheral literary languages. The literary traffic from Italian to Swedish will be exemplified by three contemporary novels that are all set in Naples. The regional culture and language are, however, treated very differently in the source texts, giving the translators three different challenges as regards finding a balance among reduction, replacement and retention.

In current Italian fiction, Neapolitan authors and writings set in Naples enjoy a privileged status even outside the national borders. In the following, three novels are analysed, with particular attention paid to the interplay between the vernacular (Neapolitan language, culture and scenery), the national (Italian) and the cosmopolitan (translations, here into Swedish). The selected novels – Erri De Luca's *Montedidio* (2001; *God's Mountain*), Valeria Parrella's *Lo spazio bianco* (2008; *The White Space*) and Elena Ferrante's *L'amica geniale* (2011; *My Brilliant Friend*) – are all set in a Neapolitan environment, which is characterized by poverty and misery, and yet they are localized in different ways. This variation of vernacular anchorage results in three different conditions when translating the novels into Swedish. *Montedidio* (*God's Mountain*) was translated by Viveca Melander and published in 2011 by the small publisher Elisabeth Grate förlag, which usually concentrates on French fiction. The same year, a newcomer on the Swedish market, Astor, published Parrella's *Lo spazio bianco*, translated by Ida Andersen. While Elisabeth Grate and Astor represent two niche market publishers, mainly issuing French, Italian and Spanish literature, Johanna Hedenberg's translation of Ferrante's best-selling *L'amica geniale* was published in 2016 by one of Sweden's largest publishing houses, Norstedts.

A current theme brings the three novels together: the linguistic intracultural opposition between Neapolitan (vernacular) and Italian (national). In the novels, the Neapolitan language appears to a different extent and has different connotations: in Ferrante's novel, *L'amica geniale*, the regional language is almost only present on a thematic level, where it is merely addressed as a class issue, but only rarely do Neapolitan words and phrases occur in the text. In Parrella's *Lo spazio bianco*, the social difference between Neapolitan and Italian is less thematized (this issue is instead addressed in the question of education and literature), but the dialogues between the adult students at an evening course and the protagonist-teacher Maria often display regional spelling. Finally, in De Luca's novel *Montedidio*, a somewhat nostalgic remembrance of the narrator's childhood in the poor Montedidio quarter, the Neapolitan language has a very prominent thematic role and is strongly present in the text itself. The main issue is to understand how the dynamics between these languages are represented and rendered in the Swedish translations. How is the interplay between these languages conveyed in the Swedish translations? And to what extent is the Neapolitan setting of the novels enacted in the peritext?

Practically all the Italian and foreign editions of Elena Ferrante's best-selling novel have women or girls on the front cover. The Swedish editions are no exception. Not surprisingly, the recent paperback edition of *L'amica geniale* has a photo from Saverio Costanzo's television series *My Brilliant Friend* (2018) on the cover. The first edition, however, was garnished with an originally black-and-white photo which had been partly coloured, a technique that emphasizes the novel's dynamic between past and presence. The photo displays two young girls walking side by side on the beach, with some modest barracks in the background and their clothes and haircuts being reminiscent of the styles of the 1950s and the 1960s.

The Neapolitan setting is less obvious in the visual parts of the Swedish cover than in the first Italian edition, where the bay of Naples and Mount Vesuvius are visible in the background. However, this is compensated for in the peritexts: all in all, Naples is mentioned five times on the Swedish flaps and back cover, while it is only mentioned twice in the first Italian edition (cf. Segnini 2017).

Quite different is the minimalist Italian front cover of Valeria Parrella's *Lo spazio bianco*, which shows a pair of black eyelashes on a white background. The French cover is similar while the German is more localized showing stylized branches of palm trees against a pale blue sky with flying birds. In this respect, the Swedish edition differs from the rest by its abstract illustration in black and white on the front cover. Interestingly, the Neapolitan setting of the novel is not at all mentioned in the Swedish peritext, nor is the city indicated in the short presentation of the author (who was born in Naples). Parrella's novel was the first publication of Astor, a publishing house focused on writers from the Italian and Spanish language areas. All their first editions were dressed in a uniform, having covers of black-and-white abstract formations that signalled modernity, exclusivity and thereby a clear alliance with the autonomous pole. The choice of uniform and easily recognizable covers, which is unusual in Sweden, associated the editions with a continental context (Schwartz 2017: 506).

An image search on Google of Erri De Luca's *Montedidio* is telling. Nearly all translated editions (English, Spanish, French, Norwegian, etc.) have the same kind of picture on the front cover: sepia coloured or black-and-white photos of children playing in the streets, with laundry hanging out to dry. The Swedish cover is no exception: it shows a young boy playing football in the street and in front of him a younger child seen from behind, dressed in a T-shirt or underwear. Interestingly, the Italian editions differ markedly from these localized covers, as the first edition is illustrated with an angel's wing on a celestial blue background, while the second edition is entirely brown, representing the porous tuff stone that the houses in the Montedidio quarter are made of. Montedidio means God's mountain and on the Italian back cover of the novel, the mountain itself is called the 'protagonist' of the novel.

The text on the Swedish back cover refers to both time (1950s) and place, highlighting the element of poverty and the characters' lack of education by expressions such as 'fattigkvarteret Montedidio' (the poor's Montedidio quarter), 'de fattigas skor' (the shoes of the poor), 'fadern som går på stuveriarbetarnas kvällskurs för att lära sig att läsa och skriva' (the father who attends the stowage workers' evening class to learn how to read and write). It also refers to Erri De Luca's own background as a construction worker and member of the left-wing organization 'Lotta continua'.

Not all translations of *L'amica geniale* have kept the word 'geniale' (ingenious, clever) in the title and even fewer have maintained the determiner before 'amica', which has sometimes been changed to the possessive pronoun 'my': *My Brilliant Friend* (English), *L'amie prodigieuse* (French), *Mi briljante venninne* (Norweigian), *La amiga estupenda* (Spanish). However, there are examples of languages in which the word *geniale* is maintained – *Meine geniale freundin* (German), *Min geniale veninde* (Danish) – and the Brazilian Portuguese is the title that comes closest to the original: *A amiga genial*. The Swedish title, *Min fantastiska väninna* (my fantastic female friend) belongs to the category of titles that have transformed both the determiner and the adjective *geniale*, which signals a certain detachment from the source text. Even though the question of dialect – *dialetto* – is continuously highlighted in the novel, the source text hardly includes any Neapolitan words at all (only on ten occasions). The translators of Elena Ferrante's *Neapolitan Novels*, in which the narrator often comments on the use of 'dialect' but rarely actually uses it (Cavanaugh 2016: 46), are frequently asked what they have done with the Neapolitan. This confusion experienced by readers of translations in which metalinguistic comments are frequent but foreign words are few is illustrated by Melinda Harvey's interview with Ferrante's American translator Ann Goldstein:

> MH: (…) One of the first questions I asked an Italian speaker when I was reading the Neapolitan novels was whether Ferrante used dialect, whether the moments in the novels where your English version says 'she answered in dialect' or 'she moved into dialect now' was your way of indicating that to English-speaking readers.
> AG: No, she doesn't write in dialect, and of course I'm grateful.
>
> (Harvey 2016)

A close reading of the source text reveals that it contains surprisingly few local references, especially in comparison with *Montedidio* and *Lo spazio bianco*. In this respect, the translation should not have caused any serious problems; actually, it is almost as if the novel was 'born translated' (cf. Walkowitz 2015).

The tendencies to replace or retain are both rare, but they do occur to a slightly greater extent than reduction, which is a very uncommon strategy applied in the translated text. Replacement can occur in cases concerning food, 'salsiccia' becomes 'korv' (sausage), and 'taralli' becomes 'tarallikringlor' (taralli pretzels). The Italian school system causes problems for translators (see below), but in the three novels analysed here, it has been replaced by the Swedish school system even though it is not parallel to the Italian one. In *L'amica geniale*, the adaptation has also been archaized so that the Italian school system of the 1950s has been transformed into the Swedish school system of the same period: the Italian primary school, 'la scuola elementare', is translated into 'folkskolan', and the secondary school, 'la scuola media', is referred to as 'realskolan'. Names of companies such as 'Manifattura del tabacco' and 'Ferrovie dello stato' are replaced by more generic forms *tobaksbolaget* (the tobacco company) and *järnvägsbolaget* (the railway company), which do not create any obstacles for the Swedish reader. Moreover, book titles mentioned in the novel are referred to with their Swedish titles and replacement is usually applied in the case of metalinguistic issues, as in the following example, where the italicized words show no semantic relation at all between source and target text:

> parole come *avvezzo, lussureggiante, ben volentieri* (44)
> [words as accustomed, luxuriant, willingly]
>
> ord som *förvisso, ofantlig och angenäm* (42)
> [words as certainly, immense and pleasant]

Italian names of streets and squares are often kept in the Swedish translation (i.e. Piazza Nazionale, Corso Garibaldi, Via Caracciolo), but the strategy wavers when it comes to names of buildings. In this sentence, for example, 'l'Albergo dei poveri' is kept while 'l'Orto botanico' is translated:

> *Source text:*
>
> Mi mostrò piazza Carlo III, l'Albergo dei poveri, l'Orto botanico, via Foria, il Museo (133)
> (He showed me Carlo III square, the Hospice of the poor, the Botanical garden, Foria street, the Museum)
>
> *Target text:*
>
> Han visade mig Piazza Carlo III, Albergo dei poveri, Botaniska trädgården, Via Foria och museet (134)
> (He showed me Piazza Carlo III, Albergo dei poveri, the Botanical gardens, Via Foria and the museum)

A similar oscillation can be observed when it comes to names of holidays: the Italian *Ferragosto* in mid-August is replaced with the Swedish name for that Christian holiday, Marie Himmelsfärd (Assumption of Mary), while the Befana, a witch-like woman who brings gifts to Italian children on Epiphany's Eve, is first explained and thereafter mentioned in Italian:

> *Source text:*
>
> Il culmine del conflitto fu raggiunto nel giorno della Befana. (175)
> (The culmination of the conflict was reached on the day of the Befana.)
>
> *Target text:*
>
> Konflikten nådde sin kulmen på trettondagen, *La Befanas* dag. (177)
> (The conflict reached its peak the day of the Epiphany, La Befana's day.)

When Neapolitan words and expressions occur in the source text, they are retained in the Swedish translation: 'strùmmolo', 'tàmmaro' and 'chillu strunz' are examples of expressions that are kept in Neapolitan, and they are accompanied by an explanation that is not always present in the source text.

The most striking example of retention is, however, the translation of the word 'dialetto' (dialect) into 'napolitanska' (Neapolitan). Despite the fact that Neapolitan is recognized as a language by UNESCO, it is often referred to as a dialect, especially at the time of the childhood of Ferrante's and De Luca's protagonists. Interestingly, De Luca uses both 'dialetto' and 'napoletano' (and so does the translation), while Ferrante almost exclusively refers to 'dialetto', while the translation refers to 'napolitanska', which retains the lingua-culturally specific origin of the text. As Segnini (2017) has observed, the Neapolitanness of Ferrante's text is more underscored abroad than it is in the Italian texts.

The title of Valeria Parrella's novel *Lo spazio bianco* (meaning 'the white space') has been translated quite differently into German (*Zeit des Wartens*, 'time of waiting'), French (*Le temps suspendu*, 'the suspended time') and Swedish (*Väntrum*, 'waiting room'). It may be noted that while the French and German titles emphasize the temporal aspect, the Swedish title remains more faithful to the spatial dimension in the Italian original. On the other hand, the Swedish title concretizes the somewhat elusive Italian title, which is better preserved in the French and German variants. None of these translational titles, however, underscore the Neapolitanness of the novel.

All three translation strategies are present in the text, even though reduction and replacement are more present than reinforcement. When it comes to the latter, the names of places (such as piazza Garibaldi, corso Vittorio Emanuele) and well-known buildings (Palasport, Castel dell'Ovo) are kept, retaining the source culture vernacular and making it stand out in the Swedish target text. However, there are cases in which the Swedish text vacillates, for instance book titles: Dante's *Purgatorio* is retained, while Manzoni's classic novel *I promessi sposi* (The betrothed) is referred to in Swedish as *De trolovade*. Names of Italian food and dishes are sometimes mentioned without any explanation (i.e. 'palatone'), but they can just as well be replaced: 'girava la frittata' (turned the frittata) is rendered as 'rörde i stekpannan' (stirred in the frying pan). The Neapolitan setting is not at all highlighted or exotified in the translation. It only comes forth when it seems inevitable, as in the following case where the reader might not know that Naples has a Greek past: 'un cardo della città greca' (a card of the Greek city) becomes 'en ullkarda från det grekiska Neapel' (a wool card from the Greek Naples). However, there is another example of retention, which is in line with Berman's idea of translating proverbs literally instead of replacing them with equivalents (Berman 1985). The phrase 'grosso come un armadio' (big as a wardrobe) could easily have been translated into the Swedish expression '*stor som ett hus*' (big as a house) but is translated literally. Another example is 'mi spaccava il cuore' (it broke/split my heart), which is not replaced by the common expression 'det krossade mitt hjärta' (it crushed my heart), but literally translated into 'det klöv mitt hjärta itu'. However, the overall tendency in the Swedish text is to reduce or replace.

In dialogues, Neapolitan colloquialisms are reduced to standard Swedish, for example where 'Sì, vabbuò' (in Italian: 'Sì, va bene') becomes 'Ja, visst' (Yes, sure), but also English expressions used in the source text, such as 'phone centre' ("telefoncenter), 'internet point' ('internetcaféer') and 'la sua body artist preferita' (his favourite body artist, 'sin favoritkroppskonstnär') (22, 27). The most obvious reduction with regard to the regional location is the somewhat comic expression 'burocrazia borbonica' (Bourbon bureaucracy), which is a historical allusion to the Spanish royal family who were the sovereigns of Naples. The Swedish translation reduces this ironic expression into 'byråkratisk process' (bureaucratic process, 29). Finally, reduction also occurs in metalinguistic passages: 'è piena di seco e pel' (it's full of *seco* and *pel* [where *seco* and *pel* are examples of compound prepositions) becomes 'den är full av sammansatta prepositioner' (it's full of compound prepositions, 41).

Replacement can be illustrated by the target text's rendering of the Italian title system into Swedish, since this system was completely abolished in Sweden after the so-called you-reform that started in 1967. Basically, Swedish translators from Italian have three options: 1) they can translate titles into Swedish, even though it sounds rather obsolete; 2) they can refrain from using forms of address; 3) they can choose to retain the Italian form (i.e. 'signora', 'dottore', 'professore') and thereby retain the foreign origin of the text. In *Lo spazio bianco*, the translator has opted for the first option: 'Dottore, va bene' becomes 'Okej, doktorn' and 'Sì, signora, quella è un'iniezione' becomes 'Jo, frun, det är en injektion', where 'frun' is the Swedish word for 'signora'. Another replacement of this kind refers to the form of address which is highlighted in the text: a student uses the more antiquated and regional form 'voi' (plural you) and the protagonist, his teacher, tries to force him to use the more modern form 'lei' (she). The translator has solved this delicate problem by using older Swedish forms of address.

As we have seen in the case of Ferrante above, replacement is the most recurring strategy when the Italian educational and administrative systems are translated into Swedish. For instance, even though the Italian school system is not parallel to the Swedish, expressions deriving from the latter are used. Likewise, the Italian political administration and authorities have been translated into Swedish equivalents. The same strategy has been applied in cases of typically Italian accommodation forms, and also in relation to building material ('le maioliche', 'case di tufo', 'il muro di tufo'). When it comes to imprecations, Italian expressions are often freely replaced by Swedish ones: 'Cristo santo', for example, becomes 'Herre jävlar'.

Reduction and replacement are not very common strategies in the Swedish translation of Erri De Luca's best-selling novel about the Neapolitan quarter called *Montedidio*. As we have seen, the peritexts vernacularize the novel, and so does the narrative text itself. Retention is therefore the most obvious strategy applied by the translator and editor. To start with, we can observe that the title has been maintained even though the Swedish reader will probably miss its semantic element: Montedidio means God's mountain (which is the English, more domesticated title of the novel). Not translating the Italian title is in line with the vernacularization in the rest of the peritexts. The language issue is a recurrent theme in the source text; the novel has plenty of vernacular words and phrases scattered throughout its pages, but instead of using footnotes De Luca provides an explanatory gloss in Italian after each Neapolitan expression. The Swedish translation imitates this strategy by retaining nearly all the Neapolitan expressions intact and inserting translations into Swedish. This can be illustrated by the very first sentence of the novel:

Source text:

A iurnata è 'nu muorzo, la giornata è un morso, è la voce di mast'Errico sulla porta della bottega. (7)

(A iurnata è 'nu muorzo, the day is a bite, it is master Errico's voice outside the door of the shop.)

Target text:

A iurnata è 'nu muorzo, dagen är en munsbit, det är master Erricos röst utanför dörren till snickarverkstan. (9)

(A iurnata è 'nu muorzo, the day is a morsel, it is master Errico's voice outside the door of the carpenter workshop.)

Since this strategy is applied throughout the whole novel, the vernacular is heavily reinforced. There are even a few cases when the gloss is left out and hence the reader has to find out the meaning of the Neapolitan words by relying on the context:

Source text:

Abbiamo messo la polvere velenosa, nel deposito c'era pure qualche topo, <u>"'o súrece, 'o súrece"</u>, ha strillato il maestro, gli fanno impressione, a me no. (10)

(We put the poisonous powder, in the deposit there were also some rats, "'o súrece, 'o súrece", the master screamed, they make an impression on him, not on me.)

Target text:

Vi lade ut giftpulver, i förrådet fanns det också en och annan råtta, <u>"'o súrece, 'o súrece"</u>, skrek mast'Errico, han är rädd för dem, inte jag. (11)

(We put poisonous powder, in the deposit there were also some rats, "'o súrece, 'o súrece", mast'Errico screamed, he's afraid of them, I'm not.)

Interestingly, the Swedish reviewers did not complain about the presence of Neapolitan in the target text. Viveca Melander's translation was explicitly praised by several critics. But are not the glossed phrases in Neapolitan obvious cases of exoticism or what Emily Apter calls 'eye dialect'? (Berman 1985, Apter 2006: 155). What are the benefits of *showing* a vernacular that the reader is not expected to understand, and then providing an explanation? Actually, the aesthetic gains are manifold. Firstly, since the language issue is a major theme in the source text, it is obvious to the reader that the glossed sentences are in Neapolitan. The translation transforms De Luca's Italian–Neapolitan text, in which Neapolitan is somewhat fetishized, into a bilingual Swedish–Neapolitan text, leaving Italian out. The absence of Italian language in the target text is perfectly consistent with the source text's attitude towards Italian: 'We live in Italy, but we are not Italians', says the narrator's father, who speaks only Neapolitan and describes Italian as a 'silent language'. According to Rebecca Walkowitz, 'multilingual works aim to reduce the importance of dominant languages' (2013: 183), an aim that could be reinforced by multilingual translations. The Swedish translation of De Luca's novel, where the dominant language Italian, for obvious reasons, is repressed, while dominated Neapolitan is maintained, creates an unusual Swedish-Neapolitan narrative.

Another aspect of the aesthetic benefits of the Swedish translation concerns how one of the characters in the book refers to Italian as 'a language without saliva', while Neapolitan is more of a 'spittle in the mouth'. This particular quality of the vernacular is visualized in the translation through the spelling out of all the Neapolitan phrases, including the many accents and double consonants at the beginnings of the words: 'e ppe fforza, comme partivo co' ll'augurio d'o schiattamuorte?' (62), 'pièttene, pettenésse, piètene larghe e stritte, ne' perucchiù, accattáteve 'o pèttene' (41). The diversity of the vernacular is underscored in this intricate play on the iconicity of the foreign words, which even a reader who does not understand Neapolitan can perceive. It is worth noting, however, that a paradox arises in the Swedish translations that retain Neapolitan or other vernacular expressions: the languages that are manifested as vernaculars in the Italian source text undergo a double exposure in the translation, because readers identify them as both real foreign languages and, if the text informs them about it, as vernaculars. This paradox creates a fascinating split between the cosmopolitan level (what is foreign) and the vernacular level (what is regional) in the translation that is non-existent in the source text.

A third benefit concerns translational norms. It is often presumed that, compared to writers, literary translators less often consider it their task to develop and change cultural norms of the target language's literature. When it comes to the representation of regional varieties, the Swedish and international norm has been to avoid translating a source language vernacular or 'dialect' into a target language vernacular (see, for instance, Englund Dimitrova 1997: 62). The possibility of consistently retaining the vernacular of the source text, providing a gloss, as Melander does, is not reported as a common procedure. Ellen McRae, for instance, suggests four different strategies for translating Italian dialect into English. The only strategy that comes close to the Swedish translator's method is what she refers to as 'compensation', which 'can be achieved by the systematic direct transfer of key "exotic" items or the occasional use of literal renderings that convey local colour and evoke foreignness' (2011: 32). In this regard, the Swedish translator of Erri De Luca's *Montedidio* approaches an innovative way of solving the eternal problem of dialect translation, confirming that the translational norms in this respect are undergoing a 'creative turn'.

To summarize, *Montedidio* is a very localized source text, which has been kept intact in the Swedish translation, mainly through using the strategy of retention and a localized peritext. Valeria Parrella's *Lo spazio bianco* is, on the other hand, a localized source text that has not been kept intact in the Swedish translation or peritexts. Reduction and replacement have rather swept away its Neapolitanness, probably in order to underscore the novel's 'universal' traits. Elena Ferrante's *L'amica geniale* surprisingly turned out to be a less localized source text than expected. Traditional culture-specific items (names of streets and places as well as trademarks, famous buildings, particular foods and so on) are actually so few that it would be difficult to locate the story if it was not for the word 'dialetto' and the peritexts. The result is that the translation does not have to adopt so many of the strategies which are analysed here. However, while reduction is not common at all, examples of both replacement and retention occur.

Two Anglophone African novels in Swedish

In analysing translations of Anglophone African literature to Swedish, we will focus on two narratives, one contemporary Zimbabwean novel and one Kenyan novel first published in the 1960s. However, the Swedish translations were published only a year apart. Both novels include distinct cases of replacement and retention, but these strategies are prompted by different source text phenomena.

The translation of Anglophone African literature in the period 1980–2018 obviously cover titles originally written in English, but also include South African authors Deon Meyer and Marlene van Niekerk, who both write in Afrikaans, since their work is translated from English. Ugandan author Moses Isegawa, whose novel *Despoternas maskerad* (*Abyssinian Chronicles*) first published in Dutch as *Abessinjse Kroniken*, was translated from the English edition. The translation of Anglophone African literature into Swedish presents a complex example of cultural transfer because of the tension between the linguistic dimensions of the fictional universe – the language or languages used by the characters and fictional narrators – and the literary text. African novels in English can be seen – and indeed have been seen – as already-translated works, where the source text covers and hides an original. Frequently, English language African novels highlight their status precisely as 'translated' texts through the insertion of phrases in other languages – which are either translated and explained in the narrative or left untranslated – or references to the fact that dialogues or narration are carried out in languages other than English. These features, characteristic of what the author Ngugi wa

Thiong'o once labelled 'Afro-English' (Ngugi 1985) literature, will be discussed as they appear in NoViolet Bulawayo's *We Need New Names* and Ngugi's *The River Between*.

Zimbabwean author NoViolet Bulawayo's novel was originally published in 2013. It was translated into Swedish as *Vi behöver nya namn* and published in 2014 by Wahlström & Widstrand, a publisher that describes itself as engaged in Swedish and translated quality literature 'med potential att nå många läsare' (with the potential to reach many) (https://www.wwd.se/om-forlaget/), with Kazuo Ishiguro, Amos Oz, Anne Tyler and Evelyn Waugh among its foreign authors. The Swedish translation is done by Niclas Hval, an established specialist translator in the field of canonized literature. Hval translates from English, often novels from regions outside Britain which display non-standard writing, for example Marlon James *A Brief History of Seven Killings* and Junot Díaz' *The Brief Wondrous Life of Oscar Wao*, but also prestigious English writers such as Ian McEwan. Hval is the vice chair of the board of the Swedish translators, and he teaches translation at Valand Academy – one of the most prestigious higher education institutes for creative writing in Sweden https://niclashval.se/.

Bulawayo's novel clearly signals its status as a (hypothetically) translated original. Most visibly, this comes out in the untranslated expressions – frequently parts of dialogues – which are included in the narrative. For a reader not familiar with the language, most of them are partly intelligible through contextual information ('You you futsekani leave her alone you bloody mgodoyis get away beSatan beRoma!', 21 [I don't want to move to a place where I will be called mkeremkere, 21), but some remain more difficult to decipher, such as the 'funeral song' sung by mourners, for instance (138). Through these features, Bulawayo's literary aesthetics sets up a logic of inclusion and (partial) exclusion where the narrative is more transparent to readers versed in Ndebele or Zulu than those who are not, all the while indicating to the latter group – through explanations or the careful selection of untranslated information – that nothing too vital is missed.

Hval's translation retains the cultural and linguistic difference emphasized in the original text. In an interview conducted while he was translating Bulawayo, Hval explained that he strove to 'really listen to the author and the book' and sought in his translation to create something that 'wasn't bland, or literal translation' (Artikelförfattare 2013). A creative translation strategy in this regard is the use of neologisms. When the young narrator refers in the original text to the USA as the 'big baboon' of the world – a phrase which draws on

African fauna for metaphorical expressiveness – it is translated as 'babianbossen' (literally 'baboon boss'), a phrase which is not part of the standard variety but arguably resonates with a Swedish youth culture used to mixing English and Swedish words. The translator's inventiveness can also be seen in a word such as 'knäklapprare' (literally 'knee-clatterer'), which is translated as 'kiss-knees' – an insult one of the characters throws in the face of another (16, 12). In Swedish, this neologism has the ring of history, evoking horse-drawn transports of earlier days. In addition to signalling the translated status of the Swedish edition, in this context the noun has the advantage of preserving the rhythm and the syntax of the original text: the equivalent to 'kiss-knees', or 'knock-knees', in Swedish is not a noun but an adjective – 'kobent' – and using this common term in the target text would require modifying the sentence. With 'knäklapprare', the clipped and fast-paced dialogue is kept, and the translator avoids inventing a noun to follow the adjective.

An intricate example of the translation's emphasis on foreignness involves the translation of the names of the characters in the novel. In the original text, the friends at the centre of the narrative have names that are either given names or nicknames: Bastard, Chipo, Godknows, Shbo and Stina. Most of these are either translated – 'Bastard' becomes 'Horungen' (literally 'child of a whore' or 'child of whoring') and 'Godknows' becomes 'Gudvet' (literally 'God knows'). 'Stina', however, while a peculiar name for a young boy in a southern African context, is a common girl's name in Sweden. Hval has therefore chosen to invent a name, 'Stinez', that sounds odd to Swedish ears – and one would presume, to Zimbabwean – to stress the foreignness of the setting the text presents.

The translation also includes strategies of replacement intended to familiarize the text to the reader. One example concerns the representation of the type of English spoken by the white Zimbabweans who briefly appear in the narrative – or more precisely the way this kind of English sounds to the main characters of the novel. In the original text, this class-based variety is unmarked. When a gang of angry Black men appear at the home of a rich white Zimbabwean couple, the hostile dialogue that ensues gives the white husband's speech as standard variety while presenting the Black leader's speech as non-standard through grammar and register:

'Can't you read? You brung English to this country and now you want it explained to you, your own language, have you no shame? […]

Bloody nonsense! This is illegal, I own this fucking property, I have the papers to prove it, the white man says. [...]

We know, sir. I'm sorry, but it's just the times, you know. They are changing, you know [...]' (117)

'Kan du inte läsa? Ni tog med engelskan till det här landet och nu vill du få det förklarat, ditt eget språk, har du ingen skam i kroppen? [...]

Struntprat! Det här är olagligt, jag äger ju för fan den här fastigheten, jag har papper på det, säger den vite mannen. [...]

Vi vet det, sir. Jag är ledsen, men sådana är tyvärr tiderna, va. Det är nya tider nu, va. [...]' (110)

The translation modifies the non-standard verb form 'brung' into the standard 'tog', but translates the informal 'you know' into 'va', a common translation of this expression. When one of the protagonist Darling's gang later mimics white speech it is spelled in a way clearly intended to reproduce the sound of Received Pronunciation: 'Wee fawgoat the fowks, wee fawgoat the fowks', Godknows says, 'sounding like a white man' (130). That this sociolect – which signals both race, as Godknows indicates, and class – has no immediate equivalent is demonstrated by the fact that Hval's rendering is not easily placed in social and geographical terms. He translates it as 'Vii gleömde fafflarna, vii gleömde fafflarna', devising a form of speech that alludes simultaneously to the posh sounds of a Stockholm suburb, and/or certain language varieties of Skåne, in southern Sweden, where diphthongs are common (120).

This strategy of replacing a locally specific form of speech with another local form of speech, can be compared with the representation of the non-standard English spoken by the Chinese workers in the narrative. In the original, the simplified English is marked, for example by simple verb forms and repetitions: 'We build you big big mall. All nice shops inside. Gucci, Louis Vuitton, Versace, and so on so on' (46). In Swedish this is marked among other things by the absence of articles and incorrect number: 'Vi bygger stor galleria till er. Bara fin affär i den, Gucci, Louis Vuitton, Versace och så' (46). A representation using the standard dialect would be 'Vi bygger *en* stor galleria till er. *Det kommer* bara *finnas* fin*a* affär*er* i den, Gucci, Louis Vuitton, Versace och så'.

A further example of replacement can be seen in the section of the novel which is set in the United States. One of the characters, Kristal, refers to her speech as 'ebonics': Black American speech. The term is used defensively when Kristal is challenged by Darling, for her way of speaking. In the Swedish translation, Kristal's 'ebonics' is represented through a combination of slang from the Stockholm region – words such as *jiddrar* for 'messing with'; and expressions such as *jag svär*, which is a literal translation of 'I swear', mostly associated with suburban slang – and retaining translations such as *Du vet inte skit*, which is not commonly used in Swedish (though the same expression with an article – *Du vet inte ett skit* – is) but transparently translates 'You don't know shit'.

What is the situation into which the translated works are released? The translation of *We Need New Names* was preceded by translations of a number of Zimbabwean authors over a long period. Doris Lessing, Chenjerai Hove, Charles Mungoshi, Dambudzo Marechera and Yvonne Vera were all translated before Bulawayo. Thus, for the reader interested in Zimbabwean literature there are several writers to choose from. Apart from Lessing and Vera, however, there are few works by each author. Of Hove's writing (three novels and two poetry collections), two have been translated into Swedish; Mungoshi and Dangarembga, admittedly less prolific writers (Dangarembga three novels, Mungoshi four short story collections), have each had only one work translated. Vera has been given a more prominent place in Swedish literature through the translation of three of her novels.

A look at the times of the translations and the publishers shows that publishers' interest in Zimbabwean authors, again excluding Lessing, has been rather temporary. Dangarembga was published by Trevi (now defunct) in 1990; Hove by Legenda (now defunct) in 1990 and B. Östling in 1995; Mungoshi by Tranan in 2003; and Marechera by h:ström in 2011. Vera has received more sustained attention through the translation of three of her novels from 1999 to 2005. It is reasonable to conclude that Swedish publishing of Zimbabwean literature, apart from Lessing and to some extent Vera, is based more on individual works than authorships.

The translation of Bulawayo's novel, though it falls into a line of translations of Zimbabwean literature, is also part of a current publishing trend focused not on country-specific literature, but on contemporary African literature in English. Bulawayo's novel belongs to a wave of African English language novels that includes authors such as Chimamanda Ngozi Adichie, Taye Selasi, Chris Abani, Teju Cole, Sefi Atta and others who have become globally successful, first by being published in Britain or the United States, and then by being translated into a number of languages (some of them, such as Adichie and Cole have also been published anew in their countries of origin). Bulawayo's Booker nomination is a testament to the attraction of this category of literature which combines aesthetic value with economic value through projected sales.

If the tradition of publishing Zimbabwean and African literature in Sweden, and the current success of serious but popular African literature indicate the reasons for *selecting* Bulawayo to be translated, the translation strategies and effects can also be explained through the broader context of Swedish publishing. One of the significant features of the target language context is the openness towards non-standard modes of speaking that a generation of Swedish authors with immigrant backgrounds have forged. Authors such as Alejandro Leiva Wenger, Jonas Hassen Khemiri, Marijane Bhaktiari and Johannes Anyuru have all turned the speech patterns and narrative modes associated with urban minorities, with the slang of the suburbs, and with hip-hop culture into literary art. All had their literary debuts, or their breakthrough novels, published between 2000 and 2005. A decade later, authors such as Athena Farrokzhad added to this tradition. Within translated literature, this broadening of representational possibilities has been accomplished through the translation of authors such as Marlon James and Junot Díaz (both translated by Hval).

The packaging of the English language edition, published by Chatto and Windus, underscores the text's contemporary and translational characteristics. The cover is aesthetically eclectic, colourful, in naïve style and apparently hand-painted. The words of the title are set in boxes, each with a different background colour, and the space around the title is seemingly sprinkled with equally manually produced, if stylized, guavas, with associations to doodling. The colours of the Zimbabwean flag are among the colours, as are the American – the word 'new' in the title clearly referencing the Star Spangled Banner. The back cover features a quotation from the first chapter (punctuation removed, all in capitals) which brings out the carefree attitude of the children, and the intensity of the narrative ('THEN WE ARE RUSHING THEN WE ARE RUNNING THEN WE ARE RUNNING AND LAUGHING AND LAUGHING AND LAUGHING').

The Swedish edition, published by Wahlström & Widstrand, retains much of the original aesthetic, but tones down the naivety in favour of a more symmetric style. The colours of the Zimbabwean and the American flags are there in the cover in the form of horizontal stripes, with the stars of the American flag appearing at the bottom and top of the front cover. Six children, silhouetted, climb a stylized guava tree positioned on the right margin. The upward movement and the stars spread at the top of the cover gives the impression of an altogether more romanticized view of childhood and children – as if they were climbing towards the stars – which contrasts with the British edition. The back cover features information about the narrative and gives some contextual information (referring, for instance, to Mugabe's 'war veterans' and township life), and describes the novel as a shocking and intense coming-of-age story ('omskakande och nervigt vital skildring av en ung flickas vuxenblivande').

The River Between is set in Kenya during the spread of British colonization. At the centre of the story are two villages, Kameno and Mukuya, on the brink of being fully integrated into the colonial management system, which are separated by the river of the title. Their separation also marks conflicting ideas as there is a clash between Christianity, represented mainly by the old man and convert preacher in Kameno, and traditional religious ideas, manifested in the old 'prophet' in Mukuya. In this struggle of ideas a younger generation are trying to negotiate the changing landscapes. At the heart of the conflict is the practice of circumcision, particularly its place in the cultural system, and its consequences for those who submit to it or refuse to do so.

Ngugi's novel was first published in 1965 by Heinemann Educational Publishers as the seventeenth publication in the 'African Writers Series' and has long had the status of a classic in African literature. This status is evidenced by the fact that the current English language edition is a fifty-year anniversary publication by Penguin Classics which includes a 'message' from Chinua Achebe (apparently drawn from his editorship of the AWR) and a foreword by Uzodinma Iweala, author of *Beasts of No Nation*, one of the more popular African novels in recent years.

The Penguin edition paratext has few features in common with the first, 1965 'African Writers Series' novel. The former presented a painted landscape with the river of the title centred and flowing through a pair of hands, symbolically invoking the bringing together needed to settle the conflict of the narrative; however, the contemporary edition appears, at least at first sight, less artistic and more general. The front cover features a photograph of an ordinary scene: an individual in a fishing canoe, in a landscape that could be anywhere outside the industrialized world. What seems to be the individual's journey across the river may echo the symbolic meaning of the river between, and the actions needed to join its sides.

Like the Penguin version, the Swedish edition confirms Ngugi's status as a canonical author. *Floden mellan bergen* is published alongside Ngugi's older and newer works, most of which are packaged with similar aesthetics to give the appearance of a series, and are equipped with prefaces by established

Swedish scholars of postcolonial literary studies. The preface to *The River Between* is written by Mikela Lundahl, historian of ideas and senior lecturer at Gothenburg University. *A Grain of Wheat* (*Om icke vetekornet*), *The Devil on the Cross* (*Djävulen på korset*) and *Weep Not, Child* (*Upp genom mörkret*) have all been translated into Swedish before (in 1980 and 1981) and were republished by Modernista between 2014 and 2015 with prefaces by well-known critics or researchers. But Modernista extends the Ngugi library in Swedish by adding a new translation of the fable *The Upright Revolution*, published in 2017, and *Wizard of the Crow* – the latter planned for publication in 2022. All the longer works (that is, excluding *The Upright Revolution*) have designs and covers that are similar, which give them the appearance of a book series. However, the Modernista edition of *Floden mellan bergen* is based on an old translation, and is published by a young publisher (Modernista was founded in 2002) with an as-yet somewhat undefined position in the publishing field. The translator Philippa Wiking (1920–2010) was a missionary to Tanzania and translated several works, mostly in the category of psychology and related fields.

Modernista's cover bears no resemblance to Penguin's. Instead, it borrows its aesthetics from the editions of Ngugi's more recent works, his memoir series *In the House of the Interpreter*, *Births of a Dream Weaver*, *Dreams in a Time of War* and *Wizard of the Crow*, which, although published by different publishers in the USA and UK, share a design based on collage technique, the inclusion of animals and graphic elements and occasionally human features or clothes items such as hats. In the Swedish edition, a blue-tinted and double-exposed landscape makes up a vague background whereas the foreground is dominated by a hyena with a human eye inserted, collage-fashion, and covering most of its head. A fragment of a recognizably African cloth also covers part of the animal's body.

The cover of Modernista's edition can be said to accomplish two goals. Firstly, its collage technique wraps Ngugi's text in an aesthetic that is recognizably modernist with a clear reference to an African cultural sphere. Secondly, though implicitly and perhaps unknown to the Swedish reader, it 'updates' Ngugi's early novel by linking it, through the similarity of its cover art, to his more recent production.

Like Bulawayo's novel, *The River Between* leaves no doubt about its characteristics of being a translated original. In contrast to *We Need New Names*, however, most of these terms are explained in the source text itself. Thus, the original gives '*thingira*, a man's hut' and '*kihii,* an uncircumcised boy' (which the Swedish translation follows: '*Kagutui ka Mucii gatihagakwo Ageni:* husets oljeduk skall inte gnida främlingars hud' (17), '*thingira*, mannens hydda' (22), '*tene na tene*, I evigheters evighet', and '*kihii*, en oomskuren pojke' (54)). The explanatory ambition includes not only terms and expressions but also customs and traditions, as in the following description of a blessing: 'a shower of saliva onto his breast in the Gikuyu way of blessing' (29), or, in a passage that addresses the heart of the conflict, the ritual of circumcision:

> Circumcision was an important ritual to the tribe. It kept people together, bound the tribe. It was at the core of the social structure, and a [*sic*] something that gave meaning to a man's life. End the custom and the spiritual basis of the tribe's cohesion and integration would be no more.

Ngugi's text, then, helps the reader unfamiliar with local traditions and vernacular terms to understand the events and their meanings, occasionally in ways that seem to confirm the argument presented by critics such as Eileen Julien and Graham Huggan that the intended audience of postcolonial African novels are American and European readers with little knowledge of the local cultural specificities (Huggan 2001, Julien 2006, 2018).

One of the significant characteristics of Ngugi's novel is the use of biblical references and terms. This relates directly to the theme and to the characterization, of course, but it also provides a template for describing Gikuyu beliefs and customs and it permeates the narrative voice so that the novelistic text approaches a biblical story. The opening of the novel displays the biblical register clearly: 'The two ridges lay side by side. One was Kameno, the other was Kamuyu. Between them was a valley. It was called the valley of life'. In other places, constatives referring to the 'people' have a biblical ring: 'People saw this and were happy'; 'There was much rejoicing everywhere' (45). This register is maintained throughout: in single words – as when the boy Kanuthia obeys his friend 'meekly' (20) – in sentence structure (like the many sentences beginning with 'And … ' [25]) – and the use of Christian words (such as 'God' and 'sacred' and 'prophecy') and phrases for local customs and traditions. The narrative voice, to exemplify this last trait, describes the end of the ritual of the 'second birth' like baptism, and in biblical style: 'She dipped him into the water and he came out clean' (26); labels Chege a 'prophet' and has Chege describe a 'prophecy' articulated by the old seer Mugo in the following terms: '"Salvation shall come from the hills. From the blood that flows in me, I say from the same tree, a son shall rise. And his duty shall be to lead and save the people!"'

The translation adheres closely to this biblical register, reinforcing it at times. The repetition of the subjective, which in Swedish is typical of this style, is one example of this, as in 'Människorna såg det och det gjorde dem lyckliga' ('People saw this and were happy'; literally 'The people saw this *and it made them happy*'; 15); and the translation of 'bulrush' as *vass*, which is the biblical word for the reeds among which Moses is found. There are occasional exceptions to this rule, as when the translation avoids the Swedish biblical equivalent of 'meekly' – which is *saktmodigt* – in favour of *fogligt* (20).

Even when not biblical, the translation uses an elevated, poetic and at times slightly archaic register when the source text is closer to standard diction. Examples are 'sorgebudet' (17) for 'sad news'; 'gulröd färgton' (67) for 'dull pale orange'; 'tvistigheter' (69) for 'strife' and 'hölja över huvudet med' for 'cover their heads with'.

Apart from the pervasive use of biblical language, the translation is characterized by strategies to reduce and replace the particularities of the Kenyan setting and text. One example of the former is the translation of 'When your stomach bites you' into as 'När du har magknip' (29) – an ingenious translation as 'magknip' literally means 'pinch-stomach', but which nevertheless familiarizes the text since it avoids what in a Swedish context would be an odd verb ('bite') for a common informal expression. Another example is the translation of 'huge cattle road' into 'kostigen' (literally 'cow path'), an expression that is familiar to Swedish readers, but also connotes something distinctly narrower and smaller than the road denoted by the text. A third example of this replacement strategy is the translation of musical instruments in the narrative. The 'beating of drums and jingles' is translated into 'trummornas dunkande och klingandet av skallror' (literally 'the beating of drums and ringing of rattles', 55). The translation does not quite conjure the sounds of the traditional instruments probably referenced here (which were probably made of metal) and which had a rather darker sound than the one connoted by 'klingandet' (in the original text, moreover, the jingles 'beat') but may seem suitable to an audience accustomed to the word 'skallra'. The translation also belittles the quality of the musical performance since 'skallra' connotes a child's instrument. In the same scene the 'whistles' used are translated as 'pipor', which to an audience familiar with older musical practices may connote a reed instrument but in contemporary Swedish connotes instruments with little musical quality – such as toys and referee instruments – and not the flutes that Ngugi must have had in mind.

Wiking's translation contains a number of footnotes. A whole range of words and concepts are explained: 'panga' (described as a kind of 'long knife for cutting grass and bush', 35), 'kiama' (translated as 'förening': 'association', 80), 'tutikwenda irigu' ('vi vill inte ha oomskurna flickor': 'we do not want uncircumcised girls', 83), 'riika' ('årsgrupp': 'year group', 112), and 'thahu' ('smitta'; 'contamination', 145). According to Lawrence Venuti, footnotes exemplify a foreignizing translation strategy since they highlight cultural differences, and provide guidance in how to understand those differences. From a more postcolonial point of view, however, footnotes may also be seen as attempts to determine and explain cultural differences, in the effort risking (or perhaps even striving) to manage and erase them. This is what happens in at least one of the footnotes in Wiking's translation (Kullberg 2011: 58). The 'kiama', which Iweala describes in his foreword as a 'governing body' and which in the literary text emerges as something akin to a regional council encompassing several ridges and villages and invested with a great deal of power, is given as 'association', a general term which says nothing about its status or its function but is familiar in Swedish contexts of sports, church and other non-professional activities.

Ngugi wa Thiong'o was the second Black African writer to be translated into Swedish. Chinua Achebe's *Things Fall Apart* was translated as *Allt går sönder* in 1967. The publishing of Ngugi four years later marks an interest in the influential voices of African intellecuals connected to political struggle and decolonization. Wole Soyinka, another prominent African writer and intellectual, was translated into Swedish in 1976, and Stockholm hosted the 'African-Scandinavian Writers' Conference' in February 1967 (in which Ngugi and Soyinka participated) with topics such as 'The Decolonization of African Literature' and 'Individualism and the Social Responsibility of the Writer'. And the seminal Ugandan magazine *Transition*, founded in Kampala in 1961, had both Swedish readers and contributors (see e.g. Falk 2019). Over the following decades, this publishing interest changed, and up to the 1980s African literature on the Swedish book market was dominated by white South African writers such as Doris Lessing, André Brink and Nadine Gordimer.

The translation of Achebe's *No Longer at Ease* and *Arrow of God* have appeared in recent years (as *Inte längre hemma*, 2014, and *Guds pil*, 2015, respectively) and thus provide the publishing context for the re-publication of *The River Between*. Modernista's edition of Ngugi also repeats the publishing pattern of Achebe in Swedish. Where the first translation of his work was published in text only, more recent editions – both new ones and re-published ones – have included contextual information in the form of prefaces. Per Wästberg, a well-known Swedish Africanist, author and member of the Swedish Academy, wrote the introduction to a 2004 edition of Achebe's *Things Fall Apart*, and Stefan Helgesson and Stephan Larsen, who have both been engaged for the Ngugi editions, have written prefaces for Achebe's other works (Helgesson for *Inte längre hemma* and Larsen for *Guds pil*, both published by Tranan).

Both David Damrosch and Lawrence Venuti have observed that translation into English continuously threatens to erase cultural differences in the name of easy communication and the ideal of standard language (Damrosch 2003). Venuti, indeed, has argued that this kind of translation, dominant in the American case, which aims to 'enhance intelligibility for a broad English language readership', amounts to 'nationalist' translation in its suppression of cultural difference in the source text in the service of national identity (2005/2013: 121). With regard to translation into the semi-peripheral language of Swedish the pattern appears to differ from the English that Damrosch and Venuti discuss. Wiking's translation and the Modernista edition include a preface by an established scholar which emphasizes the foreignness of the original text, at the same time offering a point of entry into the text. The footnotes Venuti sees as typical of foreignizing translation, in this case present a more ambiguous attitude since they partly familiarize aspects of Gikuyu cultural life. The translation's retention strategies are, further, partly offset by the source text's inclusion of untranslated words, which are kept in the target text. Hval more distinctly retains the foreignness of the text – to the extent that he invents new words – apart from a few examples, notably on minor characters' use of English – which are replaced with characteristics ostensibly familiar to the readers. *Vi behöver nya namn* and *Floden mellan bergen* were published with only a year between them. They were, then, released onto the same literary market. The translation strategies, however, or in Ngugi's case, the decision not to renew a forty-year-old translation, demonstrate that they are intended for very different audiences.

Two Lusophone novels in Swedish

This section will focus on two contemporary Swedish translations, one of a Portuguese and one of a Mozambican novel. Despite the fact that the former translation shows significant ambitions to retain the cultural particularities of the source text and the latter shows strong tendencies to reduce and replace the source culture vernacular, both translations include illustrative combinations of reduction and retention.

The internationally recognized Portuguese writer António Lobo Antunes has fourteen titles translated into Swedish (of twenty-eight novels in Portuguese) published by the mid-sized publishing house Forum from 1985 to 2015. Together with the (other) internationally consecrated Portuguese writer, José Saramago, Antunes' authorship appeared heavily in the speculations about the Nobel Prize during the 1990s. After the prize was awarded to José Saramago in 1998, finally rendering a prize for a work in the Portuguese language, the interest from the major publishing house seemed to decline somewhat. In 2014 the small-scale publishing house Modernista took up his authorship and re-published *De förrådda* (*Os cus de Judas*, 1979), and in 2017 the so-called Benfica Trilogy, including *Betraktelser över själens passioner* (*Tratado das paixões da alma*, 1990), *Tingens naturliga ordning* (*A ordem natural das coisas*, 1992) and *Carlos Gardels död* (*A morte de Carlos Gardel*, 1994). These novels were not published as a trilogy in the first place, although this was suggested by Antunes himself in a later interview. Even though not a format change, it is evident that Modernista enhances the idea of formatting these novels into a trilogy in their marketing. The Benfica Trilogy is in focus for analysing the works' epitext and, consequently, how Lobo Antunes' works were inscribed and transformed in the Swedish market in the 2010s. The novel *Tingens naturliga ordning*, translated by Marianne Eyre, will serve for analysing the translation strategies on the text level.

To transform Lobo Antunes' prose into another language brings with it many challenges. His prose is composed in the (post)modernist tradition with an advanced experimental and narrative technique. A polyphonic narrative, often containing two different narrative voices and different time perspectives in the same sentence. Extended sentences containing long monologues structured as inner dialogues between the narrator and a partner, where contemporary dialogues and events are intertwined with past ones. Deeply rooted in the vernacular geography of Lisbon (Benfica), everyday events and emotional moods, the narrative blends personal memories with historical, political and social events.

All the strategies of reducing, replacing and retaining can be traced in Marianne Eyre's translation, although they somewhat alter the expected outcomes of 'familiarity' and 'foreignness' for the reader – a shift that may be attributed to the modernist, cosmopolitan quality of the text. Replacements are evident in the translations of swear words and slang, for example 'Puta, sua puta' (whore, you whore) translated into the Swedish 'Skitmorsa' (shit mother). Indicating a transformation of the text, in some parts, into a less-offensive language in the

Swedish edition. However, it should be recognized that swear words in the Romance languages are of a blunter character than the Swedish ones.

The translation follows closely and proficiently the complicated structure of the long sentences, without losing fluency in Swedish. When Antunes starts a new paragraph or sentence without a full stop the translation does the same. The translation also maintains the experimental composition of long sentences (polyphonic narrative), separating different narrative perspectives, voices and time slots with commas, parenthesis, italics and capitals in the same sentence. The translation also keeps the Portuguese names from the vernacular geography of places, neighbourhoods, streets and, for example, the Lisbon river 'Tejo', even though a translation in Swedish exists: 'Tagus'. Both these transformation techniques can be considered as retaining the source texts' vernacular culture and experimental form in a way that reminds the target reader of another text underneath, belonging to a different linguistic and cultural sphere.

Nevertheless, in this case the retention strategy does not necessarily lead to a sense of geocultural unfamiliarity for the Swedish reader. On the contrary, it may reduce the text's vernacular rootedness and lift it to a general cultural level, something we will see is being heavily advocated for in the peritexts of Antunes' works. The vernacular setting of a specific urban geography – through naming neighbourhoods, streets, rivers and public places – and an urban 'everyday struggling life' framed in an experimental literary form are highly recognizable as a (post)modernist cosmopolitan literature. Antunes' affiliation with this tradition is expressed in the introduction to Modernista's edition of *Betraktelse över själens passioner* by Anders Cullhed: 'Antunes är trots allt lika bunden till sin hemstad som argentinaren Ernesto Sabato (en av hans favoritförfattare) till Buenos Aires, James Joyce till Dublin eller poeten Konstantinos Kavafis till Alexandria' (Antunes is just as bound to his hometown as the Argentinian Ernesto Sabato (one of his favourite writers) is to Buenos Aires, James Joyce to Dublin, and the poet Konstantinos Kavafis to Alexandria) (Cullhed 2017: viii). Even though this experimental novel form will target readers in Sweden who are familiar with modernist texts it will still require readers to be experienced and interested to access it. The success of transforming this complicated form is also highly dependent on the translator. It is worth emphasizing that the translator Marianne Eyre has been highly celebrated for her ability to transmit Antunes' musicality and experimental form, which has been pointed out in various book reviews and introductions, as well as in a dedication to her by Lobo Antunes in a Swedish edition.

Forum's dust jackets carry citations of book reviews published in the major daily papers in Sweden. Antunes' prose is celebrated as universal, experimental, innovative and extraordinary, his novels often hailed as masterpieces, for example in the national newspaper *Svenska Dagbladet*: 'Ty Lobo Antunes förefaller att representera höjdpunkten i detta sekels europeiska modernism (…). Man ska var försiktig med att använda orden "mästerverk". Att denna roman utgör ett sådant tvivlar jag inte en sekund på. Läs, tag och läs!' (As Lobo Antunes represents the peak of this century's European modernism (…). One should use the word 'masterpiece' with discretion, but that this novel constitutes such a thing I do not doubt for a second. Read, take up and read!) (Antunes 1994b).

In the dust jacket writer's presentation, Antunes is claimed to be the 'greatest Portuguese writer now living', which was modified into 'from his generation' after Saramago's Nobel Prize (Antunes 1992b). Statements like this, launching Saramago and Antunes as the best and *only* authors from Portugal in the Swedish book market, obscure other contemporary Portuguese authorships, for example equally important women writers in the source context such as Lídia Jorge and Maria Velho da Costa (cf. Helgesson 2017: viii). A startling fact is that only one novel by a Portuguese woman, namely Lídia Jorge, has been translated into Swedish since 1976. Even though Jorge has been awarded literary prizes, has a recognized important position in the source culture and, just like Antunes, writes critically on contemporary social issues and major historical events, none of this is mentioned on the dust jacket of the 2001 Swedish translation *Walters dotter* of her novel *O vale da paixão* (Jorge 2001).

In a similar manner, the introductions in the Modernista editions for the Benfica Trilogy also describe Antunes as one of the most important contemporary European writers and compare him – both in topic and style – to names such as Marcel Proust, Virginia Woolf, Vladimir Nabokov and Claude Simon. This framing of Lobo Antunes thus carries the features of 'cosmopolitan qualities' described by Es and Heilbron (2015: 303), and it is visible in the books' cover design. With photographs in black and white of artistic still lifes with a modernistic composition, the covers transmit a sophisticated and avant-garde impression.

This cosmopolitanization is strongly reinforced by the publisher's epitextual presentation of how Antunes' novels function differently in the source culture vis-à-vis the target culture, in which they sketch a transformation from a situated social critique to a universal human condition. In a Portuguese context,

Antunes' narratives inhabit tough critical reflections upon the socio-historical transformations suffered by Portuguese society in the late twentieth century. For the translation reader these topics are said, by Modernista, to represent universal questions: the Portuguese colonial war is compared with the Vietnam War, the Portuguese homecoming soldier with Odysseus, criticism of Portuguese colonial amnesia with European cultural amnesia and so forth.

From the Mozambican writer Mia Couto's over forty books (novels, short stories, poetry, chronicles, children's literature and essays), five novels have been translated into Swedish: *Sömngångarland* (Ordfront, 1995; En bok för alla, 1999), *Under frangipaniträdet* (Ordfront, 1997), *Flamingons sista flykt* (Ordfront, 2002), *Sjöjungfruns andra fot* (Leopard, 2010, reprinted, 2014) and *Jesusalem* (Leopard, 2015). The following analysis of translation strategies concerns the first edition of *Sjöjungfruns andra fot* (*O outro Pé da Sereia*, 2006), translated by Irene Anderberg. Mia Couto's two Swedish publishers are both mid-sized and independent, niched as politically engaged with a focus on public debate, cultural history, as well as fiction from Africa and Asia.

The Portuguese publisher Caminho presents Couto as an innovator and renewer of the Portuguese literary language (from the Lusophone margin to the centre). The dust jackets also emphasize his international recognition and canonization, listing his translations and many literary prizes. The peritexts accompanying Couto in the Swedish book market do not emphasize his renewal of language in the same way. On Leopard's website and on the dust jacket of *Sjöjungfruns andra fot*, Mia Couto is acclaimed as the most important writer from Portuguese-speaking Africa. Leopard does not offer an introduction to the writer's biography or literary universe. The earlier editions published by Ordfront, on the other hand, provide more extensive prefaces introducing the writer to the Swedish audience.

Leopard's framing of the novel does not inscribe his work into the discourse of the anthropological and postcolonial exotic, common for African postcolonial novels (Huggan 2001). Rather, it enhances Couto's universal values through a sophisticated image that does not exploit bright colours or stereotypical African images. Instead, Leopard's presentation of Couto's novel highlights the narrative's engagement in cosmopolitan current social issues as stereotyping and prejudices in relation to race, identity, religion and tradition: 'I Sjöjungfruns andra fot korsas nuet med det förflutna, drömmar med verklighet och med en god portion humour ifrågasätts förutfattade meningar om ras och identitet, religion och tradition' (In the mermaid's second foot, the present is intersected with the past, dreams with reality, and with a good amount of humour preconceived notions of race and identity, religion and tradition are questioned) (Couto 2010).

In the transcontinental literary circuit for the Portuguese-language literatures – especially Portugal and Brazil – Mia Couto is both a best-selling author and a renewer of the Portuguese language and literature. Couto is broadly recognized for his Mozambican vernacular language transformations of European Portuguese, using neologisms, inserting African words (Ronga) and oral narrative techniques into his literary language. The challenges of transforming Mia Couto's prose into Swedish are many. In his narrative structure, different perspectives of consciousness and spatial dimensions intertwine in a way that blurs the sharp boundaries between present reality, dreams and ancestral dimensions. The latter has caused some literary scholars to categorize his prose as magical realism (e.g. Mariano Siskind 2014). Thematically and linguistically, most of his novels are rooted in vernacular specificities (historical events, rural communities, costumes and beliefs), which fosters a situated social critique. Translators thus need to bridge a certain cultural gap when presenting Couto to a Swedish readership.

In *Sjöjungfruns andra fot* the translator mainly uses the strategies of reducing and replacing the specificities of the source vernacular in a way that strongly neutralizes and domesticates them. There are various examples of how the content and the distinctive language used in Couto's narrative are neutralized and shifted to a more familiar level. They will be discussed here mainly through the translation solutions chosen for the Ronga words, intertwined in the narrative structure of the source text. Words in Ronga are numerous in the source text and they are accompanied by explanatory footnotes placed at the end of the page (Caminho's edition). In her Swedish translation, Irene Anderberg has omitted these footnotes. Instead, she has used three other strategies to deal with the bilingual character of Couto's novel: 1) she keeps the Ronga word and adds an explanatory translation in the same sentence; 2) she replaces the African word with an equivalent word translated from European Portuguese; and 3) she omits the African word and its concept from the text without any comment:

Strategy 1:
deixara de se apresentar como um **nyanga** (*)
upphört att presentera sig som **nyanga, spåman** (22)

(ceased to present himself as a **nyanga, soothsayer**)

Strategy 2:
O magaíça (*) depôs o caixão na areia [explained in the note as the European Portuguese '**mineiro**']
Gruvarbetaren satte ner kistan i sanden (92)

(**the miner** put the chest down in the sand)

Strategy 3:
Pudessem escutar as suas vozes e todos entenderiam que bastava o português deles, **muzungos** (*), para os diferenciar dos demais, os indígenas.
Hade man kunnat höra deras röster skulle portugisiskan räckt för att alla skulle kunnat skilja dem från de övriga, de infödda. (174)

(Had their voices been audible, their Portuguese would have been enough for everyone to distinguish them from the rest, the natives.)

The footnote (in the source text) for this last omitted (in the target text) African word explains: 'Muzungos: nome dado aos brancos ou pessoas de outra raça culturalmente assimilados' (Couto 2006: 170, 'Muzungos: name given to whites or persons of another race that are culturally assimilated'). Most of the African words embedded in Couto's narrative are explained by him in a footnote which in turn describes specific Mozambican fauna, flora, religious or cultural artefacts and different, ethnic groups and their languages. This additional specific cultural knowledge of the source vernacular's landscape is probably in part directed at the Portuguese reader as Coto's novel was first published in Portugal. In this regard, the use of footnotes by Couto in his original text can be said to somewhat follow a model in postcolonial literature, presented to European audiences, of explaining cultural differences and particularities. More importantly they also function – as Christina Kullberg observes in the case of the Swedish translations of Maryse Condé – as providers of vernacular specificities that enhance the visibility and subjectivity of people and places in the source culture (Kullberg 2011: 57). Nevertheless, adapting the novel for Swedish readers, the translator and the publisher's choices were to omit a large part of this cultural information contained in the source text, which also reduced this ethical dimension of Couto's narrative.

In keeping names of places and characters in Portuguese untranslated, the translator retains the source culture vernacular to a certain degree. But with this strategy, the translation simultaneously reduces Mia Couto's technique of giving symbolically charged names for his characters, for example 'Lázaro Vivo' (literal translation Living Lazarus), 'Antigamente' (literally formerly, in the old days) and 'Vila Longe' (literally faraway village), which is an important symbolic dimension of the source text. Together with omitting the colourful specificities of fauna, flora, artefacts and people, Anderberg's tendency to retain the Portuguese proper names leads to a strong reduction of the source culture vernacular. At the same time, the strategy of keeping Ronga words and the fact that the novel has strong vernacular traits in content and plot, paradoxically, makes the text come across as a translation that still retains much of its source culture.

Three Caribbean novels in Swedish

In this last translational flow we will focus on three novels with backdrops and settings in three different Caribbean cultures, originally written in English, French and (at least partly) Spanish and translated into Swedish. In these translations, the strategies of reduction and replacement are very rarely used. Retention is thus the clearly dominating strategy used by the different translators.

Jamaica Kincaid's novel *Lucy* deals with a young woman who migrates from Antigua in the West Indies to the United States to work as an au pair in New York. It consists of the young woman's experiences in and thoughts about the new country mixed with memories from her not always happy childhood. The protagonist demasks the mendacious happy family life of her employers while contemplating love and friendship in her surroundings. The novel was first published in hardback in 1990 in New York at Farrar, Straus and Giroux and in pocket edition by the same house in 2002. It was translated into Swedish in 1994 by Lena Fagerström and published by En bok för alla. Another publisher, Tranan, used the same translation in their paperback edition from 2019.

Both the first US paperback and the Swedish 1994 edition use Paul Gauguin's painting *Poèmes barbares* from 1896 on the cover – a stereotypical exoticizing packaging at first glance, but at the same time cosmopolitanizing given the world wide fame of Paul Gauguin. Whereas the paperback only includes a detail from the painting, the Swedish cover has a full representation, where also the monkey is visible – which could be seen as a reinforcement of the foreign character of the novel. In the Swedish paperback there is no exoticizing painting on the cover. Instead the cover lacks imagery and is only covered by the title of the novel *Lucy*, standing out in red handwriting on a yellow background.

Opening the source novel there is a photograph of Jamaica Kincaid, a short biographical note and a list of her other published novels. This is a formal presentation of the author focusing on her literary production and literary prizes – an authority argument aimed at convincing the source reader of the quality of the novel at hand. The target presentation of Kincaid is on the contrary placed at the back of the cover. This placement makes the presentation more direct and visible. The Swedish presentation is more personal than the English, informing us of her birth name and birthplace, playing more on pathos than on authority arguments in the beginning, but then recovering the authority by placing her as a professor at Harvard University. She is exotic (Caribbean), but still highly regarded within the American culture – a sign of high prestige.

The novel is a first-person narrative without footnotes. We follow the experiences of Lucy as she tells us about them. They are effectively narrated in a plain and precise style with touches of colloquialisms and with surprising turns in the syntax. There is no specific Caribbean variety of English in the source text, not even in the few dialogue sections. If we examine the first paragraph of the chapter 'The Tongue', 'Tungan', the translation strategy will unfold.

At 14 I had discovered that a tongue had no real taste.

Redan vid fjorton års ålder hade jag upptäckt att tungor egentligen inte har någon direkt smak.

(Already at the age of 14 I had discovered that tongues really do not have any taste.)

In this sentence, the translator makes the prose more wordy, emphasizing the oral narration character of the text. This strategy is, however, compensated for in the next sentence:

I was sucking the tongue of a boy named Tanner, and I was sucking his tongue because I had liked the way his fingers looked on the keys of the piano as he played it, and I had liked the way he looked from the back as he walked across the pasture, and also, when I was close to him, I liked the way behind his ears smelled. (44)

Jag stod och sög på en pojkes tunga, han hette Tanner, och orsaken till att jag smaskade på hans tunga var att jag gillade hans fingrar när de spelade piano, och jag hade också tyckt att than såg fin ut bakifrån när han gick över betesmarken och dessutom, på närmare håll, tyckte jag om lukten bakom hans öron. (45)

The present participle, the -ing form, needs a complement in Swedish which is 'stod och' (standing and) and 'because' becomes 'orsaken till' (the reason for). The clause 'I was sucking his tongue because' is translated with a colloquialism 'smaskade' (munched) retaining the colloquial style in the target text. The syntax is eased up and more concentrated, producing a fine rendering of the stylistic level of the narrative by compensation. This is an adequate translation in the sense of Toury (2012). It is source-oriented and keeps the overall structure distinctive of the source text, often by compensation as we have seen in examples one and two. The syntax, however, is idiomatically rebuilt in Swedish, but it follows the rhythm of the source text, and its idiosyncratic experiences come across as products of Lucy's mind. The colloquial style in vocabulary and syntax of the source text are retained.

If *Lucy* is the story of a West Indian immigrant in the United States, Maryse Condé's *Traversée de la mangrove* is a story about domestic migration within the Caribbean Sea. A body has been found in the mangrove swamps near the small town of Rivière de Sel in Guadeloupe. The novel is constructed around the victim, a suspicious character named Sancher. During the wake, each character in the novel relates his or her relationship and experiences with Sancher. The man is dead, possibly murdered, but he is resurrected in the stories told by the villagers. In the act of telling they discover their own complex history filled with shame, blood and rape. It is not as much the strange man Sancher that they fear, but the past that they never confronted. And surrounding the village there is the mangrove swamp – a dangerous place that acquires a proper voice in the narrative, reflecting the colonial heritage of the Caribbean.

Condé is the most translated Caribbean author in Sweden, with seven novels in Swedish. *Traversée de la mangrove* was translated by Helena Böhme and published by Leopard in 2007 as *Färden genom mangroven*. Studying the covers of the source and target texts of the novel there is a common denominator: the form of a mangrove plant, whether in an actual picture or in a stylized abstract form. The source cover is presented to the reader by the distinct design of the Folio publishing house with the white top where the name of the author is written in the left corner – the most important space according to Western visual grammar (Kress and van Leeuwen 2021) – where also the title of the novel in a slightly bigger font is printed. The rest of the cover consists of a photograph of a Black woman in bright colourful clothing who is crossing a water by help of an old tree reaching over to the other side. The woman is carrying a red saucepan on her head and is using two large sticks to keep her balance. In the foreground there is a plant with green leaves. The whole picture is reflected in the water, where you also catch a glimpse of the pale blue sky. The setting in the picture is clearly exotic and the photograph gives the cover a touch of authenticity. But this feeling of authenticity is revoked by the mirror effect, suggesting that everything is not as clear as it seems to be.

The Swedish hardcover from 2007 includes an abstraction of a mangrove tree and plays with the colours brown, black and baby blue. The title in baby blue heads the cover. The name of the publishing house Leopard is printed in small characters under the title and the name of the author Maryse Condé in white and on the cover is placed at the bottom of the cover in a larger font than the title – a kind of mirror effect from the front distribution on the source cover. The design of the abstraction plays with Western conceptions of naïve African art and conveys a modest exoticization of the cover focusing mainly on the name of the author. The Swedish paperback edition takes the exoticization a step further and depicts the mangrove in dark brown, blue and pink surrealistically scary on the cover. At the very bottom there is a quote from the newspaper *Dagens Nyheter* stating: 'Detta är en författare i Nobelprisklass' (This is an author of Nobel Prize quality), lifting the prestige of the author to the highest possible position.

In the French original, there is a quite lengthy presentation of Condé, presenting her as a prominent figure on the French literary scene:

> Maryse Condé (de son vrai nom Maryse Philcox) est née le 11 février 1937 à Pointe-á-Pitre (Guadeloupe) d'une famille aisée de huit enfants. Elle a fait ses études secondaires en Guadeloupe puis au Lycée Fénelon à Paris, et ses études de lettres à la Sorbonne. Elle se marie à un Guinéen et en 1960 part pour l'Afrique où elle enseigne pendant douze ans (en Guinée, au Ghana et au Sénégal). De retour en France en 1972, elle prépare une thèse de doctorat en littérature comparée à Paris-III sous la direction du professeur René Etiemble. Dès 1975 elle enseigne à l'université en France et est invitée sur de nombreux campus américains. Si à Paris elle obtient en 1987 le Grand Prix Littéraire de la Femme pour *Moi, Tituba sorcière ...*, en 1993, elle est la première femme à obtenir aux Etats-Unis le prix Puterbaugh pur l'ensemble de som oeuvre. *Les derniers rois mages* est son huitième ouvrage de fiction. Remariée à un anglais, Maryse Condé vit aux Etats-Unis où elle enseigne la littérature antillaise.

> (Maryse Condé (today Philcox) was born on February 11, 1937 at Pointe-á-Pitre (Guadeloupe) in a wealthy family with eight children. She completed her high school studies in Guadeloupe and then at the Lycée Fénelon in Paris, continuing with literature studies at the Sorbonne. She married a Guinean man in 1960 and left to live in Africa for 12 years (in Guiane, Ghana and Senegal). Returning to

France in 1972, she worked on a thesis in comparative literature at Paris III with professor René Etiemble as her supervisor. Starting in 1975, she gave classes at a French university and was repeatedly invited to several American universities. Back in Paris she was awarded the Grand Prix Littéraire de la Femme for the novel *Moi, Tituba sorcière* ..., and in 1993 she was the first female writer ever to receive the Puterbaugh Prize for her entire œuvre. Her eighth novel is *Les dernier rois mages*. Today, remarried to an Englishman, Maryse Condé lives in the United States where she teaches Caribbean literature.)

Condé is a professor of literature and an awarded fiction author from a French region in the Caribbean, but she has studied in France and at the Sorbonne. She is cosmopolitan, with experience of both Africa and the United States, who has won several prestigious literary prizes. The mere fact of being published at Folio by the Gallimard publishing house is in itself a sure sign of literary consecration.

In the Swedish target text the author is presented to the Swedish audience on the inside of the back of the dust jacket. There is a black-and-white photograph of Maryse Condé and a short peritext:

> Maryse Condé, född 1937 på Guadeloupe, anses vara en av den karibiska litteraturens främsta författare. Hon har skrivit ett tjugotal romaner, är flerfaldigt prisbelönad och har undervisat vid bland annat Harvard och Columbia University i New York.
>
> (Maryse Condé, born in 1937 in Guadeloupe is considered one of the most prominent Caribbean writers. She has written some twenty novels and has received several literary awards. She has given classes in literature, for instance at Harvard and Columbia Universities in New York.)

This formal presentation evaluates Condé as one of the most important writers in the Caribbean. In this text Condé's importance for French literature has no relevance and is not even mentioned. Her literary prizes are in focus as well as her connections with prestigious American universities. The American experience of Condé seems more important than her French literary consecration, possibly because of the importance of Anglo-American culture in Sweden.

The Swedish publication includes a short peritextual note giving the reader an insight into Helena Böhme's challenges in translating Condé's novel:

> De kreolska orden i kursiv stil finns förklarade i ordlista på sidan 252. Citatet på sidan 174–175 är hämtat ur Daggens härskare av Jacques Roumain i översättning av Jan Larsson, Ord & Visor förlag 2004. Bibelcitaten är hämtade ur 1917 års översättning: Svenska kyrkans diakonistyrelses bokförlag 1972.

(The Creol words in italics are explained in a glossary on page 252. The quotations on page 174–175 are fetched from Daggens härskare [The dynast of the dew] by Jacques Roumain in translation by Jan Larsson, Ord & Visor Publishing house 2004. The quotations from the Bible all stem from the 1917 translation by the Swedish church diaconical board publishing house, 1972.)

The first sentence states that the Creole words in italics are explained in a glossary at the end of the novel, thereby informing the reader about the function of the italics in the novel: to signal something deviant in the source text, i.e. the French Creole variety. This strategy seems to follow in Swedish what Lennon (2010: 10) identifies as the most important convention for managing other languages than English in bilingual novels in the American book market. They are retained and put into italics. In Sweden it seems that the same convention applies. The translator Helena Böhme has then chosen another way to deal with the novel's bilingual elements than the author or editor of the source text, in which there are added footnotes with French standard translations. At the end of the Swedish book there is hence an 'Alfabetisk ordlista över kreolska ord och uttryck' (an alphabetical glossary of Creole words and expressions), where thirty-four Creole expressions are translated and explained in Swedish. This is a distinct strategy of retention that reminds the reader that the text is a translation, in fact a translation of a translation, a meta-translation. The translator trusts in the reader's ability to interpret culturally specific references and understand foreign words in context.

The Swedish glossary covers about one-third of the Creole variety used in the source text. Another third of the local Creole vocabulary was translated into standard Swedish, a strategy that reduces the source text's vernacular from the culturally specific to a more general level. The remaining third of the Creole variety are kept in the target text, followed by a translation or explanation in standard Swedish. These cases often consist of whole proverbs or strophes from a song incorporated in the narrative as in the example that follows.

> Quand TI-Tor s'était installé, il avait eu beaucoup de gens pour s'offusquer et chanter méchamment:
> Kouli malaba
> Isi dan
> Pa peyiwl
> Coolie Malabar (injurieux.) Ce pays n'est pas le vôtre. (20)

(OBS: When Ti-Tor had settled, there were here many people, who were offended and maliciously sang:
Kouli malaba
Isi dan
Pa peyiwl
Coolie Malabar (insulting) This is not your country.)

När Ti-Tor bosatte sig här var det många som hade tagit anstöt och elakt sjungit:
Kouli malaba. Kuli Malabar
Isi dan Det här landet
Pa peyiw är inte ditt. (17)

(OBS:When Ti-Tor settled here many people were offended nd maliciously sang:
Kouli malaba. Kuli Malabar
Isi dan This country
Pa peyiw is not yours.)

In this example the translator keeps the Creole words in the target text and opts for the standard variety of French in the footnote from the source text and translates it adequately into Swedish, but then she also keeps the swear word in Creole, probably wanting to give the target text an exotic flavour even in the explained part, making the cultural Other manifest in the target text.

The most salient transformation in the target text is retention. In the source text the setting of the novel corresponds to the literary language – a mixture of standard French and the local Creole variety. In the target text the setting is merely evoked by the retention of Creole words and phrases vernacularizing the text, a translation strategy that challenges the expectancy norms of the Swedish readership.

Migration is also the central theme in Junot Díaz' *The Brief Wondrous Life of Oscar Wao*. The novel tells the story of an overweight New Jersey adolescent with Dominican roots who dreams of becoming the Dominican Tolkien and who longs for love. But the *fukú* – the ancient curse that has haunted his family for generations, dooming them to prison, torture and tragic accidents – is constantly in his way. We follow the nerdy hero Oscar, his runaway sister Lola and their ferocious mother Belicia from Santo Domingo to New Jersey and back again. The story is told in a mixture of street-smart English mixed with Spanish Dominican, giving authenticity to the struggling characters. The setting and the code-switching language of the novel thus correspond in the source text. Leah

Hager Cohen characterizes Díaz' literary technique and style in *The New York Times Sunday Book Review* as follows:

> Junot Díaz writes in an idiom so electrifying and distinct it's practically an act of aggression, at once alarming and enthralling, even erotic in its assertion of sudden intimacy [...]. Breaking easily and often out of first-person narration to address his readers directly, Díaz flatters us with his confidence. Yet his prose also throws up walls, equally abruptly and equally seductively. Refusing to condescend or even pause for edification, the narrative moves along at speed, exciting us with its demands. This, then, is the Díaz rhythm: a syncopated stagger-step between opacity and transparency, exclusion and inclusion, defiance and desire.
>
> (Hager Cohen 2012)

Doris Sommer underlines that '[c]ode switching prefers the surprise element of an estranged expression to the predictability of one legitimate language: it values artistry over stable identity. And it invites an acknowledgement of aesthetic agency over a politics of cultural recognition' (Sommer 2004: 37).

Díaz' novel was first published in the USA in 2007 by Penguin, and in the UK in 2008 by Faber & Faber. It was translated into Swedish by Niclas Hval and published in 2009 by Bonniers as *Oscar Waos korta förunderliga liv*. Before the narrative starts, the source text paperback, which is the text examined here, has a presentation of the author followed by four appraising quotes from *The New York Times* and *The Times Literary Supplement*. The presentation is focused on authority arguments informing about the author's university degrees, literary prizes and current position teaching creative writing at MIT (Massachusetts Institute of Technology), all very prestigious tokens of a highly consecrated author within the American literary culture. The presentation reads as follows:

> Junot Díaz was born in Santa Domingo, Dominican Republic. He is a graduate of Rutgers University and received his master of fine arts degree from Cornell University. His collection of short stories, *Drown*, was described as a 'dazzlingly talented first book' by Hermione Lee in the Independent on Sunday. He teaches creative writing at MIT. *The Brief Wondrous Life of Oscar Wao* won both the Pulitzer and the American National Book Critics Circle Award for Fiction.

Then follows a quote from the *Fantastic Four* from 1966 and an excerpt from a poem by Derek Walcott. In the Swedish paperback the author is presented on the back cover:

> Junot Díaz, född 1968 i Dominikanska republiken, har rönt stora framgångar i sitt hemland USA. Han har skrivit för the New Yorker, undervisar i kreativt

skrivande och har publicerat en novellsamling. Oscar Waos korta förunderliga liv är hans första roman. Den har tilldelats Pulitzerpriset och hyllats av en enig kritikerkår.

(Junot Díaz, born in 1968 in the Dominican Republic, is very successful in his homeland USA. He has written for *The New Yorker* and teaches creative writing and has published a collection of short stories. *The Brief Wondrous Life of Oscar Wao* is his first novel. It has been awarded the Pulitzer Prize for Fiction and has been unanimously praised by critics.)

This presentation is more general and distant than the American one, but just like the source text presentation it is based on authority arguments. One peculiar thing is that the target text stresses that Díaz has written in *The New Yorker* before mentioning his works. To write for that prestigious literary magazine is a sure sign of consecration – a token that he shares with Jamaica Kincaid. In the Swedish book, the reader finds translations of the *Fantastic Four* quote and the Walcott poem. An addition above the colophons is the information on who translated the poem and the novel's quotes from J. R. R. Tolkien's *The Lord of the Rings* into Swedish, which is a distinct reminder of the fact that the following text is a translation.

An interesting fact having to do with the occurring code-switching between the American slang and the Dominican Spanish is that the translator has opted for a very source-oriented translation strategy translating titles of chapters and subsections that are in English in the source text but retaining its Spanish titles, surprising the Swedish reader and challenging the expectancy norms for translated fiction in Sweden. For instance, the fifth subsection in the first chapter 'Oscar Comes Close' is translated as 'Oscar är nära', followed by the sixth subsection 'Amor de Pendejo' left untranslated as 'Amor de Pendejo' and the seventh 'Oscar in Love' translated literally as 'Oscar är kär'. This strategy distinctly underlines the translated status of the Swedish target text.

The translator uses similar retention strategies throughout the novel. He consequently leaves the Dominican vernacular untouched also on the syntactic and lexical levels. The Swedish reader is thus estranged by the fact that the setting and the code-switching of the novel do not correspond in the target text. The first term to come to mind when trying to describe the language mixture in the novel is Spanglish, since the novel is written in English but with a great many inserted Spanish/Dominican words, phrases and whole sentences. Spanglish is often used as a term implying an insecurity in one language or the other, but Díaz and his narrator Yunior are fluent in both languages, which is why this term cannot be used to describe the special 'Diaz dialect' in the novel. Tactical bilingualism on the other hand, as proposed by Laura Fennell (2015: 19), captures this specific literary idiom better. It not only represents the ability to speak and write in two languages, but also the ability to seamlessly integrate one language into another simultaneously. Consequently, Díaz never identifies Spanish insertions with footnotes or italics as Condé does with the Creole variety in the French novel studied. The result is a seamless language blending. Italics are only used in the English variety to convey emphasis.

The sociolinguist Lourdes Torres identifies an ascending order of accessibility for the monolingual English speakers in bilingual texts. Her categories cover three different strategies used by the bilingual narrator: 1) easily accessed or cushioned Spanish; 2) gratifying the bilingual reader; and 3) radical bilingualism (Torres 2007: 77). The first category includes words or phrases that most monolinguals in the United States know and feel comfortable with, for example 'abuelo', 'ojo' and 'buenos dias'. It is used in a novel as a trick to lure monolingual readers with exoticism. This category might also work for monolingual Swedish readers and can be considered as an expected part of the retention translation strategy. The second category is more difficult for monolingual English-speaking readers and more enjoyable for bilinguals. In the translation even more so, considering that the Swedish-Spanish bilingual population is much smaller in Sweden than the English–Spanish population is in the United States. This strategy uses Spanish words that are less known to English speakers, for instance 'maricón', 'pendejo' and 'carajito'. They are translatable but do not possess the exact same emotional charge in English or Swedish. In the Swedish translation they are even less accessible to the monolingual but tolerant reader. This is an example of Torres' second category of literary bilingualism:

[…] what every single Dominican, from the richest Jabao in Mao to the poorest güey in El Buey, from the oldest anciano sanmarcorisano to the littlest carajito in San Francisco […] (3)

([…] det som varenda dominikan visste, från den rikaste jabao i Mao till den fattigaste güey i El Buey från den äldste anciano sanmarcorisano till den minsta carajito i San Francisco […])

The vocabulary used in the Swedish translation is not transparent for the Swedish reader. The phrases 'jabao i Mao' and 'güey i El Buey' can perhaps be approximately understood from the sound effects, but 'anciano sanmarcorisano' and 'carajito' remain unclear. In the following quote, Niclas Wahl has also retained all of Díaz' Spanish words:

> Listen, palomo: You have to grab a muchacha, y metérselo. That will take care of everything. Start with a fea. Coje that fea y metérselo. Tío Rudolfo had four kids with three different women so the nigger was without doubt the family's resident metéselo expert. (24)

> (Hör på här, palomo: du måste få tag i en muchacha, y metérselo. Då fixar sig allting. Börja med en fea. Coje den där fean y metéselo! Tío Rudolfo hade fyra barn med tre olika kvinnor och var helt klart familjens metéseloexpert.) (25)

With the word 'metéseloexpert' Hval has created a neologism by mixing Swedish and Dominican vernacular morphemes, a clear example of retention. In these examples the co-text helps the Swedish monolingual reader, but the effect of exclusion is often distinct. The last quote also includes a rare exception to Hval's retention strategy when Díaz' controversial word 'nigger' is omitted. In this particular case, the narrator's use of vernacular language is reduced by the translator.

Torres' third category, radical bilingualism, speaks entirely to bilinguals. It gives the monolingual the feeling of the immigrant's situation in the new country meeting a new language. It may even be hard to understand for bilinguals, if they do not have access to the specific slang variety of Spanish such as the Dominican slang word 'parigüiayo'. When these vernacular words are retained in the Swedish translation, the exclusion of the monolingual reader is complete, fully breaking the expectancy norms of Swedish translation:

> Tú ta llorando por una muchacha? She hauled Oscar to his feet by his ear. Mami, stop it, his sister cried, stop it! She threw him to the floor. Dale un galletazo, she panted, then see if the little puta respects you. (14)

> (Tú ta llorando por una muchacha? Hon tog tag i Oscars öra och drog upp honom på fötter. Mami, sluta! Skrek hans syster. Sluta! Hon kastade honom till golvet. Dale un galletazo, flämtade hon. Sedan får vi se om den lilla putan visar dig någon respekt.) (25)

In this example a full sentence in Dominican is starting the scene. It is Oscar's mother giving him a lesson in life. The whole sentence is retained in the target text, even the oral variety of incorrect verb declination in 'Tú ta' instead of 'Tú estás'. The complete sentence 'Dale un galletazo' is also retained and the word 'puta' has been transformed into a Swedish word by adding the Swedish definite article -n, 'putan'.

In some cases, Hval has retained English expressions to create new compound words of English and Swedish, using the fact that English is the second language of most Swedes. Here, the bilingual source text turns into a multilingual target text, creating an additional level of the 'Díaz dialect' in the Swedish target text.

Footnotes are abundant in the source text. They are mostly written in English and are adequately translated into Swedish. They have three main functions in the narrative. Firstly, they serve as reminders of important historical persons and events in the Dominican Republic mostly connected to the former dictator Rafael Trujillo. Secondly, they explain some of the references to science fiction and fantasy. And thirdly, they are used by the omnipotent storyteller (who turns out to be Oscar's former brother-in-law, Yunior) to apostrophe the reader with literary meta-comments on how to start a chapter or to explain the macho culture of the average Dominican male.

In sum, the most salient transformation in Jamaica Kincaid's *Lucy*, Maryse Condé's *Traversée de la mangrove* and Junot Díaz' *The Brief Wondrous Life of Oscar Wao* is the different translators' ascending degree of source-orientation. These different degrees correspond to Gideon Toury's concept of adequate translation (1995), Lawrence Venuti's concept of foreignizing translation (1995) and Philip Lewis' of abusive fidelity (2004). In *Lucy*, retention is noticeable as a result of the adequate translation strategy adopted by the translator. As Itamar Even-Zohar reminds us, an adequate translation realizes in the target language the textual relationships of a source text with no breach of its own basic linguistic system (1975: 43). If adequacy is adopted, the translation will be dominated by attempts to have the ensuing text reflect the source text along with the norms embodied in it (Toury 2012: 79). The translator of *Lucy* has worked very much according to an adequate translation strategy on the textual level, thereby meeting the demands of the Swedish reading public as expressed in the expectancy norms for translations of high prestige literature (cf. Chesterman 1997: 64). This orientation is perspicuous in *Lucy* where the translator constructs a monolingual translation from a monolingual source text.

In *Traversé de la mangrove*, retention is made more obvious by the foreignizing translation strategy chosen by the translator when working with words and phrases in the source text in the local vernacular French Creol. The foreign in foreignizing translation is not a transparent representation of an essence that resides in the foreign text, but a strategic construction whose value is contingent on the current target language situation (Venuti 1995: 20). The Swedish translator of *Traversée de la mangrove* has adopted the foreignizing strategy in her work with conveying the French Creole variety of the source text in Swedish. She standardizes one-third of the occurring Creole variety, keeps one-third with an explanation and leaves the last third unexplained. These are three ways of gradually challenging the expectancy norms of the Swedish reading public – which is a tolerant readership when it comes to foreign cultural phenomena. A bilingual code-switching source text is thus rendered as a bilingual code-switching target text. However, the reader is rarely excluded from understanding.

Finally, in *The Brief Wondrous Life of Oscar Wao* retention is constructed by the risk-taking abusive fidelity translation strategy of the translator (Lewis 2004: 262–4). This strategy involves supplementing the source text and giving it renewed energy. It is a strong forceful translation that values experimentation, tampers with usage and seeks to match the polyvalencies or plurivocities or expressive stresses of the original by producing its own (Lewis 2004: 262). The risk-taking in the translation follows and sometimes exaggerates that of the source text, seamless mixing languages and code-switching, sometimes excluding the Swedish reader from the radical bilingualism in the source text, but also adding a new layer when creating neologisms of mixed Dominican–Swedish and English–Swedish morphemes as a way of conveying and amplifying the 'Díaz dialect' in Swedish. A bilingual code-mixing source text then becomes a multilingual code-mixing translation. The abusive fidelity risks testing the tolerance of the Swedish readers by breaking and abusing the translation expectancy norm for high-prestige literary translation and by challenging two of the most profound ethical rules of translation: trust and understanding (cf. Chesterman 1997).

Concluding remarks

The case studies above have dealt with twenty translations: two translations from Swedish into French (Katarina Mazetti's *Grabben i graven bredvid* and Therese Bohman's *Den drunknade*); eight translations from Swedish into

English (Jan Fridegård's *Jag Lars Hård, Tack för himlastegen* and *Barmhärtighet*, Moa Martinson's *Kvinnor och äppelträd* and *Mor gifter sig*, Ivar Lo-Johansson's *Godnatt, jord* and *Bara en mor* and Stieg Larsson's *Män som hatar kvinnor*); three from Italian into Swedish (Erri de Luca's *Montedidio*, Valeria Parrella's *Lo spazio bianco* and Elena Ferrante's *L'amica geniale*); four from English into Swedish (NoViolet Bulawayo's *We Need New Names*, Ngugi wa Thiong'o's *The River Between*, Jamaica Kincaid's *Lucy* and Junot Díaz' *The Brief Wondrous Life of Oscar Wao*); two from Portuguese into Swedish (António Lobo Antunes' *A ordem natural das coisas* and Mia Couto's *O outro pé da Sereia*); and one from French into Swedish (Maryse Condé's *Traversée de la mangrove*). According to the world system theory of translation patterns, these twenty editions include four translations from the hyper-central language into a semi-peripheral language; eight from a semi-peripheral language into a hyper-central one; one from a central language into a semi-peripheral language; two from a semi-peripheral language into a central one; three from one semi-peripheral into another semi-peripheral language; and two from a peripheral language into a semi-peripheral one. Most kinds of literary traffic to and from semi-peripheral literatures are thus represented in these cases.

In these twenty translations, translators and publishers have dealt with source culture vernaculars in different ways. In six of the translated texts, we find instances of reduction. Source culture specificities in novels by Maryse Condé, Junot Díaz, Katarina Mazetti, Therese Bohman and Mia Couto have been somewhat neutralized in the translation process, in a variety of ways. Proper names of persons, places and brands have been omitted or neutralized, and so have culturally specific words for fauna, flora, artefacts, food and behaviour. The source texts' cultural specificities are also reduced by translators' tendency to remove or neutralize colloquialisms and idiomatic expressions. Another kind of reduction occurs when the inclusion of bilingual elements is omitted and the use of non-standard syntax is standardized in the target text. Furthermore, translators and editors reduce vernacular rootedness by omitting italics, footnotes and source culture references on book covers, as well as through cosmopolitanizing acclaim in dust jacket citations.

Five of the translations show an extensive use of replacement. In Katarina Mazetti's, Elena Ferrante's, Valeria Parella's, NoViolet Bulawayo's and Ngugu wa Thiong'o's novels, source culture specificities have been replaced by target culture particularities. In these target texts the vernaculars have been dislocated, a process that can be divided into two different strategies: source culture specificities are replaced by 1) existing or 2) made up target culture counterparts. In our material, the first strategy is the most common one. Source culture-specific proper names, food, musical instruments, building materials, school systems, administrative systems, accommodation forms, expressions, colloquialisms, sociolect and the way persons address each other are often replaced by real target culture versions.

The most common strategy is retention. Eleven of the novels include significant instances of retaining source culture references and phenomena, thereby reinforcing the distance between target and source culture. The source culture vernaculars in the novels by Jamaica Kincaid, Maryse Condé, Junot Díaz, Jan Fridegård, Moa Martinson, Ivar Lo-Johansson, Therese Bohman, Elena Ferrante, Erri De Luca, NoViolet Bulawayo, António Lobo Antunes, Mia Couto and Ngugi wa Thiong'o have all been made more salient and explicit. Instances of retention are to be found on every level of these target texts. In the narratives as such, the source culture vernacular is acknowledged when names of persons, places, buildings, artefacts, holidays and food are kept, and when source culture references are maintained and unexplained. Another distinct acknowledgement of the source culture vernacular is the inclusion of source language words in the target text. Retention also occurs when the translator has invented proper names and used literal translations of source language expressions, and when non-standard source text grammar, words and expressions – including bilingual elements – are maintained by the translator. A special case of this kind of retention is the translators' invention of bilingual neologisms – composed of either target and source languages or target language and non-standard languages in the source text. Peritextual retention of the source culture vernacular include localized front covers, the translator's visibility on the cover, added back cover presentations of the author, introductory translator notes, added footnotes and endnotes, added glossaries of non-standard words and expressions, stress on the text's or the author's foreignness and comparisons with other source culture phenomena. It seems, then, that cultural exchange involving the semi-periphery permits an openness towards what is foreign and unfamiliar. In the case of the Swedish literary culture, Sweden's growing importance in the world republic of letters has not erased the memory of what it means and feels like to be peripheral in relation to a powerful other. Even though Sweden, as will be shown in the following, is becoming a more closed literary culture – in the sense that the number of translations into Swedish is decreasing in relation to the number of

Swedish originals – the translations themselves still show important signs of openness towards the world.

One of the translations studied, Reg Keeland's English version of Stieg Larsson's thriller *Män som hatar kvinnor*, *The Girl with the Dragon Tattoo*, does not include any significant transformation of the story's rootedness in source culture specificities. The widely distributed English translation is definitely transformed, as Larsson's prose is significantly slimmed, almost paragraph by paragraph, but these continuous shortenings do not reduce domestic Swedish references. *The Girl with the Dragon Tattoo* is thus just as rooted in the Swedish vernacular setting as *Män som hatar kvinnor*.

One conclusion to be drawn from these case studies is that one kind of transformation does not rule out the use of other strategies. In many of the translations, translators and publishers have made significant use of more than one of these three transformations. In some cases, a kind of balance is achieved in which the source culture vernacular is diminished in some ways and amplified in others. Another observation is that one and the same strategy can have opposite effects on the visibility of the source culture vernacular. Translator Marianne Eyre's ability to maintain António Lobo Antunes' experimental prose in her Swedish rendition of the novel, for example, simultaneously prompts both vernacularizing and cosmopolitanizing effects. A third conclusion is that genre and market position seem to be important factors prompting different strategies to deal with source culture vernaculars. Highbrow status and small-scale distribution tend to prompt retention and thus enhance cultural particularities and stress cultural differences, whereas lowbrow status and large-scale distribution tend to prompt reduction and replacement and thus blur distinctions and even out cultural differences.

Literary translators' challenging task to handle source texts' cultural specificities is not a binary choice between two mutually exclusive alternatives. There are at least three distinct strategies available, and an extensive variety of combinations between them. If we go beyond Friedrich Schleiermacher's tenacious two-way model, we will also have a clearer view of the complex set of objectives behind specific translational choices. Reducing source culture particularities and thereby evening out the cultural difference between reader and text, is usually done to give access to the text, to make it understandable, but the strategy of reduction also avoids forcing the reader to focus on insignificant elements of the narrative. When Lena Grumbarch and Catherine Marcus neutralize the Swedish newspaper *Dagens Nyheter* to 'le journal' and the Swedish bank 'Föreningsbanken' to 'le banque' in Katarina Mazetti's *Grabben i graven bredvid*, for example, they give the French-speaking reader smooth access to the Swedish story but they also avoid creating an unnecessary interpretive uncertainty. A different kind of reduction occurs when a narrative is lifted from a culturally specific position to a cosmopolitan sphere through stylistic retention. This is what happens in the Swedish translation of António Lobo Antunes' *A ordem natural das coisas* when the translator maintains Antunes' stylistic idiosyncrasies in her Swedish prose, thus neutralizing the novel's vernacular rootedness and positioning it in the cosmopolitan canon of modernism.

Plainly giving access is not the only desirable effect when source culture particularities are replaced with target culture phenomena. When the use of Received Pronunciation in NoViolet Bulawayo's *We Need New Names* is replaced with a posh Stockholm dialect, for example, the translator wants to keep the impression of social hierarchy between the novel's characters. The replacement strategy thus helps to maintain a socially nuanced cultural setting, respecting the distinctions and diversity within the depicted source culture. And when the metalinguistic issues addressed in Elena Ferrante's *L'amica geniale* are replaced with totally dissimilar Swedish examples, the Swedish translator respects the untranslatability of specific Italian words and expressions. The target text does not attempt to convey what it cannot convey.

The strategy of retention leads to many different effects and is pursued for different reasons. Adding an extensive number of footnotes to Swedish proletarian novels has an educational objective, besides reminding the reader that what she or he is reading is a translation. This strategy gives the translators opportunities to teach the readers about a foreign culture, but the limited text in the footnote might give an inadequate impression of the source culture vernacular, at odds with literature's potential of conveying nuances and complexity. When a whole and very particular socioeconomic system is summed up in a couple of sentences, for example, culturally and historically remote conditions are generalized and simplified, giving the target text reader the impression that the cultural Other can be totally explained, known and understood. According to Venuti, footnotes are exemplary of foreignizing translation strategies, since they highlight cultural difference, and provide guidance in how to understand that difference. However, it has also been suggested that footnotes produce almost the opposite effect, by 'sweeping the floor' for the reader, eliminating all kinds of resistance, while at the same time dictating a specific kind of reading, namely a mimetic one (Kullberg 2011: 58). In our analysis, we have discussed both these perspectives.

A very different reason to retain cultural difference governs the Swedish translation of Junot Díaz' *The Brief Wondrous Life of Oscar Wao*. Instead of educating, the translator wants to expose the target reader to the same kind of lack of control and limited understanding that many source text readers have to deal with. When the translator retains the bilingual character of Díaz' prose, he is in fact creating a very different kind of bilingual – and to a certain extent even trilingual – target text. Whereas the American translators of Swedish proletarian realism tend to nationalize the novels' vernacular settings, Díaz' Swedish translator works against stereotypical ideas of national identity and portrays the foreign setting as culturally diverse. A similar effect is evident in the Swedish translation of Erri De Luca's *Montedidio*. When the regional Neapolitan culture and language are retained and made explicit while the national Italian frame is obscured, the translator erases national identities and puts forward the regional vernacular as the primary context in which we live.

5

Positioning the Swedish literary semi-periphery

Chapter 2 described how cultural intermediaries allow literary texts to move in and out of the Swedish literary semi-periphery through translation and publishing. Using information such as book publishing data from the National Library of Sweden, we were able to sketch the contours of each translation flow, and to discuss similarities between source and target language publication patterns. By looking at the position of the publishers in the respective literary fields, and the publishers' *selection* and *framing*, we noted a few instances of affinity – *horizontal isomorphism* – and cases in which the translated literary work underwent a form of transformation as a source publisher of one kind was replaced with a target language publisher of another. In the case of Swedish translation of Lusophone literatures, we noted, such transformation is very common as micro-publishers play a major role in making this literature available to Swedish readers.

Turning to the translation of Nobel laureates – including the 'alternative' Nobel laureate Maryse Condé – in Chapter 3, we described the positions of the translators involved in bringing the Nobel laureate's work into Swedish, but also the nuances and the shifting effects on the authors' career before and after the award. While the reception of the Nobel Prize is one of the highest forms of consecration, it has not always led to wider circulation for all the authors we looked at. For Wole Soyinka for instance, already relatively widely translated, being awarded the Nobel in 1986 did not generate a wave of translations, even if the rapid translation of his Nobel lecture into French signalled an interest in the prize in French literary culture. For earlier Swedish laureates Martinson and Johnson, on the other hand, the prize had a clear impact and sustained their continuing translation into French (as well as other languages).

Chapter 4 took a case-based approach to the translation into Swedish and looked at a number of literary texts with a focus on translation strategies. In critical dialogue with Lawrence Venuti's theorization of translation strategies as expressing either *domestication* or *foreignization*, we investigated translation strategies through an optic composed of *reduction*, *retention* and *replacement*. In an extension of Venuti's hypothesis that translation strategies are coherent through a literary work – which are marked by being *either or* – we noted that all three strategies were used in the translation of several of the texts, but that 'reduction' and 'replacement' appeared more common at the popular end of the literary spectrum and a tolerance for the unidiomatic was more common at the literary end. This is a conclusion which confirms earlier studies (e.g. Lindqvist 2002). In answer to the question of whether particular translation strategies dominate the literary semi-periphery we conclude that the literary status of the work, the scope of distribution, the level of narrative localization and the level of un-standardized language used in the source text are key determining features which shape translation.

In this chapter, we turn from the decisions made by publishers and other agents in the literary fields, and translation strategies shaping the texts, to the broader characteristics of literary translation flows. This is because we consider Sweden's *position* in the world literary space to be best conceived as a *constellation of relations*. In what follows, we examine significant features and some of the changes that have occurred over the period studied. We look at aspects to do with the position of translated works close to the small-scale or large-scale pole of production, and further, at variations in genre, changes over time and the composition of the total volume of translations with respect to gender. The examination will allow us to sketch some of the *conditions* that underlie the transfer of literary works through translation

Three significant features of the Swedish semi-periphery

In the last decades, the publishing business across the world has undergone a number of changes, the broad outlines of which are well documented. Globalization in the literary sphere has meant an extension of the 'market logic'; waves of mergers and acquisitions have made publishing houses part of media conglomerates; and the increasing significance of marketing departments and budget allocation have put new pressure on books in more segments to sell. In addition, the emergence of the profession of literary agents has contributed to higher advances for authors and the increasing importance of 'cross-over' books which combine traits of popular literature with literary fiction (Brouillette 2007, Thompson 2010, Sapiro 2016). These developments have also transformed publishing in Sweden (e.g. *Böckernas tid* 2018).

Another effect of literary globalization, as Rebecca Walkowitz has argued, is the diminishing hold between author and place among some of the contemporary literary stars. 'Born-translated' literature, she writes, whose originators include the likes of J. M. Coetzee and Haruki Murakami who receive wide critical acclaim and sell well (as well as more popular authors such as J. K. Rowling and Dan Brown), does not originate within one literary system but exists in several systems at once. One concrete manifestation of the transnational life of this type of literature is that it may appear in translation simultaneously to, or even before, its original publication (Walkowitz 2015). Walkowitz' argument cuts against Casanova's insistence on the significance of particular metropoles, and their role as literary arbiters determining the literary 'now'.

Despite these developments, we hold that the division of the field of literary production into a large-scale and a small-scale circuit remains a useful analytical approach, not least in the study of translated literature, and this is because translation at opposite ends of the literary spectrum involves different *actors*, different *logics* and different *genres*. In addition, the temporal dimension of literary consecration – through which recognition is granted first in one location and subsequently in others – is still important for the large majority of writers.

Moving towards a description of the Swedish literary semi-periphery, we proceed in two steps. First we describe what we see as three significant general characteristics: the importance of the state in literary exchange, the existence of a specific northern translation field and the strong position of Swedish translators, grounded in the fact that Sweden has a relatively autonomous translation field. With respect to the transnational – more precisely Scandinavian – translation field, we describe some of the trends occurring during the period studied in this book. In the second part of the chapter, we provide overviews of the respective translation flows.

The state's role in the Swedish literary semi-periphery is at once similar to other states' and marked by specifically national characteristics. Translations of fiction are often enabled through support programmes aiming to export national literature or allow literary cultures to access literature which has been recognized as valuable (van Es and Heilbron 2015: 307; Sapiro 2016: 84; Brems et al. 2017: 13). In Sweden, the cultural agency Kulturrådet is one of the government authorities that channel state funding to translation projects aimed at disseminating Swedish literature across the globe. But the agency also supports literary translations into Swedish, and the volume and character of Kulturrådet's support is large enough to make it a central facilitator of literary exchange. Its significance is further amplified by including translations from English in the support programmes. Support is also granted to the largest publishers, and extends well into the segment of 'mid-brow' literature, or literature with a wide global readership. In the years 2004–2018, for instance, Kulturrådet sponsored translations of authors such as Elena Ferrante, Umberto Eco, Dario Fo, Alessandro Baricco, José Saramago, António Lobo Antunes, Philip Roth, Chinua Achebe and Margaret Atwood.

Författarfonden (the Author's Fund), also funded by the Swedish government (more precisely through a compensation system for royalty losses caused by book loans in public libraries) is another important, if indirect, supporter of translated upmarket literature through scholarships to translators. Providing a range of working scholarships for translators – from one-year to ten-year grants, and including a renewable ten-year plan of economic support – the state finances the pillars of a relatively autonomous translation field.

Initiatives by other states, it should be added, also affect Swedish literary imports. Cartaditalia, a publisher of Italian literature in Sweden, is an example of a literary actor established with the help of the Italian cultural institute. For 'smaller' literatures like the Lusophone the financial support of Portuguese cultural institutes such as Camões and the Portuguese General Directorate for Books, Archives and Libraries (Direcção-Geral do Livro e das Bibliotecas) is crucial for a large portion of the Portuguese and Afro-Portuguese translations that come to be published in Sweden (Schwartz and Edfeldt forthcoming). This state-sponsored exchange of literature, Sapiro and others have observed, has historically favoured what she calls 'national' authors, but has recently, due to sociocultural struggles and shifting discourses, become more diverse.

The existence of a relatively autonomous Scandinavian translation field is central to the Swedish semi-peripheral position. Taking the globally high ranking of Swedish and Danish as literary source languages in global translation flows, and using data from the Scandinavian National Bibliographies, Lindqvist has recently shown that domination patterns in the global translation field are reproduced on a smaller scale within the Scandinavian literary geography. The most dominant source languages (English, French, German) have a given position even within Scandinavian literatures, but the regional languages also play a crucial role in being the most translated languages – except English – in this space. Examining four relevant dimensions of publishing and translation – 1) general translation rates, i.e. the amount of translated literature within the total output of published literature; 2) the non-translation rate, i.e. the number of published works in (mainly) English in relation to the total output of published literature; 3) the top five source languages; 4) the position of the Scandinavian languages as source languages in the global translation field – Lindqvist unveils a regional struggle between literary languages which indicates the existence of a regional translation field in which Swedish literature occupies the centre.

Over the nearly four decades covered in this study, has Sweden's regional central position changed? If so, in what ways, and what might possible changes tell us about the literary semi-periphery? Placing the focus on publishing in Sweden, and on the publishing of Swedish literature (as opposed to the Scandinavian focus and total publishing output referenced above), in what follows, we will outline the tendencies of literary import through translation.

The data is retrieved from the Swedish National Bibliography (NB) and Svensk bokkatalog (the Swedish Book Transcript) and organized in Tables 1–4, each table covering the publication data for one decade, 1981–1990, 1991–2000 and so forth. It may be noted that the numbers published in the National

Table 1 The relation of published original fiction and translated fiction (new works and new editions) expressed as percentages of translated fiction during the period 1981–1990 (National Bibliography, 1981–1990, Svensk Bokförteckning [Swedish Book Transcript] 1981–1990)

Published fiction in Sweden							
Year	Swedish fiction			Translated fiction			Translation
	New lit.	New ed.	Total	New lit.	New ed.	Total	%
1981	624	134	758	1,019	267	1,286	62
1982	586	147	733	871	300	1,171	61
1983	549	136	685	852	264	1,116	61
1984	743	161	904	930	319	1,249	58
1985	586	167	753	892	369	1,261	62
1986	694	172	866	1,029	363	1,392	63
1987	675	219	894	894	459	1,353	60
1988	687	195	882	989	506	1,495	63
1989	668	170	838	878	424	1,302	61
1990	712	195	907	927	441	1,368	60
Total no.	6,524	1,696	8,220	9,281	3,712	12,993	61
Total %	31	8	39	44	17	61	

Bibliography do not exactly correspond with the real numbers for published literature during the current year since there is a delay in the reporting and registration at the National Library of Sweden. But the delay is constant over the years and does not really affect the outcome. The numbers in the NB are still the best source of information available.

In the tables the column 'Translation %' accounts for the percentage of translations in the total output of published *fiction* (original plus translations) during each year of the decade and for the decade as a whole. It is the most interesting column in the tables since it readily delivers numbers for a comparison of the development over the decades. But the other columns both concerning new works and new editions for domestic and translated literature reveal the interplay of translated literature with domestic confirming its central or more marginal position within specific time spans.

Thus, from Table 1 we can conclude that the Swedish literary space was extremely open during the 1980s, when translated fiction had an exceedingly central position. More than half of the published fiction, 61 per cent, during the decade consisted of translations, showing that translated fiction constituted a dominant force in literary renewal well in the centre of literary production. The variation over the decade is very stable ranging from 58–63 per cent. It is worth noticing also that the numbers of new translated works and new editions exceed the domestic production of fiction, which confirms the centrality of translated fiction during the period. Hence, in the 1980s approximately 60 per cent of the published fiction in Sweden consisted of translations.

This strong position of translated fiction was probably an aftermath of the abolishment of the regulation of the Swedish book market in the 1970s, when book prices and distribution channels were fixed. Unregulated distribution channels and free book prices raised fears about the domination of bestsellers at the expense of quality literature, which led to a reform of government subsidies for literature in 1975 (Svedjedal 1993: 794–5). According to Rüegg (2020: 5), these subsidies played an important role for publication of translated fiction and for minor publishing houses working with translated literature in the Swedish literary market.

During the 1990s, as we can see in Table 2, the translation rate within the Swedish literary space for fiction decreased, starting off with a rather high percentage of 58, reaching the lowest level in 1994 and 1996 with 52 per cent, then slowly recovering to 56 per cent at the turn of the millennium. The decrease might reflect the introduction of a new player in the Swedish book

Table 2 The relation of published original fiction and translated fiction (new works and new editions) expressed as percentages of translated fiction during the period 1991–2000 (National Bibliography 1991–2000, Svensk Bokförteckning [Swedish Book Transcript] 1991–2000)

Published fiction in Sweden							
Year	Swedish fiction			Translated fiction			Translation
	New lit.	New ed.	Total	New lit.	New ed.	Total	%
1991	690	205	895	859	392	1,251	58
1992	687	259	946	716	317	1,033	52
1993	746	215	961	759	346	1,105	53
1994	686	231	917	672	314	986	52
1995	623	212	835	625	384	1,009	53
1996	618	247	865	589	345	934	52
1997	647	184	831	664	335	999	54
1998	620	220	840	598	428	1,026	55
1999	574	256	830	617	403	1,020	55
2000	535	261	796	627	402	1,029	56
Total no.	6,426	2,290	8,896	6,726	3,666	10,392	54
Total %	33	12	46	35	19	54	

market affecting translated literature – the literary agent (Göthberg 2001: 27). Literary agents hardly existed in Sweden prior to the 1990s. The dip in numbers for translated literature during the mid-1990s might mirror the instability created by the new conditions of the book market induced by this literary intermediary. Agents play an important role as gatekeepers introducing foreign literature to publishers. Publishers had to redefine their ways of doing business in relation to both foreign writers and the agents, especially since 'Ramavtalet' – a general agreement between the literary agents concerning remuneration and fees – ceased to exist in 1996. A new space was thus created for the literary agent. This re-organization of the book market might also have affected the decade as a whole, since the average translation rate for the decade amounted to 54 per cent, 7 per cent lower than in the 1980s, indicating that translated fiction lost ground. Nevertheless, translations still constitute more than half of the published fiction in Sweden. This weakened but still rather strong position is also demonstrated by the fact that translated fiction and new editions of translated fiction still exceed domestic production. However, the decrease can now be seen as a tendency.

Table 3 shows that during the first two years after the turn of the century the translation rates within Swedish fiction surmounted the numbers of the previous decade average at 57 per cent and 55 per cent. However, after a fairly steep decrease to 42 per cent in 2004 the numbers never exceeded 50 per cent

Table 3 The relation of published original fiction and translated fiction (new works and new editions) expressed as percentages of translated fiction during the period 2001–2010 (National Bibliography 2001–2010, Svensk Bokförteckning [Swedish Book Transcript] 2001–2010)

Published fiction in Sweden							
Year	Swedish fiction			Translated fiction			Translation
	New lit.	New ed.	Total	New lit.	New ed.	Total	%
2001	543	244	787	650	386	1,036	57
2002	599	245	844	621	434	1,055	55
2003	752	249	1,001	663	431	1,095	52
2004	1,341	255	1,566	737	404	1,141	42
2005	1,065	251	1,316	721	397	1,118	46
2006	976	271	1,247	691	402	1,093	47
2007	1,016	305	1,321	765	449	1,214	48
2008	1,406	345	1,751	801	406	1,207	41
2009	1,215	314	1,529	757	257	1,014	40
2010	1,523	443	1,966	814	250	1,064	35
Total no.	10,436	2,922	13,328	7,220	3,816	11,037	45
Total %	43	12	55	30	16	45	

and fell as low as to 35 per cent in 2010. The first decade in the new millennium bore the stamp of crisis in the Swedish publishing business, since sales and publishing numbers as a whole diminished severely (Rüegg 2020: 15), partly due to the increasing consolidation in the world of publishing where Transnational Media Conglomerates, for instance Wolters Kluwer and Hachette Livre, were constantly gaining ground (Steiner 2012: 29). The two largest Swedish publishing houses then responded to the situation by discharging in-house staff, thereby opening up a new possibility for smaller publishing houses to work with translated fiction but not with the same quantity as before (Hedberg 2016). Another factor influencing the decrease of translated fiction was probably the relatively high costs of the production of translations in comparison with the production of domestic literature. The prices of translation rights were peaking from year to year, especially for the 'notable' writers, which we have seen in previous chapters to be the most translated into Swedish. The average translation rate of the decade amounted to 45 per cent, and for the first time in this study new Swedish published works exceeded new translated works by number, but translated new editions still outnumbered the new domestic editions. The decreasing importance of published translated fiction within Swedish literary space can now with hindsight be considered as a confirmed trend.

Table 4 The relation of published original fiction and translated fiction (new works and new editions) expressed as percentages of translated fiction during the period 2011–2019 (National Bibliography 2011–2019, Svensk Bokförteckning [Swedish Book Transcript] 2011–2019).

Published fiction in Sweden							
Year	Swedish fiction			Translated fiction			Translation
	New lit.	New ed.	Total	New lit.	New ed.	Total	%
2011	1,184	322	1,506	834	239	1,073	42
2012	1,225	519	1,744	818	337	1,195	41
2013	1,248	382	1,630	743	352	1,095	44
2014	1,493	452	1,945	875	319	1,194	38
2015	1,533	486	2,019	756	399	1,155	36
2016	1,352	368	1,720	732	264	996	37
2017	1,833	203	2,036	1,151	119	1,270	38
2018	2,030	160	2,190	977	82	1,059	32
2019	2,051	162	2,213	983	73	1,059	28
Total no.			17,003			10,096	
Total %							37

As can be seen in Table 4, the falling trend for translated fiction during the three preceding decades was further accentuated during the 2010s, where the general translation rate only reached 37 per cent. It seems that there was a rather steady decrease of translated fiction by approximately 7 per cent per decade. No numbers for the year 2020 are yet available, which explains the empty slots.

It is possible that there was a correlation between increasing rates of private publishing (self-financed and not published by a publishing house: through services such as Författarens bokmaskin [The Author's Book Machine], a print-on-demand service) and decreasing numbers of literary translations. Private publishing increased from very low numbers at the turn of the century to 13 per cent of all published literature in Sweden 2019. More than 40 per cent of the private publishing was composed of novels – a fact influencing the percentages of the total of book publishing as well as of the output of fiction and translated fiction in Sweden, where the novel has been the most favoured genre of domestic and translated fiction during the last forty years. In fact, novels represented more than 80 per cent of all translated literature during the last decades. Nevertheless, the decreasing trend reached an extreme in 2019 with the lowest amount of translated fiction since the middle of the previous century, 28 per cent of the annual output of published fiction in Sweden.

This overview has shown a steady trend of falling numbers for translated fiction, thus demonstrating its decreasing importance within the Swedish literary space. Nevertheless, the percentage of translated fiction in Sweden is still relatively high in comparison with other European countries, both counting the total translation rate and the specific translation rate for fiction, constituting one of the specific traits of the semi-peripheral Swedish literary geography. The decreasing importance of translated fiction indicates that Swedish literature has undergone a development towards more closeness in this regard and hence towards a more firm centrality in the northern literary geography. Simultaneously, the number of translations *from* Swedish has risen dramatically. This trend has accelerated during the last decade, the value of rights sold to Swedish literature tripling between 2008 and 2018 (Hedberg 2019). It is hardly surprising that these trends occurred at the same time, since 'closed' literary markets tend to be strong literary exporters.

A third characteristic of the Swedish literary semi-periphery is the strong position of its translators. It has been shown in previous studies (Lindqvist 2006, 2021a) that the Swedish literary translation field – in contrast to other translation spaces within other literary geographies (Gouanvic 1997, Simeoni 1998, 2007, Wolf 2006, Sela-Sheffy 2008) – can be characterized as a relatively autonomous field. A relatively autonomous field presupposes a market and experts capable of distinguishing good quality from ordinary work – in this case good translations from ordinary. It requires cultural magazines and journals, where these specialists scrutinize, evaluate and discuss translations. It also requires possibilities for institutional consecration in the form of stakeholding organizations, for instance membership-based agencies and translator unions offering grants and scholarships after selective entrance requirements, and literary societies and academies providing consecration in the form of translation prizes, grants and appointments. One should also not forget the importance of government funding, i.e. state subsidizing of highly esteemed translators in the form of guaranteed annual wages, which is probably the most solid basis for institutional consecration of Swedish translators in their relative autonomous translation field (Lindqvist 2021a). All of these characteristics – some of which have also been mentioned in the previous chapter on translators of Nobel laureates – are present in Sweden.

From these general characteristics of the Swedish literary semi-periphery, we turn now to the specifics of our translation flows. We are concerned both with what could be called the 'profile' of literary exchange to the changes that occur over time. Three dimensions of each literary flow are in focus: the temporal 'translation gap'; the composition of authors (categorized as 'vanguard', 'popular', 'aesthete' and 'notable' – the categories used in Chapter 2); and the balance between women and men authors. In addition, we note whether particular genres (children's literature and/or poetry, for instance) are conspicuously missing or present.

Swedish literature in English translation 1980–2018

During the period 1980–2018, literary translations from Swedish into English amounted to approximately 1,800 publications, including new editions. The period showed no univocal overall tendency as to the amount of translations being published. Rather, the numbers oscillated significantly between different, shorter periods of time, a phenomenon that becomes visible if we divide the four decades into five-year units and start in the late 1970s (Table 5).

During the latter part of the 1970s the amount of translations was quite substantial. In the early 1980s the number dropped drastically just to rise again in the next period. In the late 1980s and early 1990s approximately 175 books were published in each five-year period. Then there was another drop at the end of the 1990s, and another rise after 2000. However, it was not until the period 2005–2009 that the amount of translations equalled that of the late 1970s. In the next period there was another rise. Between 2010 and 2014 more books were published than during any former five-year period. This rise continued during 2015, but in 2016 and 2017 the numbers fell yet again. The highest quantity of titles were published in 2012, but also 2008, 2011, 2014 and 2015 were good years for English

Table 5 Publications, including new editions, of literary translations from Swedish to English 1975–2018

Period	Number of editions
1975–1979	263
1980–1984	145
1985–1989	177
1990–1994	174
1995–1999	146
2000–2004	191
2005–2009	263
2010–2014	350
2015–2018	260

translations of Swedish literature. The lowest quantity of titles appeared in 1981. Also, few translations were published in 1982, 1984, 1994 and 1998.

The whole time span also shows a great variety in the kinds of literature being translated. In the 1980s, children's books were by far the most translated genre, and the translations in this category were dominated by a single author: Astrid Lindgren. In the 1980s, Lindgren belonged to the absolute canon of domestic children's literature. She was still productive, but her works from the 1940s and the 1950s had already become modern classics. One of the characteristics of children's books is that successful titles often are published again and again in different editions. The same stories are continuously presented to new generations of children readers. This also affected the English translations of Astrid Lindgren in the 1980s. Older translations were re-issued, older original titles were translated for the first time, but newer original titles were also translated and published in the UK and the USA. There were thus quite significant temporal gaps between source and target texts in many of these titles, whereas there were no such gaps in others.

Apart from Astrid Lindgren's books for school children, the picture book was the most translated children's book genre, in the 1980s as well as during the whole period 1980–2018. These publications were quite varied. Many of them were classic Swedish picture books. The little Scottish publishing house Floris Books was, for example, responsible for many translations of Elsa Beskow's idyllic picture books from the early twentieth century. Here, there were significant delays between the appearance of target texts and the original source texts, but we must not forget that Beskow's classic books were continuously re-issued in Sweden throughout the twentieth century. The historical gaps were then just as present in the source culture as in the target culture. On the other hand, these gaps were not as obvious in the latter as in the former. Other picture book translations are more surprising and less in line with source culture canon formation. One example is the translations issued by the Illinois publisher Albert Whitman, who published two Swedish picture books in 1994, six in 1995 and two in 1996, all of which were translations of Maj Lindman's contemporary titles. Another example is Gunilla Ingves, whose books for small children were profusely translated in the first half of the 1980s: between 1982 and 1985, fifteen titles by Ingves were published by the London publisher A & C Black. Whereas Beskow was an aesthete, Lindman and Ingves were notables, and the Albert Whitman and A & C Black translations were published with no significant gaps between source and target texts.

When it comes to adult literature, translations of contemporary Swedish prose fiction were very sparse during the early 1980s. Instead, translations for adults were dominated by older Swedish titles, which were either re-issued or translated belatedly. More often than not, there was thus a significant gap in this period between the Swedish source texts and the English translations. Quite a few notables from twentieth-century Swedish literature were published. The 1950s translation of Vilhelm Moberg's epic narrative on Swedish emigration to the United States was re-issued, and so was Moberg's late novel *A Time on Earth* (*Din stund på jorden*), originally published in 1963 and translated by Naomi Walford in 1965, a story narrated by a Swedish emigrant in California. Other translations in this category included the first English translation of Jan Fridegård's modern classic *I, Lars Hård* (*Jag Lars Hård*), a modern classic of proletarian realism from 1935, and a re-issue of the 1956 translation of Frans G. Bengtsson's historic novel about the Viking age, *The Long Ships* (*Röde Orm*, 1941 and 1945).

Most of the older Swedish titles published in English in the early 1980s were, however, works by aesthetes. We find one title by the literary giant August Strindberg, and as many as eight titles by the Nobel laureates Selma Lagerlöf, Pär Lagerkvist and Eyvind Johnson. Selma Lagerlöf, who became the first female laureate in 1909, was the author of two of these translations, and Lagerkvist, who received the prize in 1951, had as many as five translated titles in 1982 and 1983. Eyvind Johnson, who shared the prize in 1974 with fellow Swedish author Harry Martinson, had only one title translated in the early 1980s, a first translation of the historical novel *Dreams of Roses and Fire* (*Drömmar om rosor och eld*, 1949), a fact that illustrates the tendency of belated English translations of Swedish prose fiction during this period. Johnson's and Martinson's shared Nobel Prize led to translations into many languages in the latter half of the 1970s. Books by the two Swedish laureates appeared in French, German, Spanish, Turkish, Hebrew, Japanese and Korean. However, this Nobel effect did not reach the English markets. No title by either Johnson or Martinson was published in English between 1974 and 1984. It takes longer, it seems, for canonized Swedish authors to be acknowledged in the UK and the USA than on many other literary markets.

During the latter part of the 1980s, the publication of contemporary fiction increased significantly, mostly due to swift translations of Swedish notable authors. Recent novels by Sara Lidman, P. O. Enquist, Lars Gustafsson, Torgny Lindgren and P. C. Jersild quickly found Anglophone readers on each side of the Atlantic. Lindgren and Jersild had as many as four publications each in English in the latter half of the 1980s. More surprising is perhaps the translations of the less-known authors Margareta Ekström and Margareta Bergman, each of them with two publications during these years. A special case was film director Ingmar Bergman's autobiography *The Magic Lantern* (*Laterna magica*, originally published in Swedish in 1987), which was published in English in four different editions in 1988 and 1989. Also related to the film industry was the translation of Reidar Jönsson's novel *My Life as a Dog* (*Mitt liv som hund*, 1983), which was adapted into a film in 1985. The Swedish film was a success in US movie theatres and led to Lasse Hallström's international breakthrough as a director. This new interest in contemporary fiction does not mean, however, that Swedish literary classics were less translated during this period. Books by the solidly canonized older authors August Strindberg, Hjalmar Söderberg, Selma Lagerlöf, Pär Lagerkvist, Karin Boye and Eyvind Johnson were published in the late 1980s, as well as modern classics by Moa Martinson, Jan Fridegård and Stig Dagerman.

This tendency remained intact throughout the 1990s: contemporary prose was translated alongside older Swedish prose, but the former category was distinctly more frequently published. Apart from Lars Gustafsson, Torgny Lindgren and P. O. Enquist, a range of contemporary notable women writers were translated during the 1990s, for example Sigrid Combüchen, Agneta Pleijel, Cordelia Edvardsson, Majgull Axelsson and Kerstin Ekman. Ekman alone had as many as nine books in English during the decade. The 1990s also saw the rise of Swedish popular fiction in English translation, notably thrillers by Jan Guillou and existential novels by Marianne Fredriksson. Among the translations of Swedish literary classics we find, apart from the usual suspects August Strindberg, Selma Lagerlöf, Hjalmar Söderberg and Pär Lagerkvist, nineteenth-century novelists Victoria Benedictsson, Fredrika Bremer and Carl Jonas Love Almqvist, eighteenth-century botanist Carl Linnæus and fourteenth-century religious writer Saint Bridget of Sweden.

The increase in translated prose fiction, and especially the rise of contemporary Swedish fiction in English, changed the imbalance between literary genres. During the 1990s the relation between children's literature and literature for adults evened out, and at the beginning of the 2000s, fiction for adults became the most translated genre. During the first two decades of the new millennium, then, this development was not only confirmed but strongly reinforced. The number of titles for adults distinctly increased during this period, whereas the number of translated children's books slightly decreased.

From the turn of the millennium, the rise of Swedish prose fiction in English was mainly due to an increasing amount of translated popular fiction, mostly suspense literature. This increasing dominance of popular authors rather than notables and aesthetes was closely connected to the international popularity of the so-called Nordic noir phenomenon, i.e. dark suspense narratives in literature, film or television, set in northern Europe, predominantly Scandinavia. Already in 2000, crime novelist Henning Mankell had four publications in English, but the rise of translated Swedish suspense novels started for real a couple of years later and exploded in 2006 with fourteen publications. After that it kept rising until reaching an all-time-high of thirty-three Swedish Nordic noir publications in English in 2012. By that time, the number of suspense authors being translated every year was also very high. In 2013 as many as nineteen different Nordic noir authorial signatures were published, including the two double pen names Roslund/Hellström (Anders Roslund and Börge Hellström) and Hjort/Rosenfeldt (Michael Hjort and Hans Rosenfeldt).

Related to this increase in suspense novels was a significant decrease in translated Swedish fiction classics. Between 2000 and 2004 no more than nine English translations of older Swedish fiction were published. During the following two five-year periods these numbers only slightly increased: eleven older works were translated or re-issued between 2005 and 2009, and sixteen between 2010 and 2014.

The quite dramatic rise of translated popular fiction in the two first decades of the twenty-first century must not, however, hide the fact that Swedish suspense literature was translated into English throughout the period 1980–2018. The police novels of the writing couple Per Wahlöö and Maj Sjöwall have been available in English since the 1970s, with new editions published in the 1990s. Another successful popular Swedish novelist before 2000 is Kjell-Olof Bornemark, whose spy novels *The Messenger Must Die* (*Legat till en trolös*, 1982), *The Dividing Line* (*Skiljelinjen*, 1983) and *The Henchman* (*Handgången man*, 1986) were published between 1986 and 1990 by the New York publisher Dembner Books.

Two literary genres enjoy a quite stable history of publication and distribution in the UK and the USA: theatre and poetry. The translations of Swedish drama are highly dominated by the works of August Strindberg; almost forty books of his theatrical works were published in English during these four decades. All in all, there were only eight Swedish dramatists represented in Anglophone books, not counting contributions to anthologies. The second most translated – and printed – dramatist was Ingmar Bergman, who had as many as nine publications during the period, all of them from the 1980s. Being mostly known internationally as a film director, it is no surprise that Bergman's translated books consist of screenplays. The only other dramatic writer with more than one publication was contemporary aesthete Lars Norén with four translated and printed plays in 2003, 2014 and 2017.

When it comes to poetry, Tomas Tranströmer is by far the most available Swedish poet in English with as many as twenty-seven publications during the four decades. From this amount of collections, which were spread out throughout the period and thus by no means only an effect of Tranströmer's Nobel Prize in 2011, there is a huge gap down to Gustaf Fröding, Harry Martinson, Werner Aspenström, Aase Berg and the UN general director Dag Hammarskjöld, who had four poetry publications each in English. The number of books of Swedish poetry collections that became available in English during these decades was, on the other hand, quite high: fifty-seven. Half of these can be categorized as written by established contemporary poets, whereas slightly more than one-third were either written by deceased modern poets or by older canonized poets. Only five of these, however, were published before 1900: eighteenth-century poets Carl Michael Bellman and Anna Maria Lenngren, and late-nineteenth-century to early twentieth-century authors August Strindberg, Ola Hansson and Gustaf Fröding. Slightly less than one-third of all the published poets were only available – in Swedish as well as in English – through self-financed publications.

Apart from the self-financed poets, the Swedish dramatists and poets available in English should all be considered as aesthetes, which is one probable reason why these two categories of translations were so quantitatively stable from 1980 onwards. When it comes to historic gaps between source and target texts, the two dominant authors make the two categories quite different from each other. The English translations from this period of August Strindberg's plays were either belated translations or re-issued older translations, whereas the translations of Tomas Tranströmer's poetry were made historically close to the poems' original publication in Swedish.

The overall tendency for English translations of Swedish literature from 1980 to 2018 was, then, that the number of drama and poetry publications remained stable throughout the period, whereas the balance between other genres shifted. In the 1980s, children's literature was the most translated kind of literature. During the 1990s, contemporary notable prose fiction caught up with children's literature and took over its dominant role. After 2000, there was a more radical change of scene due to a dramatic rise of translated popular fiction. Throughout the 2000s and the 2010s, the suspense novel was by far the most available kind of Swedish literature in English.

Swedish literature in French translation 1980–2018

The 1980s marked an important breakthrough for the proliferation of Swedish language fiction in translation to French. During the first decades of the postwar era, translation from Swedish to French had to a large degree been supply-driven, an issue for cultural diplomacy rather than publishers and literary agents. Cultural transmitters, among them several Swedish expatriates, worked hard to raise interest in a small number of aesthete authors among the elite of Parisian publishing houses, often with very limited results, especially when it came to sales. Among the authors published in French were the surrealist poet Gunnar Ekelöf (1907–1968), one of Sweden's most highly esteemed authors of the twentieth century, and Birgitta Trotzig (1929–2011), an experimental catholic novelist living in Paris and later (1993) elected to the Swedish Academy, where she replaced another author of the same ideal-typic calibre, also translated into French in the 1960s, Per Olof Sundman (1922–1992).

Cultural transfer from Sweden to France, then, was very much an elite project. If there was an ambition to make Swedish literature 'world literature', it was in the sense of making highly esteemed Swedish authors known among the French intelligentsia, whose appreciation might have a positive effect on the status of Swedish literature in the rest of Europe and worldwide. These efforts, however, were mostly in vain, as it has been repeatedly shown that Swedish authors, with very few exceptions, are absent from the Damroschian *hypercanon*.

But at the beginning of the 1970s, the total number of translations from Swedish to French quite suddenly began to rise. This was not an immediate result of the work done by the cultural transmitters mentioned above. Rather, it was Swedish children's fiction that started to attract the interest of French publishers. Literature for children had enjoyed a considerable rejuvenation in Sweden from the late 1960s and into the following decade, a development that now started to have an international impact, the number of translations rising from 138 in 1966 to 214 in 1974. When it came to translations into French, the number of translations of this kind of literature also soared, more than doubling between the 1960s and 1970s.

Literature aimed at an adult audience, however, did not enjoy the same success. Numbers remained as low as before. It was not until the early 1980s that things began to change in this regard. There was then talk of a 'Swedish wave', i.e. a growing number of translations of Swedish authors, most of them notables, especially to German and French (Ballu 2016: 912). From the middle of the 1980s and during the following thirty years, Swedish fiction aimed at an adult audience gradually gained in importance on the French book market. This rising interest can be partly explained with reference to a number of important changes in the publishing field. The 1980s saw the establishment of new publishing houses, several of them devoting themselves especially to translations. Some of the publishers spoke of this as an attempt to alter the French discussion on literature, making it more cosmopolitan, but it can also be seen simply as a way for the publishers to enrich themselves in cultural capital. These new houses also engaged a new generation of translators, several of them with university backgrounds. An overall trend during the 1980s was a move from domesticating to foreignizing translation.

New publishers and new translators also meant new kinds of literature; the 1980s saw a broadening of the 'translation flow' from Sweden to France. Still, the aesthete and notable writers were seen as important, although there was a shift towards contemporary and still developing authorships. A noteworthy example is Torgny Lindgren (1938–2017, elected to the Swedish Academy in 1991), whose novels were quickly translated and published by the Arles-based Actes sud (mostly within a couple of years from the first original language edition). New publishers also made room for works that were harder to fit into the catalogues of the traditional Parisian houses, for example those dealing specifically with Swedish phenomena (which is true of Lindgren's works), which shows the growing acceptance of foreign elements in translated fiction. At the same time, storytelling qualities tended to be increasingly highlighted, rather than, as was more common before, philosophical or intellectual content. These tendencies in the book market were to some extent underpinned by the French state, channelling financial support (through the Centre national du livre) for translations in an attempt to counter the growing hegemony of English language literature.

During the first half of the 1990s, the situation for Swedish literature in French translation remained mostly the same, i.e. the number of translations per year was still relatively high compared to the period before 1980. At the end of the decade, however, numbers declined, both for children's fiction and literature aimed at adult readers; the turn of the century marked one of the least successful periods for Swedish literature in France since the 1970s. But this tendency came with an exception that would prove to become very significant: the number of translations of crime novels did not decline but instead started to rise. This development continued during the first decade of the twenty-first century, reaching an impressive peak in the early years of the 2010s, when crime fiction became the quantitatively most important type of literature translated from Swedish to French. Crime fiction even overshadowed children's literature, which to a large degree had remained popular among French publishers since the 1970s. Nevertheless, the 'boom' of Swedish crime novels (which cannot be described as an isolated phenomenon, but rather coincided with the success of similar novels from other Scandinavian countries) did not mean a limiting of the space for other kinds of literature. Rather the opposite, since the number of translations of children's books and non-genre fiction also rose around the turn of the decade 2010. Taken together, this meant that the number of editions of Swedish literature in French translation exceeded a hundred per year in 2013, the highest confirmed number to date, leaving the 'success' of the 1980s 'Swedish wave', with forty to fifty editions per year, far behind.

The difference between the periods, of course, lies in the types of literature that were translated. While aesthete and notable authors achieved a remarkable degree of success in the 1980s, this in no way compared to the impact of Swedish crime fiction, the work of 'popular' authors, thirty years later. On the other hand, it seems that success in one part of the spectrum of literature also has an effect on the others, e.g. when there is talk about Swedish crime fiction this also helps to promote translations from the same language in other genres. Another tendency is that the translation flow from Sweden to France has become increasingly demand-driven. This has meant that translation happens faster, shortening the time gap between source and target language edition. A good example is *The Girl with the Dragon Tattoo*, the first instalment of Stieg Larsson's now globally successful Millennium trilogy. The French publisher Actes sud acquired the right to this novel before it was published in Swedish. The overall quickening of the book marketplace was also a result of the establishment of a system of international literary agents, to which Swedish publishers were relatively early adopters.

To conclude, then, the yearly number of editions of Swedish literature in translation to French has doubled since the 1980s. This is especially noteworthy since the 1980s has been described as a breakthrough decade for Swedish authors in France. In the 1990s, this 'new system' was consolidated, resulting in a broader selection of literature translated from Swedish. In the 1950s, 1960s and 1970s, this 'translation flow' had been dominated by consecrated fiction, translations often seen as a kind of cultural diplomacy. From the 1980s onwards, the infrastructure of translation became increasingly structured around the demands of the target culture market. As a result, popular authors were translated besides the aesthetes and notables. The work of several Swedish authors was also marketed as distinctly Swedish, rather than cosmopolitan or global.

Today, Sweden is internationally known for its crime fiction authors. They have made Swedish literature an issue for 'the man on the street', also promoting a broader interest in Sweden and Scandinavia. The 'boom' of crime fiction is also the main explanation behind the doubling of the number of editions of Swedish literature in France. However, under this flood of crime novels, the number of editions of other types of literature (children's books, contemporary novels, etc.) is the same (or slightly higher) as in the 1980s. These changes – the growing importance of the demands of the target market, the success of crime fiction, etc. – have also influenced the number of female writers being translated from Swedish. In the first years of the 1980s, only 13 per cent of the editions were of books by female writers. In the 2010s, the same number was 55 per cent.

Italian literature in Swedish translation 1980–2018

The number of editions of Italian literature translated into Swedish in the time period 1980–2018 constantly increased, starting with 126 editions in the 1980s and arriving at 218 editions in the years 2010–2018. Considering the period as a whole, two important observations can be made: firstly, that the Swedish import of Italian literature suffered from an extreme male bias with 84 per cent male writers (versus 16 per cent female). One reason for the male predominance is related to the second observation, namely the large proportion of classics translated from Italian. No less than 13.5 per cent were 'old classics', i.e. works written more than a century ago (in fact often several centuries ago), while 15 per cent consisted of translations of what can be termed 'modern classics', i.e. literary works originally published in the source language twenty to a hundred years before. Taken together, old and modern classics represent a third of the Italian literature in Swedish. Interestingly, the number of older classics

Table 6 Editions of Italian literature in Swedish translation 1980–2018

Period	Total number of editions	Number of old classics	Number of modern classics
1980–1989	126	26	13
1990–1999	138	22	18
2000–2009	155	18	20
2010–2018	217	20	47
Total	636 (100%)	86 (13.5%)	98 (15%)

seems to diminish, while the number of modern classics recently increased considerably (Table 6).

From these figures it can be deduced that Italian literature has what Sapiro calls 'a past symbolic capital' (Sapiro 2015: 321), which is probably one of the explanations for Italy's prominent position in the global literary exchange where it accounts for at least 3 per cent of the entire translation market. It should therefore be stressed that Italy's strong position among the so-called semi-peripheral literatures relies on the number of long-selling classics by Dante, Petrarch, Boccaccio, Machiavelli, Tasso, Goldoni, Leopardi, etc. In the following, we will go deeper into each decade by discussing genres and analysing the ideal-typic categories of authors translated into Swedish.

In the 1980s, the proportion of old classics – aesthetes – was higher (21 per cent) compared to the subsequent decades, which might be explained by the slow recovery of the Swedish book market after the crisis in the early 1970s. As a result of the crisis, the large publishers tended to concentrate on 'safe cards', which in the case of Italian literature meant canonized authors: *le tre corone* Dante, Petrarch and Boccaccio, but also Marco Polo's stories about his travels to the Far East in the *Milione* from the thirteenth century, Niccolò Machiavelli's somewhat cynical analysis of renaissance power strategies in *The Prince*, Carlo Goldoni's droll comedies from the eighteenth century and Leopardi's romanticist meditations on the meaninglessness of life. Another longseller was Carlo Collodi's *Pinocchio* (1883), which in the 1980s was issued in four different Swedish editions.

Parallel to the steady translation of classics, a very different genre started to enter the Swedish sphere: comics for an adult readership and the graphic novel, a genre which had enjoyed a longer tradition in countries such as France and Italy, but which in mid-1980s Sweden was a literary outsider. The importation of graphic novels in the 1980s represented more than a fifth of all the translations from Italian, which significantly increased the figures of Italian *populars* in Sweden. It is noteworthy, however, that most of the graphic novels translated from Italian in the 1980s fell into the category of erotic literature, featuring the work by Guido Crepax and published by the notorious publisher Medusa/RSR Epix. Soon, the genre would be complemented by many distinguished Italian creators of graphic novels, such as Milo Manara and Hugo Pratt. After a crisis in the first decade of the new millennium, the graphic novel again became a vital part of the literary inflow from Italy.

Besides the inflow of popular authors (comics, graphic novels) on the one hand and aesthetes (old and modern classics) on the other, some Italian notables were also introduced in the 1980s, for instance Umberto Eco's *The Name of Rose*, which was published in 1983 in Swedish (and in English). Despite the huge worldwide success of his first novel, Eco remained faithful to the small publisher who believed in him from the very start, Brombergs. In the following decades, Eco remained a stable presence in the Swedish book market as Brombergs published all his new titles, often in many editions. Another constant in the whole time period studied is Italo Calvino. He was first translated into Swedish in the late 1950s and the publications went on as Calvino's literary fame grew stronger. In the 1980s some of his most important works were translated: *If on a Winter's Night a Traveler* and *Palomar*. It is interesting that while Calvino belonged to the notables in the 1980s, the new editions of his works in recent years should rather be relegated to the canonized group of the aesthetes. Another notable of the 1980s is Primo Levi, who passed away in 1987, many decades after his survival of the Nazi concentration camp Auschwitz. A considerable translation gap can be noticed between Levi's seminal novel *Se questo è un uomo* from 1947 (the English translation received the title *If This Is a Man* in the UK and *Survival in Auschwitz* in the USA), which was translated more than four decades later in 1988. The novel had already been proposed to Bonniers in 1960, but the publisher refused it with the argument that there were already many stories about the Holocaust on the market. When Levi's work was recognized in the United States in the mid-1980s, Bonniers bought two titles at a reduced price: *The Periodic Table* and *If Not Now, When?* The latter was launched in 1986 in the presence of Levi himself, who had been invited to Stockholm. When he learned that *If This Is a Man* had not been translated into Swedish he told Bonniers' editor that it was necessary to translate it immediately. *If This Is a Man* came out in 1988, followed in the 1990s by other Levi titles.

In Italy, the 1990s was a decade when a new generation of writers (born in the 1950s and 1960s) succeeded the great names of the twentieth century (Pavese, Calvino, Moravia, Morante, etc.) and became part of the literary establishment. This generational shift is mirrored in the international markets (including Sweden) where many Italian newcomers were introduced. In Sweden, we notice the arrival of writers such as Paola Capriolo, Daniele Del Giudice, Marta Morazzoni, Susanna Tamaro, Alessandro Baricco, Margaret Mazzantini among many others. Their titles were generally published in Swedish translation only one or two years after the publication in Italy, which in some cases was related to the fact that the writers had received prestigious Italian awards. More importantly, however, is the fact that the lion's share of these writers and titles had previously been translated into English. Considering the fact that English is a global language, we can conclude that a great proportion of the titles and authors selected for translation to Swedish were so-called 'global notables' (cf. Schwartz 2021). However, there are a number of authors who were translated into Swedish before they received their first book-length translation in English, and in two cases the writers were never translated into the language. In one case the Swedish version came out in the same year as the English translation; Susanna Tamaro's global bestseller *Va' dove ti porta il cuore* was translated into both languages in 1995. What these cases show is that the Swedish field is partly independent of the Anglophone literary field and might even contribute to enriching the global market by introducing new names. Beside these 'new' notables we can observe the presence of writers who had become notables during the previous decade and maintained this position even in the 1990s (Eco, Magris, Tabucchi), as well as another group of notables whose works continued to be published many years after their death (Calvino, Pasolini, Levi), moving towards the space of aesthetes. The 1990s also illustrate how the Nobel Prize can initiate the removal of an author who is positioned on the unusual continuum between the avant-garde and the popular, to the quadrants of the aesthetes, as in the case of politically radical dramatist Dario Fo, who was awarded the prize in 1997.

The old and modern classics (aesthetes) kept their stable proportion in the 1990s, representing 29 per cent of all the publications, and likewise the publications of graphic novels were still prominent, even though the category of populars was complemented with other genres, for instance *La piovra*, a book based on the homonymous television series about the mafia. The interest in Italian organized criminality is also reflected in the three Swedish editions of Giovanni Falcone's and Marcelle Padovani's *Cose di Cosa nostra* (1991), which was translated into Swedish the year after Falcone, an anti-mafia judge, was murdered by the Sicilian mafia.

The upturning trend for Italian literature in Sweden continued at the beginning of the new millennium (155 editions). A fourth consisted of old and modern classics, but this was the first decade in which the 'modern' classics prevailed over the older ones (see Table 1). Most of these authors are obviously to be regarded as aesthetes, but as both Eco and Fo were still alive and active at the beginning of the new millennium, they should rather be placed among the notables. Even among the older classics (dominated by Dante, Boccaccio, Petrarch, Machiavelli and Collodi) it is noteworthy that Pietro Aretino's famous erotic work from the 16th century *The ragionamenti: The lives of Nuns, The Lives of Married Women, The Lives of Courtesans* was published by the vanguard publisher Vertigo. Actually, it could be argued that Aretino's work, taken together with the erotic adult comics as well as the tendency to publish sexually outspoken writers, gives Italian literature a somewhat erotic bias. This observation seems particularly interesting to consider with regard to the strong gender imbalance among the authors of imported titles (only 16 per cent of the editions were authored by women in the years 2000–2009, which was in line with the low average of the whole period studied).

During the first decade of the new millennium around thirty new Italian writers were introduced to the Swedish readers, and most could be placed in the categories of the notables or popular. Among the popular we notice a radical decrease in graphic novels, but on the other hand subgenres which usually were not imported from Italy were translated, i.e. crime fiction (Andrea Camilleri, Marcello Fois, Giorgio Faletti, Michele Giuttari and Gianrico Carofiglio) as well as international bestsellers in historical settings (Valerio Massimo Manfredi and Giulio Leoni).

Some of the new names among the notables were Andrea De Carlo, Niccolò Ammaniti, Melania Mazzucco, Simona Vinci, Paolo Giordano and Roberto Saviano. They were all well-established authors on the Italian market but remained quite anonymous among Swedish readers, except for Saviano, who received worldwide recognition in 2007 with his anti-mafia reportage book *Gomorra*. This anonymity also characterized many of the notables who were introduced during the previous decade and continued to be published in the 2000s: Margaret Mazzantini, Alessandro Baricco, Marta Morazzoni, Antonio Tabucchi and Giuseppe Pontiggia.

In comparison to the 1980s and the 1990s, the new millennium offered more contemporary Italian poetry. The authors were mainly male and even though some of them were well known in Italy (Sebastiano Grasso, Luciano Erba, Paolo Ruffilli) others were definitely less established: Mimmo Morina, Marta Bertolotti, Corrado Calabrò. The latter, who was rather ignored in his source culture, is today the most translated contemporary Italian poet in Sweden, with no less than six book-length editions translated by seven different translators (often working together in couples). As a comparison, the Nobel laureates Salvatore Quasimodo and Eugenio Montale are represented by four volumes each (cf. Schwartz 2019).

The most recent years, 2010–2018, confirm the tendency that Italian literature is an increasing presence in the Swedish book market, featuring not only the largest number of editions (217 editions) but also of classics (sixty-seven editions). Among the classics, however, the modern (forty-seven) prevail significantly over the older ones (twenty). The explanation for the large number of modern classics is related to different strategies of publishing houses, for instance: Natur & Kultur's initiative to translate and re-issue the work of Italo Calvino; the profile of the publisher Modernista whose principal publishing strategy implies the re-publication of older translations (Bassani, Camilleri); the initiative taken by the Italian Institute in Stockholm to fill in the gaps in the Swedish list of Italian literature by founding the book series Cartaditalia (cf. Schwartz 2017). Perhaps the renewed interest in modern classics should be contextualized in a broader setting, including a new interest in the past century that was manifested in very different ways (from the worldwide success of the TV series *Mad Men* to the re-issuing of John Williams' novel *Stoner* from 1965). Another explanation might lie in the effects of a more digitalized book market where the 'long tail' (the large number of titles sold in very small numbers on internet sites) proved that there was a demand for all sorts of books. Actually, the total sales of these low sellers turned out to constitute a larger market than that of the bestsellers (cf. Anderson 2008, Steiner 2011).

In 2010–2018, no less than forty-three Italian authors were translated for the first time into Swedish, and among these names there are two female writers in particular, and they have reached a large audience both among readers and critics, Silvia Avallone and Elena Ferrante. It is interesting to notice, however, that no new crime fiction writers were introduced (but representatives of the genre such as Camilleri and Carofiglio were still present), which suggests that these titles had difficulty in squeezing themselves into the already crowded national field of

Swedish noir. Instead, some titles were introduced in the wake of the enormous success of Roberto Saviano's non-fiction novel *Gomorra*, for instance Fabrizio Gatti's undercover journalism in *Bilal* (Italian 2007/ Swedish 2013) and Nicolai Lilin's autobiographical *Educazione siberiana* (Siberian Education It. 2009). The almost complete lack of *popular* titles among the imported Italian novels was balanced by a renaissance of the graphic novel launched by the new publishing house Ades media, which published at least twenty-five Italian titles in the years 2010–2018.

The dominant category of ideal-typical authors was represented by the notables, including the previously introduced names (e.g. Ammaniti, Eco, Magris, Mazzantini, Mazzucco, Morazzoni) as well as the new arrivals (e.g. Agus, Cognetti, Lagioia, Murgia, Parrella, Starnone, Veronesi). Editions by women writers rose to 26 per cent, but this upswing was only related to the 'Ferrante Fever'; if we exclude the many Ferrante editions published in the years 2010–2018, the proportion of women writers would be 17 per cent, just slightly exceeding the average of the whole period studied.

When it comes to Italian poetry, the new interest we witnessed in the previous decade grew stronger in the years 2010–2018. A whole range of new poets were introduced for the first time in book-length editions (for instance Valerio Magrelli, Eugenio De Signoribus, Andrea Zanzotto and Alda Merini), even though some of them had been included before in literary magazines and anthologies. Even more interesting is the fact that previously translated poets received a second or third collection of translations into Swedish (Calabrò, Del Serra, Erba, Grasso, Bevilacqua, etc.).

To conclude, in the period studied, Italian literature clearly strengthened its position in the Swedish literary field. One reason for this improved situation is that the old classics never cease to gain new attention, a fact that seems to apply even to some of the notable poets and narrators from the twentieth century, whose works have now become modern classics as they are still being translated and published in new editions (Pasolini, Calvino, Morante, Primo Levi, etc.). Moreover, Italian literature provided Sweden with the graphic novel, a genre which hardly existed in the national field at the time. Another phenomenon that contributes to Italy's strong position is that the nation, every now and then, produces worldwide bestsellers, often by unexpected names: who would have predicted that an established university professor of semiotics (Eco), a young Neapolitan student (Saviano) and an anonymous author (Ferrante) would produce worldwide bestsellers?

Anglophone African literature in Swedish translation 1980–2018

The translation of Anglophone African literature into the Swedish literary semi-periphery is, over the period covered here, a process in which a highly selective group of authors widens slightly to include more authors and more racial and national diversity. But it is also a literary flow in which there are significant gaps, and some unexpected changes of place.

One of the early introductions of African printed literature in Sweden was made by the popular publisher Ljus ('Light'), which translated Alan Paton's *Cry the Beloved Country* (1948) as early as 1949. Ljus, emerging out of a magazine with the same name established around the turn of the last century, sought to enlighten the working classes through cheap editions of what it considered significant writers (Svedjedal 1988). The Swedish poet Arthur Lundkvist's anthology of Caribbean, South American and African poetry, a decade later (1957) titled *Den mörke brodern* ('The Dark Brother'), presents a second important introductory effort of Anglophone African literature, here in the context of an emerging literary and publishing interest in literature from outside Europe. In the same year as Ljus published Paton, Lundkvist edited a special issue of the poetry publication *Poesi* devoted to Francophone literature by Black authors, and that year also saw the publication of an anthology of poetry by African American authors. The discursive labelling of this writing – and the interest that fuelled it – depended on exoticism and othering: what holds the selection of writers together in the eyes of editor and publisher is blackness, and the label 'negro' is used to categorize the writing (Alvstad and Lundahl 2010).

Even against the background of these pioneering efforts, Per Wästberg's remarkably ambitious anthology of fifty-seven authors, entitled *Afrika berättar* ('Africa narrates') and published by small publisher Cavefors in 1961, constituted a landmark publication in the introduction of Anglophone African literature in Sweden. The volume appeared in a landscape in which the relationship to Africa and African cultural production was changing. Underpinned by interest in the sociopolitical situations in African countries – not least in South African apartheid and the ongoing independence struggles – Wästberg noted about his own anthology that the writers included in it thematized 'the revolt against colonialism, the difference between country and city, and the break with tradition' rather than eternal subjects such as 'loss, longing, love' since 'they did not have time to calibrate emotions and were suspicious towards the private and the fictional' (Wästberg 2007: 291–2, my translation).

The socially driven opening towards African literary production which was achieved by individual efforts such as Wästberg's anthology was part of a wider cultural and political interest in African matters. In 1962, The Scandinavian Institute of African Studies (later to become the Nordic Africa Institute), was founded, and in 1967 the Institute organized the conference 'The Writer in Modern Africa' together with the Swedish Institute for Cultural Relations with Foreign Countries and the Council for Swedish Information Abroad – a conference for which Wästberg was on the organizing committee and which featured many of the renowned authors from the continent (Wästberg 1968). In the educational world, courses on African literature began to emerge, first outside the formalized education system – in 'folk high schools' and adult study circles – and eventually within higher education (Granqvist 1988: 469). The decade also saw a small burst of translations – of Nadine Gordimer, Ezekiel Mphahele, Chinua Achebe, Peter Abrahams and Doris Lessing, among others.

The stirring interest in Anglophone African literature and the connections that formed between Swedish intellectuals and African writers forged during the 1960s did not result in a flood of translations of African literature in the following decade. The 1970s was rather characterized by a comparatively narrow reception of the continent's literary output. From 1970 to 1980, out of the translated Anglophone literature, eighteen editions (seventeen titles) were by African authors. Thirteen (twelve) of these were by Doris Lessing. The Nigerian Wole Soyinka, represented by a single text – *Laglöshetens tid* (*The Season of Anomy*), published by small, radical publisher Cavefors in 1976, was the only non-white author.

Two things may be noted, then, about the patterns of translation of Anglophone African literature in the period that precedes the period focused on in this study. First, that the interest in Africa that propelled introductory efforts a decade earlier was replaced by interest in a few individual authorships handled by large or mid-size publishers. Second, that the political interest in – and protest against – South Africa's apartheid regime did not result in immediate and large-scale translation of South African authors, but instead yielded a slightly delayed and highly selective number of titles.

In the period 1980–1989, ninety-six editions of Anglophone African literature were translated and published by Swedish publishers. Major and mid-size publishers remained committed to the authors they had previously taken

Table 7 The total number of editions by Anglophone African writers published in Swedish translation 1980–2018 divided by decade. (The table excludes four editions – all books by Doris Lessing – which have uncertain publication dates all of which are new editions of previously published novels.)

Period	Number of editions
1980–1989	101
1990–1999	52
2000–2009	152
2010–2018	116
Total	430

on – Gordimer, Lessing, Brink. By contrast, Athol Fugard, who continued to be translated, was published by smaller publishers and/or theatres which staged his drama. Through the small literary publisher Bromberg, another future Nobel Prize winner, J. M. Coetzee, was introduced to the Swedish reading audience through the publication of three novels in rapid succession: *I väntan på barbarerna*, 1982 (*Waiting for the Barbarians*), *Historien om Michael K*, 1984 (*The Life and Times of Michael K*) and *Mr Foe*, 1989 (*Mr Foe*). In addition, publishing signalled a broader interest in South African literature also in terms of racial representation with the publishing of works such as Alex La Guma's *I dimman då sommaren dör* (*In the Fog of Season's End*) in 1982, Alan Paton's *Vad ert land är vackert* (*Ah, But Your Country is Beautiful*) in 1984, Lewis Nkosi's *Parningslek* (*Mating Birds*) in 1986 and Zoe Wicomb's *Du kan inte gå vilse i Kapstaden* (*You Can't Get Lost in Cape Town*) in 1988. The diversification of South African literature was achieved by smaller publishers such as Legenda (Nkosi) and Hammarström & Åberg (Wicomb), or popular publishers such as Bra böcker (La Guma). It can be noted that the effort was not a stable trend: Wicomb was not translated again until 2011 despite the fact that she established a literary reputation and career in the English-speaking world, and La Guma, though not a highly productive author (La Guma had four novels, one novella and a travel account published during his lifetime – several of them first published in the East Germany and the USSR), has had none of his other books translated into Swedish – not even 'A Walk in the Night', whose Shakespearean narrative of Black life under apartheid was to become one of the most important literary works of the period.

The publishing of South African literature (partly including the new literary voices from that country translated into Swedish) by and large had a contemporary focus. Bonniers, Trevi and Forum all translated and published their authors at the same time as they were published in the UK. The translation of literature from other African countries was more retrospective. Works by Nigerian authors published during the decade – Amadi Elechi, Buchi Emecheta and Chinua Achebe – had all been written in previous decades; so had Ghanaian Ayi Kwei Armah's *De ännu inte födda* (*The Beautyful Ones of Not Yet Born*) in 1984.

The publishing of Kenyan author Ngugi wa Thiong'o, and Somalian Nuruddin Farah were at least in part exceptions to this temporal lag. Cavefors and Corona published three of Ngugi's works in 1981 and 1982: *Upp genom mörkret* (*Weep Not, Child*), *En blomma av blod* (*Petals of Blood*) and *Om icke vetekornet* (*A Grain of Wheat*). While *Upp genom mörkret* and *Om icke vetekornet* are among Ngugi's first works, *En blomma av blod* appeared only four years after its original publication as *Petals of Blood*. The rapid-sequence publishing of Ngugi, then, had the appearance of a committed effort to establish him on the Swedish literary market. The case of Farah is more ambivalent. As described in Chapter 2, *Kartor* (*Maps*) was published by Bonnier in 1987 and followed by *Gåvor* (*Gifts*) in 1990. A decade later the publisher continued its efforts with (*Secrets*) in 2000, *Länkar* (*Links*) in 2006, and *Adams revben* (*From a Crooked Rib*) in 2008, before it abandoned the author, who was later picked up by small publisher Modernista.

The delay that characterized some of the publishing with regard to non-South African literature indicates a lingering and strong interest in the postcolonial moment and/or its immediate aftermath among Swedish readers – or at least among the publishers who provide their reading. In this way, because the literature perceived as important enough to translate and publish in the Swedish literary semi-periphery is apparently selected on the basis of its socio-historical topicality, it appears that a version of what Graham Huggan has called an 'anthropological' approach to literature directs publishing efforts (Huggan 2001: 37–57). In contrast to Gordimer, Brink and Lessing who are continuously imported to Sweden, some of the authors in question here appear to be seen as important because their narratives valuably illuminate particular historical events and experiences. The rather uneven and truncated representation of authors such as Soyinka (who, in addition to *Season of Anomy* has had three works translated into Swedish), Farah and Ngugi (both of whom, until 2015, with efforts by a new and small publisher, Modernista, each had four novels translated), in the Swedish literary landscape are indications that support such an interpretation. All three authors, at the time they were introduced in Swedish, had long writing careers behind them and were internationally recognized.

The pattern is not unequivocal, however. Soyinka's awarding of the Nobel Prize in 1986 stirred renewed publishing interest and *The Interpreters* was published that year alongside a new edition of *Season of Anomy*. The national 'Nobel effect' had been preceded by the publishing of Soyinka's memoir, *Aké: barndomsåren* (*Aké: The Years of Childhood*) in 1983. A year after the Nobel award, *Aké* was re-published, and a few years later, *Isara* followed in 1990.

The decade 1990–1999 saw a declining interest in Anglophone African literature. English as a source language for translations strengthened its domination of the Swedish literary market, but the share captured by Anglophone African literature decreased; over the ten-year period, sixty-one editions were published; that is 13 per cent of the period total. South African literature in Swedish translation remained contemporary – and predominantly white. Bromberg, Bonniers, Forum and Trevi continued to publish 'their' authors, and, as noted, some South Africans introduced in the preceding decade dropped off the list: Wicomb, Galgut, Paton, Nkosi. Small-scale publisher Brutus Östling put out Njabulo Ndebele's short story collection, *Fools and Other Stories*, another one-off by a small actor, which went against the tendency of white domination of South African literature.

The 1990s was a strong decade for André Brink, who had seven editions (six titles) published by Forum, almost the same number as Gordimer, who was awarded the Nobel Prize in 1991 and consequently saw a number of her works published and re-published that year (seven out of eight editions were published in 1991). The equal presence of Gordimer and Brink in the Swedish literary market is noteworthy, even considering the higher productivity of the latter, because of the different positions they would hold in literary history, Gordimer becoming over time far more consecrated – as shown, for instance through the different number of scholarly articles written about them.

Apart from the 'modern classic' – used here in the sense of the Italian literature above, that is, first published more than twenty years ago – Amos Tutuola's *Palmvindrinkaren* (*The Palm-Wine Drunkard*) – a novel that has often, controversially, been labelled the first 'African novel' praised for its authenticity (wa Ngugi 2018: 71–102) – the Swedish publishing of African literature in the 1990s was becoming more up to date. Njabulo Ndebele, Nigerian Ben Okri, whose *The Famished Road* was the Booker Prize winner in 1991, Kenyan-Tanzanian M. G. Vassanji and Zimbabwean Yvonne Vera are new additions to the gathering of authors available in Swedish, and whose translated novels were written only a few years before translation.

Apart from the discovery of Ndebele by Brutus Östling, the publishing of Zimbabwean writer Yvonne Vera in 1999 was a publishing event which cut against South African white dominance. Vera's Swedish publishing was a distinctly person-driven affair. She was introduced to Swedish readers by crime fiction author Henning Mankell, who had a strong engagement in African cultural matters and was a long-term resident in Mozambique. Mankell established the literary prize Afrikas röst ('The Voice of Africa'), which was awarded to Vera in 1999. The same year, her novel *Under the Tongue* was published by Ordfront, Mankell's publisher at the time, as *Under tungan*. Over the following six years Vera was to have two more novels translated into Swedish and published by Ordfront.

The first decade of the new millennium constituted a minor breakthrough period for Anglophone African literature in Swedish translation. Publishing tripled, with a total of 157 editions of the period's 440 total, or approximately 36 per cent. The overall trend in the decade was for wider representation and update of literary publishing. In total, nineteen authors from seven countries were published (the number excludes an anthology of new South African writing published by Tranan which present more than twenty authors, many of whom had not previously been translated). With respect to South African literature, the decade was characterized by the discovery by Swedish publishers of more South African authors, also race-wise. Zakes Mda, Patricia Schonstein and Achmat Dangor were among the new and contemporary authors who were introduced to Swedish readers.

As in the 1980s, small-scale and niche publishers drove the broadening of the base, in this case Leopard and Tranan. Dambudzo Marechera, Chris Abani, Ivan Vladislavic, Achmat Dangor, Patricia Schonstein, Zakes Mda and Yvonne Vera were all published by minor publishers with a profile concerning social issues or literature outside Europe and the United States. The commitment of these publishers, whose drivers were less economic than symbolic, varied, however, and an overall impression is that they were interested in individual books – perhaps with particular themes – rather than seeing themselves as permanent homes for authors. One example of this tendency is Celanders, which published three of Abani's works during the decade but left out *Virgin of Flames* and *The Secret History of Las Vegas*, both of which are set in Las Vegas, and showed no interest in his poetry (a genre which is among the publisher's profile). Another was Leopard, which translated Mda but then seemed to lose interest as they did not translate and publish *Madonna of Excelsior*, nor *Cion* which were both published after *The Whale Caller*. They also ignored his earlier works, such as

Ways of Dying – internationally widely acclaimed – or *She Plays with Darkness*. A similar fate befell Achmat Dangor, whose *Bitter Fruit*, shortlisted for the Man Booker Prize 2004 (and IMPAC Dublin Literary Award 2003) was published by Leopard as *Bitter frukt* in 2005. The book was a one-off and Leopard did not translate either previous (such as *Kafka's Curse*, 1997) or later (such as *Dikeledi*, 2017) works by the author.

The years leading up to the present, 2000–2018, saw a slight downturn in the total volume (and the proportion) of translation and publishing of Anglophone African literature: 106 editions. The representation was wider, however, with twenty-eight authors from eight countries. The decade saw a definitive breakthrough for Nigerian literature, which became distinctly contemporary in Swedish translation with the temporal delay between original publication and publishing of translation shrinking to one or two years. Nigeria also became the great literary nation in the African literary flow, overtaking South Africa in terms of number of authors (eleven to six – leaving out South African authors Marlene van Niekerk and Deon Meyer who had novels translated and published but who originally write in Afrikaans), and contributing almost a third of the authors published (eight out of twenty-eight).

In the period studied here, Anglophone African literature had become much more diverse on the Swedish literary market. The number of countries and authors has increased, and the stirring of Nigeria as a large literary culture has begun to be felt. The temporal emphasis has also shifted distinctly to the present, and to notable rather than canonical literature, even as the publishers' commitment to literary authors have waned. The decreasing representation of women authors in the flow is in part explained by the small numbers of total translations which, due to Lessing's and Gordimer's strong presence, gave a skewed baseline image.

Lusophone literature in Swedish translation 1980–2018

The translation flow of Lusophone literatures into Swedish does not form a homogeneous entity as it is represented by literary works originating from such different geographical locations as East Timor, Brazil, Portugal and Portuguese-speaking African countries. This literary flow was thereby composed of several diverse literary cultures and facets, which can each contain a specific historical and cultural interrelationship of cultural exchange guiding their pathways into the Swedish literary landscape. In order to identify some significant aspects of, and trends in, what gets translated (and what does not) the following analysis will approach the Lusophone translation flow both as an entity and as different flows of African, Brazilian and Portuguese literatures. Considering the modest annual number of publications of Lusophone literatures in the Swedish literary market some features stand out in this comparison which seem to affect the annual translation outcome, such as the emergence of single consecrated or popular authorships, the establishment and prevalence of new niche publishers, the impact of Swedish literary prizes and participation in the Gothenburg Book Fair. Equally important in characterizing the translational field of Lusophone literature into Swedish is that it is supported and enabled by a limited pole of common cultural mediators, often multitasking as translators, micro-publishers (as was addressed in Chapter 2) and agents in cultural networks of dissemination and cultural exchange. These phenomena will be explored by decade, including a discussion on the gender distribution of translated authors and a reflection on what literature gets translated and what does not (Table 8).

For the whole period there is a steady increase in the total amount of published translations. The majority of these translations are from Brazilian authors, 58 per cent, over Portuguese authors, 28 per cent, and African authors, 13 per cent (included in this category is the author Luís Cardoso from East Timor). Notably, starting in the 2000s there is a steady increase in the publication rate for African and Brazilian literatures, while there is a slight decrease from the 1990s to today for Portuguese literature. This substantial increase is a tripling of Brazilian literature (from twenty-two titles in the 1990s to sixty-five in the 2000s) and African literature (from five to sixteen) while leaving the Portuguese works at a stagnant rate. When it comes to the 2010s there is nearly the same number of translations from African authors (seventeen books) as there is of

Table 8 A total number of 317 editions of Lusophone literature were translated and published in Sweden during the studied period. The total number of publications is broken down by decade and number of editions, corresponding to the geographical regions of these source cultures

Period	Total	African	Brazilian	Portuguese
1980–1989	44	4	25	15
1990–1999	55	5	22	28
2000–2009	106	16	64	26
2010–2018	112	17	64	20
Total	317 (100%)	42 (13%)	185 (58%)	89 (28%)

Portuguese authors (twenty books), which is quite remarkable considering that the Portuguese literary market produces much higher numbers of annual publications, and has a stronger position as a source country in international translations than its African counterparts. The explanation for the increased numbers of translated works from Africa and Brazil, while not including Portugal, seems to be explained by changes in the Swedish publishing landscape, as will be addressed when discussing the development in the 2000s.

During this whole period, the Portuguese and Brazilian classics from the *aesthetes* – in this case considered as canonized authorships in their national literary histories – do not attract the same interest as we can see in the Italian case. In comparison, we do not see the same impact of a 'past symbolic capital' in the cultural transfer that could have resulted in new publications of Portuguese 'old classics' from the Middle Ages or Renaissance, or romanticism such as Gil Vicente, Luís de Camões or Almeida de Garett. We do however find translations from early twentieth-century *aesthetes*, although these are quite modest in number, counting approximately five titles per decade. Among these we find three novels each by Eça de Queirós (Portugal) and Machado de Assis (Brazil), several volumes of poetry by Ferando Pessoa and the modernist novel by Mário de Sá-Carneiro (both Portuguese first-wave modernists), published by the small-scale niche publishing house Pontes.

Instead, the intercultural relations promoting the Lusophone literary translations, produced during the decades before the studied period, were to a high degree politically tinged, connected to leftist intellectual ideas of solidarity and human rights. In the 1960s and 1970s, Swedish governmental, as well as non-governmental, organizations and solidarity groups supported, in different ways, the struggle for independence (from the colonial power Portugal) in African countries. Already in the 1970s, translations of writers such as Luandino Vieira (Angola) and Agostinho Neto (a poet and Angola's first president), as well as writings by leaders of liberation movements, Eduardo Mondlane (Mozambique) and Amilcar Cabral (Cabo Verde and Guiné-Bissau) were presented to the Swedish audience. The same political interest now invested in the political opposition to the totalitarian Brazilian and Portuguese contemporary regimes showed the pathways of the translated works from these source cultures. In 1976, the feminist classic and globally translated and circulated *Novas Cartas Portuguesas* (Barreno, Horta and Costa, 1972, *New Portuguese Letters*) was published, entitled *De tre Mariornas bok. Nya portugisiska brev*, by Forum. Apart from expressing liberating feminist intellectual thought in an advanced hybrid aesthetic form, the work also contained strong criticism of the Portuguese fascist regime and its colonial war (for a thorough analysis of the book's global circulation and reception, see Amaral et al. 2015). From Brazil, the professional and award-winning translator Marianne Eyre translated Augusto Boal's political theatre and the internationally known socialist novelist Jorge Amado.

In the 1980s, the number of publications was still very modest, only forty-four altogether, and the literary genres represented were quite evenly distributed between novels, poetry and short stories. The publishers were quite diversified, ranging from generalist larger publishers such as Norstedts to non-profit, non-governmental solidarity groups, such as Afrikagrupperna, which published the Angolan novelist Pepetela. The tendency of a political interest showing the path for the translations of Lusophone literatures into Swedish continued. The publishers' framing (prefaces and covers) of the African and Portuguese literary works highlighted the sociopolitical contexts of contemporary historical events, such as the end of Portuguese colonial rule, the revolution of 1974 and the struggle for African independence. For example, the introduction of Agostinho Neto's poetry placed his poems in the independent struggle from Portuguese colonialism, and the back covers of novels by the Portuguese writer Almeida Faria contextualized his narrative of family history in the backdrop of the Portuguese Carnation Revolution of 1974. Besides these more contemporary translations, that dominated this flow, it was mainly single titles by male novelists and poets in the categories of *aesthetes* and *notables* from Portugal and Brazil (as mentioned above) that were included. The only exception from the single title phenomenon was the Brazilian poet Carlos Drummond de Andrade who had four volumes translated. As evidenced in released protocols from the Swedish Academy's discussion of the Nobel Prize, Drummond de Andrade was placed several times on the list as a possible candidate in the 1960s. The Brazilian flow also included the novelty of eight works of children's literature, thereby introducing to the Swedish reader the women writers Lygia Bojunga and Ana Maria Machado.

During the 1990s, the features that started to crucially influence the translation flow were the strong prevalence of the novel as a literary genre and the emergence of single contemporary consecrated authorships (*notables*). As many as 87 per cent (forty-eight of fifty-five editions) of the translated literary works of this decade were novels. The 1990s was also the only period when the number of translations was highest for Portuguese works. Leading up to the Portuguese Nobel Prize for José Saramago in 1998, several novels by him and, the other widely critically acclaimed and considered Nobel candidate, the Portuguese writer, António Lobo Antunes were translated by Marianne Eyre and published by the large-scale publishers Wahlström & Widstrand and Forum, respectively. Out of the total amount of twenty-eight Portuguese publications, Saramago with eleven editions and Lobo Antunes with nine editions were together responsible for twenty of them. Another feature was the start-up of the small-scale niche publishers Pontes and Fabian, which published nearly all the other Portuguese publications, as well as several of the Brazilian ones. This niche publisher specialized in *aesthetes* from Portugal (e.g. Pessoa), and Brazil (e.g. Machado de Assis and Graciliano Ramos).

In the 1990s, Brazilian literature introduced the novelty of women novelists to the Lusophone flow: Helena Morley (Pontes), Ana Miranda (Wahlström & Widstrand), Lýgia Fagundes Telles (Natur och Kultur) and Clarice Lispector (Tranan). With Clarice Lispector as the only exception, the trend for these women authorships, as well as for the majority of the Brazilian male authorships published was that these writers, *notables* in their source culture, rarely had their first translated novel followed up by a second. This was a trend that continued throughout the following decades, especially in large-scale publishing, as in the cases of the contemporary notables Milton Hatoum, Michel Laub, Andréa de Fuego and Barbara Vanessa.

By the new millennium, the number of Lusophone translated works doubled due to a substantial increase in Brazilian and African translations. The feature that strongly dominated these translation flows between 2000 and 2018 was the entrance of niched small-scale and micro-publishers in the contemporary landscape for the Lusophone literatures in the Swedish market. Niche publishers taking over from the larger more generalist publishers of these literatures were visible in several cases. After the Nobel Prize, new translations of José Saramago's literary production continued to be published during the 2000s as well as translations of António Lobo Antunes. However, in the 2010s, after Saramago's death, the publications decreased and the latest translation of his work *Kain* (*Cain*) was published by Tranan in 2013. Also, the publishing of António Lobo Antunes has been taken over from Forum by the publishing house Modernista, who re-published the Benfica Trilogy in 2017.

A large proportion of the Brazilian increase can again in part be contributed to a single authorship, the worldwide best-selling popular Paulo Coelho. The 'Paulo Coelho effect' took off in the 2000s when the publishing house Bazar took over from the publishing house Forum, which belonged to the Bonnier Group.

A sign of Coelho's popularity in Sweden was the 2008 publication of Staffan Vahlqvist's debut novel *Jag sköt Paulo Coelho* ('I shot Paulo Coelho'), in which the main character gets so frustrated with Coelho's popularity, which he regards as an effect of bad taste among the reading public, that he decides to assassinate the Brazilian author. Forum had published Coelho's first translated work in Swedish, *Alkemisten* (*The Alchemist*) in 1995. Since Bazar (a niche publisher specializing in best-selling works) published Coelho's first title in 2002 they had up until 2018 published sixty-one editions and re-editions of Coelho's novels. In the first decade (the 2000s) alone he was the author of thirty-one of the forty-seven Brazilian novels published. This left sixteen translated Brazilian novels, and as many as thirteen of these were published by the new niche publisher Tranan, including authors such as Ruben Fonseca, Bernardo Carvalho, João Ubaldo Ribeiro, Paulo Lins and Chico Buarque.

The publishing house Tranan, established in 1992 and specialized in literature from the world outside Europe, is in the 2000s the publisher behind a major part of the increased number of publications from Brazil, Africa and East Timor. Tranan's translations include a rich variety of published authors from these source cultures, such as, besides the Brazilian ones mentioned above, several novels by Ondjaki and Pepetela from Angola, Luís Cardoso from East Timor and Germano Almeida from Cape Verde. Tranan also published separate volumes of translated short stories from Mozambique and Brazil. The fact that Tranan established itself as a major player in publishing Lusophone literatures, although not including European Portuguese literature in their profile, is probably one of the reasons behind the decrease in translations from Portuguese literature in the overall flow. One interesting illustration of this is the fact that Tranan recently included two translated titles by the Portuguese notable Gonçalo M. Tavares in their backlist. In doing so the publisher incorporated this internationally recognized and circulated Portuguese authorship in their profile through extending Tavares' geographical affiliation to include Angola, and emphasizing it as his birthplace (in the epitext on Tranan's website).

During the 2010s, Tranan also had company from other niche publishers in publishing Luso-African contemporary notables, such as Mia Couto and Agualusa, published by the mid-scale publisher Leopard (publishing fiction from Africa and Asia) and the micro-publisher Almaviva (specializing in Portuguese and Luso-African literatures). Another micro-publisher, Panta rei, managed by the cultural mediator (translator, editor and publisher) Gunilla Winberg, was behind titles from Angolan authors that represented novelties in this translation flow. Among the translations from Panta rei we find two crime novels, with a socially critical perspective, by the *notable* Pepetela and a volume of chronicles, *Salomes huvud* (2014; *A Cabeça de Salomé*, 2004) by Paula Tavares. Panta rei also published a children's book by Maria Celestina Fernandes, which placed this micro-publisher as the force behind two of the – stunningly – only three existing translations of women writers in the Portuguese language from Africa in the whole period investigated here.

When it comes to translations of poetry, these volumes constitute approximately 11 per cent of the total number of the publications during the period. Translations of poetry started in a modest way and increased by the turn of the millennium due to the establishment of the small and micro-publishers Fabian, Pontes, Almaviva and Edition Diadorim. These are all very small enterprises, managed by single multitasking individuals: the translators Margareta Marin and Lars Axelsson (Pontes) translating Fernando Pessoa, Ulla Gabrielsson (Edition Diadorim) who translated five volumes of Ferreira Gullar (Brazil) and the Portuguese poet Ana Luísa Amaral, Marianne Sandels (Almaviva) who translated the Portuguese poets Ana Luísa Amaral, Nuno Júdice, Vasco Graça Moura, Jorge de Sena and Eugénio de Andrade. Besides the titles these translators published in their own companies they were also the translators of the Lusophone poetry published by other publishing houses, which made them crucial nodal persons in the cultural networks of cultural exchange and dissemination of Lusophone poetry in Sweden.

The other literary genre that occupies approximately 10 per cent of the total number of translations in the whole period is children's literature. This is especially due to the Brazilian translations which offer a steady number of books by Maria Machado de Assis and Lygia Bojunga. In 2004, Lygia Bojunga received the prestigious Swedish prize Astrid Lindgren Memorial Award (ALMA) which led to a republishing of several of her works. By the 2010s, this genre had introduced a diversity of authors from Brazil: Ilan Brenman, André Neves, David Cali and Silvana Talvano. Additionally, there was one title each by Ondjaki from Angola and the Portuguese authors Isabel Minhós Martins, Rita Nabais and Catarina Sobral. This is the only literary genre in the Lusophone translation flow that presents a gender balance by numbers, which is not the case for any other genres.

The overall predominance of translations from Brazil (58 per cent), in general allowed for a more diversified translation flow when it comes to literary genres. Among the Brazilian translations we also find biographies, memoirs and a series of comic books that we do not see represented in the Portuguese or African translations. The comic books were about the football stars Neymar Jr. and Ronaldinho Gaucho and introduced new translators of the Portuguese language. Another feature that influenced the annual number of publications was the possibility of being the focus country of the largest book fair in Sweden. In 2014, Brazil was the focus country in the Gothenburg Book Fair, which spawned an increase of published titles to twenty-five, compared to the five to eight translations published in the years before and after. The Brazilian translations also presented a higher number of women authors compared to translated Portuguese and African literatures, which nevertheless did not mean a positive shift in the gender balance. This raises the question of what has not been translated from the Lusophone literature so far, namely notable women authors.

Just as in the case of Italian literary translations into Swedish, the operating gender bias, in favour of male writers, is striking in the Lusophone flow. When calculating the gender of translated Lusophone authors with their own published volume, eighty-three (79 per cent) were men and twenty-two (21 per cent) were women. The proportion of women authors' representation in all the three translations flows was roughly the same; that is, Brazilian women authors constituted 20 per cent, Portuguese women reached 23 per cent and African women 21 per cent. Out of a total of 317 published editions (including re-editions) only fifty-four (17 per cent) were authored by women. Moreover, of these fifty-four translations of women authors twenty-five (that is as much as 46 per cent) were in the genre of children's literature. Although the overall, predominant literary genre in the published translations of this period was the novel (64 per cent of the total amount), women were mainly represented in the historical stronghold for women authors, that is, children's literature. There was thereby a void of untranslated novels from important contemporary women also belonging to the categories of aesthetes and notables in their source cultures. For example, as regards critically acclaimed women authors in the Lusophone source cultures such as Agustina Bessa-Luís, Maria Judith de Carvalho and Maria Velho da Costa from Portugal, Nélida Piñon and Raquel de Quieroz from Brazil, and Paulina Chiziane from Mozambique, to name but a few, if they appeared at all it was only with a short story in an anthology. Moreover, the notable Lídia Jorge, with a dense novel production translated into other languages, and receiver of literary awards, had one novel translated into Swedish. In fact, this was the only translated novel from a Portuguese woman author in the whole period. Among established notable and aesthete women authors from these source cultures, Clarice Lispector was the only novelist granted consistency of publication, with eight titles translated. This same picture of contemporary gender inequality in the representation of Lusophone women authors in translation is supported by the results of researchers looking at this question in the UK (Odber de Baubeta 2012, Fernandes 2013, Atkin 2020).

The Lusophone translations being a limited phenomenon in the Swedish literary sphere, combined with favouritism towards only the very most consecrated notables and aesthete authors (read men) in these source cultures, seems to leave little room for women authors' translations, no matter how critically acclaimed they are in their source cultures. Furthermore, it is highly likely that consecration processes and critical acclaim of women authors in their national literary history and establishment can significantly influence which authors will be up for consideration to cross borders in translation. In any case, to be able to give a thorough answer to this gender question, a more in-depth case study, encompassing the whole circulation process, than is possible to conduct here will be needed (cf. Atkin 2020).

To conclude, although translated Lusophone literary works in Sweden still constitute a modest phenomenon in terms of numbers, the quantity of publications more than doubled from the first decade to the last in the period studied. During this time, the number of Brazilian and African translations tripled, while the Portuguese publications decreased in number slightly, a trend that can be explained by the emergence of new niche publishers such as Tranan, with a profile encompassing African and Brazilian literatures while leaving European Portuguese literature outside their scope. The overall picture shows a strong predominance of the contemporary novel, authored by notables – authors receiving prestigious international, Lusophone and national awards, and with high sales figures in their source cultures. With the exception of a handful of novelists such as Paulo Coelho, Mia Couto, Agualusa, António Lobo Antunes, José Saramago and Clarice Lispector the overall trend for these authors was to have one novel published (probably for the publisher to test the waters) without the title being followed up with a second one. Nevertheless, it was above all the 'smugglers', the networking culturally engaged mediators – translators and micro-publishers – that constituted the force behind the publishing consistency of Lusophone translations in general, and of poetry in particular, into Swedish (cf. Roig-Sanz and Meylaerts 2018).

Francophone and Hispanic Caribbean bibliomigration to Sweden 1980–2018

The Caribbean literary space is a heterogeneous and multifaceted culture interconnected by the sea, but also divided by different colonial experiences and languages, landscapes and seascapes. Since translation on top of this is never neutral and always ideological, Caribbean bibliomigration resists generalizing descriptions. Despite this heterogeneity and diversity some salient features of the Francophone and Hispanic literary flows from the Caribbean literary periphery to the Swedish literary semi-periphery will be explored in this segment – flows which were marked by the unwillingness of Swedish publishers to risk publishing an unknown Caribbean writer, who had not previously been consecrated by literary prizes and awards within the Anglo-American literary space. The success of the studied peripheral writers in the Swedish literary market thus seems to depend on the consecration and success within the Anglo-American literary culture. Bibliomigrancy from this part of the world to the northern hemisphere, and particularly to Sweden, seems to a large extent to depend on a kind of double consecration – first within the centre of the former colonial power and secondly within the centres of the Anglo-American literary culture. This double consecration process is decisive for the lion's share of both Francophone and Hispanic Caribbean literature in Swedish translation. On the contrary, Anglophone Caribbean writers, whether they are presented as Cuban or Haitian writers to the Swedish readers – as in the case of for instance Esmeralda Santiago and Edwidge Danticat – do not need double consecration in the same way in order to be selected for translation into Swedish. This is due to the Americanization of Swedish literary space – a long-term process, which reaches back as far as the mid-nineteenth century (Torgerson 1982). More recently in 2018, 71 per cent of all fiction published and translated in Sweden comprised translations from English. Generally, examining the years between first publication in original language and Swedish translation the works of 'Hispanic writers' writing in English migrate faster than their Spanish language counterparts to Sweden. Furthermore, bibliomigration of Francophone Caribbean literature is usually even more long-lasting.

The following presentation and comparison start with two Francophone writers confirming the bibliomigration pattern of double consecration; they continued with an exception to that rule and conclude with a supposedly Francophone Haitian author writing in English. Then Hispanic bibliomigration is further explored with a representative example of double consecration and another exception to the most common patterns of the Hispanic literary flow to Sweden. Finally, the salient features of the two flows are compared.

Bibliomigration patterns of the Caribbean Francophone literature form part of the French mono-centric literary consecration culture (Casanova 2004) where most authors are *made* in Paris:

> [...] on the literary front France is still institutionally and intellectually the *locus princeps*. Not only are literary texts, essays and histories published in Paris, but it is first and foremost there that they are commissioned, reviewed and commended. The majority of established Caribbean authors become famous originally in France, and the United States has only really courted French Caribbean writers to the extent that Paris has already made their reputation.
>
> (Gallagher 2002: 206)

The literature of the Francophone part of the Caribbean translated into Swedish, stems from the islands Haiti, Guadeloupe and Martinique. The database Världslitteratur.se, which is the most important source for this research, lists sixteen authors from this literary space. Of these sixteen authors, nine have been translated into Swedish (Table 9). In this Francophone context, Martinique can be singled out as the 'island of poetry and politics', since the island has fostered important poets such as Aimé Cesaire and Joseph Zabel and major thinkers such as Édouard Glissant, Franz Fanon and Partick Chamoiseau, also a Goncourt prize winner. However, Cesaire and Zabel were not translated within the researched time span and will therefore not be commented on. Four authors will be examined in the following: Danny Laferrière, Maryse Condé, Patrick Chamoiseau and Edwidge Danticate. The consecration processes for Laferrière, Condé and Chamoiseau are rather similar to those demonstrated by the Gallagher quote above. They have been published within several literary genres in France and they have received high acclaim in the form of literary

Table 9 Overview of the Francophone Caribbean literature per region and according to the selection criteria of the study

Region	Authors presented in Världslitteratur.se	Authors in Swedish translation	Translated novels 1980–2019
Haiti	6	2	4
Guadeloupe	5	2	9
Martinique	5	5	1
Total	16	9	14

prizes and awards. They were all published in Paris by prestigious publishing houses and they have been translated into English by translators who hold large amounts of translation capital (Lindqvist 2019).

Maryse Condé, nevertheless, has been the most successful of the four in establishing herself in the Swedish literary market, with six translated novels, a translated youth novel and a biography, in comparison with one novel each for Laferrière and Chamoiseau. Condé stands out due to her high consecration within Anglo-American literary culture, marked by the American and British literary prizes and awards she has received. As we have shown in earlier chapters, these constitute important selection criteria for Swedish translations. The category of notable authors are the most translated into Swedish in the majority of the flows explored in this book. In the Anglophone literary space, Condé has been awarded the 1993 Puterbaugh Prize, the 1999 Prix Marguerite Yourcenar and the 2005 Hurston/Wright Legacy Award. In 2015, she was also shortlisted for the Man Booker International Prize. These consecration processes can probably, apart from her demiurgic literary skills, be ascribed to her eminent academic career in the United States. Additionally, among her more than twenty novels, twelve have been translated into English. Another factor contributing to her American consecration might be her systematic collaboration with her (second) husband, English translator Richard Philcox. He frequently writes paratexts, for instance translator's notes explaining his translation strategies when working with Condé's novels. As we have seen, paratexts are an efficient way of framing a foreign experience for a new audience (Watts 2005). A case in point is Philcox's three-page preface in his translation of *Traversée de la mangrove*, which following Genette's (1987: 169) terminology, can be characterized as allographic, since it evaluates the narrative to follow more than discussing the translation strategies. Philcox explains that his translation was very much influenced by Virginia Woolf's novel *To the Lighthouse* (1927), since its interior monologue corresponds exactly to the twenty monologues in Condé's novel. Moreover, he finds a kinship between Condé's and Woolf's style, tone, register and characters, despite differences in time and location. Philcox claims that he translated Condé's novel with the voice of Virginia Woolf in the back of his mind (Lindqvist 2019). Consequently, he presents Condé as a worthy member of the hyper canon in Damrosch's terms (2009).

Furthermore, Condé's œuvre initially needed double consecration to be selected for inscription in the Swedish literary canon by translation. After three translated novels, however, no previous English translation was needed. She had found the way to her Swedish readers. The temporal gap between the first source publication and translation in the early stages of her bibliomigration was twenty years, but during the last decades this gap has constantly diminished to a few years (Lindqvist 2016). For Francophone Caribbean literature translated into Swedish, the degree of symbolically past capital (cf. Sapiro 2015) is low, close to non-existent, since Caribbean literature is young in comparison with its colonial counterparts. Nevertheless, today Condé is an established French Caribbean author held in high esteem by the Swedish reading audience – a fact demonstrated by her selection for the 2018 alternative Nobel Prize for Literature (cf. Chapter 4).

For the Haitian author, Dany Laferrière's translation, bibliomigration and its sequel within the Swedish literary space is quite different from that of Maryse Condé. The consecration processes of Laferrière mainly remain within the Francophone cultural sphere. Laferrière has not been awarded any Anglo-American tokens of consecration. This circumstance might explain the fact that only one of his fifteen novels so far has been translated into Swedish. Laferrière grew up in Port-au-Prince, Haiti, during the Duvalier regime. He worked as a journalist before emigrating to Montréal, Canada and later on to the United States. Laferrière refers to his œuvre as 'an American autobiography' (Jaggi 2013). It ranges from vernacularizing fiction drawing on his Haitian childhood to field notes from travels across North America. It also touches upon absent fathers and nourishing family females, interracial relations and sex tourism, which are more cosmopolitan themes. The narrative style is more often than not provocative and ironic. He defines his style as direct, North American, without any unnecessary flourishes, but written in French (Jaggi 2013), the latter probably the reason for the non-translation into Swedish of most of his œuvre. His production comprises fifteen novels, but only one has been translated into Swedish, namely *Comment faire l'amour avec un nègre sans se fatiguer* published in 1985 at VLB Editions at Quebéc, in Canada (Lindqvist 2019). The novel was translated into Swedish in 1991 with the Swedish title *Konsten att älska med en neger utan att bli utmattad* (*The Art of Making Love to a Negro Without Getting Exhausted*). The inflammatory n-word is here translated literally from the Canadian title. However, the word was not as controversial at the beginning of the 1990s as it is today, a fact underlined by the reduction strategy employed concerning the same word in the Swedish translation of *The Brief Wondrous Life of Oscar Wao* in 2009.

Concerning the literary consecration within the studied cultures, Laferrière has received several important literary awards and prizes, for instance the Prix

Carbet de la Caraïbe 1991, for the novel *L'odeur du café* (1991) translated in 1993 with the title *An Aroma of Coffee* (1993), the Prix Médicis 2009 for *L'Énigme du retour* (2009; *The Return*, 2011) and the Grand Prix Metropolis bleu 2010 for the novel *Je suis un écrivain japonais* (2008; *I am a Japanese Writer*, 2010). Laferrière is published by the prestigious French publishing house Grasset in Paris, which holds the global rights to his works. Exceptions are Québec and other Francophone areas in the Americas, as he remains faithful to his Montréal-based publishers, Éditions du Boréal and Mémoire d'encrier. In December 2013 Laferrière was elected to the French Academy. His election constituted the culmination of Laferrière's French literary consecration. He is the first Haitian and the first Canadian writer ever inducted into the French Academy (Lindqvist 2019).

Laferrière's translator into English, David Homel, is himself an established Canadian prize-winning writer, also receiving the Governor General's Literary Award for Translation in 1995 and 2001. His English translation from 1987 was published by Coach House Press in Toronto and by Bloomsbury in London the same year. The Swedish translator Tony Andersson, published by Tidens Publishing house in 1990, remembers how he struggled with the Koran verses that initiate each chapter. He collaborated with a pious Koran specialist in these translations and was worried that the specialist would ask to see a sample from the book, which he found too audacious for the specialist. Andersson is today a well-established translator with a large amount of accumulated translation capital (Lindqvist 2019). That Dany Laferrière's novel was published within both the French and English literary spheres before it was translated into Swedish, not to forget the success of the Canadian drama film directed by Jaques W. Benoit made in 1989 and based on the novel, probably influenced the decision to undertake a translation into Swedish.

Patrick Chamoiseau's work sheds light on the dynamic processes of creolization that have shaped Caribbean history and culture. In fact, the contemporary vitality of Antillean literature is frequently linked to him (McCusker 2007: 14). Chamoiseau lives and works in Fort-de-France, Martinique. According to Knepper (2012), Chamoiseau is one of the most important living Caribbean writers today. His literary production comprises twelve novels, several essays and plays. In addition to his fictional output, Chamoiseau is a major postcolonial theorist. He is the author of several non-fiction works dealing with the colonial history of Martinique and the Manifest of the Creole movement (Bernabé et al. 1989).

His novels deplore the loss of Creole traditions among the Martinican people, especially of the ancient oral literary traditions, which he tries to preserve and develop as 'le marqueur de paroles', the word scratcher (Gigoley 2013: 161). What is most striking about Chamoiseau's work is his foregrounding of language. His works are judged 'a potential nightmare for the translator', in view of his eclectic play between Creole and French, his code-switching, his register and sociolectal shifts, as well as his neologisms, creolisms and non-standard syntax (Gigoley 2013: 161). Consequently, Chamoiseau has felt the need to explain his four writing principles to his translators. First, he stresses the importance of the Creole language and the Creole 'conception of the world' (Volk 1999: vii), including the ideological and humanistic benefits of opacity. Second, he uses the 'totality' (vii) of the French language. This leads to his third principle, namely the arrangement of language to undermine and relativize its coherence as a 'formal' (vii) system, to 'feel it trembling' (vii) and to open it up to the possibilities of other languages. Finally, writing should 'sacrifice everything to the music of the phrase' (viii).

Chamoiseau's third novel *Texaco* (1992), originally published by Gallimard, is his only literary work translated into Swedish. It was awarded the most important and prestigious literary prize in France, the Prix Goncourt. *Texaco* was translated into English in 1997 by Rose-Myriam Réjouis, an associate professor of literature at Lang New School in New York with Haitian roots, and her American husband Val Vinokurov. According to N'Zengou-Tayo and Wilson (2000: 91), *Texaco*'s success in English translation, despite many potential pitfalls, can be attributed to Réjouis, who together with Vinokurov was awarded the American Translation Association's Lewis Galantière Prize for Best Book in 1998. After the English translation appeared, critical acclaim for Chamoiseau's work and his international stature as a writer grew. Nonetheless, as in the case of Dany Laferrière, Chamoiseau's literary consecration mainly remains within the French-speaking cultural sphere (Lindqvist 2019). This is reflected in the literary awards he has received, including the 1993 Prix Carbet de la Caraïbe for his novel *Antan d'enfance* (1993) and the 2002 Prix Spécial du jury RFO for *Biblique des derniers gestes* (2002).

In Sweden, *Texaco* was translated by Anders Bodegård as early as 1994 and published by Bonniers, only two years after its first publication in France and before the English translation. Thus, the double consecration hypothesis is not supported in this case – an exception confirming the rule in the Caribbean Francophone flow. One possible explanation could be that the Swedish translation was not initiated by a publishing house, but by the very prestigious and hence charismatic translator. Indeed, Bodegård fell in love with the novel after reading it in 1993 in Paris. He travelled to Martinique and studied the local language to better recreate the Creole sound in Swedish. Bodegård is considered one of the most prominent Swedish literary translators of modern times (Ekenberg 2014), which is confirmed by the fact that he is the only Swedish translator ever to be nominated for the European Aristeion Translation Prize (Lindqvist 2019).

The second most translated supposedly French Caribbean author is Edwidge Danticat, with three novels: *Breath, Eyes and Memory* (1994), *The Farming of Bones* (1998) and *Claire of the Sea Light* (2013), the first two originally published by Soho Press and the latter by Knopf. They were all translated into Swedish by Dorothee Sporrong – a prolific and highly recognized translator – and published under the titles *Magiska länkar* (Magic links) in 1996 by Natur och Kultur and *En skörd av tårar* (A harvest of tears) in 2000, by Norstedts and *Claire, som havets ljus* (Claire as the light of the sea), in 2019 by Tranan. The original language of the novels is English, Edwidge Danticat having moved from Haiti to the United States at the age of twelve. However, her English is marked by reminiscent layers of the different languages of the Caribbean – French, Creole and even Spanish – which affect the English syntax. Her novels are in this sense multilingual, where the multilingualism simultaneously expresses the lack of belonging and a new freedom (Kullberg 2016: 61). Danticat has received more than twenty-five literary prizes and awards, starting with the Caribbean Writer award in 1994, and the most recent the Neustadt International Prize for literature in 2019, which is sometimes called the American Nobel Prize. No double consecration is thus necessary to reach Swedish readers in translation. Having explored the Francophone Caribbean bibliomigrancy to Sweden we now turn to some further examples from the Hispanic literary flow.

An examination of the Hispanic Caribbean literature in Världslitteratur. se results in fifty-nine listed authors. Of these fifty-nine authors fifteen are translated into Swedish. Literature presented as Cuban represents the highest number of translated authors in comparison with Puerto Rican literature and literature from the Dominican Republic (Table 10).

From examining Table 10 one could reach the conclusion that each author translated into Swedish is represented by approximately two novels, but by the majority of the authors – nine out of fifteen – there is only one novel translated into Swedish, which seems to be symptomatic of the Caribbean literary flow to Sweden. Bibliomigration patterns from the Spanish Caribbean to the Swedish

Table 10 Overview of the Spanish Caribbean literature per region and according to the selection criteria of the study

Region	Authors presented in Världslitteratur.se	Authors in Swedish translation	Translated novels 1980–2019
Cuba	39	12	24
Dominican Republic	9	2	2
Puerto Rico	11	1	2
Total	59	15	28

literary space are highly complex, since the authors studied write in Spanish and/or in English, thus belonging to two different kinds of consecration cultures. Of the twelve authors presented as Cuban, only five live in Cuba. Two of them work and live in Spain and of the remaining five, four live in the United States and one in Sweden. Both authors from the Dominican Republic live and work in New York. They write in both Spanish and English and sometimes use both languages simultaneously in the same novel. The Puerto Rican author Esmeralda Santiago for instance, writes in English, but is very well aware of the Spanish literary market and hence translates her novels herself into Spanish. These dynamics reveal some of the inherent difficulties in working with literature stemming from the Spanish Caribbean space. The following sections will examine one author representative of the most common bibliomigration pattern of Hispanic Caribbean literature to Sweden and – as in the Francophone flow – an exception confirming the rule.

A representative writer from the most important Hispanic flow to Sweden, the Cuban, is Zoé Valdés. Valdés spent her childhood and part of her studies in Cuba. Before finishing her studies, she was employed by UNESCO and moved to Paris. She returned to Cuba at the beginning of the 1990s and led the cultural journal *Cine Cubano* during that time. In 1994, she was officially exiled from Cuba for political reasons. Today, Valdés shares her time between France and Spain, working as a poet, writer and critic. To date, she has written more than fifteen novels and ten collections of poems. Valdés collaborates frequently with French and Spanish cultural journals and daily press. She also writes film scripts. Her themes are fictionalized autobiographical and she writes about her native Cuba with nostalgia and explores sexuality in writing, where she also criticizes Cuban politics.

Valdés has received many literary prizes and awards in France and Spain both for her production of novels and her poetry, for example the Planeta prize

(Premio Planeta) in 1996, the Liberateur Prize in 1997 and the Chevalier de l'Ordre des Arts et des Lettres in 1999. In the year 2013, Valdés was awarded the Azorín Prize for the novel *La mujer que llora* (*The Crying Woman*). The Planeta prize is a Spanish literary prize founded by the Planeta Publishing house rewarding a novel written in Spanish. The sum of money of the prize is the second highest sum for a literary prize in the world, except for the Nobel Prize. The Liberateur Prize existed during the period 1987–2012 and was an annual literary prize for writers from Africa, Asia and Latin America at the Frankfurt book fair, and the Valdéz Azorín Prize is a Spanish annual literary award presented by the municipality of Alicante and the Planeta publishing house. Two novels by Valdés have been translated into Swedish: *Vårt dagliga intet* (*La nada cotidiana*) and *Jag skänkte dig mitt liv* (*Te di la vida entera*). They were published in 1999 and 2000 in Sweden by Norstedts publishing house and translated by Yvonne Blank – a recognized translator specializing in Spanish language literature. In the English language sphere, Valdés' novels were published by Arcade Publishing New York with the titles *Yocandra in the Paradise of Nada: A Novel of Cuba* in 1997 and *I Gave You All I Had* in 1999, both translated by Nadia Benabid. Arcade Publishing was founded by Jeanette and Dick Seaver in 1988. They specialized in translated fiction. Nadia Benabid, born in Morocco, took her degree at Princeton University and works today as a translator from Arabic, French and Spanish. She translates both poetry and fiction but specializes in non-fiction literature for academic purposes, for instance anthologies of Arabic, French and Latin American modern literature and philosophy. As we have seen, the double consecration hypothesis was also confirmed by the bibliomigrancy pattern of the two translated novels by Zoé Valdés (Lindqvist 2018).

The exception to the discovered patterns in the Hispanic material is the novel by the Cuban author Senel Paz *El lobo, el bosque y el hombre nuevo* (The Wolf, the Forest and the New Man) which was published by Edición Homenaje del Ministerio de Cultura in Cuba in 1990. The novel is better known under the title *Fresas y Chocolate* (*Strawberry and Chocolate*) after a movie based on the novel directed by Tomás Gutiérrez Alea and Juan Carlos Tabío. Senel Paz is an important screenwriter and playwright in Cuba, where he is the principal of and teacher at the International School for Theatre and Cinema. His plays and tales have been translated into seven languages and published in international anthologies.

In Sweden, the novel *El lobo, el bosque y el hombre nuevo* was published by Carlsson Publishing house in 1994 on the personal initiative of the translator Eva

Sjöblom. The breaking of the pattern of double consecration might be explained by the fact that the personal initiative set aside 'normal' consecration processes in this case. It was not until 1995 that the novel appeared at Bloomsbury Publishing in London in Peter R. Bush's translation and that the film based on the novel had its Swedish premiere (Lindqvist 2019).

Comparing bibliomigration patterns of the Caribbean Francophone and Hispanic literatures some shared and decisive features can be discerned, notably the fact that these literary flows are not important in numbers, that there are no niched publishing houses for this kind of literature in Sweden, that the majority of the translated authors are so-called 'notables', that it is more common that Swedish publishers only publish one novel of each writer than several, that the majority are published by medium-sized publishers in Sweden, that the literary translators are highly consecrated and that double consecration seems to be a favourable process for choosing which literature to translate. Two exceptions to the succession of events in the bibliomigration – one in the Francophone flow and the other in the Hispanic – point to the influence of highly consecrated translators within the Swedish literary space. Their personal intervention persuading node persons within the publishing houses to translate novels of their choice actually set aside double consecration processes. However, to sum up, bibliomigration patterns for the Hispanic Caribbean writers are more complicated and windling than the mono-centric Francophone bibliomigration, which is due to the pluri-centrality of the Hispanic language and consecration culture.

Concluding remarks

As has been indicated by the overviews of the six translation flows given above, the conclusions that can be drawn from our empirical material confirm, complement and in some respects seemingly contradict each other. This is not surprising and might even constitute a fourth conclusive significant trait of the semi-peripheral position in the world literary geography – a position which is not an 'either/or', but rather an entangled relational constellation of in and out flux of contemporary literature. However, three relevant dimensions will be singled out here.

The first is the overall changes over time in the make up of the Swedish literary landscape and the significant geographies studied in this volume. The overall tendencies do not always coincide with the specific bibliomigration patterns, but the contradictions might be quite easy to explain after a closer look and some pondering. As always when one juggles with statistics, it is important to keep in mind which entities you are actually comparing and that if you are working with percentages it is the proportionality that you are discussing. In the introductory section of this chapter the overall statistics of all literary publications in Scandinavia were examined in order to understand how it is possible that such relatively 'small' languages as Danish and Swedish could make their way into the top ten list of most important source languages in the world republic of letters, according to the UNESCO statistics. One answer is that there is a local Scandinavian translation field in play asserting the Scandinavian languages' position. With the help of variables such as translation rates and non-translation rates and most translated languages it was also shown that the Swedish position was the relational centre in the Scandinavian literary geography (Lindqvist 2016).

Narrowing down the focus and examining solely the Swedish literary geography and only fiction – domestic and translated – during the last forty years, it was also shown that this literary space has become increasingly closed, which probably entails a more central position in the Scandinavian geography. These changes in openness over time were partly related to structural developments of the literary markets, economic fluctuations and new agents in the literary field. In this context it might be considered a contradiction that the number of publications within both Italian and Lusophone translated fiction actually increased during the researched period. However, as we know, numbers and percentages are not comparable. High numbers say very little about proportionality, which is what percentages are all about. Here it suffices to underline that the important results from our investigations are that even though Sweden is evolving into a more closed literary geography and the numerical importance of specific flows varies over time, the translations themselves still show important signs of openness towards the world. This is possibly a significant trait of the semi-periphery.

In line with studies on the effect of globalization of the publishing industry, our material demonstrates an overall trend of 'contemporanization' in translations both into and from Swedish. The narrowing temporal gap between the first publication of literary works and their translation is not only a matter of an accelerated translation process but also illustrates a shift in the kinds of authors and the types of literature that are translated. Here, too, however, some of the translation flows contradict the overall pattern, indicating that they follow specific dynamics.

In the case of Swedish literature, the historically large proportion of canonical authors (aesthetes) such as August Strindberg and Selma Lagerlöf in translation into English and French have been complemented in both language areas by children's literature from the 1970s on. While many of the children's books were translated relatively quickly, some 'classics' (by Elsa Beskow, Astrid Lindgren) continued to be translated through the period, a trend that mirrored a steady interest in the Swedish source culture where they continue to be re-published. The broadening selection of authors of children's books translated which is noticeable, for instance, in the French literary field, resonates with Franssen's conclusion that literary cultures can be considered 'good' at particular genres (Franssen 2015: 304–5). The success of one children's book, in other words, opens the door for others.

From the 1980s, the export of Swedish literature acquired a more contemporary and notable slant, exemplified by authors such as Torgny Lindgren and Kerstin Ekman. This was a tendency that was tied both to a more demand-driven translation pattern, and, in the French case, to a cultural politics of openness, which in turn allowed new publishers, such as Actes sud, to establish themselves.

The combination of global interconnection and specific exchange dynamics is also seen in later developments, notably in the boom of 'Nordic noir', which, from the millennium, came to dominate the translation flows from Swedish into other languages. In the UK and the USA, the increase in popular crime novels coincided with a decrease in 'classics' (aesthete authors from the late nineteenth and first part of the twentieth century). In France, on the contrary, the success of this literature appeared to pull other genres. To Franssen's conclusion that global success is often genre-bound, then, our material indicates that there may be 'spill-over' effects, but that these have to do with the dynamics of particular exchange dynamics.

Incoming translations similarly demonstrate an overall trend of contemporanization. Against this background, however, the changes differ. Italian literature was made more contemporary in two phases, beginning in the 1900s and the 2000s respectively, where the first introduced a number of notables such as Saviano and Tamaro, and the second authors such as Avallone and Ferrante. Particularly the latter two were immediately translated because of their global success. The 'updating' of translations of Italian literature partly occurred by way of English – an indication of the globalization of literary culture – but also retained some specific, bilateral dynamics, such as the establishment of a publisher of Italian with the support of the Italian Institute. Throughout the period, the continuous translations and editions of 'classics' of varying stripes ('old' and 'modern') made up around a third of the translated literature, far above the other flows, which shows that Italian literature carries a large degree of 'past symbolic capital'.

Italian literature's divided face in the Swedish literary market can be compared with Portuguese literature. Portugal's rich literary history does *not* register in Swedish translations, and canonical authors such as Camões and de Garett who are translated and circulate transnationally, were not published in Sweden in the period studied, and the literary flow remained dominated by notable authors. Being a small translation flow, general trends are hard to discern, however, and individual actions by publishers and the commitment to particular authors affect numbers greatly. This is the case with the rather rapid translations of notables Saramago and Antunes, who were both translated continuously through the 1990s up to the former's Nobel award in 1998 and until the early 2010s.

Portuguese literature is part of the larger Lusophone flow, whose other literary cultures exhibit the same variations caused by individuals and small actors. The translation of Brazilian and Lusophone African authors, highly contemporary with the exception of Clarice Lispector, suddenly increased in the 2000s, thanks to small new publishers, with the introduction of new authors, but the higher numbers reveal one-time efforts. The increase in translations of Brazilian literature was caused exclusively by Coelho.

Anglophone African literature, although in the printed sense a young literature, shows a similar development from 'modern classics' to contemporary fiction – and this, arguably, despite the fact that the translation flow is a small one where individual authors affect the percentages greatly. In temporal terms, a few authors – Nadine Gordimer, Doris Lessing and J. M. Coetzee – though their introduction on the Swedish market occurred at different times, were all translated continuously and rather quickly. For most of the others, translation was rather retrospective until the 1990s. That decade marked a shift towards contemporary literature, and considerable broadening of both the number of authors and the number of countries represented. In the years leading up to the present, the comparably large number of rapid translations of Nigerian notable authors – with Chimamanda Ngozi Adichie as the star – stands out.

Caribbean literature, which is joined by archipelago and sea, is also, as noted above, divided by consecration cultures. A young literary space seen from the point of view of printed literature, translation patterns are by necessity contemporary, and they involve notable writers. However, there are significant differences in the rhythms that bring, or do not bring, literary works into Swedish. The general mechanism of 'double consecration' – which in turn is an effect of Anglo-American influence on Swedish publishing – means that literature written in Spanish or French becomes available for translation only after it has been consecrated in the anglo sphere. This is the case with Maryse Condé, whose position in the American and British literary markets has ensured her continued translation also into Swedish – and with increasing speed. The absence of such consecration not only widens the temporal distances, but more profoundly means that authors risk invisibility to Swedish publishers. That there are individual cases expecting this rule, such as the early translation of Patrick Chamoiseau, does not change the overall picture but testifies to the existence of alternative literary routes.

Caribbean literature originally written in English and first published in Britain or the United States is more immediately eligible for translation. Edwidge Danticat's novels – whose surface English reveals marks of several other Caribbean languages – exemplify this pattern. Danticat's fiction has been continuously translated since the late 1990s, albeit at a somewhat uneven pace.

A shifting gender balance towards a greater proportion of women writers is a trend in several of our translation flows, but not in all. The changes vary significantly, moreover, and in some cases tip the scales from quite extreme positions. The most outstanding example is the translation of Swedish literature into French. In the years 1980–1982, women authors made up 13 per cent of the editions; in 2016–2018 this had changed to 55 per cent. In Lusophone literature the pattern is one of back and forth through the period, beginning at 20 per cent in the 1980s, decreasing to 12 per cent in the 1990s, then rising again to 21 per cent in 2010s, before reaching an all-time low of 15 per cent again in the 2010s. As in the Italian case, there is overall a strong favouring of male authors in the Lusophone flow and for both these literatures women authors account for more or less 20 per cent. Anglophone African literature, on the other hand, presents a trend towards male dominance, from a remarkably high representation of women authors at the beginning of the period to a lower proportion towards the end: 42 per cent in the period 1980–1982 to 28 per cent in 2014–2016. In real terms the numbers present a somewhat different picture: out of the nineteen editions published in the first three years, Doris Lessing and Nadine Gordimer alone make up the female share. The tendency of an increase in female writers is not noticeable in Hispanic translated literature in Sweden. The gender distribution in the Hispanic Caribbean bibliomigration is surprisingly even, with eight female authors and seven male.

Gisèle Sapiro's observation that, within canonical literature, the world has seen a global trend of 'feminization' – albeit changing the balance quite modestly – is not confirmed in our material, which presents a more varied pattern (2016: 92). However, in the translation flows where changes occur, they are directly linked to 'contemporanization' and popularization. In the Swedish literary export boom to France, in which crime novels make up the largest share, followed by children's books and non-genre contemporary fiction, women authors are well represented. Conversely, the translation of Italian literature into Swedish, which is clearly divided into a canonical and a contemporary stream, presents the changing gender balance in the latter, where Silvia Avallone and Elena Ferrante are stark examples. Likewise, in the Lusophone case it is three consecrated Brazilian women authors, namely Ana Maria Machado, Lýgia Bojunga and Clarice Lispector, that are the reason behind the rise to 20 per cent in the 1990s and 2000s.

Obviously, a few female authorships that single-handedly and temporarily improve the gender balance in publication figures cannot be regarded as a reliable change in trend. It cannot be confirmed by our findings that a gender balance in published translations automatically follows upon a general increase in published female authorships – or a 'feminization' of canon formations – in national or international literary cultures. Rather, just as in human societies and practices in general, gender functions in various ways and on different levels as a mediating category in the circulation processes of literature. Depending on the access to literacy, creative conditions, social status and critical (canonical and consecration) recognition of women in different societies and literary establishments, there could be many 'gatekeepers' to bypass on the path to wider circulation of their literature (Edfeldt 2018).

6

General conclusion

We set out to highlight and analyse a position that has been left unnoticed or under-studied by earlier research on world literature: the semi-periphery. Perhaps it is not the most extreme of positions, nor the most exciting. It cannot be summarized in striking phrases, revealing shocking oversights or prejudiced treatment. This, however, does not mean that it is less interesting, or less worthy of this kind of study. In fact, it has proved itself to be highly productive, since the concept moves beyond the binary centre-periphery model to uncover more decentralized, transversal and inter-peripheral literary communication.

We have also used the concepts of the cosmopolitan and the vernacular in order to engage with the intermingled forces of local specificity and global outreach inherent in world literature. This paradigm has proved an efficient tool in our attempts to understand cultural transfer and the different fields of translation. We have, however, used the concepts in a specific way. Cosmopolitanizing and vernacularizing have been seen as movements in opposite directions on a scale from the most limited circulation of cultural goods to the largest possible one. Crucially, cosmopolitanization and vernacularization can exist alongside one another (e.g. in a text) and can be differently configured on different levels. This use has yielded a more fruitful understanding of the often complex and nuanced world of literary translation. Our collective studies have shown the following.

In Chapter 2, 'Infrastructure of the Semi-peripheral Exchange', our main hypothesis was that the semi-periphery is an intermediate literary space where boundaries between the cosmopolitan and the vernacular are blurred and, more importantly, where ideas of the cosmopolitan and the vernacular are negotiated and transformed. In many cases, the analyses of the selection and framing of translated works confirmed this main hypothesis. The blending of the cosmopolitan and the vernacular concerned all kinds of publishers, from large-scale to small-scale houses. The semi-peripheral Swedish translation field allows for both domesticating and foreignizing translation and framing, in a way hardly possible in central or hyper-central target cultures, where domestication is a prerequisite (Casanova 2015).

In Chapter 3, 'Translators of Nobel Prize Literature', our discussion of Nobel prize laureates and their translators emphatically showed that high-prestige literature in translation is a field for enthusiasts. Among the translators discussed, only a few are or have been writers and translators exclusively. Several of our examples showed the central role of literary translators in and around the Nobel Prize. When it comes to translated high-prestige literature in general, the act of translation is more often than not made explicit. The name of the translator might even be printed on the book cover. It is, however, of equal importance to stress literature's capacity to consecrate those who handle it – publishers, academies, translators, etc. Our analysis also stressed the fact that literary prestige is created, and that the autonomy of high-prestige literature is consequently being emphasized by the literary establishment.

In Chapter 4, 'Translation Strategies to and from the Literary Semi-periphery', we undertook an in-depth analysis of the translation strategies in twenty translated novels, in which translators and publishers dealt with source culture vernaculars in different ways. Eleven of the novels included significant instances of retaining source culture references and phenomena, thereby reinforcing the distance between target and source culture. We also found instances of replacement and reduction, although to a lesser extent. The strategy of retention, we found, leads to many different effects and is pursued for different reasons.

In Chapter 5, 'Positioning the Swedish Literary Semi-periphery', we used the findings from Chapters 2 to 4 in order to position and discuss the Swedish semi-periphery. Narrowing down the focus and examining solely the Swedish literary geography and fiction exclusively – both domestic and translated – during the last forty years, we could show that this literary space has become more and more closed, which probably entails a more central position in the Scandinavian literary geography. At the same time, the number of translations *from* Swedish steadily increased, supporting the claim that the stronger source languages are relatively less common as target languages. In line with studies on globalization's effect on the publishing industry, our material also demonstrated an overall trend of 'contemporanization' in translations both into and from Swedish. A shifting gender balance towards a greater degree of women writers proved to be a trend in several of our translation flows. The changes varied significantly, however, and in some cases tipped the scales from quite extreme positions. Consequently,

Gisèle Sapiro's observation that, within canonical literature, the world has seen a global trend of 'feminization' – albeit changing the balance quite modestly – was not confirmed in our material, which presented a more varied pattern.

Taken together, Chapters 2, 3, 4 and 5 have shown the conditions of translated literature on the micro, meso and macro levels, specifically with a connection to the literary semi-periphery. Different agents and different practices have been in focus, some of them not often studied in the field of world literature. Although overarching trends have not always been identified, the work undertaken in this volume has given deep insights into the multifaceted world of translated literature.

So, how do literary texts circulate between languages and literary cultures? Well, that all depends. Our studies do not show a general tendency, but rather a range of diverse minor patterns. From the point of view of cosmopolitanizing and vernacularizing processes, literary circulation to and from the Swedish semi-periphery has proved to be shaped by a set of conditions due to particular relations between specific literary cultures and markets, publishing agendas, authorial positions, temporal gaps between source and target texts, translator profiles, genre, stylistic qualities and ambitions, and narrative techniques. These disparate conditions definitely affect each other, but not in a regular, predetermined way.

The semi-peripheral literary space does not only work in relation to three other kinds of space – minor peripheral spaces, major central spaces and other semi-peripheral spaces – but also according to disparate strands of circulation mechanisms that function beyond these hierarchies: infrastructures that moves freely across spaces of different sizes and statuses. Indeed, the hierarchical world system of literary markets and literary cultures are often overshadowed by differences in technique, style, genre, positions, gaps, profiles and specific relations. The dynamics between dominance and subordination is far from the only mechanism at play in international literary circulation, at least from a median undominant and undominated perspective.

But how special is Sweden as a case of the possible? Does its position as a major Scandinavian literary culture lead to a particular kind of central semi-periphery? And does that fact that the Swedish literary culture each year – through the Nobel Prize – significantly affects the formation of the world literary canon make it unlike other semi-peripheral positions? No, we don't think so. Every semi-peripheral culture has its own idiosyncrasies that cannot be directly compared to any others. But the set of conditions governing the literary traffic to and from these different semi-peripheral positions are probably quite similar, in their complexity and diversity. That is, at least, our suggestion. It remains to be validated by further studies.

Is, then, semi-peripheral translation a particular kind of translation? Our answer is yes and no. On the one hand, translation to and from the semi-periphery shows a larger diversity than translation to and from the centre and to and from the periphery. On the other hand, we believe that the multifaceted qualities evident in the semi-peripheral translational processes studied in this book make a general diversity at work on all levels and between all kinds of positions extra apparent. The complexity is everywhere, but it's at its thickest in the in-between.

References

Ahlmark, P. (1997), *Det öppna såret. Om massmord och medlöperi*, Stockholm: Timbro.
Albuquerque, J. Lins de (2019), *Maldita Prêmio Nobel: O Reverso da Medalha*, Cultura.
Allt om böcker (1991), special issue 'Portugal', no. 6, Lund.
Almeida, M. Vale de (2004), *An Earth-Colored Sea: Culture and the Politics of Identity in the Postcolonial Portuguese-speaking World*, Oxford: Berghahn.
Almeida, P. (2019), 'Prêmio Nobel de Literatura – Quando será a nossa vez?', *Publishnews*, 13 August. Available online: https://www.publishnews.com.br/materias/2019/08/13/premio-nobel-de-literatura-quando-sera-a-nossa-vez (accessed 14 September 2020).
Alvstad, C. and Lundhahl, M. (2010), 'Den mörke brodern: svensk negrifiering av svart poesi', *Tidskrift för litteraturvetenskap* 2: 39–53.
Amaral, A. L., Ferreira, A. P. and Freitas, M., eds (2015), *New Portuguese Letters to the World: International Reception*, Oxford: Peter Lang.
Anderson, C. (2008), *The Long Tail: Why the Future of Business is Selling Less of More*, New York: Hyperion.
Andersson, A. (2013), 'Boken som händelse – Adam Helms och svensk marknadsföringshistoria'. Available online: http://www.axelandersson.se/wp-content/2013/06/Boken-som-h%C3%A4ndelse-%E2%80%93-Adam-Helms-och-svensk-marknadsf%C3%B6ringshistoria.pdf (accessed 1 May 2021).
Antunes, A. L. (1979), *Os Cus de Judas*, Lisbon: Vega.
Antunes, A. L. (1990), *Tratado das paixões da alma*, Lisbon: Dom Quixote.
Antunes, A. L. (1992a), *A ordem natural das coisas*, Lisbon: Dom Quixote.
Antunes, A. L. (1992b), *Tingens naturliga ordning*, Stockholm: Forum.
Antunes, A. L. (1994a), *A morte de Carlos Gardel*, Lisbon: Círculo de Leitores.
Antunes, A. L. (1994b), *Betraktelser över själens passioner*, Stockholm: Forum.
Antunes, A. L. (1996), *Handbok för inkvisitorer*, Stockholm: Forum.
Antunes, A. L. (2014), *De förrådda*, Stockholm: Modernista.
Antunes, A. L. (2017a), *Betraktelser över själens passioner*, Stockholm: Modernista.
Antunes, A. L. (2017b), *Carlos Gardels död*, Stockholm: Modernista.
Antunes, A. L. (2017c), *Tingens naturliga ordning*, Stockholm: Modernista.
Apter, E. (2001), 'On Translation in a Global Market', *Public Culture* 13.1: 1–12.
Apter, E. (2006), *The Translation Zone: A New Comparative Literature*, Princeton: Princeton University Press.
Apter, E. (2013), *Against World Literature: On the Politics of Untranslatability*, London and New York: Verso Books.
Ariel: litterär tidskrift (1994), special issue 'Lissabon fados fäste' (nos 4–5), Tollarp: Studiekamraten.

Atkin, R. (2020), 'Does Size Matter? Questioning Methods for the Study of "Small"', in R. A. Chitnis, J. Stougaard-Nielsen, R.R. Atkin and Z. Milutinović (eds), *Translating the Literatures of Small European Nations*, 247–66, Liverpool: Liverpool University Press.

Ballu, D. (2016), *Lettres nordiques. Une bibliographie 1720–2013*, Stockholm: Kungliga biblioteket.

Barile, L. (1977), *Bibliografia montaliana*, Milan: Mondadori.

Barreno, M. I., Horta, M. T. and Costa, M. V. da (1976), *De tre Mariornas bok*, Stockholm: Forum.

Bassnett, S., ed. (2019), *Translation and World Literature*, London and New York: Routledge.

Beecroft, A. (2015), *An Ecology of World Literature: From Antiquity to the Present Day*, London and New York: Verso.

Berman, A. (1985), 'La traduction et la lettre ou l'auberge du lointain', in G. Granel (ed.), *Les Tours de Babel. Essais sur la traduction*, 31–50, Mauvezin: Trans-Europ-Repress.

Bernabé, J., Chamoiseau, P. and Confiant, R. (1989), *Éloge de la Créolité*, Paris: Gallimard.

Bgoya, W. and Jay, M. (2013), 'Publishing in Africa from Independence to the Present Day', *Logos* 26.3: 9–22.

Bode, K. (2012), *Reading By Numbers*, London: Anthem Press.

Bosch Santana, S. (2018), 'The Story Club: African Literary Networks Offline', in M. Adejunmobi and C. Coetzee (eds), *Routledge Handbook of African Literature*, 358–98, London: Routledge.

Boschetti, A. (2012), 'How Field Theory can Contribute to Knowledge of World Literary Space', *Paragraph* 35.1: 10–29.

Bouquet, P. (2004), *Tankar vid en prisutdelning*, Nantes: L'Élan.

Bourdieu, P. (1986), *Kultursociologiska texter*, Stockholm: Salamander.

Bourdieu, P. (1993), *The Field of Cultural Production: Essays on Art and Literature*, Cambridge: Polity Press.

Bourdieu, P. (2008), 'A Conservative Revolution in Publishing', *Translation Studies* 1.2: 123–53.

Brems, E., Réthelyi, O. and Van Kalmthout, T., eds (2017), *Doing Double Dutch: The International Circulation of Literature from the Low Countries*, Leuven: Leuven University Press.

Brouillette, S. (2007), *Postcolonial Writers in the Global Literary Marketplace*, Basingstoke: Palgrave Macmillan.

Böckernas tid. Svenska Förläggareföreningen och svensk bokmarknad sedan 1943 (2018), ed. Johan Svedjedal, Stockholm: Svenska förläggareföreningen.

Casanova, P. (2002), 'Consécration et accumulation de capital littéraire. La traduction comme échange inégal', *Actes de la recherche en sciences sociales* 144: 7–20.

Casanova, P. (2004), *The World Republic of Letters*, Cambridge, MA: Harvard University Press.

Casanova, P. (2010), 'Consecration and Accumulation of Literary Capital: Translation as Unequal Exchange', in M. Baker (ed.), *Critical Readings in Translation Studies*, 287–303, London: Routledge.

Casanova, P. (2014), 'Literature as a World' (2005), in D. Damrosch (ed.), *World Literature in Theory*, 275–88, Chichester: Wiley Blackwell.

Casanova, P. (2015), *La langue mondiale. Traduction et domination*, Paris: Seuil.

Cavanaugh, J. (2016), 'Indexicalities of Language in Ferrante's Neapolitan Novels: Dialect and Italian as Markers of Social Value and Difference', in G. R. Bullaro and S. Love (eds), *The Works of Elena Ferrante: Reconfiguring the Margins*, 45–70, New York: Palgrave Macmillan.

Chesterman, A. (1997), *Memes of Translation: The Spread of Ideas in Translation Theory*, Amsterdam and Philadelphia: John Benjamins.

Chesterman, A. (2014), 'Proposal for a Hieronymic Oath', *The Translator* 7 (2): 139–54.

Chitnis, R., Stougaard-Nielsen, J., Atkin R. and Milutinovic, Z., eds (2020), *Translating the Literatures of Small European Nations*, Liverpool: Liverpool University Press.

Cochrane, K. (2011), 'Stieg Larsson's partner: "It's odd to have to prove our life together existed"', *Guardian*, 4 October.

Couto, M. (2006), *O Outro pé da Sereia*, Alfragide: Caminho.

Couto, M. (2010), *Sjöjungfruns andra fot*, Stockholm: Leopard förlag.

Cullhed, A. (2017), 'Förord', in A. L. Antunes, *Betraktelser över själens passioner*, Stockholm: Modernista.

Damrosch, D. (2003), *What is World Literature?*, Princeton, NJ, and Oxford: Princeton University Press.

Damrosch, D. (2009), 'Framing World Literature', in S. Winko, J. Fotis and G. Lauer (eds), *Grenzen der Literatur. Zum Begriff und Phänomen des Literarischen*, 496–515, Berlin and Boston: De Gruyter.

Davis, C. (2012), 'Publishing Wole Soyinka: Oxford University Press and the Creation of "Africa's own William Shakespeare"', *Journal of Postcolonial Writing* 48.4: 344–58.

Dubini, P. (2009), 'La fortuna commerciale degli autori italiani', in F. Arnoldo and A. Mondadori (eds), *Copy in Italy*, 3–36, Milan: Mondadori.

Ducourneau, C. (2011), 'From One Place to Another: the Transnational Mobility of Contemporary Francophone Sub-Saharan African Writers', *Yale French Studies* 120: 9–61.

Edfeldt, C. (2018), 'Gender and the Circulation of African Lusophone Literature into the Portuguese Literary System', in S. Helgesson, A. Mörte Alling, Y. Lindqvist and H. Wulff (eds), *World Literatures: Exploring the Cosmopolitan-Vernacular Exchange*, 369–82, Stockholm: Stockholm University Press.

Ekenberg, K. (2014), 'Översättaren får skina', *Arbetarbladet*, 8 May.

English, J. F. (2005), *The Economy of Prestige: Prizes, Awards and the Circulation of Cultural Value*, Cambridge, MA, and London: Harvard University Press.

Englund Dimitrova, B. (1997), 'Translation of dialect in fictional prose – Vilhelm Moberg in Russian and English as a case in point', in *Norm, Variation and Change in Language. Proceedings of the centenary meeting of Nyfilologiska sällskapet, Nedre Manilla 22–23 March 1996*, 49–65, Stockholm: Almqvist och Wiksell.

Erherenberg, M. (2011), 'Frånvarande mödrars bok', *Kristianstadsbladet*, 11 October. Available online: https://www.kristianstadsbladet.se/bokrecensioner/franvarande-modrars-bok/ (accessed 30 January 2020).

Espmark. K. (2001), *Litteraturpriset. Hundra år med Nobels uppdrag*, Stockholm: Norstedt.

Even-Zohar, I. (1975), 'Decisions in Translating Poetry', *Ha-sifrut/Literature* 21: 32–45.

Falk, E. (2019), 'World Literature, Kampala 1961–968: Literary Circulation in Transition', *Études litteraires africaines* 48: 55–72.

Fennell, L. (2015), 'Across Borders: Migrancy, Bilingualism, and the Reconfiguration of Postcolonialism in Junot Díaz's Fiction', Lund University Papers: Lund.

Fernandes, A. R. (2013), 'Women Authors in (Ex)Change: Short Fiction in Portugal and the United Kingdom (1980–2012)', *Comparative Critical Studies* 10.3: 355–76.

Feuser, W. (1988), 'Wole Soyinka: The Problem of Authenticity', *Black American Literature Forum* 22.3: 555–75.

Flakiersk, G. (2007), 'Nobelpris till Karibien?', *LO-tidningen*, 5 October.

Franssen, T. and Kuipers, G. (2013), 'Coping with Uncertainty, Abundance and Strife: Decision-making Processes of Dutch Acquisition Editors in the Global Market for Translations', *Poetics* 41.1: 48–74.

Franssen, T. (2015), 'Diversity in the Large-scale Pole of Literary Production: An Analysis of Publishers' Lists and the Dutch Literary Space, 2000–2009', *Cultural Sociology* 9.3: 382–400.

Fridegård, J. (1935), *Jag Lars Hård*, Stockholm: Schildt.

Fridegård, J. (1936), *Barmhärtighet*, Stockholm: Schildt.

Fridegård, J. (1936), *Tack för himlastegen*, Stockholm: Schildt.

Fridegård, J. (1983), *I, Lars Hård*, trans. R. E. Bjork, Lincoln and London: University of Nebraska Press.

Fridegård, J. (1985), *Jacob's Ladder & Mercy*, trans. R. E. Bjork, Lincoln and London: University of Nebraska Press.

Gallagher, M. (2002), *Soundings in French Caribbean Writing since 1950: The Shock of Space and Time*, Oxford: Oxford University Press.

Genette G. (1987), *Paratexts. Thresholds of Interpretation*, Cambridge: Cambridge University Press.

Gibbs, J. (1986), *Wole Soyinka*, London: Palgrave.

Gilogley, C. (2013), 'Subverting Subversion? Translation Practice and Malpractice in the Work of Patrick Chamoiseau', in K. Batchelor and C. Bisdorff (eds), *Intimate*

Enemies: Translation in Francophone Contexts, 161–80, Liverpool: Liverpool University Press.

Gouanvic. J.-M. (1997), 'Pour une sociologie de la traduction. Le cas de la littérature américaine traduite en France après la Second Guerre Mondiale (1945–1960)', in M. Snell Hornby, S. Jettmarová and K. Kaindl (eds), *Translation as Intercultural Communication*, 33–45, Amsterdam and Philadelphia: Benjamins.

Granqvist, R. (1988), 'Wole Soyinka, Nobel Prize Winner: Sweden Acknowledges Africa', *Black American Literature Forum* 22.3: 467–74.

Griswold, W. (2000), *Bearing Witness: Readers, Writers, and the Novel in Nigeria*, Princeton, NJ: Princeton University Press.

Gunder, A. (2011), 'In the wake of a Nobel Prize on modern Icelandic literature in Swedish 1940–1969', in P. Broomans and E. Jiresch (eds), *The Invasion of Books in Peripheral Literary Fields: Transmitting Preferences and Images in Media, Networks and Translation*, 105–16, Barkhuis, Groningen.

Göthberg, L. (2001), 'Man måste fan tro på en författare … ', Master's thesis, Uppsala: Institutionen för ABM, estetik och kulturstudier, Biblioteks- och informationsvetenskap.

Hager Cohen, L. (2012), 'Love stories', *The New York Times Sunday Book Review*, 20 September.

Harlitz-Kern, E. (2018), 'A Closer look at the Alternative Nobel Prize in Literature Longlist', *Book Riot*, 18 July. Available online: https://bookriot.com/alternative-nobel-prize-in-literature-longlist/ (accessed 3 February 2020).

Harvey, M. (2016), 'Ann Goldstein on Translating Elena Ferrante and the Inner Workings of The New Yorker', *The Literary Hub*, 1 September. Available online: https://lithub.com/ann-goldstein-on-translating-elena-ferrante-and-the-inner-workings-of-the-new-yorker/ (accessed 18 June 2021).

Hatoum, M. (2010), *Den förtrollade staden*, Stockholm: Bonniers.

Healey, R. (2019), *Italian Literature Since 1900 in English Translation*, Toronto: University of Toronto Press, Scholarly Publishing Division.

Hedberg, A. (2016), 'Small Actors, Important Task: Independent Publishers and their Importance for the Transmission of French and Romance Language Fiction to Sweden Since the Turn of the Millennium', *Moderna språk* 110: 21–30.

Hedberg, A. (2017), 'The Knife in the Lemon: Nordic Noir and the Glocalization of Crime Fiction', in D. Damrosch, T. D'haen and L. Nilsson (eds), *Crime Fiction as World Literature*, 13–22, New York: Bloomsbury Academic.

Hedberg, A. (2019), *Svensk litteraturs spridning i världen*, Stockholm: Svenska Förläggareföreningen.

Heilbron, J. (2000), 'Translation as a Cultural World System', *Perspectives: Studies in Translatology* 8.1: 9–26.

Helgesson, S. (1996), 'Det viktigaste för en översättare är att resa', *Dagens Nyheter*, 6 May.

Helgesson, S. (2008), *Transnationalism in Southern African Literature: Modernists, Realists, and the Inequality of Print Culture*, London: Routledge.

Helgesson, S. (2017), 'Förord', in A. L. Antunes, *Carlos Gardels död*, Stockholm: Modernista.

Helgesson, S. (2018), 'Translation and the Circuits of World Literature', in B. Etherington and J. Zimbler (eds), *The Cambridge Companion to World Literature*, 85–99, Cambridge: Cambridge University Press.

Helgesson, S. and Rosendahl Thomsen, M.(2020), *Literature and the World*, Literature and Contemporary Thought, New York: Routledge.

Hertzman, O. (2013), *En kämpande poet. Sture Axelsons liv och diktning*, Lund: Ellerströms.

Hodapp, J., ed. (2020), *Afropolitan Literature as World Literature*, New York: Bloomsbury Academic.

Hodkinson, P. and Sparkes, A. C. (1997), 'Careership: A Sociological Theory of Career Decision Making', *British Journal of Sociology of Education* 18.1: 29–44.

Hofmeyr, I. (2004), *The Portable Bunyan: A Transnational History of The Pilgrim's Progress*, Princeton, NJ, and Oxford: Princeton University Press.

Huggan, G. (2001), *The Postcolonial Exotic: Marketing the Margins*, New York: Routledge.

Håkanson, N. (2012), *Fönstret mot öster. Rysk skönlitteratur i svensk översättning 1797–2010, med en fallstudie av Nikolaj Gogols svenska mottagande*, Stockholm: Ruin.

Jaggi, M. (2013), 'Danny Laferrière: A Life in Books', *Guardian*, 1 Februry. Available online: https://www.theguardian.com/books/2013/feb/01/dany-laferriere-life-in-books (accessed 25 October 2016).

Jonsson, S. (2007), 'Maryse Condé: Färden genom mangroven', *Dagens Nyheter*, 18 September.

Jorge, L. (2001), *Walters dotter*, Stockholm: Bromberg.

Julien, E. (2006), 'The Extroverted African Novel', in F. Moretti (ed.), *The Novel vol 1: History, Geography, and Culture*, 667–98, Princeton, NJ: Princeton University Press.

Julien, E. (2018), 'The Extroverted African Novel, Revisited: African Novels at Home, in the World', *Journal of African Cultural Studies*, vol. 30: 371–381.

Khachaturyan, E. and Llosa Sanz, A., eds (2019), *Scandinavia through Sunglasses: Spaces of Cultural Exchange between Southern/Southeastern Europe and Nordic Countries*, Berlin: Peter Lang.

Kleberg, L. (2007), *Konsten att översätta. Föreläsningar vid skönlitterära översättarseminariet 1998–2008*, Huddinge: Södertörns högskola.

Kovala, U. (1996), 'Translations, Paratextual Mediation, and Ideological Closure', *Target* 8.1: 119–47.

Kress, G. and Van Leeuwen, T. (2021), *Reading Images: The Grammar of Visual Design*, 3rd edn, London and New York: Routledge.

Kullberg, C. (2011), 'Textens fönster mot världen. Om översättning och fotnoter hos Maryse Condé och Patrick Chamoiseau', in E. Bladh and C. Kullberg (eds), *Litteratur i gränszonen. Transnationella litteraturer i översättning ur ett nordiskt perspektiv*, 53–63, Falun: Högskolan Dalarna.

Kullberg C. (2016), 'Edwidge Danticat: Skriva i transit. Christina Kullberg om skrivandets rörelse mellan språk och platser', *Karavan* 2: 58–65.

Laachir, K., Marzagora, S. and Orsini, F. (2018), 'Significant Geographies in Lieu of World Literature', *Journal of World Literature* 3: 290–310.

Lagerqvist, D. (2016), 'Så ska Contempo få svensken att läsa italienska böcker'. Available online: https://driva-eget.se/nyheter/starta-eget/sa-ska-contempo-fa-svensken-att-lasa-italienska-bocker/ (accessed 28 March 2021).

Larsson, S. (2005), *Män som hatar kvinnor*, Stockholm: Norstedts.

Larsson, S. (2008), *The Girl with the Dragon Tattoo*, trans. R. Keeland, London: MacLehose Press.

Lewis, P. E. (1985/2004), 'The measure of translation effects', in L. Venuti (ed.), *The Translation Studies Reader*, 2nd edn, 256–75, London and New York: Routledge.

Lindberg, Y. (2018), 'Nobelpriskandidat #5 Maryse Condé', *Falköpings tidning*, 6 December. Available online: https://www.skaraborgslanstidning.se/artikel/nobelpriskandidat-5-maryse-conde (accessed 30 January 2020).

Lindqvist, Y. (2002), *Översättning som social praktik. Toni Morrison och Harlequinserien Passion på svenska*, Acta Universitatis Stockholmiensis, Stockholm Studies in Scandinavian Philology, new series, 26, Stockholm: Almqvist & Wiksell International.

Lindqvist, Y. (2006), 'Consecration mechanisms – The reconstruction of the Swedish Field of High Prestige Literary Translation during the 1980s and 1990s', in M. Wolf (ed.), *Übersetzen – Translating – Traduire: Towards a 'Social Turn'?*, 65–75, Münster, Hamburg, Berlin, Vienna and London: LIT.

Lindqvist, Y. (2008), 'Att manipulera matrisen. En jämförelse mellan den svenska, engelska och franska översättningen av den spanska romanen *La caverna de las ideas* av Carlos Somoza', *Språk och stil* 18: 187–208.

Lindqvist. Y. (2016), 'The Scandinavian Literary Translation Field from a Global Point of View – A Peripheral (Sub)field?', in S. Helgesson and P. Vermeulen (eds), *Institutions of World Literature – Writing, Translation, Markets*, Routledge Interdisciplinary Perspectives on Literature, 174–87, New York and London: Routledge.

Lindqvist, Y. (2018), 'Bibliomigration från periferi till semi-periferi. Om den spansk-karibiska litteraturen i svensk översättning', *Tidskrift för litteraturvetenskap*, 1–2: 90–104.

Lindqvist, Y. (2019), 'Translation Bibliomigration: The Case of French Caribbean Literature in Sweden', *Meta. International Journal for Translation Studies* 64.3: 600–30.

Lindqvist, Y. (2021a), 'Institutional consecration of 15 Swedish translators – "Star translators" or not?', in K. Kaindl, W. Kolb and D. Schlager (eds), *Staging the Literary translator*, 137–54, Amsterdam and New York: Benjamin Publishing.

Lindqvist, Y. (2021b), 'Det sverigesvenska översättningsfältet och det skönlitterära översättarkapitalet – 15 översättares arbete med nutida spanskkaribisk litteratur som exempel', *Finsk tidskrift*: 7–37.

Lo-Johansson, I. (1933), *Godnatt, jord*, Stockholm: Bonniers.

Lo-Johansson, I. (1939), *Bara en mor*, Stockholm: Bonniers.
Lo-Johansson, I. (1990), *Breaking Free*, trans. R. Wright, Lincoln and London: University of Nebraska Press.
Lo-Johansson, I. (1991), *Only a Mother*, trans. R. E. Bjork, Lincoln and London: University of Nebraska Press.
Lönnroth, L. (1990), 'Den svenska litteraturen på världsmarknaden', in H.-E. Johannesson and L. Lönnroth (eds), *Den svenska litteraturen, 7: Bokmarknad, bibliografier, samlingsregister*, 38–43, Stockholm: Bonniers.
Lundkvist, A. (1976), 'Våldsorgier i Nigeria', *Arbetet*, 26 November.
Magnusson, L. (2018), 'Det enda som är värre än den gamla Akademien är den nya', *Dagens Nyheter*, 10 September. Available online: https://www.dn.se/ledare/signerat/lisa-magnusson-jag-skams-for-den-nya-akademien/ (accessed 14 April 2020).
Maia, R. B., Pinto, M. P. and Pinti, S. R. (2015), 'Introduction: Portugal and Translation Between Centre and Periphery', in R. B. Maia, M. P. Pinto and S. R. Pinti (eds), *How Peripheral is the Periphery? Translating Portugal Back and Forth*, xvii–xxix, Newcastle upon Tyne: Cambridge Scholars Publishing.
Mani, V. (2014), 'Bibliomigrancy: Book Series and the Making of World Literature', in T. D'haen, D. Damrosch and D. Kadir (eds), *The Routledge Companion to World Literature*, 283–96, London: Routledge.
Mani, V. (2017), *Recoding World Literature: Libraries, Print Culture, and Germany's Pact with Books*, New York: Fordham University Press.
Martins, A. M. (2012), *Magic Stones and Flying Snakes: Gender and the Postcolonial Exotic in the Work of Paulina Chiziane and Lídia Jorge*, Oxford: Peter Lang.
Martinson, H. (1933), *Kap Farväl!*, Stockholm: Bonniers.
Martinson, H. (1934a), *Cape Farewell*, trans. N. Walford, London: The Cresset Press.
Martinson, H. (1934b), *Cape Farewell*, trans. N. Walford, New York: Putnam.
Martinson, H. (1935), *Nässlorna blomma*, Stockholm: Bonniers.
Martinson, H. (1936), *Flowering Nettle*, trans. N. Walford, London: The Cresset Press.
Martinson, M. (1933), *Kvinnor och äppelträd*, Stockholm: Bonniers.
Martinson, M. (1936), *Mor gifter sig*, Stockholm: Bonniers.
Martinson, M. (1985), *Women and Appletrees*, trans. M. S. Lacy, New York: Feminist Press.
Martinson, M. (1987), *Women and Apple Trees*, trans. M. S. Lacy, London: The Women's Press.
Martinson, M. (1988), *My Mother Gets Married*, trans. M. S. Lacy, New York: Feminist Press.
McCusker, A. (2007), *Patrick Chamoiseau: Recovering Memory*, Liverpool: Liverpool University Press.
McGrath, C. (2010), 'The Afterlife of Stieg Larsson', *The New York Times*, 23 May.
Moberg, V. (1935), *Sänkt sedebetyg*, Stockholm: Bonniers.
Moberg, V. (1937a), *Sömnlös*, Stockholm: Bonniers.

Moberg, V. (1937b), *Memory of Youth*, trans. E. Björkman, New York: Simon & Schuster.

Moberg, V. (1939), *Giv oss jorden!*, Stockholm: Bonniers.

Moberg, V. (1940), *The Earth is Ours*, trans. E. Björkman, New York: Simon & Schuster.

Moretti, F. (2000), 'Conjectures on world literature', *New Left Review* 1 (Jan–Feb): 54–68.

Moretti, F. (2020), 'The Roads to Rome: Literary Studies, Hermeneutics, Quantification', *New Left Review* (Jul/Aug): 125–36.

Murray, S. (1998), '"Books of Integrity"': The Women's Press, Kitchen Table Press and Dilemmas of Feminist Publishing', *The European Journal of Women's Studies*: 2.

Nergaard, S. (2004), *La costruzione di una cultura. La letteratura norvegese in traduzione italiana*, Rimini: Guaraldi.

Nergaard, S. (2013), 'The (In)visible Publisher in Translations. The Publisher's Multiple Translational Voices', in H. Jansen and A. Wegener (eds), *Authorial and Editorial Translation 2: Editorial and Publishing Practices*, 177–208, Quebec: Éditions québécoises de l'œuvre.

Ngugi, M. (2018), *The Rise of the African Novel: Politics of Language, Identity, and Ownership*, Ann Arbor: University of Michigan Press.

Ngugi wa Thiong'o (1985), 'The Language of African Literature', *New Left Review* 150.2. Available online: https://newleftreview.org/issues/i150/articles/thiongo-ngugi-wa-the-language-of-african-literature (accessed 22 June 2021).

Nilsson, L. (2017), 'Covering Crime Fiction: Merging the Local into Cosmopolitan Mediascapes', in D. Damrosch, T. D'haen and L. Nilsson (eds), *Crime Fiction as World Literature*, 109–30, New York: Bloomsbury Academic.

'Nu startar Henning Mankell bokförlag' (2001), *Aftonbladet*, 6 June. Available online: https://www.aftonbladet.se/nyheter/a/VR1vJ3/nu-startar-mankell-bokforlag (accessed 20 September 2019).

N'Zengou-Tayo, M.-J. and Wilson, E. (2000), 'Translators on a Tight Rope: The Challenges of Translating Edwidge Danticat's *Breath, Eyes, Memory* and Patrick Chamoiseau's *Texaco*', *TTR: traduction, terminologie, rédaction* 13.2: 75–105. Available online: http://id.erudit.org/iderudit/037412ar (accessed 25 October 2016).

Odber de Baubeta, A. (2012), 'The Intersection of Translation Studies and Anthology Studies', *New Directions in Translation Studies*, Special Issue of *Anglo Saxonica* 3.3: 71–83.

Österling, A. (1921), *Dagens gärning. Essayer och kritiker 1916–1921*, Stockholm: Bonniers.

Perera, Y. (2018), 'Den Nya Akademiens litteraturpris är intressant som process och protest – men spelar det nån roll vem som får det?', *YLE*, 4 October. Available online: https://svenska.yle.fi/artikel/2018/10/04/den-nya-akademiens-litteraturpris-ar-intressant-som-process-och-protest-men (accessed 14 April 2020).

Pettersson, J-E. (1994), 'Femtio år med Bokförlaget Forum', *Svensk Bokhandel*, 20: 12–21.

Roig-Sanz, D. and Meylaerts, R. (2018), 'General Introduction. Literary Translation and Cultural Mediators: Toward an Agent and Process-Oriented Approach', in D.

Roig-Sanz and R. Meylaerts (eds), *Literary translation and cultural mediators in 'peripheral' cultures: customs officers or smugglers?*, 1–37, Cham: Palgrave Macmillan.

Ruëgg, J. (2020), *Utgivningen av översättningar på den svenska bokmarknaden 1970–2016*, Uppsala: Litteraturvetenskapliga institutionen.

Rundle, C. (2010), *Publishing Translations in Fascist Italy*, Italian Modernities 6, Berlin: Peter Lang.

Sapiro, G., ed. (2008), *Translatio. Le marché de la traduction en France à l'heure de la mondialisation*, Paris: CNRS Éditions.

Sapiro, G. (2008), 'Translation and the Field of Publishing', *Translation Studies* 1.2: 154–66.

Sapiro, G. (2015), 'Translation and Symbolic Capital in the Era of Globalization: French Literature in the United States', *Cultural Sociology* 9.3: 320–46.

Sapiro, G. (2016), 'How Do Literary Works Cross Borders (or Not)? A Sociological Approach to World Literature', *Journal of World Literature* 1: 81–96.

Sapiro, G. (2020), *Peut-on dissocier l'œuvre de l'auteur?*, Paris: Seuil.

Sapiro, G. and Bustamante, M. (2009), 'Translation as a Measure of International Consecration Mapping the World Distribution of Bourdieu's Books in Translation', *Sociologica: Italian Journal of Sociology on line*: 2-3, Bologna: Società editrice il Mulino, Bologna. Available online: https://www.researchgate.net/publication/336878465_Translation_as_a_Measure_of_International_Consecration_Mapping_the_World_Distribution_of_Bourdieu_s_Books_in_Translation (accessed 16 August 2021).

Saramago, J. (1993), *Historien om Lissabons belägring*, Stockholm: Wahlström & Widstrand.

Saramago, J. (1994), 'Kätteri – en mänsklig rättighet', trans. M. Eyre, *Idag*, 14 February.

Schiöler, N. (2010), 'På jakt efter den osynliga dikten. Tranströmer–Bly tur och retur', in D. Möller and P. Tenngart (eds), *Kasta dikt och fånga lyra. Översättning i modern svensk lyrik*, 133–72, Lund: Ellerströms.

Schmidt, T. (2001), 'Inledning', in T. Schmidt (ed.), Tomas Tranströmer and Robert Bly, *Air Mail. 150 brev 1964–1990*, Stockholm: Bonniers.

Schwartz, C. (2015), 'Montale svedese', *Bollettino di italianistica* 12.2: 48–76.

Schwartz, C. (2017), 'Semi-peripheral dynamics. Inclusion modalities of Italian literature in Sweden', *Journal of World Literature* 2: 488–511.

Schwartz, C. (2018), 'Östen Sjöstrand', *Svenskt översättarlexikon*. Available online: https://litteraturbanken.se/%C3%B6vers%C3%A4ttarlexikon/artiklar/%C3%96sten_Sj%C3%B6strand (accessed 30 June 2021).

Schwartz, C. (2019), 'Semi-peripheral relations – the status of Italian poetry in contemporary Sweden', in J. Blakesley (ed.), *Sociologies of Poetry Translation. Emerging Perspectives*, 173–96, London: Bloomsbury.

Schwartz, C. (2021), *La letteratura italiana in Svezia. Autori, editori, lettori (1870–2020)*, Rome: Carocci.

Schwartz, C. (n.d.), 'Karin Alin, 1892–1974', *Svenskt översättarlexikon*. Available online: https://litteraturbanken.se/översättarlexikon/artiklar/Karin_Alin (accessed 30 June 2021).

Schwartz, C. and Edfeldt, C. (forthcoming), 'Supporting Inter-peripheral Literary Circulation: The Impact of Institutional Funders of Italian and Portuguese Language Literatures in Sweden', *Perspectives: Studies in Translation Theory and Practice*.

Segnini, E. (2017), 'Local Flavour vs. Global Readerships: The Elena Ferrante Project and Translatability', *The Italianist* 37.1: 100–18.

Seixo, M. A., ed. (1999), 'José Saramago: O Ano de 1998', *Colóquio Letras* 151/152, Lisbon: F. C. Gulbenkian.

Sela-Sheffy, R. (2008), 'The Translators' Personae: Marketing Translatorial Images as Pursuit of Capital', *Meta* 53.3: 609–22.

Simeoni, D. (1998), 'The Pivotal Status of the Translator's Habitus', *Target* 10.1: 1–39.

Simeoni, D. (2007), 'Between sociology and history: Method in context and in practice', in M. Wolf and A. Fukari (eds), *Constructing a Sociology of Translation*, 187–204, Amsterdam and Philadelphia: John Benjamins.

Simonetti, G. (2018), *La letteratura circostante. Narrativa e poesia nell'Italia contemporanea*, Bologna: Il Mulino.

Siskind, M. (2014), *Cosmopolitan desires: global modernity and world literature in Latin America*, Evanston, Illinois: Northwestern University Press.

Sjöstrand, Ö. (1983), 'Om Wole Soyinkas lyrik', *Artes* 1: 64–71.

Smedberg Bondesson, A. (2010), 'Montale och Medelhavet – i Norden', in D. Möller and P. Tenngart (eds), *Kasta dikt och fånga lyra. Översättning i modern svensk lyrik*, 53–79, Lund: Ellerströms.

Smith, T. R. (2013), 'Crossways: Pages from a Literary Friendship', in *Airmail: The Letters of Robert Bly and Tomas Tranströmer*, Minneapolis: Greywolf.

Snell-Hornby, M. (2006), *The Turns of Translation Studies*, Amsterdam: John Benjamins.

Sommer, D. (2004), *Bilingual Aesthetics: A New Sentimental Education*, Chicago: University of Chicago Press.

Steiner, A. (2011), 'World literature and the book market', in T. D'haen, D. Damrosch and D. Kadir (eds), *The Routledge Companion to World Literature*, 316–24, London and New York, Routledge.

Steiner, A. (2012), 'Läsarnas marknad och marknadens läsare – reflektioner över materiella villkor på bokmarknaden', in U. Carlsson and J. Johannisson (eds), *Läsarnas marknad och marknadens läsare*, 27–43, SOU 2012:10.

Steiner, A. (2018), 'The Global Book: Micropublishing, Conglomerate Production, and Digital Market Structures', *Publishing Research Quarterly* 34: 118–32. Available online: https://doi.org/10.1007/s12109-017-9558-8 (accessed 30 June 2021).

Steiner, A. (2019), *Litteraturen i mediesamhället*, Lund: Studentlitteratur AB.

Strängberg, U. (2012), Interview with Maryse Condé, Sveriges Radio Kultur, 10 December 2013.

Suhr-Sytsma, N. (2013), 'Ibadan Modernism: Poetry and the literary present in mid-century Nigeria', *Journal of Commonwealth Literature* 48.1: 41–59.

Suhr-Sytsma, N. (2018), 'The Extroverted African Novel and Literary Publishing in the Twenty-first Century', *Journal of African Cultural Studies* 30.3: 339–55.

Svedjedal, J. (1988), 'Henrik Koppel, Ljus förlag och enkronasböckerna', *Samlaren* 109: 71–99.

Svedjedal, J. (1993), *Bokens samhälle. Svenska bokförläggareföreningen och svensk bokmarknad 1887–1943*, vol. 2, Stockholm: Svenska bokförläggareföreningen.

Svedjedal, J., ed. (2012), *Svensk litteratur som världslitteratur*, Uppsala: Avdelningen för litteratursociologi.

Svensson, R. (2015), 'Afrikansk skönlitteratur på svensk bokmarknad 1961–1981: Bo Cavefors och *Afrika berättar*', *Tidskrift för litteraturvetenskap* 2–3: 33–44.

Swaan, A. de (2001), *Words of the World: The Global Language System*, Cambridge: Polity.

Swedish Academy (n.d.), https://www.svenskaakademien.se/nobelpriset/nobelpriset-i-litteratur-pristagarna.

Thompson, J. (2010), *Merchants of Culture: The Publishing Business in the Twenty-first Century*, Cambridge: Polity.

Torgerson, S. (1982), *Översättningar till svenska av skönlitterär prosa 1866–1870 1896–1900 1926–1930*, Gothenburg: Litteraturvetenskapliga institutionen vid Göteborgs universitet.

Torres, L. (2007), 'Code-mixing as a narrative strategy in a bilingual community', *World Englishes* 11. 2–3: 183–93.

Toury, G. (1995), *Descriptive Translation Studies and Beyond*, Amsterdam and Philadelphia: John Benjamins.

Toury, G. (2012), *Descriptive Translation Studies and Beyond*, 2nd edn, Amsterdam and Philadelphia: John Benjamins.

Tranströmer, T. (1973), *Stigar*, Stockholm: Författarförlaget.

Tranströmer, T. (1987), *Collected Poems*, trans. R. Fulton, Newcastle upon Tyne: Bloodaxe.

Tranströmer, T. (1989), *För levande och döda*, Stockholm: Bonniers.

Tranströmer, T. (1990), poems in *World Literature Today*: 4.

Tranströmer, T. (1995), *For the Living and the Dead*, trans. R. Bly, New York: Ecco Press.

Van Es, N. and Heilbron. J (2015), 'Fiction from the Periphery: How Dutch Writers Enter the Field of English-Language Literature', *Cultural* Sociology 9.3: 296–319.

Van Uffelen, H. (2017), 'Is it only the original which unfolds anew in the reception?', in E. Brems, O. Réthely and T. Van Kalmthout (eds), *Doing Double Dutch: International Circulation from the Low Countries*, 93–109, Leuven: Leuven University Press.

'The Women's Press' (2016), http://www.writewords.org.uk/directory/detail_page. asp?subtypeid=11&directory_id=4835.

Venuti, L. (1995), *The Translator's Invisibility: A History of Translation*, London and New York: Routledge.

Venuti, L. (1998), *The Scandals of Translation: Towards an ethics of difference*, London and New York: Routledge.

Venuti, L. (2005/2013), 'Local Contingencies: Translation and National Identities', in *Translation Changes Everything: Theory and Practice*, 177–202, Abingdon: Routledge.

Verboord, M., Kuipers, G. and Janssen, S. (2015), 'Institutional Recognition in the Transnational Literary Field, 1955–2005', *Cultural Sociology* 9.3: 447–65.

Vimr, O. (2020), 'Supply-driven Translation. Compensating for Lack of Demand', in R. Chitnis, J. Stougaard-Nielsen, R. Atkin and Z. Milutinovic (eds), *Translating the Literatures of Small European Nations*, 46–68, Liverpool: Liverpool University Press.

Volk, C. (1999), 'Translator's Note', in P. Chamoiseau, *Childhood*, Lincoln: University of Nebrasca Press.

Walkowitz, R. L. (2013), 'Close Reading in an Age of Global Writing', *Modern Language Quarterly* 74.2 (June): 171–95.

Walkowitz, R. L. (2015), *Born Translated: The Contemporary Novel in an Age of World Literature*, New York: Columbia University Press.

Wallerstein, I. (1974), *The Modern World System I: Capitalist Agriculture and the Origins of the European World-Economy in the Sixteenth Century*, New York: Academic Press.

Wallis, K. (2018), 'Exchanges in Nairobi and Lagos: Mapping Literary Networks and World Literary Space', *Research in African Literatures*, 49.1: 163–86.

Watts, R. (2005), *Packaging Post/Coloniality. The Manifacture of Literary Identity in the Francophone World*, New York, Toronto and Oxford: Lexington Books.

Westerström, J. (2013), *Den ständige Anders Österling. En litteraturmänniskas alla sidor (1919–1981)*, Stockholm: Atlantis.

Widestam, A. (2001), 'Marianne Eyre', Amnesty Historia. Available online: http://www2.amnesty.se/amnestyshistoria.nsf/ff998d5be1d1df0dc1256ae300387a29/804e7bc97c5f5410c1256ae30038ba98?OpenDocument (accessed 30 June 2021).

Wolf, M. (2006), 'Translating and Interpreting as a Social Practice – Introspection into a New Field', in M. Wolf (ed.), *Übersetzen–Translating–Traduire: Towards a 'Social Turn'?*, 9–23, London: Transaction Publishers.

Wolf, R. (1999), 'Maryse Condé', *Bomb Magazine*, 68. Available online: https://bombmagazine.org/articles/maryse-cond%C3%A9/ (accessed 3 December 2010).

WReC (2015), *Combined and Uneven Development: Towards a New Theory of World-Literature*, Liverpool: Liverpool University Press.

Wrede, H. (2018), 'Ingen skillnad på nobelpriset och det alternativa nobelpriset', SVT nyheter, 10 December. Available online: https://www.svt.se/kultur/maryse-conde-ingen-skillnad-pa-nobelpriset-och-det-alternativa-nobelpriset (accessed 30 June 2021).

Wästberg, P., ed. (1968), 'The Writer in Modern Africa: African-Scandinavian Writers' Conference', Stockholm 1967, Uppsala: The Scandinavian Institute of African Studies.

Wästberg, P. (2007), *Vägarna till Afrika. En memoar*, Stockholm: Wahlström & Widstrand.

Zell, H. (2011), 'James Currey Africa Writes Back: The African Writers Series & the Launch of African Literature', *Logos: The Journal of World Book Community* 22.3: 7–69.

Zorn, H. (1994), 'En lämplig, inte helt ung man', *Svensk Bokhandel* 19: 6–9.

Index

abbreviation of text 126, 134–6
academic dimension of a publication 131
Achebe, Chinua 101, 162, 166–7
Actes sud (publisher) 48, 140, 210–11
'adequate' translation, concept of 185
Ades media 218 (publisher) 218
Adichie, Chimamanda Ngozi 5, 52, 54, 57, 160, 246
aesthetes and aesthetic qualities 23, 25, 39, 74, 161, 163, 205, 208, 213, 227
African Books Collective 51
African literature 6–13, 50–9, 64, 78, 99–100, 105, 156–67, 220–5, 246
'Afro-English' label 156–7
agents, literary 194, 198–9, 211
Agualusa, José Eduardo 61–8
Ahndoril, Alexander and Alexandra 53
Alberti, Barbara 43
Aleksijevitj, Svetlana 116
Aleramo, Sibilla 43–4
Alfabeta (publisher) 140–1
Almaviva (publisher) 63–8, 79
Almeida, Germano de 60
Almqvist, Carl Jonas Love 206
Alves, Inger M. 65
Amado, Jorge 65, 228
Amaral, Ana Luisa 65
Ammaniti, Niccolò 48
Anderberg, Irene 172
Andersson, Gösta 94–8
Andersson, Tony 238
Anglo-American literary culture 12, 76, 178, 247
Anglophone literature 7, 50–9, 78, 84, 156, 205, 220–5, 246
Angola 63, 68
Antunes, António Lobo 42, 61, 68, 107–13, 168–71, 189–90, 229, 246
Anyuru, Johannes 117
Appelius, Mario 95
Apter, Emily 99, 154

Aretino, Pietro 216
Armah, Ayi Kwei 58
Åsberg, Stig 133
Aspenström, Werner 208
Assis, Machado de 61, 227
Astor (publisher) 146, 148
Attallah, Niam 32
Avallone, Silvia 47, 217, 248
Avenard, Étienne 89, 91
Axelson, Sture 95–8

Balzac, Honoré de 57
Bankier, Joanna 84
Bao, Viola 59
Barile, L. 94
Bassnett, Susan 4
Bazar (publisher) 61, 70, 72, 79
Bellman, Carl Michael 208
Benedictsson, Victoria 206
Bengtsson, Frans G. 39–40, 205
Benni, Stefano 46
Berg, Aase 53, 208
Berggren, Henrik 109
Bergman, Ingmar 34, 132, 206–8
Bergman, Margareta 206
Bergsten, Staffan 98
Bergstrand, Mikael 39
Berman, A. 152
Beskow, Elsa 204
Bessora, Sandrine 114
bestsellers 26, 33–4, 41–2, 49, 79, 92, 198, 216, 218
bias 43, 212
biblical language 165
bibliomigration 11, 69, 88, 234–5, 243–4
bilingualism 183–7, 191
Bjork, Robert E. 128–31, 134, 138–9
Bjurström, Carl Gustaf 91
Black, A. and C. (publishers) 204
Bly, Robert 84–8, 119–20
Boal, Augusto 111, 228

Bode, Katherine 17
Bodegård, Anders 115, 239–40
Bohman, Therese 142–6
Böhme, Helena 113–16, 176–9
Bojunga, Lýgia 248
Bolaño, Roberto 53, 71
Bonemark, Kjell-Olof 207
Bonnier, Albert 111
Bonniers (publishers) 35, 41, 44, 52–7, 61, 64, 72, 78–9, 96, 99, 104, 110, 181, 214
Booker Prize 29, 53, 55
Börjlind, Cilla and Rolf 34
Boschetti, Anna 14
Bouquet, Philippe 39–40, 90–3, 119–20
Bouraoui, Nina 117
Bourdieu, Pierre 6, 12–16, 23, 26, 33–7, 42, 58, 71, 79, 114
Bourgois, Christian 36
Boye, Karin 206
Brazilian literature 10–11, 60–1, 68, 106, 111, 172, 229–32
Bremer, Fredrika 206
Bridget, Saint 206
Bright, Freda 42
Brink, André 166, 223
Bromberg (publisher) 43, 52, 221
Brouillette, Sarah 53
Brown, Dan 76
Bruy, Carine 144–6
Bufalino, Gesualdo 44
Bulawayo, No Violet 157, 160–1
Bunyan, John 123

Caen University 90
Calabrò, Corrado 217
Calvino, Italo 94, 217
Caminho (publisher) 171
Camões, Luis de 246
canonical authors 39, 157, 205–6, 209, 214, 245, 248
Cárdenas, Teresa 71
Cardoso, Luis 60
Caribbean literature 7, 11–12, 69–80, 113, 174–86, 234–43, 246–8
Carofiglio, Gianrico 45
Carreyru, John 30
Cartaditalia (publisher) 196

Casanova, Pascale 12–16, 19, 21–2, 34–7, 78, 81, 90, 92, 95, 99, 106, 108, 119, 195
case studies 4–5
  conclusions drawn from 189
Cassatt, Mary 133
Cassava (publisher) 51
Cather, Willa 30
Cavefors, Bo (and publishing business) 101–3, 220
Caverinha, José 66
Cederroth, Maria 75
centre-periphery model 2–4, 13, 249–50
Chagall, Marc 45
Chamoiseau, Patrick 238–9, 247
Char, René 104
Charters, Samuel 86
Chatto & Windus (publishers) 161
Chaviano, Diana 75
Chevalier, Caroline 91
children's books 7–8, 31, 33, 39–40, 71, 78, 121, 138–9, 203–11, 231
Chinese literature 71
Chinweizu, Jemie & Madubike 101
Chraibi, Driss 114
circumcision 164
classic literature 7–8, 25, 31, 41, 44, 57–8, 119, 206, 212–17, 245–6
  modern 218, 223
code-switching 180–2, 186
Coelho, Paulo 61, 70, 229–30, 246
Coetzee, J.M. 10, 52, 195, 221, 246
coffee 45
Cognetti, Paolo 47
Cole, Teju 5, 160
Coles, Don 84, 86
collaborative research 18–19
Collings, Rex 100
Collins, Jackie 43
Colombian literature 15
colonial history 9–11, 113
The Color Purple 32
commercial success 33–4, 37, 42–52, 57, 76
Condé, Maryse 11, 62, 82, 113–20, 173, 176–8, 183–5, 193, 236–7, 247
conglomerate companies, international 200

Conran, Shirley 42
consecration, literary 23–4, 112–16, 119–20, 182, 193, 195, 250
'double' 247
institutional 202
consecration pathways 107
Contempo (publisher) 46–50, 79
contemporary writing 8, 11, 39, 60, 160, 206, 208, 246
contemporization 244–5, 248, 250
cosmopolitanizing 1–2, 6, 9, 18–26, 30, 33–8, 41, 45–6, 55, 64, 68, 75–8, 123–5, 155, 187, 190, 210, 249–51
meaning of 2
Coursaud, Jean-Baptiste 40–1
Couto, Mia 61–4, 79, 111, 171–4
Covacich, Mauro 50
covers of books 123, 133–7, 140, 143, 147–8, 161, 170, 250
Creole language 179–80, 183, 186
Crepax, Guido 214
crime writing 7–8, 27, 34–6, 39, 121, 134, 144, 211–12, 245, 248
Croce, Benedetto 93, 96
'cross-over' books 194–5
Cuban literature 69, 75–7
Cuenca, João Paulo 60
cultural context 10, 131, 251
cultural differences 145, 190
stressing or evening out of 189
cultural transfer 2, 4
Culture House, Stockholm 116
Currey, James 100

Dagerman, Stig 91, 206
Damrosch, David 5, 12, 123–5, 167
Dangor, Achmat 62
'dansband' genre 142
Danticat, Edwidge 11, 240, 247
Darrieussecq, Marie 114
Davis, Caroline 16, 99–100
Deane, John F. 84
De Carlo, Andrea 46
Deforges, Régine 110
Delargy, Marlaine 144
Delaroche, Paul 143
De Luca, Erri 146–8, 151–5, 191
Denmark 5

Desplechin, Marie 114
Díaz, Junot 11, 74–5, 157, 161, 180–5, 191
Dickens, Charles 57
Diehl, Marguerite 40
digitization 6, 217
'Dirty Realism' movement 76
discourse networks 16
Ditlevsen, Tove 32
Djebar, Assia 62
domestication of text 23, 79–80, 120, 153, 172, 194
dominance, linguistic 251
Dongala, Emmanuel 62
Drummond de Andrade, Carlos 228
Den drunknade 142–6
Duffy, William 84
Duranti, Francesca 45
dust jackets *see* covers of books
Dutch literature 3–4, 25–6

Eco, Umberto 216, 218
Edfeldt, Chatarina 18–19
Éditions Balland 144, 146
Egan, Jennifer 29
Ekelöf, Gunnar 85, 139, 209
Ekelund, Kristina 114–15
Ekman, Kerstin 245
Ekström, Margareta 206
Elechi, Armand 58
Eliot, T.S. 104
Emecheta, Buchi 52
Emitslöf, Göran and Malin 46–7
emotional charge 183
English expressions 152
English language 14, 69, 76, 83, 88, 92–4, 127, 167, 185, 196–7, 210, 215
translation into 203–9, 236, 238
translation out of 223
Enquist, P.O. 205–6
environment, *cultural, political* and *social* 2
Enwonwu, Ben 101
epitext 24–5, 28, 49, 125
Eriksson, Kjell 39
Ernestam, Maria 39–40
erotic literature 214–16
Escarpit, Robert 33
establishment, literary 78, 121, 215, 250

ethnographic gaze 131
Etiemble, René 178
European Union Literary Prize 110
Even-Zohar, Itamar 185
exoticism and exoticization 138, 154, 177, 183
Eyre, John 67
Eyre, Marianne 107–12, 168, 189, 228–9

Faber & Faber (publishers) 181
Falcone, Giovanni 215–16
Falk, Erik 19
Fanon, Frantz 62
Farah, Nuruddin 10, 52, 55–9, 64, 79
Faria, Almeida 66, 228
Farrokzhad, Athena 161
'feelgood' literature 39
Felicetti, Si 43
feminism 227
Feminist Press 31–2
feminization 248, 251
Fennell, Laura 183
Fernandes, Maria Celestina 65
Ferney, Alice 114
Ferrante, Elena 47, 146–53, 156, 190, 217–18, 248
fiction, translation of 198–202, 205
    support for 195–6
film 136, 206, 208
Fioretos, Mikael 83
Fitzgerald, Scott 57
Floris Books 204
Fo, Dario 94, 215–16
foreignness and foreignizing 128–30, 133, 145, 158, 167, 185–8, 194
Författarfonden fund 196
Författarens bokmaskin 201
format of literary work, changes in 126, 131
Forum (publisher) 41–8, 55, 61, 72, 78–9, 168, 170
framing 23–6, 40
France 4, 8, 17, 33–41, 88–92, 103, 114–15, 119, 139–46, 193, 209–12, 245, 248
Francophone literature 234–43
Franssen, T. 245
Fredriksson, Marianne 206

Fridegård, Jan 128, 130, 133, 205–6
Friesen, Gunnel von 114
Fröding, Gustaf 208
Fugard, Athol 52, 221
Fulton, Robin 84, 86

Gabrielsson, Ulla M. 65
Gaïa (publisher) 37–41, 78–9, 140, 142
Gaiman, Neil 118
Gainsborough, Thomas 40
Gallagher, M. 235
Gappah, Petina 54–7
Gardell, Jonas 39–40
Gaspar, Martin 4
Gatti, Fabrizio 218
Gauguin, Paul 174
gender balance 248
generalizable propositions 7
Genette, Gérard 125
genres, literary 17
Gentile, Giovanni 93
German language 92–3, 103
Ghasi, Yaa 5
Gibb, James 103
Gibson, Anna 36
Giordano, Paolo 45
The Girl with the Dragon Tattoo 27–9, 136, 138, 143, 189, 211
global flows 14
global literary space 13
globalization of the publishing industry 194–5, 244, 250
'glögg' 142
glossary provision 179
Godin, Stig-Lennart 90
Goldoni, Carlo 213
Goldstein, Ann 149
Gombrowicz, Witold 53
Gordimer, Nadine 52–9, 78, 166, 246–7
Gothenburg University 42
Grann, David 30
Granqvist, Raoul 101
graphic novels 213–18
Grate-förlag, Elisabeth (publisher) 146
Greece and Greek poetry 5, 83
Gripenberg, Georg 31
Grisham, John 53
Griswold, Wendy 9

Grossi, Paolo 46
Grumbach, Lena 40–1, 140–2, 189–90
Guerra, Wendy 71
Guillou, Jan 91, 206
Gullar, Ferreira 65
Gustafsson, Lars 205–6
Gutiérrez, Pedro Juan 75–6

Hachette (publisher) 140
Hager Cohen, Leah 180–1
Hallström, Lasse 206
Hammarskjöld, Dag 208
Hamsun, Knut 87
Handke, Peter 81
Hansson, Ola 208
Hansson, Svante 114–15
Hård, Lars 133
Harlitz-Kern, Erika 117
Harvey, Melinda 149
Hatoum, Milton 61
Healey, Robin 94
Hedberg, Andreas 18
Hedenberg, Johanna 146
Hedgesson, Stefan 16
Heilbron, Johan 14–17, 21–5, 34–5, 44
Heinemann Educational Publishers 162
Helgesson, Stefan 6, 111, 167
Helms, Adam 41–2
Helms, Elisabeth 74
Hemingway, Ernest 41
Hermansson, Gunilla 5
hermeticism 93
Himmelsfärd, Marie 150
Hispanic literature 69, 72–3, 79, 234–5, 243, 248
Hodapp, James 5–6
Hofmeyr, Isabel 123
Höglund, Anna 34
Holberg, Ludvig 31
Holt, Anne 144
Homel, David 238
horizontal isomorphism 19, 35, 38, 44, 68, 193
Hornby, Nick 48
Hove, Chenjerai 160
Huggan, Graham 5, 164, 222
Hval, Niclas 157, 161, 167, 181, 184–5

Ibadan University College (UCI) 99–100
Ibsen, Henrik 103
Icelandic literature 31
ideal-type writers 23, 71–2, 75, 79
Ingves, Gunilla 204
inscription, process of 22–3
intercultural transfer 107
internationalization 26, 28, 70
Iperborea (publisher) 48
Isegawa, Moses 156
isomorphism *see* horizontal isomorphism
Israel, Daniel 61–2
Italian Institute, Stockholm 217, 245
Italian language and literature 23, 41–50, 93–9, 146–56, 196, 212–18, 246–8
Italy and Italianness 5, 8, 49, 103
Iweala, Uzodinma 162

ja, use of 129–30
Jaffe, Rona 42
James, Marlon 53, 157, 161
Jansen, Hanne 5
Janzon, Åke 97
Jersild, P.C. 205–6
Johanson, Kerstin 76
Johansson, Ingela 5
Johnson, Eyvind 88–91, 193, 205–6
Jonasson, Jonas 144
Jönson, Johan 53
Jönsson, Reidar 206
Jorge, Lídia 232
Julien, Eileen 5, 164
Juul, Susanne 37–8

Kadaré, Ismail 110
Käll, Bertil 41
Kampala conference (1962) 100–1
Karavan (journal) 116
Keeland, Reg (pseud.) 29, 134–9, 189
Kenya 162
Kepler, Lars (pseud.) 53
Key, Ellen 52
Khemiri, Jonas Hassen 53, 117
Kincaid, Jamaica 117, 174–5, 182, 185
Knopf, Alfred A. (and publishing business) 29–30, 72, 134

Kuipers, G. 17
Kullberg, Christina 173
Kulturrådet 195–6

Läckberg, Camilla 36, 143
Lacy, Margaret S. 128–34, 138–9
Laferrière, Dany 237–8
Laffont, Robert 40
Lagerkvist, Pär 31, 52, 205–6
Lagerlöf, Selma 52, 57, 88–9, 205–6, 245
La Guma, Alex 221
Lambert, Jean-Clarence 34
Lampedusa, Giuseppe Tomasi di 43–4
Landelius, Peter 76
Larsen, Stephan 167
Larson, Erik 30
Larsson, Åsa 144
Larsson, Björn 34, 91
Larsson, Lisbeth 117–18
Larsson, Martha 95
Larsson, Stieg 27–9, 36, 76, 134–40, 143, 211
Latin America 15
Laub, Michel 61
Leffler, Yvonne 5, 42
Lehane, Dennis 53
Lema, Elieshi 9, 51
Lenngren, Anna Maria 208
Leopard (publisher) 61–4, 67, 72, 79, 171, 176–7, 213
Lessing, Doris 9, 160, 166, 220, 246–7
Levi, Primo 214
Lewis, Philip 185
Lidman, Sara 205
Lilin, NicolaI 218
Lindgren, Astrid 143, 204
Lindgren, Torgny 205–6, 210, 245
Lindman, Maj 204
Lindqvist, Jon Ajvide 144
Lindqvist, Yvonne 19, 82, 112, 194–7
Lindström, Lasse 75
linguistico-literary capital 14
Linnaeus, Carl 206
Linto, António 111
The Lion and the Jewel 100
Lisboa, Adriana 60
Lispector, Clarice 60, 71, 111, 233, 246, 248
literariness 21–2, 35
literary culture 1, 8, 15–16

literary space 8, 14–15, 194, 202
  closed 250
  open 198
Ljungberg, Sven 133
Lo-Johansson, Ivar 88–91, 128–33
Louis, Édouard 117
Lundahl, Mikela 163
Lundqvist, Artur 75, 105
Lusophone literature 10, 59–69, 79, 111, 167–74, 193, 196, 225–33, 246–8

McCall Smith, Alexander 9, 52, 54
McCarthy, Cormac 29
MacDiarmid, Hugh 93
McEwan, Ian 157
McGrath, Charles 29
Machado, Maria 248
Machiavelli, Niccolò 213
MacLehose, Christopher (and MacLehose Press) 27–9, 33, 78–9, 134–8
McRae, Ellen 155
Magris, Claudio 42, 46, 79
Magritte, René 45
male violence 137
Mallon, Gui 65
Malmström, August 142
Manara, Milo 214
Mandela, Nelson 101
Manifesto of the Anticommunist Intellectuals 93
Manifesto of Fascist Intellectuals 93
Mankell, Henning 36–9, 61–4, 79, 143, 207
Mansfield, Kathereine 57
Marcus, Catherine 140–2, 189–90
Marechera, Dambudzo 160
Marin, Margareta 65
Martinson, Harry 82, 85, 88–93, 120, 193, 205, 208
Martinson, Moa 31–2, 128–9, 132–3
master classes in translation 115–16
masterpieces, literary 4
'mazarin' pastry 142
Mazetti, Katarina 39–40, 139–41, 144, 186, 189–90
Mazzantini, Margaret 48–50
Mazzucco, Melania 48–9, 79
Melander, Viveca 146, 154–5
Melo, Patricia 61

Mendonça, José Luis 65
Mengestu, Dinaw 56–7
Mercer, Christine 133
meso level of publication 21
meta-data 17
meta-language 121
Methuen (publisher) 100
Meyer, Deon 52, 156
Meylaerts, R. 65
micro level of publication 21
micro-publishers 60, 65, 68–9, 79, 193
Miller, Arthur 103
minority groups 32
Missiroli, Marco 47
Mo Yan 71
Moberg, Vilhelm 39–40, 79, 88, 91, 205
modernism 166
Modernista (publisher) 52, 56–9, 113, 163, 167–70, 217
Modersohn-Becker, Paula 133
Mondlane, Eduardo 227
Montale, Eugenio 82, 93–9, 119–20, 217
Morais, Fernando 111
Moravia, Alberto 94
Moretti, Franco 12, 17
Moretti, Nanni 48
Morgan, Edwin 94
Morrison, Mona 206
Mozambique 66, 172–3
multilingual works 154
Mungoshi, Charles 160
Murakami, Haruki 30, 118, 195
Murray, Simone 32
Murray, Steven T. 27, 29, 136, 138
Mussolini, Benito 93
Myrdal, Jan 57

Nabokov, Vladimir 170
Naert, Pierre and Denise 91
Naipaul, V.S. 15
Namara Group 32
names
    of places and characters 173–4
    of TV shows and magazines 138
Naples and Neapolitanism 146–56, 191
narrative technique 126–7, 138
'national' authors 196
Natur & Kultur (publishing house) 217

Nazism 137
Ndebele, Njabulo 223–4
Nebraska University Press (UNP) 30–1, 79
Nellinge, Solveig 42
neologisms 158, 184–8
Nergaard, Siri 48
Neruda, Pablo 84
Nesser, Håkan 36, 39
Neto, Agostinho 227
New Academy Prize in Literature 116–20
New York City University 31–2
Ngugi wa Thiong'o 58–9, 156–7, 162–7, 222
niche strategies 9, 24–5, 33–4, 39, 47, 60, 64–9, 146, 229–30
Nicholl, David 48
Nietzsche, Friedrich 57
Nigeria 9, 101–2, 105, 225, 246
Nkosi, Lewis 221
Nobel Committee 102
'Nobel effect' 19–20, 29, 52, 55, 59, 95, 98–9, 103, 107, 109, 205
Nobel Foundation 81
Nobel laureates 19–20, 71, 116, 119, 193, 205, 217, 223, 250
    female 83, 88
    Italian 93–9
Nobel Prize in Literature 56, 81–3, 88–9, 92–109, 112, 116–21, 170, 208, 246, 251
    mediators for 82
    shared 205
'noir' phenomenon 138, 143, 207, 217–18, 245
non-fiction 8, 62, 64
non-profit regimes 128
Norén, Lars 208
norms 15, 155, 186
Norstedts (publishers) 35, 61, 72, 79, 136, 142–3, 146
northern translation field 195
notes (footnotes and endnotes) 130–3, 145, 165–6, 172–3, 179, 185, 190
novels 7, 10–11, 15, 27, 36, 38, 69, 95–6, 201
Nyorican movement 73
Nyssen, Hubert 38

Official Artist Salary for translators 112, 114
Okri, Ben 56, 58, 223
Olofsson, Lennart 105–6
Ordfront (publisher) 171
Oreglia, Giacomo 96
Österling, Anders 95–9, 119–20
Østvær, Giorgia D'Aprile 5
Oumassine, Damia 114
Oxford University Press (OUP) 100–3, 106

Padovani, Marcelle 215–16
Pallavicini, Lucia 97
Palm, Anna Karin 39–40
Pålsson, Ann 117–18
paratext 20, 28, 40, 236
Parks, Tim 17
Parrella, Valeria 146–8, 151, 155–6
Pascalidou, Alexandra 116–17
Patoni, Alan 221
Paz, Senel 242
pen names, double 207
Penguin Books 56, 162, 181
Penser, Erik 138
peritext 24–5, 43, 47–50, 68, 125–7, 130–2, 153, 171, 187
Pessoa, Fernando 61
Philcox, Richard 11, 236
Philox, Maryse 177
Piazza, Emma 46
picture books 204
Pirandello, Luigi 94, 96
place-names 137–8
Plato 57
plays 207–8
Pleijel, Agneta 117
poetry 104, 203, 207–8, 217–18, 231
  negative attitudes to 98
  by women 95
Polo, Marco 43, 213
Pontes (publisher) 61, 65, 227
popular fiction 207
popularity of literature 24, 50, 75
portraits of authors 46
Portugal 3, 10, 106–9, 172, 196, 246; see also Lusophone literature
post-colonialism 8–9, 15–16, 53, 120, 164

Pratt, Hugo 214
prestige, literary 8, 24, 33, 55, 74, 81–2, 92–3, 97–8, 107, 114, 119–21, 185–6, 250
private publishing 201
Prix Goncourt 33
prizes and awards, literary 12, 19–20, 23, 33, 36, 44, 55–6, 60, 63–4, 73–4, 111–12, 116–18, 202, 215, 236, 239, 241; see also Booker Prize; Nobel Prize; Prix Goncourt; Pulitzer Prize
professionalization of translation 19
proletarian literature see working-class narratives
Proust, Marcel 170
publication strategy 28, 55–7, 62, 70–1
publishing houses 23, 26, 48–9, 139, 217
  division into large- and small-scale operations 79, 195, 200, 213
  recent changes in 194, 197–9
  small 37–41, 48, 52, 60, 68, 72, 78–9
Pulitzer Prize 29, 32, 182

Quasimodo, Salvatore 93–5, 98, 217
Queirós, Eça de 61, 227
Quercus Publishing 27
Quveval, Jean 91

'radhus' design 142
Radice, Marco Lombardo 43
'Ramavtalet' agreement 199
Ranung, Björn 105–6
Ravera, Lidia 43
reduction strategy used by translators 124–9, 139–41, 144–6, 151, 156, 174, 187, 189 194, 250
regulation of book market 198
Réjouis, Rose-Myriam 239
religious controversy 110
replacement strategy used by translators 124–9, 139–46, 149–53, 159, 165, 174, 187, 194, 250
retention strategy used by translators 124–7, 130, 133–4, 139, 144–6, 151–3, 156, 174, 180–90
Roberts, Nora 53
Roig-Sanz, D. 65
romantic fiction 42

Rome University 95
Ronga words 172, 174
Rowling, J.K. 195
Royal Court theatre, London 103
Rüegg, J. 198
Rushdie, Salman 53, 56, 59, 110
Russian language 16–17

sa, omission of 136
Sá-Carneiro, Mário de 227
Said, Sami 35
Saint-Bonnet, Bernard 37–8
Salviano, Roberto 218
Samartin, Cecilia 75–6
Samfundet de nio 111
Sandel, Cora 32
Sandels, Marianne 66, 111
Sandin, Gunilla 117–18
Santiago, Esmeralda 73–4, 241
Sapiro, Gisèle 4, 12–13, 17, 23, 34, 57, 196, 213, 248, 251
Saramago, José 61, 68, 82, 106–13, 168, 170, 228–9, 246
Sartre, Jean-Paul 46
Saviano, Roberto 216, 218
Scego, Igiaba 50
Schaper, Edzard 93
Schleiermacher, Friedrich 125, 189
Schöler, Niklas 83, 86
Schwartz, Cecilia 18, 104
Ségol, Agneta 40
Ségol-Samoy, Marianne 40
Seixo, Maria Alzira 106
Sekwa (publisher) 38
Selasi, Tayie 5
selection
    of literary works 26, 34
    of target language 24
semi-peripheral context 1–2, 5–7, 13, 18–22, 32, 35–8, 41, 77–80, 119, 124, 126, 133, 187, 194, 202, 243–4, 249–52
Le Seuil (Éditions du Seuil) 33–9, 44, 55, 79
Simon, Claude 170
Simonetti, Gianluigi 44
Sjöblom Eva 242–3
Sjögren, Örjan 111

Sjöstrand, Östen 95, 104–5
Sjöwall, Maj 91, 207
'small' languages 244
'small-nation' literatures 4
small-scale operations 24–5
Smaragdi, Marianna 5
Smith, Patti 117
Smith, Thomas R. 85
Smith, Wilbur 52
social capital 24
Söderberg, Hjalmar 206
Söderberg, Lasse 95
Sommer, Doris 181
source culture and text for translation 123–33, 141, 156, 174–5, 179–80, 185–9, 193, 196–7, 204, 245, 250
South Africa 220–3
Soyinka, Wole 82, 99–106, 166, 193, 220, 223
    comments on poetry and prose of 104–5
    delay in Swedish translations of 102–5
    identity as an African 100–1
    international career 102, 104
    introduction to Swedish audiences 99–101, 105
    place in British culture 102–3
    reputation as a dramatist 105–6
    translators of 104–5
Spain 5
'Spanglish' 182
sponsorship of translation 196
state support for literature 5, 195, 198, 202, 210
Steiner, Ann 60, 63
Stenson, Peter 117–18
Stockholm Conference (1976) 166
Stockholm University 96
Stolpe, Jan 115
Strawberry Publishing 70
Strindberg, August 52, 205–8, 245
style, literary 126–7, 138
subordination, linguistic 251
subversive literature 4, 24, 76
Sundman, Per Olof 209
suspense literature 207, 209
Svensk Bokkonst 67
Svenska Dagbladet 94–5

Svensson, Lars-Håkan 95
Swaan, Abram de 12
Swamp Dwellers (play) 101
Sweden
  culture and society in 131-2, 137-8
  growing importance in the world republic of letters 188
  as literary space 194, 202
  National Biography (NB) 197-8
Swedish Academy 81-2, 88, 97-8, 106-11, 117, 120
Swedish language 22, 234-43
  literary 1
  spoken 130
  translation from 7-8, 78, 80, 90, 92, 127-39, 202, 210-12, 250
  translation into 10-13, 70-3, 94-5, 102-3, 113, 119, 225-33, 146-67, 172-89, 193, 196, 200, 212-18
Swedish literature 6-8, 20, 245
  in English translation 26-32, 203-9
  in French translation 33-41, 139-46, 209-21
  status of 209
Swedish model (*modèle suédois*) for dealing with the epidemic 41
'Swedish wave' 210-11
Swedishness 40, 212, 251-2
Swinburne, Algernon Charles 145
symbolic capital 23-4, 33-5, 55-8, 64, 139

Tamaro, Susanna 215
target culture and text 123-6, 130-4, 180, 187-8, 193, 204, 250
Tartt, Donna 117
Tavares, Gonçalo M. 68, 230
Tavares, M. 65
Tavares, Paula 65
Tenggren, Estrid 95, 102-6
Tenngart, Paul 18
themes in literary work 127
Theorin, Johan 144
Thomsen, Mads Rosendahl 6
three-level model of translation 19-20
Thúy, Kim 118
Tokarczuk, Olga 81, 116
Tolkien, J.R.R. 180, 182

tonal particularities of a language 130
Torres, Lourdes 183-4
Toury, Gideon 125, 176, 185
tradition, literary 14
Trakl, Georg 84
Tranan (publisher) 51-2, 60, 65, 71, 78-9, 230
transformation by means of translation, three strategies for 123-7, 144, 189
'translatability' 92
translation
  particular kinds of 252
  strategies for 3-10, 18-20
  studies of 69
Tranströmer, Tomas 82-9, 92, 120-1, 208
Troell, Jan 40
Trotzig, Birgitta 57, 75, 139, 209
Trujillo, Rafael 185
Tutuola, Amos 223

Ungaretti, Giuseppe 93
United Kingdom (UK) 127
United States (US) 127, 204
university presses 30, 32, 128-9, 132-3
Uppsala University 95

Vahlqvist, Staffan 230
Valdés, Zoe 241-2
Vallejo, César 84
values, educational and scholarly 128
van Es, Nicky 21-5, 34-5, 44
van Gogh, Vincent 45
vanguard authors 24, 76
van Niekerk, Marlene 52, 156
Världsbiblioteket, Stockholm 70
Världslitteratur.se (database) 235, 240
Vásquez Díaz, René 74-5
Venuti, Lawrence 20, 23, 104, 120, 125, 128, 166-7, 185, 190, 193-4
Vera, Yvonne 160, 224
Verboord, M. 17
vernacularizing 1-2, 6, 9-11, 18, 21-9, 32, 37-41, 45-6, 54-5, 68, 77-8, 123-5, 153, 155, 180, 187-90, 249-51
  meaning of 2

Veronesi, Sandro 47–8
Vertigo (publisher) 216
Vicenzi, Penny 53
Vieira, Alice 65
Vimr, Ondřej 5
Vinde, Viktor 89
Virago (publishers) 32

Wahl, Niclas 184
Wahlin, Claes 113
Wahlöö, Per 91, 207
Wahlström (publisher) 8, 52, 61, 101–2, 107, 109, 157, 161
Walcott, Derek 181–2
Walford, Naomi 205
Walker, Alice 32
Walkowitz, Rebecca 6, 154, 195
Wallenberg, Peter 138
Wallenström, Ulrika 115
Wallerstein, Immanuel 12
Warwick Research Collective (WReC) 17–18
Wästberg, Per 101–7, 166, 220
welfare state 128
Weyler (publisher) 52

Whitman, Albert 204
Wicomb, Zoe 221
Widstrand (publisher) 101–2, 107, 109
Wiking, Philippa 165–7
Williams, John 217
Winberg, Gunilla 230–1
Wizelius, Ingemar 97
Wollstonecraft, Mary 31
women writers 5, 42–3, 69, 203, 212, 216–18, 228–9, 232–3, 247–50
Women's Press 31–2
Woolf, Virginia 57, 170
working-class narratives 88, 127–9, 132–4, 138–9, 190–1, 205
world literary space 8, 14–15
world literature 3–6, 12, 17, 51, 68, 70, 104, 120, 209, 251
world systems theory 12–19, 187, 251
Wright, Jim 85
Wright, Rochelle 128–34, 138–9

Yourcenar, Marguerite 116

Zimbabwean literature 160–1

www.ingramcontent.com/pod-product-compliance
Lightning Source LLC
Chambersburg PA
CBHW052154300426
44115CB00011B/1664